THE PLANTS OF ACADIA NATIONAL PARK

THE PLANTS OF ACADIA NATIONAL PARK

compiled and edited by Glen H. Mittelhauser, Linda L. Gregory, Sally C. Rooney, *and* Jill E. Weber

photographs by Marilee Lovit, Donna Kausen, Glen H. Mittelhauser, *and others*

THE UNIVERSITY OF MAINE PRESS, ORONO, MAINE

IN ASSOCIATION WITH THE GARDEN CLUB OF MOUNT DESERT,

FRIENDS OF ACADIA, AND THE MAINE NATURAL HISTORY OBSERVATORY

University of Maine Press
126A College Avenue
Orono, Maine 04473
www.umaine.edu/umpress

FIRST EDITION

14 13 12 11 10 1 2 3 4 5

ISBN: 0-89101-120-X / 978-0-89101-120-0

The paper used in this publication meets the minimum requirements of the American National Standard for Information Sciences—Permanence of Paper for Printed Library Materials, ANSI Z39.48–1984.

Printed and bound in the United States of America by Shapco Printing, Inc., Minneapolis, MN.

Book design by Michael Alpert and Betsy G. Rose.

Cover photograph of Mount Desert Island mountains by Tom Blagden, Jr.

TABLE OF CONTENTS

Edgar T. Wherry was born in Philadelphia in 1885. He received his Ph.D. from the University of Pennsylvania in geology and mineralology in 1909. He worked first at the Smithsonian Institution, then at the U.S. Department of Agriculture in the general area of geology. He married Gertrude Smith in 1914 and settled in Chevy Chase, Maryland. About that time, he became interested in plants, and with characteristic energy soon became an expert. This interest, which quickly narrowed to native American wild plants, became the dominant factor in his life. He became the country's leading authority on ferns, on native phlox, and on native wildflowers, writing definitive books on each. He was a tireless writer; in his lifetime, he published more than 400 papers on geological and horticultural subjects.

In 1930, he joined the faculty of the University of Pennsylvania as Professor of Plant Ecology and Soils, and moved back to the Philadelphia area. He was the first ecologist at the Morris Arboretum, a founder of Bowman Hill Wildflower Preserve, and, in the 1950s, a member of the faculty at the Arboretum of the Barnes Foundation. He was the first editor of the *Bulletin of the American Rock Garden Society*, and also served as editor of *Bartonia*, the journal of the Philadelphia Botanical Club. He ended his life as Professor of Botany, University of Pennsylvania.

Courtesy of The Pennsylvania Horticultural Society (excerpted from PHS's *Green Scene* magazine, January, 1987).

DEDICATED TO DR. EDGAR T. WHERRY

1885–1982

Edgar T. Wherry, *circa* 1925. Wherry was a soft-spoken man with a wry sense of humor. An early conservationist, he once described the vandals who dug up an entire stand of *Gentiana autumnalis* (the pine barren gentian) presumably for commercial purposes, as "a herd of *Swinus vulgaris.*"

In July 1928 the Garden Club of Mount Desert published *Wild Flowers of Mount Desert Island, Maine* by Edgar T. Wherry, then working for the U.S. Department of Agriculture Bureau of Chemistry and Soils.

It is fitting that in 2010, the Garden Club of Mount Desert is again helping to publish a book, *Field Guide to the Plants of Acadia National Park*, with the help of Friends of Acadia, Maine Natural History Observatory, and Julie and Ted Leisenring.

THE GARDEN CLUB OF MOUNT DESERT

The Garden Club of Mount Desert, located in the town of Mount Desert, was founded in 1923, at a time when women's groups were forming all over the country. With the encouragement of the celebrated landscape gardener Beatrix Farrand, a small group of enthusiastic gardeners on Mount Desert established the first garden club on the island. In 1926, the Club was accepted as a member of the Garden Club of America. In accordance with its original mission to stimulate interest and increase knowledge in horticulture, and to protect native flora and fauna, the Garden Club of Mount Desert has throughout its history sponsored Open Garden Day tours and flower shows, which are open to the public; provided scholarship aid and internships to students; and encouraged conservation through symposia. It has also contributed to the community by giving financial assistance to organizations involved in conservation and preservation.

One of the Club's early projects was the funding of an important book by renowned botanist and soil scientist Dr. Edgar T. Wherry entitled *Wild Flowers of Mount Desert Island, Maine.* It is therefore a fulfillment of our mission as well as a great pleasure to support this new publication, *The Plants of Acadia National Park.* In the summer of 2005, Mrs. William Benjamin, president of the Club, invited Acadia National Park botanist Linda Gregory to present to the Club's Board a proposal for a vascular plant guide. With the approval of Club members, the Garden Club of Mount Desert, Friends of Acadia, and the Maine Natural History Observatory formed a partnership in 2006 to work on the book. The Garden Club and Friends of Acadia then financed the production of the manuscript by the Maine Natural History Observatory. Funds for the publication and distribution of the plant guide were generously provided by Mrs. Edward B. Leisenring, a member of the Garden Club, as a tribute to Dr. Wherry. An oversight committee, chaired by Mrs. Gilbert H. Kinney, with Mrs. William E. Benjamin representing the Garden Club of Mount Desert, and Mrs. Kevit R. Cook and Mrs. Benjamin Emory representing Friends of Acadia, managed the plant guide project during the tenures of Garden Club presidents Mrs. William E. Benjamin, Mrs. Persifor Frazer, and Mrs. W. Clayton Hamner.

It is our wish that the current publication will foster knowledge and appreciation of the plants of Acadia National Park, and enhance the enjoyment of its visitors.

FRIENDS OF ACADIA

Friends of Acadia is pleased to partner with the Garden Club of Mount Desert and the Maine Natural History Observatory to produce this guide to the plants of Acadia National Park. Since 1986, Friends has worked to preserve, protect, and promote the natural beauty, ecological vitality, and distinctive cultural features of Acadia National Park and the surrounding communities. Members and volunteers have joined as citizen stewards and funders, enabling Friends to grant more than fourteen million dollars to Acadia National Park and the local communities for conservation projects that include the restoration and maintenance of Acadia's trails and carriage roads, internships in the park, volunteer programs, youth initiatives, and projects that protect Acadia's natural resources. *The Plants of Acadia National Park* is an invaluable tool to understanding the plants essential to Acadia's natural beauty and the ecological systems within and surrounding the park. Friends of Acadia partners, as well, in efforts to reduce the encroachment of invasive plant species in Acadia—a great threat to the continuing ecological vitality of the park. We hope that this plant guide will inspire you to explore Acadia and discover the wonder of its native vascular plants, taking away only photographs and memories. If, in the course of your explorations, you find a plant not identified in this guide, please let us know. You may find a native species previously thought extinct or an invasive species to be noted. But most of all, we hope that you will find great enjoyment and inspiration in discovering the diverse plant life in Acadia National Park. You can find out more about Friends of Acadia at www.friendsofacadia.org, and at P. O. Box 45, Bar Harbor, Maine 04609.

MAINE NATURAL HISTORY OBSERVATORY

Maine Natural History Observatory is a small nonprofit research organization located in Gouldsboro, Maine. Our mission is to advance the knowledge of Maine's natural history and resources. We coordinate efforts to inventory and monitor the local and regional flora, fauna, and habitats of Maine, and compile and publish summaries of Maine's natural history. The Observatory also facilitates cooperation and exchange of information among organizations, agencies, and individuals conducting natural history research in Maine or caring for natural history collections.

Maine Natural History Observatory is proud to cooperate with The Garden Club of Mount Desert, Friends of Acadia, and University of Maine Press to provide researchers, visitors, and residents of the Acadia National Park region with a comprehensive field guide of the flora of the area.

To learn more about our mission, current projects, and publications, visit The Observatory's web site at www.mainenaturalhistory.org.

ACKNOWEDGMENTS

Dr. Craig Greene.

We fondly remember our late friend and colleague Dr. Craig William Greene. Craig's keen knowledge of the Mount Desert Island flora and enthusiasm for sharing it with others inspired many an hour botanizing—exploring and enjoying the wonders of our unique flora—with students, colleagues, friends, and family. Craig's love of hiking, canoeing, swimming, cycling, and photography made him the ultimate field biologist. Professor of Biology at College of the Atlantic (COA) in Bar Harbor and an avid researcher, he studied pollination biology and completed inventories of rare plants and fresh water aquatic vegetation, and a bibliography of natural resource studies in Acadia National Park before his death in October 2003. Craig's extensive botanical work significantly increased the understanding and appreciation of the vegetation in this unusual part of the Maine coast. He initiated research on the plants of Acadia National Park in the 1980s, including the authors of this publication in his forays and inspiring them to complete this work. With this field guide we honor Craig's lasting legacy and hope it will inspire both residents and visitors to appreciate and protect Acadia's unique flora.

We thank The Garden Club of Mount Desert, whose long tradition of making the knowledge of our flora available to all plant lovers has made this guide possible. They, in collaboration with Friends of Acadia and Julia and Ted Leisenring, have generously funded the creation of this pictorial field guide to the flora of Acadia National Park. Special thanks go to Elise Felton and Eliot Paine for their unwavering encouragement. We are grateful for the Maine Natural History Observatory's commitment to the project from its inception.

This field guide was brought to completion with the help of many people. Drafts were field tested by Matt Arsenault, Arthur Haines, and Susan Hayward. David Manski, Chief of Resource Management at Acadia National Park, made numerous helpful comments during its development. We thank Tom Vining, Arthur Haines, and Nishanta Rajakaruna for their careful reviews of all or portions of this guide. Karen Anderson, geographer at Acadia National Park, created the maps. We are grateful to Ann Kinney, Marla O'Byrne, Ian Marquis, Betsy Rose, and Michael Alpert for helping to keep this field guide on schedule throughout its development.

We thank Christopher Campbell for opening the University of Maine Herbarium (MAINE) for our research and allowing us to photograph specimens. Thanks go also to the staff of New England Botanical Club Herbarium (NEBC) and Albion Hodgdon Herbarium at University of New Hampshire (NHA) for allowing us to consult their collections. We are grateful to the many botany students at COA, who over the last twenty-five years have contributed to specimen collection and identification, especially "Queen of the Herbarium" Geneva Langley, whose dedicated efforts have made the COA herbarium (HCOA) a top-notch research collection for coastal Maine.

Obtaining good photographs of each species included in this guide was no small task! We thank Matt Arsenault, Donald Cameron, Bob Gibbons, Carol Gracie, Craig W. Greene, Peter Greenwood, Arthur Haines, C. Barre Hellquist, John Kartesz, Ron Lance, Ed Monnelly, Jason Sacs, Wesley Smith, and Mario Vallejo-Marin for generously allowing us to use their excellent photographs. Thanks to Carol Hess and Daaby Tingle for photo formatting and editing, and to Janet Christrup for her research on species descriptions for selected plant families.

We thank the dedicated staff of Acadia National Park for support of the project over many years, with special thanks to Michael Blaney, Brooke Childrey, Judy Hazen Connery, and David Manski of the Resource Management staff. We also acknowledge C. Smoot Major, who was there in the beginning of this project, for his camaraderie and enthusiasm; together we covered a lot of botanical ground! Heartfelt thanks to Bo and Will Greene, who allowed us unlimited access to Craig's home office and photograph collection.

And finally, we are grateful for our families' love and support always.

—G.H.M., L.L.G., S.C.R., & J.E.W.

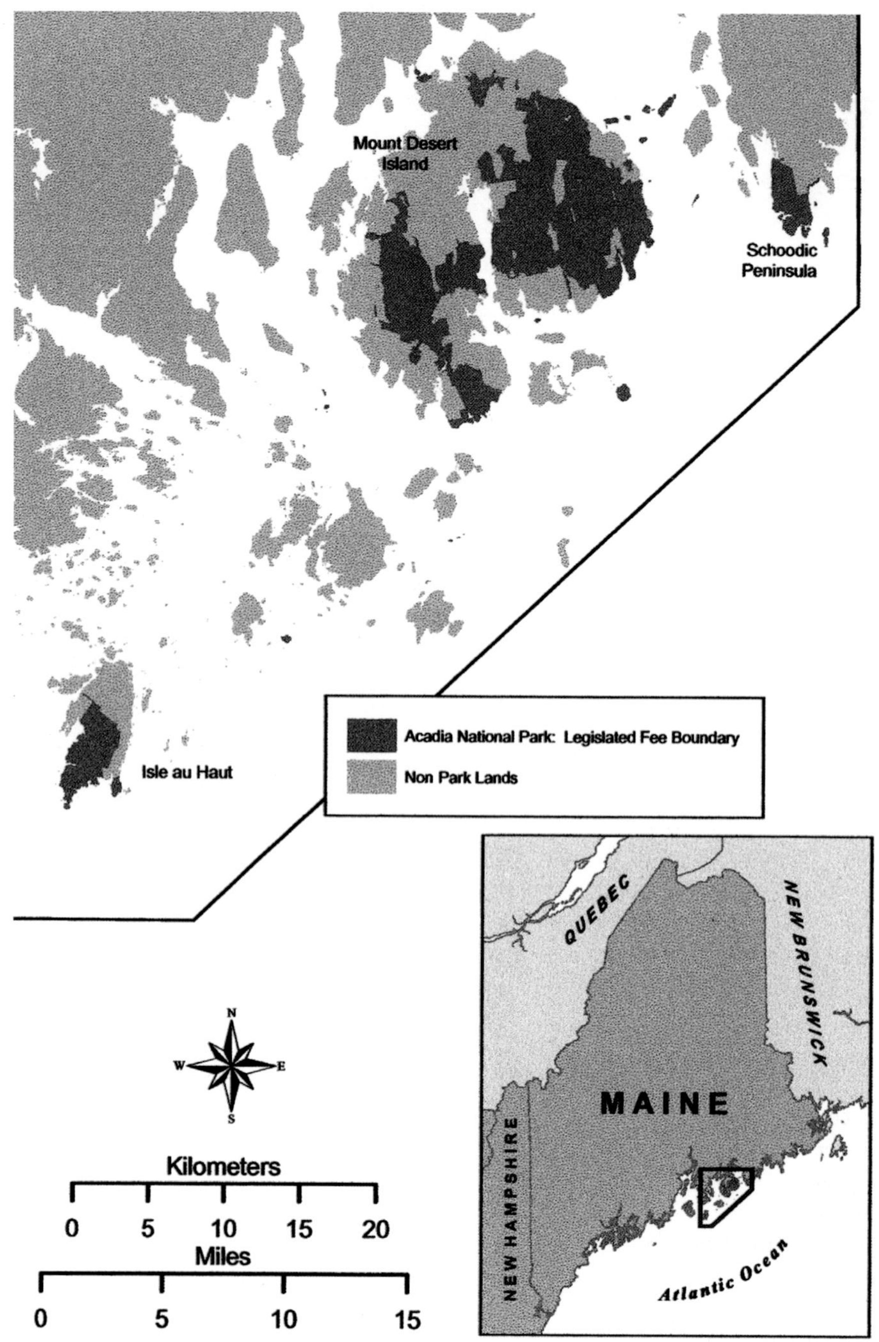

The region covered by this field guide includes all of Mount Desert Island (MDI), all of Isle au Haut (IAH), and park lands on Schoodic Peninsula (SCH).

INTRODUCTION

New Mill Meadow on Mount Desert Island. Photograph by Craig Greene.

This guide covers the plants of Acadia National Park (ANP) and surrounding lands. Acadia National Park comprises parcels on Mount Desert Island (MDI) in Frenchman Bay, Schoodic Peninsula (SCH) east of Frenchman Bay, and Isle au Haut (IAH) in Penobscot Bay. Acadia National Park's main unit of 31,000 acres is on Mount Desert Island, and other units include 2,730 acres on Isle au Haut, 2,265 acres on Schoodic Peninsula, and 200 acres on fifteen small islands near the main units. We also included plants that have been documented on nonpark lands on Mount Desert Island and Isle au Haut. Over 2,100 plant taxa are listed as growing wild in Maine (Campbell et al. 1995). This guide includes 862 plants, or 41% of the state's flora. Our goal in preparing the guide is to provide a reference that will help both the casual plant appreciator and the botanical professional to identify the plants of the region. Like many who have come before us, we have a deep appreciation of the local flora, and we hope to inspire the same in users of the guide.

Seasonal visitors have enjoyed the Acadia National Park region for centuries. Archaeological evidence tells us that Native Americans came to Mount Desert Island to harvest shellfish and fin-fish and to gather coastal fruits and other plant material. When Samuel Champlain arrived in 1604, he named the island Isle des Monts Desert, loosely translated as "Island of barren mountains"—not exactly a place likely to attract travelers! Subsequent visitors reported that this "barren island" was a land of plenty. Large numbers of visitors began traveling to this region of Maine in the mid-nineteenth century after work by painters from the Hudson River School publicized the area's great natural beauty. A portion of what is now Acadia National Park was first designated as Sieur de Monts National Monument in 1916, renamed Lafayette National Park in 1919, and finally established as Acadia National Park in 1929.

The plants of the Acadia National Park region have long fascinated those who have encountered them. Botanical explorations of the area were initiated in 1880 by the Champlain Society, a group of Harvard University students who cataloged the flora and geology of Mount Desert Island from their encampment on Somes Sound. John Redfield, an attorney and amateur botanist, began his own study of the flora two years later. In 1888, Champlain Society member Edward Rand began to collaborate with Redfield to compile and consolidate botanical discoveries by the Champlain Society and reports from other botanists. Their results were published as *Flora of Mount Desert Island, Maine* (Rand and Redfield 1894). Although subtitled a "preliminary catalogue," it included abundance, rarity, and collection locations of nearly 1,500 species of vascular plants, bryophytes, lichens, and algae, and covered Mount Desert Island as well as many of the adjacent islands. Their work was well documented with numerous pressed specimens deposited at the New England Botanical Club Herbarium (NEBC) and Gray Herbarium (GH). Many duplicates from their work were scattered among herbaria in the region; significant collections are currently found at the University of Maine Herbarium (MAINE), Albion Hodgdon Herbarium (NHA), College of the Atlantic Herbarium (HCOA), and Philadelphia Academy of Natural Sciences Herbarium (PH). Over the years that followed, additions to this catalogue were reported in various manuscripts (Chamberlain 1908; Fassett 1927; Fellows et al. 1908; Hill 1914; Norton 1913; Rand 1899a, 1899b, 1903, 1907, 1908; Redfield 1884, 1889; Stebbins 1929a; Taylor 1921). Edgar Wherry, to whom this book is dedicated, conducted additional field work, compiled these additions, and published them (Wherry 1928), along with a guide illustrating the more common wildflowers of the area.

From left to right, Craig Greene, Glen Mittelhauser, Smoot Major, and Linda Gregory inventorying the flora of Acadia National Park in the mid-1980s.

By the early 1900s, botanists also regularly visited other islands in the Acadia National Park region. Wise (1970a, 1970b) published the first flora of Isle au Haut, building upon the efforts of Albert Hill (1919, 1923) and Nathaniel Kidder (1921, 1923a, 1923b, 1928). Vouchers from Isle au Haut made by Hill, Kidder, and Wise are preserved at Albion Hodgdon Herbarium with many duplicates at the New England Botanical Club Herbarium. In contrast, little botanical work has been conducted on the Schoodic Peninsula portion of Acadia National Park. At Schoodic Peninsula, early records of vascular plants were generally single-species reports (Norton 1913; Rand 1889; Redfield 1889; Stebbins 1929b, 1930). Historical vouchers indicate that botanists made occasional collecting forays to Schoodic Peninsula, but few published reports exist. In the early 1980s, Dr. Craig Greene rekindled interest in compiling a flora of the Acadia National Park region. These efforts included collaboration with numerous botanists, College of the Atlantic students, and Acadia National Park biologists. Several progress reports were published based on fieldwork conducted in portions of the Acadia National Park region (Glanz and Connery 1999; Greene 1990; Greene et al. 1999, 2002, 2004; Mittelhauser et al. 1996; Reiner and McLendon 2002). Rand and Redfield had published their flora "with the hope that it can serve as a means of exciting interest in the undertaking, and thus make possible a more complete catalogue in the near future." Over a century after Rand and Redfield's 1894 preliminary catalogue, we presented a comprehensive vascular flora of the Acadia National Park region in our 2005 paper *Vascular Flora of the Acadia National Park Region, Maine*, published in *Rhodora*, the journal of the New England Botanical Club (Greene et al. 2005). We were encouraged by many plant enthusiasts to use our scientific paper as the basis of an up-to-date identification guide to the plants that grow here.

The region covered by this guide includes all portions of Acadia National Park in Hancock and Knox Counties (with the exception of three islands and all easement lands) and some adjacent private lands described below. We separated our study area into three units: Mount Desert Island, Isle au Haut, and Schoodic Peninsula. The Mount Desert Island unit included all of the public and private lands on Mount Desert Island and nine adjacent islands: Baker Island, Bald Porcupine Island, Bar Island (off Bar Harbor), Bar Island (in Somes Sound), Great Cranberry Island, Little Cranberry Island, Sheep Porcupine Island, The Hop, and Thompson Island. This unit excluded the adjacent mainland and Great Duck Island, which was included by Rand and Redfield (1894). The Isle au Haut unit included all of public and private lands on Isle au Haut and Western Ear, a tiny island off the southwestern tip of Isle au Haut. The Schoodic Peninsula unit comprised only Acadia National Park lands and included three adjacent islands: Little Moose Island, Pond Island, and Schoodic Island.

Plants grow in specific places through the interaction of many factors, including topography, geology, soils, and climate. Acadia National Park is in the southwestern-most portion of what scientists call the east coastal biophysical region, which extends east from Mount Desert Island and Schoodic Peninsula to the Canadian border and about 32 km (20 miles) inland. Glacial action created the regional topography, with ridges and mountains running north–south, separated by deep, U-shaped valleys. This region is characterized by small ridges with elevations generally under 30 m (100 ft), which are surrounded by poorly drained lowlands. Because seven of its mountains are over 270 m (900 ft) elevation, Mount Desert Island is exceptional in the region. When people think of the Acadia region, expanses of granite usually come to mind, whether it is the stone of the bold coast, the varied hues of the mountaintops, or the lichen-covered rocks of the forests.

Glaciers also formed the soils of the region, which include acidic tills and clay-rich sediments deposited after the last glacier melted and the sea covered Mount Desert Island and the surrounding land. Mountaintop soils are extremely shallow or even absent, and any precipitation runs off very quickly. Soils of slopes and valleys are deeper and hold enough water and nutrients to support tree growth. Clay deposits are thickest in low, flat areas, where the clay forms a layer that seals water in; this is where wetlands of various types have formed. For example, Big Heath on Mount Desert Island and the smaller peatlands on Isle au Haut and Schoodic Peninsula have clay deposits under them.

Strong and varied environmental gradients at Acadia National Park produce diverse habitats. Over a distance of only a few kilometers, topography on Mount Desert Island ranges from sea level to 466 m (1528 ft) elevation at Cadillac Mountain summit, and ecosystems transition from saltwater to subalpine. Similarly, rocky headlands with minimal soils occur within a few kilometers of bogs where peat is several meters thick. Acadia National Park's vegetation map identifies 53 vegetation types within Acadia National Park, including 23 upland forest and woodland types, five wetland forest and woodland types, six nonforested upland types, six shrub or dwarf shrub wetland types, and 13 herbaceous wetland types. Maine, which is 51,376,000 acres in extent, supports 105 natural communities. Although it represents less than one percent of the state's land area, surprisingly, Mount Desert Island supports more than 50% of Maine's types of natural communities.

The Atlantic Ocean has a moderating effect on Acadia National Park's climate, which is characterized by cool summers and mild winters. Mean July high temperatures are low in the east coastal bioregion, with an average high temperature of 77° F (25° C) in Bar Harbor and only 63° F (17° C) in the town of Eastport, near Maine's coastal border with New Brunswick, Canada. The mean minimum January temperature for Bar Harbor on Mount Desert Island is 14° F (-10° C), and region-wide January minimum temperatures are the warmest in Maine. Average annual precipitation of 122 cm (48 inches) and frequent summer fog cover provide abundant moisture to Acadia National Park, where, unlike the rest of Maine, more precipitation is received in the winter than in the summer.

A number of plant species reach the northern or southern limit of their range in Acadia National Park. Arctic blue flag (*Iris hookeri*), marsh-felwort (*Lomatogonium rotatum*), blinks (*Montia fontana*), baked-apple berry (*Rubus chamaemorus*), and roseroot (*Rhodiola rosea*) are at their southern range limit in the Acadia National Park region. A suite of woody taxa that are either extant or historically documented from Acadia National Park reach their northern or eastern range limits in this ecoregion, including sweet pepperbush (*Clethra alnifolia*), water-willow (*Decodon verticillatus*), mountain laurel (*Kalmia latifolia*), pitch pine (*Pinus rigida*), beach plum (*Prunus maritima*), bear oak (*Quercus ilicifolia*), and purple-flowering raspberry (*Rubus odoratus*).

Some of the species at their range limits in our area are also listed as rare in Maine, as are several others that grow in the region. Plants in this guide that are included on Maine's rare plant list are presented in the table below.

Scientific Name	**Common Name**	**State Rank***
Amelanchier nantucketensis	Nantucket shadbush	S2, T
Bartonia paniculata	Twining screwstem	S1, T
Botrychium lunaria	Moonwort	S1, E
Calamagrostis pickeringii	Pickering's bluejoint	S1, T
Calamagrostis stricta ssp. *inexpansa*	Northern New England reedgrass	S1, E
Carex vacillans	Salt marsh sedge	S2, E
Huperzia appressa	Mountain firmoss	S2, SC
Ilex glabra	Inkberry	S1, E
Isoëtes acadiensis	Acadian quillwort	S2, SC
Isoëtes prototypus	Prototype quillwort	S1, T

Juncus secundus	Lopsided rush	S1, T
Lomatogonium rotatum	Marsh-felwort	S1, T
Minuartia glabra	Appalachian sandwort	S3, SC
Montia fontana	Blinks	S2, SC
Piptatherum canadense	Canada mountain ricegrass	S2, SC
Proserpinaca pectinata	Comb-leaved mermaid-weed	S1, E
Suaeda calceoliformis	Northern sea-blite	S2, T
Vaccinium boreale	Alpine blueberry	S2, SC
Zannichellia palustris	Horned pondweed	S2, SC

* **S1**: Critically imperiled in Maine because of extreme rarity (five or fewer occurrences or very few remaining individuals or acres) or because some aspect of its biology makes it especially vulnerable to extirpation from the State of Maine; **S2**: Imperiled in Maine because of rarity (6–20 occurrences or few remaining individuals or acres) or because of other factors making it vulnerable to further decline; **S3**: Rare in Maine (20–100 occurrences); **E** (endangered): Rare and in danger of being lost from the state in the foreseeable future; or federally listed as Endangered; **T** (threatened): Rare and, with further decline, could become endangered, or federally listed as Threatened; **SC** (special concern): Rare in Maine, based on available information, but not sufficiently rare to be considered Threatened or Endangered.

Acadia National Park provides protected habitat vital to the persistence of these species within the region. In addition, Acadia National Park monitors the rare plant populations that occur on park lands and will conduct management activities if necessary to ensure their survival in the park.

If rare plants are the bonus of our flora, then nonnative, invasive plants might be considered the bane. Nonnative, invasive plants are those not part of the regional flora prior to European settlement and that have been introduced by humans. Many of these species originated in Asia and some are European. In many cases specific insects have coevolved with plants and ultimately control plant population size. When plants were collected in distant lands for food, medicinal, or horticultural use, more often than not, the organisms controlling their spread were left behind, allowing these nonnative species to become established and run rampant in the natural landscapes of their new land. Why is this problematic? One might think that the addition of new species would enhance diversity, but the opposite tends to be true. Most often, these invasive plants are so fast-growing and aggressive that they crowd out and even eliminate natives, resulting in plant communities that comprise only a few species. Undisturbed natural areas typically have a complex structure, with low-growing and mid-sized herbaceous plants, low and taller shrubs, and a multispecies tree canopy. When invasive plants become dominant, the structure becomes more simple, with just a couple of layers and a greatly reduced number of species.

Maine does not have an official list of invasive plant species, but Acadia National Park has developed one. Acadia National Park tracks the locations of these plants and manages some of them, usually with the goal of control, and sometimes of eradication. Invasive species tracked by Acadia National Park are: amur maple (*Acer ginnala*), Norway maple (*Acer platanoides*), garlic mustard (*Alliaria petiolata*), barberries (*Berberis* ×*ottawensis*, *B. thunbergii*, *B. vulgaris*), narrowleaf bittercress (*Cardamine impatiens*),

Asiatic bittersweet (*Celastrus orbiculatus*), Canada thistle (*Cirsium arvense*), winged euonymus (*Euonymus alatus*), Japanese knotweed (*Fallopia japonica*), alder buckthorn (*Frangula alnus*), shrubby St. Johns-wort (*Hypericum prolificum*), nonnative honeysuckle species (*Lonicera* spp.), privet (*Ligustrum* spp.), forest woodrush (*Luzula luzuloides*), purple loosestrife (*Lythrum salicaria*), ninebark (*Physocarpus opulifolius*), black locust (*Robinia pseudoacacia*), multiflora rose (*Rosa multiflora*), bittersweet nightshade (*Solanum dulcamara*), and coltsfoot (*Tussilago farfara*). Several traits of invasive species allow them to proliferate. Many of the shrubby, invasive plants produce fleshy fruits that are eaten by birds and then widely dispersed. Garlic mustard, narrowleaf bittercress, shrubby St. Johns-wort, forest woodrush, purple loosestrife, and ninebark produce thousands of seeds per plant. And Japanese knotweed can produce new plants from root fragments as small as a few cells, making eradication all but impossible. There is little or no control of these plants on private lands, but Acadia National Park's control efforts continue.

In addition to the biophysical conditions described above, the region's land use history has undoubtedly influenced what plants grow here. Evidence shows that Native Americans inhabited the region for about 5,000 years. Their primary influence on plant distribution was probably repeated, small fires they ignited to drive game and keep blueberry lands from becoming forested. Europeans arrived in the seventeenth century, and occupation has been continuous since then with concomitant land clearing, grazing, and timber harvesting. Ships from the Maine coast routinely traveled around the world to engage in trade. Each return voyage likely brought the intended cargo from foreign ports as well as plant seeds, which were introduced to the region both intentionally and unintentionally. Significant changes to the Mount Desert Island flora occurred when a forest fire burned a large portion of the eastern half of the island in 1947, resulting in the creation of thousands of acres of habitat suitable for colonizing plant species and likely eliminating others growing here, such as *Kalmia latifolia*.

Other changes to the local flora have occurred since early botanists compiled lists of the region's plants. Over 200 species historically reported as occurring in the region have not been documented for more than 20 years (Greene et al. 2005). Two orchids, yellow lady's-slipper (*Cypripedium parviflorum*) and showy lady's-slipper (*C. reginae*), may have fallen prey to collection by avid gardeners. In addition, these species and Michaux's sedge (*Carex michauxiana*), long-styled sweet cicely (*Osmorhiza longistylis*), and black snakeroot (*Sanicula marilandica*) require a higher pH than is currently found in most of the region. Land use and climate changes may have caused modifications in soil chemistry that have eliminated these plants from our flora. Several brome grasses (*Bromus commutatus, B. hordeaceus, B. secalinus*) and crested dog's-tail grass (*Cynosurus cristatus*) are agricultural weeds that may have been prevalent when more of the local land was farmed but have now disappeared due to declining agricultural use. Water level changes caused by increased beaver activity may have drowned other plants, including appressed bog clubmoss (*Lycopodiella appressa*).

Some of the 200 plants that have not been reported in more than 20 years undoubtedly are still present and need only to be rediscovered by eager botanizers. Like Rand and Redfield, we hope this field guide will inspire professional botanists and amateurs alike to enjoy, appreciate, and protect our unique flora.

LITERATURE CITED

Campbell, C. S., H. P. Adams, P. Adams, A. C. Dibble, L. M. Eastman, S. C. Gawler, L. L. Gregory, B. A. Grunden, A. D. Haines, K. Jonson, S. C. Rooney, T. F. Vining, J. E. Weber, and W. A. Wright. 1995. *Checklist of the vascular plants of Maine,* third revision, Bulletin 844. Maine Agricultural and Forest Experiment Station, Orono, ME.

Chamberlain, E. B. 1908. Meeting of the Josselyn Botanical Society. *Rhodora* 10: 172.

Fassett, N. C. 1927. A plant new to Mt. Desert. *Rhodora* 29: 253.

Fellows, D. W., C. H. Knowlton, and E. B. Chamberlain. 1908. Josselyn Botanical Society of Maine: fourteenth annual meeting. *Bulletin of the Josselyn Botanical Society of Maine* 2: 3–23.

Glanz, W. E., and B. Connery. 1999. *Biological inventories of Schoodic and Corea Peninsulas, Coastal Maine, 1996.* Technical Report NPS/BSO-RNR/NRTR/00-4. U.S. Department of the Interior, National Park Service, Boston, MA.

Greene, C. W. 1990. *Rare vascular plants of Acadia National Park and the Mount Desert region of Maine.* Technical Report. North Atlantic Region, National Park Service, Boston, MA.

———, L. L. Gregory, G. H. Mittelhauser, S. C. Rooney, and J. E. Weber. 2005. Vascular flora of the Acadia National Park region, Maine. *Rhodora* 107(930): 117–185.

———, C. B. Hellquist, and L. Gregory. 1999. *Survey of fresh water aquatic vegetation of Acadia National Park.* Technical Report NPS/BSO-RNR/NRTR/00-3. U.S. Department of the Interior, National Park Service, Boston, MA.

———, J. Weber, and S. Rooney. 2002. *Rare plant monitoring in Acadia National Park.* Technical Report NPS/BSO-RNR/NRTR/2002-10, Dept. of the Interior, National Park Service, Boston Support Office, Boston, MA.

———, J. Weber, S. Rooney, and K. Anderson. 2004. Invasive plant species distribution and abundance in Acadia National Park. Unpublished report to Acadia National Park, Bar Harbor, ME.

Hill, A. F. 1914. Notes on the flora of the Penobscot Bay region, Maine. *Rhodora* 16: 189–192.

———. 1919. Vascular flora of the Penobscot Bay region. *Proceedings of the Portland Society of Natural History* 3: 119–304.

———. 1923. The vegetation of the Penobscot Bay region, Maine. *Proceedings of the Portland Society of Natural History* 3: 305–438.

Kidder, N. T. 1921. Additions to the flora of Isle au Haut. *Rhodora* 23: 26.

———. 1923a. Isle au Haut plants. *Rhodora* 25: 16.

———. 1923b. Further notes on the plants of Isle au Haut. *Rhodora* 25: 147–148.

———. 1928. *Lemna trisulca* at Isle au Haut, Maine. *Rhodora* 30: 121.

Mittelhauser, G. H., J. H. Connery, and J. Jacobs. 1996. *Inventories of selected flora and fauna on 10 islands of Acadia National Park, Maine.* Natural Resources Technical Report, NPS/NESO-RNR/NRTR/96-01, National Park Service, New England System Support Office, Boston, MA.

Norton, A. H. 1913. Some noteworthy plants from the islands and coast of Maine. *Rhodora* 15: 137–143.

Rand, E. L. 1889. *Pinus banksiana* on the coast of Maine. *Bulletin of the Torrey Botanical Club* 16: 294–295.

———. 1899a. *Pinus banksiana* on Mt. Desert Island. *Rhodora* 1: 135–136.

———. 1899b. *Subularia aquatica* on Mt. Desert Island. *Rhodora.* 1: 155–156.

———. 1903. *Galinsoga* in Maine. *Rhodora* 5: 258.

———. 1907. *Arceuthobium pusillum* at Mt. Desert. *Rhodora* 9: 75–76.

———. 1908. Additions to the plants of Mount Desert Island. *Rhodora* 10: 145.

Rand, E. L., and J. H. Redfield. 1894. *Flora of Mount Desert Island, Maine: a preliminary catalogue of the plants growing on Mount Desert and the adjacent islands.* Cambridge University Press, Cambridge, MA.

Redfield, J. H. 1884. *Corema conradii* and its localities. *Bulletin of the Torrey Botanical Club* 11: 97–101.

———. 1889. *Pinus banksiana* with *Corema conradii. Bulletin of the Torrey Botanical Club* 16: 295–296.

Reiner, D., and T. McLendon. 2002. *Assessment of exotic plant species of Acadia National Park.* Dept. of Interior, Technical Report NPS/BSO-RNR/NRTR/2002-5. National Park Service, New England System Support Office, Boston, MA.

Stebbins, G. L. Jr. 1929a. Further additions to the Mt. Desert Flora. *Rhodora* 31: 81–87

———. 1929b. *Lomatogonium rotatum* (L.) Fries in Maine. *Rhodora* 31: 143.

———. 1930. *Thelypteris fragrans* (L.) Nieuwl. var. *hookeriana* Fernald on the Maine coast. *American Fern Journal* 20: 86–87.

Taylor, W. R. 1921. Additions to the flora of Mount Desert, Maine. *Rhodora* 23: 65–68.

Wherry, E. T. 1928. *Wild flowers of Mount Desert Island, Maine.* Lancaster Press Lancaster, PA.

Wise, D. A. 1970a. The vascular flora of Isle au Haut, Knox County, Maine. Dissertation, University of New Hampshire, Durham, NH.

———. 1970b. The flora of Isle au Haut, Maine. *Rhodora* 72: 505–532.

ABOUT THIS GUIDE

This guide includes the wildflowers, ferns, grasses, sedges, rushes, trees, and shrubs that grow in the Acadia National Park region, which we define as Mount Desert Island (MDI), Isle au Haut (IAH), and Acadia National Park lands on Schoodic Peninsula (SCH). Because the flora of the region is diverse and comprises many species found elsewhere in Maine, especially in coastal habitats, we are confident that the guide will be useful for making plant identifications in other areas of Maine. We encourage users out of the Acadia National Park region to confirm their findings with a guide that specifically covers the area where the plant is growing.

It is illegal to collect plants within the bounds of Acadia National Park. We also discourage the picking of wild plants outside park lands and suggest that you take this book into the field to make your identifications of plants first-hand. If you identify the plant as it is growing, you are less likely to have the frustration of having a crucial part unavailable, as might happen if you collect only a few flowers and a leaf, return home, settle in with your guide to identify the plant, and discover that basal leaves are necessary to separate your plant from three closely related ones! You may find it useful to use a field notebook to record key features and make sketches or to take digital photographs. We encourage everyone to visit the Wild Gardens of Acadia at Sieur de Monts Spring in Acadia National Park, which displays many of the plants in this guide.

HOW THIS GUIDE IS ORGANIZED

In this guide, we separate the plant species into 4 groups: wildflowers (pages 53–363); ferns and other spore-producing plants (pages 365–389); conifers (pages 391–399); and sedges, grasses, and rushes (pages 401–498). Plant families are arranged alphabetically within these groups, as are genera within families and species within genera. We have chosen to arrange this guide by plant family to help users become familiar with the characteristics shared by species within each family. Once practiced in the art of family recognition, plant lovers can often jump ahead several steps in a key and make their identifications more quickly. In an effort to make this guide accessible to as many plant lovers as possible, we have attempted to keep our plant descriptions nontechnical, although the use of some technical terms is necessary for accurate identification. A glossary of the technical terms begins on page 501.

Plant names: We include both scientific and common names for the plants in this guide. Each plant has only one scientific name that is recognized by botanists throughout the world but may have numerous common names, some of which may be identical to unrelated plants. For example, the plant most commonly known in Maine as Indian paintbrush is in the aster family, but in the Rocky Mountain region, the plant called Indian paintbrush is closely related to snapdragons. Scientific names may seem intimidating at first, but after a few trips to the glossary or other reference, you will likely find that the names are descriptive and even entertaining. Scientific plant names used in this field guide are those used in *Flora Novae Angliae* (A. Haines, in preparation). In general, hybrids between two species are not included in this guide unless recent

evidence suggests a nonhybrid treatment of the species is appropriate.
Nonnative species: An asterisk (*) is placed before the scientific name of any plant that is not native to the Acadia National Park region.

Species description: We include measurements of the flowers, leaves, fruits, and seeds. Other characteristics are also described if useful. Italicized text indicates key information used to distinguish a species. We have used the metric system throughout the text because it facilitates the accurate measurement of small plant features. A scale in both metric and English units is printed on the last page inside of the back cover to help users unfamiliar with metric units or those whose rulers routinely disappear from their backpacks.

Occurrence: We base our abundance estimates for the plants in the Acadia National Park region on how often a species has been documented in the region, population size, and on the number and rarity of habitats in which that plant grows. The abundance terms and their definitions are as follows: **common** – species that are widespread and occur in large numbers; **occasional** – species that are sporadic or scattered; **uncommon** – species that occur infrequently; **rare** – species usually restricted to small areas, specialized habitats, or consisting of one or a few populations. We have also record the areas in the Acadia National Park region where each species has been documented: **MDI** – Mount Desert Island and adjacent park islands; **IAH** – Isle au Haut and adjacent park islands; and **SCH** – Acadia National Park lands on Schoodic Peninsula and adjacent park islands.

Notes: This section includes additional information that readers may find interesting. Any reference to a plant's edibility or medicinal use is listed for interest only; we do not encourage consumption of wild plants.

Other names: Other common names and older scientific names are listed at the end of each species' section.

Plant photographs: We have attempted to include photographs of plant features that are useful for identification. Despite our best attempts, we were unable to find and photograph some species at the optimal time to capture their identifying features. Many people have generously allowed us to use their photographs so that we could complete this guide. Photographs used in this guide that were not taken by the authors are identified by the photographer's initials: **AH** – Arthur Haines; **BG** – Bob Gibbons; **CBH** – C. Barre Hellquist; **CG** – Carol Gracie; **CWG** – Craig W. Greene; **DSC** – Donald Cameron; **JS** – Jason Sachs; **MA** – Matt Arsenault; **MV** – Mario Vallejo-Marin; **PG** – Peter Greenwood; **RL** – Ron Lance; and **WS** – Wesley Smith.

NEW PLANT RECORDS

Nearly 200 species that were historically documented in the region have not been reported in more than 20 years. Some of them may still be present and need only be discovered by eager botanists. If you think that you have found a species not included here that is freely reproducing in the guide region, please send details via the contact link at www.mainenaturalhistory.org or mail the information to Maine Natural History Observatory, 317 Guzzle Road, Gouldsboro, ME 04607. Please include the following details: your name and the names of the people who checked the identification; the scientific name of the plant; a detailed description of where the plant was found (a sketch map or coordinates recorded with a GPS are very useful); the day, month, and year when this plant was observed; additional information on the abundance of the species at the site and other species present; and digital photographs, if available. If you encounter a species listed as having a Maine Rarity Ranking, please report it to the Maine Natural Areas Program at www.maine.gov/doc/nrimc/mnap/ or 93 State House Station, Augusta, ME 04333-0093.

FURTHER READING

Technical floras, guides, and reference books

Flora of Maine: a manual for identification of native and naturalized vascular plants of Maine. 1998. A. Haines and T.F. Vining.

Flora Novae Angliae. In preparation. A. Haines.

Manual of vascular plants of northeastern United States and adjacent Canada. 1991. H.A. Gleason and A. Cronquist.

The illustrated companion to Gleason and Cronquist's manual – illustrations of the vascular plants of northeastern United States and adjacent Canada. 1998. N.H. Holmgren.

Aquatic and wetland plants of northeastern North America. 2 volumes. 2000. G.E. Crow and C.B. Hellquist.

Gray's manual of botany, 8th edition. 1950. M.L. Fernald.

The genus Viola *of Maine: a taxonomic and ecological reference.* 2001. A. Haines.

The families Huperziaceae and Lycopodiaceae of New England: a taxonomic and ecological reference. 2003. A. Haines.

Plant identification terminology: an illustrated glossary. 1999. J.G. Harris and M.W. Harris.

Photographic or illustrated field guides

Newcomb's wildflower guide. 1977. L. Newcomb.

Wildflowers in the field and forest: a field guide to the northeastern United States. 2006. S. Clemants and C. Gracie.

Ferns of northeastern and central North America. 2005. B. Cobb, E. Farnsworth, and C. Lowe.

Forest trees of Maine. 2008. Maine Forest Service.

Wildflowers of the eastern United States. 1999. W.H. Duncan and M.B. Duncan.

HOW TO USE THIS GUIDE

Whether you are a first time plant observer or a seasoned professional, we welcome you to the beautiful and exciting world of coastal Maine botany! This guide is designed to help all users identify plants that grow in and around Acadia National Park; it is not designed to replace technical guides that have broader geographic and taxonomic scopes. Users will not be able to accurately identify all plants they encounter solely by using this guide. Rather, for particularly complex taxonomic groups such as grasses, sedges, and willows, users can use this book to arrive at what you suspect to be a correct identification, but you will then need to verify their result by consulting a more technical manual that considers more subtle characteristics than are included here (see previous page for a list of suggested publications). In most instances, users will be pleased to find that this guide will lead them to a correct answer without the use of a dissecting scope and technical identification keys.

Below are several approaches for using this book to identify a plant you encounter:

• **Use the index:** If you know the common or scientific name of the plant or the family to which the plant belongs, simply use the index to find the name and page number and confirm your identification.

• **Browse the plant family photographs:** Turn to page 28 and scan the thumbnail photographs for plants that match your specimen. This section contains thumbnail photographs for all families and most genera of plants in this guide.

• **Skim through the species pages:** When all else fails, thumb through the book to find your mystery plant. Although this method is inefficient, it is a great way to become familiar with the plants of the Acadia National Park region.

• **Use the keys:** The **Master Key**, the **Flower and Leaf Keys**, and **Plant Family Photographs** are very useful features of this book, and we encourage you to use them. These keys and summary photographs are designed to help you determine and, in some instances, separate similar looking plants. Plant keys can be intimidating, but the **Flower and Leaf Keys** in this guide are simple to follow and will often quickly limit the number of species you need to consider. To use the keys, take the following steps.

1. First, have a close look at your plant to determine flower type, leaf type, and the arrangement of the leaves on the plant. Consult the **Definitions** table on page 15 or the glossary beginning on page 501 to become familiar with the terms used in the keys.

2. Use the **Master Key** on page 16 to help you decide which **Flower and Leaf Key** to use. Choose the option that best describes your plant. Some highly variable or confusing plants are in multiple keys and categories within a key. In the aster family (Asteraceae), the "flower" is actually an inflorescence of many tiny flowers (disc

flowers or ray flowers) that are grouped together to form a flower head (capitulum). For all species in the aster family, the number of petal-like parts referred to in the keys is the number of petal-like ray flowers in a capitulum.

3. Go to the appropriate **Flower and Leaf Key** and find the row that best represents the arrangement of leaves on your plant (basal only, alternate, opposite or whorled, or none) and the column that best represents the leaf type (entire, toothed or lobed, or divided). Find the cell in the table where the row and column you have chosen cross.

4. In the table cell you will usually find a list of flower colors (refers to the color of the petal-like parts) in capital letters followed by a list of plant families (in bold letters) and genera (in italics). Although flower colors can be quite variable from plant to plant, we have chosen basic color categories to help account for this variability: MOSTLY WHITE, BLUE to PURPLE, PINK to RED (we include magenta and brown-red here), ORANGE, YELLOW, GREEN, and BROWN. Plants with highly variable flower color are listed under more than one color. If there are many plant families listed under a particular color, we have included a simple key to help narrow down your choices. For example, you may encounter the following two options under FLOWERS MOSTLY WHITE: "❖Stems woody at base:" and, a few lines below, an alternate "❖Stems herbaceous:". This is known as a dichotomous key, which offers two contrasting alternatives known as a couplet. In the above example, if your plant is woody at the base (a shrub or a tree for example), you should look at the plant families and genera listed directly beneath "❖Stems woody at base:". If your plant is not woody at the base and is instead herbaceous, you should consider the plant families and genera listed directly beneath "❖Stems herbaceous:".

5. Next, go to the **Plant Family Photographs** section, which starts on page 28. Read the family descriptions and look at the photographs that represent the genera within the families. Choose the family whose description and photographs best match your specimen.

6. Return to the **Flower and Leaf Key** and note the genera (in italics) within your chosen plant family and then return to the **Plant Family Photographs** section to compare your unknown plant with the photographs of those particular genera. Look through the photographs and find one or two that look most similar to your plant. Remember that flower color often varies, and the photographs are unlikely to match your specimen exactly.

7. In the species pages (starting on page 53) find each genus you have selected and look at the photographs within each genus. When you find a species that seems to match your specimen, read the species description carefully. If the description matches, Eureka, you've identified your plant. If not, return to the keys and try other options.

EXAMPLE 1: WILDFLOWERS

Almost everyone is familiar with daisies. Let us assume that you are standing next to a tuft of daisies in full flower and you want to see if you can use this guide to correctly identify them. First, you may want to consult the definitions table on page 15 to determine if the flower is bilaterally symmetric or radially symmetric. Because the daisy flower has petal-like parts that radiate out from the center like spokes on a wheel, you decide that it is radially symmetric. It has more than seven petal-like parts, so from the **Master Key** on page 16, you select the **Flower and Leaf Key** for "radially symmetric flowers, 7 or more petal-like parts" on page 25. In this key, first look at the rows to determine the leaf arrangement. Based on the **Definitions** on page 15, you decide that the leaves are alternate, because they are present on the stem and occur singly, rather than in groups of two or more. Next, you examine the daisy's leaf edges and notice that rather than being entire, the edges have teeth and lobes, but the sinuses between the lobes do not extend all the way to the middle of the leaf, so you choose: toothed or lobed. If you look in the cell that is in both the toothed or lobed column and in the alternate row, and look under the heading FLOWERS MOSTLY WHITE, you will see two plant families listed in bold letters (Aquifoliaceae and Asteraceae) and a list of plant genera (in italics) under each family. Look up these two families in the **Plant Family Photographs** section. A quick glance at the thumbnail photographs and description of the families should suggest that the family Asteraceae is the correct family. Glancing back at the **Flower and Leaf Key**, you will find that the list of genera under the Asteraceae family includes *Achillea, Erigeron, Leucanthemum, Nabalus, Oclemena, Petasites, Solidago*, and *Symphyotrichum*. Return to the **Plant Family Photographs** section, and find Asteraceae and examine the photographs for these genera. You might decide that *Leucanthemum* and *Symphyotrichum* look most similar to your plant and decide to check both. As noted in the **Plant Family Photographs** section, the species pages in the Asteraceae family begin on page 78. Turn to the Asteraceae family and search alphabetically to find the genus *Leucanthemum*. The description and photographs on page 100 match your plant well, but you decide to check *Symphyotrichum,* just to make sure. You see five species of *Symphyotrichum* on pages 114–116, but none of them looks as much like your plant as the *Leucanthemum* photographs do. You decide that your daisy is an ox-eye daisy, and its Latin name is *Leucanthemum vulgare.*

Some groups of plants do not have flowers (ferns and other spore-producing plants, conifers) or may have flowers without showy petals (sedges, rushes, and grasses). Identification of these plants can be a little intimidating at first, but with a little practice it is fun and rewarding to identify and see some of the features that characterize these groups.

EXAMPLE 2: FERNS

As you descend a mountain trail along a brook in Acadia National Park, you encounter an area where the ground levels out, the brook widens, and the habitat becomes marsh-like. You see some large ferns, almost a meter tall and wonder what they are. You pull out your Plants of Acadia National Park field guide and settle down to identify them.

As usual, you start on page 16 with the **Master Key**. Because ferns (and a few other related species) reproduce by spores rather than seeds and have no flowers, you choose "Petal-like parts indistinguishable, trees & shrubs, spore-producing plants, and grass-like plants" on page 26. Looking at this key, there is a row for spore-producing plants. The leaves of your unknown fern are cut all the way to the middle of the leaf, so you choose the leaves divided column. You look in the cell that is in both the spore-producing plants row and in the leaves divided column, and you find a couplet of a dichotomous key: "❖Veins of leaves in a net-like pattern" and "❖Veins of leaves not in a net-like pattern". After closely examining the veins of your unknown fern, you decide that the veins are not in a net-like pattern. You now encounter another couplet: "♦Leaves dissected into pinnae but not pinnules:" or the alternative "♦Leaves dissected into pinnules:". After using the glossary to look up the definitions of pinnules and pinnae, you decide that your fern frond is highly dissected into pinnules. Now you have six fern families to check (Dennstaedtiaceae, Dryopteridaceae, Ophioglossaceae, Osmundaceae, Pteridaceae, and Woodsiaceae). You examine the photographs and family descriptions in the **Plant Family Photographs** section and in your search, you find that your unknown fern looks exactly like one of the *Osmunda* photographs in the Osmundaceae family. You turn to the Osmundaceae family on the species pages and look at the two species in the genus *Osmunda*. The leaves of your unknown fern have green parts at the bottom and top, but have darkened, spore-containing curled areas in the middle. When you look at the book, you see that it looks exactly like interrupted fern (*Osmunda claytoniana*).

EXAMPLE 3: SEDGES, RUSHES, AND GRASSES

You are sitting on the summit of Cadillac Mountain, admiring the view when you feel something tickle the exposed part of your shorts-clad leg. You look down and find that a delicate grass is blowing in the wind and wonder what its name might be. You remember reading earlier in this guide that users will not be able to accurately identify all plants they encounter solely by using this guide, but you decide to give it a try anyway. Even when you look closely, you cannot distinguish petal-like parts, and this species is grass-like, so guided by the **Master Key** on page 16, you decide to check page 26 of the **Flower and Leaf Keys** "Petal-like parts indistinguishable, trees & shrubs, spore-producing plants, and grass-like plants." In the key, there is a row for grass-like plants and under leaves entire, you find five plant families (Cyperaceae, Juncaceae, Juncaginaceae, Poaceae, and Zosteraceae). By searching through the **Plant Family Photographs** section and reading the family descriptions, you decide that your plant is probably a member of the Cyperaceae or Poaceae families. After looking through the Cyperaceae and Poaceae pages a while longer, you decide that your plant is in the Poaceae family and is probably either wavy hairgrass (*Deschampsia flexuosa*) or Canada mountain ricegrass (*Piptatherum canadense*). It has also become clear that this guide has reached the limits of its scope and, if you want to correctly identify this grass, you will need more information. Ready for a challenge, you stop at the library on your way home, use some technical manuals, search for additional pictures on the internet, and decide that the plant that tickled you on Cadillac was wavy hairgrass.

FLOWER TYPE	BILATERALLY SYMMETRIC	A type of flower that can be divided through the center into two equal parts by only one plane.
	RADIALLY SYMMETRIC	A type of flower with petal-like parts radiating from a common point, like the spokes of a wheel.
LEAF TYPE	ENTIRE	Margin of the leaves without teeth or lobes; occasionally species with only basal lobes included here.
	TOOTHED OR LOBED	Margin of the leaves with more or less regular serrations, notches, points, or lobes.
	DIVIDED	Leaves deeply cut into distinct parts; divisions must reach to the midrib.
ARRANGEMENT OF LEAVES	OPPOSITE or WHORLED	Plants with 2 (opposite) or more (whorled) leaves at each node along the stem.
	ALTERNATE	Plants with only 1 leaf at each node along the stem.
	BASAL ONLY	Leaves growing only from the base of the plant; without leaves along the stem.
	NONE	No leaves present during flowering.

MASTER KEY

Bilaterally symmetric flowers		pages 17–18
Radially symmetric flowers, 2 petal-like parts		page 19
Radially symmetric flowers, 3 petal-like parts		page 20
Radially symmetric flowers, 4 petal-like parts		page 21
Radially symmetric flowers, 5 petal-like parts		pages 22–23
Radially symmetric flowers, 6 petal-like parts		page 24
Radially symmetric flowers, 7 or more petal-like parts		page 25
Petal-like parts indistinguishable: trees & shrubs, spore-producing plants, and grass-like plants		page 26
Petal-like parts indistinguishable: herbaceous and non-grass-like plants		page 27

Bilaterally symmetric flowers

	LEAVES ENTIRE	LEAVES TOOTHED or LOBED	LEAVES DIVIDED
LEAVES BASAL ONLY	FLOWERS MOSTLY WHITE Araceae – *Calla* Campanulaceae – *Lobelia* Orchidaceae – *Goodyera, Spiranthes* FLOWERS BLUE to PURPLE Araceae – *Symplocarpus* Campanulaceae – *Lobelia* FLOWERS PINK to RED Orchidaceae – *Arethusa, Calopogon, Cypripedium*	FLOWERS MOSTLY WHITE Violaceae – *Viola* FLOWERS BLUE to PURPLE Violaceae – *Viola*	FLOWERS MOSTLY WHITE Fabaceae – *Trifolium*
LEAVES ALTERNATE	FLOWERS MOSTLY WHITE Orchidaceae – *Platanthera, Spiranthes* Plantaginaceae – *Digitalis* FLOWERS BLUE to PURPLE Plantaginaceae – *Nuttallanthus* Polygalaceae – *Polygala* Pontederiaceae – *Pontederia* FLOWERS PINK to RED Ericaceae – *Rhododendron* Orchidaceae – *Platanthera, Pogonia* Plantaginaceae – *Digitalis* Polygalaceae – *Polygala* Polygonaceae – *Persicaria* FLOWERS YELLOW Euphorbiaceae – *Euphorbia* Fabaceae – *Genista, Laburnum* Orchidaceae – *Epipactis, Platanthera* Plantaginaceae – *Linaria* FLOWERS GREEN Orchidaceae – *Corallorhiza, Epipactis, Malaxis, Platanthera* Polygalaceae – *Polygala*	FLOWERS BLUE to PURPLE Campanulaceae – *Lobelia* Plantaginaceae – *Veronica* Violaceae – *Viola* FLOWERS PINK to RED Campanulaceae – *Lobelia* Orobanchaceae – *Pedicularis* FLOWERS YELLOW Balsaminaceae – *Impatiens* Orobanchaceae – *Pedicularis*	FLOWERS MOSTLY WHITE Fabaceae – *Amphicarpaea, Lupinus, Robinia, Securigera, Trifolium* Papaveraceae – *Adlumia* FLOWERS BLUE to PURPLE Araceae – *Arisaema* Campanulaceae – *Lobelia* Fabaceae – *Amorpha, Amphicarpaea, Lathyrus, Lupinus, Medicago, Trifolium, Vicia* FLOWERS PINK to RED Fabaceae – *Lupinus, Robinia, Securigera, Trifolium, Vicia* Orobanchaceae – *Pedicularis* Papaveraceae – *Adlumia, Capnoides* FLOWERS YELLOW Fabaceae – *Lathyrus, Lotus, Medicago, Melilotus, Thermopsis, Trifolium* Orobanchaceae – *Pedicularis* Papaveraceae – *Capnoides*

Continued on the next page

Bilaterally symmetric flowers

	LEAVES ENTIRE	LEAVES TOOTHED or LOBED	LEAVES DIVIDED
LEAVES OPPOSITE or WHORLED	FLOWERS MOSTLY WHITE Caprifoliaceae – *Lonicera* Orobanchaceae – *Melampyrum* Plantaginaceae – *Veronica* FLOWERS BLUE to PURPLE ❖Stems square: Lamiaceae – *Prunella* ❖Stems round: Orchidaceae – *Listera* Plantaginaceae – *Veronica* Polygalaceae – *Polygala* FLOWERS PINK to RED Orobanchaceae – *Agalinis* FLOWERS YELLOW Caprifoliaceae – *Lonicera* Euphorbiaceae – *Euphorbia* Orobanchaceae – *Melampyrum* FLOWERS GREEN Polygalaceae – *Polygala*	FLOWERS MOSTLY WHITE Lamiaceae – *Lycopus, Mentha* Orobanchaceae – *Euphrasia, Melampyrum* Plantaginaceae – *Chelone* FLOWERS BLUE to PURPLE Balsaminaceae – *Impatiens* Lamiaceae – *Mentha, Prunella, Scutellaria, Teucrium* Orobanchaceae – *Euphrasia* Plantaginaceae – *Veronica* FLOWERS PINK to RED Lamiaceae – *Galeopsis, Mentha, Stachys, Thymus* Orobanchaceae – *Euphrasia, Odontites* Plantaginaceae – *Chelone* FLOWERS YELLOW Caprifoliaceae – *Diervilla* Orobanchaceae – *Melampyrum, Rhinanthus* FLOWERS GREEN Scrophulariaceae – *Scrophularia* FLOWERS BROWN Scrophulariaceae – *Scrophularia*	FLOWERS BLUE to PURPLE Araceae – *Arisaema*
LEAVES NONE	FLOWERS MOSTLY WHITE Orobanchaceae – *Epifagus* FLOWERS BLUE to PURPLE Araceae – *Symplocarpus* Lentibulariaceae – *Utricularia* FLOWERS PINK to RED Lentibulariaceae – *Utricularia* Orchidaceae – *Arethusa* FLOWERS YELLOW Lentibulariaceae – *Utricularia* FLOWERS GREEN Orchidaceae – *Corallorhiza*		

Radially symmetric flowers with 2 petal-like parts

	LEAVES ENTIRE	LEAVES TOOTHED or LOBED	LEAVES DIVIDED
LEAVES ALTERNATE	FLOWERS YELLOW Euphorbiaceae – *Euphorbia*		FLOWERS MOSTLY WHITE Papaveraceae – *Adlumia* PINK to RED Papaveraceae – *Adlumia*
LEAVES OPPOSITE or WHORLED	FLOWERS PINK to RED Elatinaceae – *Elatine*	FLOWERS MOSTLY WHITE Onagraceae – *Circaea*	

Radially symmetric flowers with 3 petal-like parts

	LEAVES ENTIRE	LEAVES TOOTHED or LOBED	LEAVES DIVIDED
LEAVES BASAL ONLY	FLOWERS MOSTLY WHITE Alismataceae – *Alisma, Sagittaria* Hydrocharitaceae – *Vallisneria* FLOWERS BLUE to PURPLE Iridaceae – *Iris* FLOWERS YELLOW Xyridaceae – *Xyris*		
LEAVES ALTERNATE	FLOWERS BLUE to PURPLE Ericaceae – *Empetrum* Iridaceae – *Iris* FLOWERS PINK to RED Cistaceae – *Lechea* FLOWERS GREEN Scheuchzeriaceae – *Scheuchzeria*	FLOWERS YELLOW Asteraceae – *Solidago* FLOWERS GREEN Haloragaceae – *Proserpinaca*	FLOWERS MOSTLY WHITE Ranunculaceae – *Actaea*
LEAVES OPPOSITE or WHORLED	FLOWERS MOSTLY WHITE Hydrocharitaceae – *Vallisneria* Melanthiaceae – *Trillium* Rubiaceae – *Galium* FLOWERS BLUE to PURPLE Ericaceae – *Empetrum*		

Radially symmetric flowers with 4 petal-like parts

	LEAVES ENTIRE	LEAVES TOOTHED or LOBED	LEAVES DIVIDED
LEAVES BASAL ONLY	FLOWERS MOSTLY WHITE Brassicaceae – *Draba, Subularia*		
LEAVES ALTERNATE	FLOWERS MOSTLY WHITE ❖Stems woody at least at base: Aquifoliaceae – *Ilex* Cornaceae – *Swida* Ericaceae – *Gaultheria, Vaccinium* ❖Stems herbaceous: Gentianaceae – *Bartonia* Polygonaceae – *Persicaria* Potamogetonaceae – *Potamogeton* Ruscaceae – *Maianthemum* FLOWERS BLUE to PURPLE Brassicaceae – *Boechera* FLOWERS PINK to RED Crassulaceae – *Rhodiola* Ericaceae – *Vaccinium* Onagraceae – *Chamerion, Epilobium* FLOWERS YELLOW Brassicaceae – *Boechera, Erysimum* Crassulaceae – *Rhodiola, Sedum* Euphorbiaceae – *Euphorbia* Hamamelidaceae – *Hamamelis* Onagraceae – *Oenothera* Portulacaceae – *Portulaca* FLOWERS GREEN Potamogetonaceae – *Potamogeton, Stuckenia*	FLOWERS MOSTLY WHITE Aquifoliaceae – *Ilex* Brassicaceae – *Alliaria, Capsella, Hesperis, Lepidium, Thlaspi* FLOWERS BLUE to PURPLE Brassicaceae – *Boechera, Cakile, Hesperis* FLOWERS PINK to RED Brassicaceae – *Hesperis* Crassulaceae – *Rhodiola* Onagraceae – *Chamerion, Epilobium* FLOWERS YELLOW ❖Stems woody at least at base: Hamamelidaceae – *Hamamelis* ❖Stems herbaceous: Asteraceae – *Solidago* Brassicaceae – *Boechera, Brassica, Erysimum* Crassulaceae – *Rhodiola* Onagraceae – *Oenothera*	FLOWERS MOSTLY WHITE Asteraceae – *Achillea* Brassicaceae – *Capsella, Cardamine, Lepidium* Ranunculaceae – *Actaea* FLOWERS PINK to RED Brassicaceae – *Cardamine* FLOWERS YELLOW Brassicaceae – *Barbarea, Brassica, Raphanus, Sisymbrium* Papaveraceae – *Chelidonium* FLOWERS GREEN Haloragaceae – *Myriophyllum*
LEAVES OPPOSITE or WHORLED	FLOWERS MOSTLY WHITE ❖Stems woody at least at base: Cornaceae – *Swida* Ericaceae – *Calluna* Oleaceae – *Ligustrum* ❖Stems herbaceous: Caryophyllaceae – *Sagina* Cornaceae – *Chamaepericlymenum* Linaceae – *Linum* Onagraceae – *Epilobium* Plantaginaceae – *Veronica* Rubiaceae – *Galium, Mitchella* FLOWERS BLUE to PURPLE Gentianaceae – *Lomatogonium* Plantaginaceae – *Veronica* Rubiaceae – *Houstonia* FLOWERS PINK to RED Ericaceae – *Calluna* Onagraceae – *Epilobium* FLOWERS YELLOW Gentianaceae – *Bartonia* Rubiaceae – *Galium*	FLOWERS MOSTLY WHITE ❖Stems square: Lamiaceae – *Lycopus, Mentha* ❖Stems round: Asteraceae – *Galinsoga* Onagraceae – *Circaea* Plantaginaceae – *Veronica, Veronicastrum* FLOWERS BLUE to PURPLE Lamiaceae – *Mentha* Plantaginaceae – *Veronica* FLOWERS PINK to RED Celastraceae – *Euonymus* Lamiaceae – *Mentha* Melastomataceae – *Rhexia* Onagraceae – *Epilobium* FLOWERS YELLOW Saxifragaceae – *Chrysosplenium* FLOWERS GREEN Celastraceae – *Euonymus* Saxifragaceae – *Chrysosplenium*	FLOWERS GREEN Haloragaceae – *Myriophyllum*

Radially symmetric flowers with 5 petal-like parts

	LEAVES ENTIRE	LEAVES TOOTHED or LOBED	LEAVES DIVIDED
LEAVES BASAL ONLY	FLOWERS MOSTLY WHITE **Droseraceae** – *Drosera* **Ericaceae** – *Orthilia, Pyrola* **Menyanthaceae** – *Nymphoides* FLOWERS BLUE to PURPLE **Plumbaginaceae** – *Limonium* FLOWERS YELLOW **Nymphaeaceae** – *Nuphar* FLOWERS GREEN **Ericaceae** – *Pyrola*	FLOWERS MOSTLY WHITE **Ericaceae** – *Moneses, Orthilia* **Rosaceae** – *Rubus* **Saxifragaceae** – *Micranthes* FLOWERS PINK to RED **Sarraceniaceae** – *Sarracenia* FLOWERS YELLOW **Ranunculaceae** – *Ranunculus* FLOWERS GREEN **Saxifragaceae** – *Mitella*	FLOWERS MOSTLY WHITE ❖Plant aquatic: **Menyanthaceae** – *Menyanthes* ❖Plant terrestrial: **Apiaceae** – *Aralia* **Oxalidaceae** – *Oxalis* **Ranunculaceae** – *Coptis* **Rosaceae** – *Fragaria* FLOWERS YELLOW **Rosaceae** – *Argentina*
LEAVES ALTERNATE	FLOWERS MOSTLY WHITE ❖Stems woody at least at base: **Aquifoliaceae** – *Ilex* **Ericaceae** – *Andromeda, Arctostaphylos, Chamaedaphne, Epigaea, Gaylussacia, Rhododendron, Vaccinium* **Rhamnaceae** – *Frangula* ❖Stems herbaceous: ♦Plant a vine: **Convolvulaceae** – *Calystegia* **Polygonaceae** – *Fallopia* ♦Plant not a vine: **Campanulaceae** – *Campanula* **Menyanthaceae** – *Nymphoides* **Polygonaceae** – all genera except *Rumex* FLOWERS BLUE to PURPLE **Boraginaceae** – *Mertensia, Myosotis* **Campanulaceae** – *Campanula* FLOWERS PINK to RED **Convolvulaceae** – *Calystegia* **Ericaceae** – *Andromeda, Arctostaphylos, Epigaea, Gaylussacia, Vaccinium* **Polygonaceae** – *Persicaria, Polygonum* FLOWERS YELLOW ❖Leaves fleshy: **Crassulaceae** – *Sedum* **Portulacaceae** – *Portulaca* ❖Leaves not fleshy: **Asteraceae** – *Solidago* **Cistaceae** – *Hudsonia* **Ericaceae** – *Hypopitys* **Scrophulariaceae** – *Verbascum*	FLOWERS MOSTLY WHITE ❖Stems woody at least at base: **Aquifoliaceae** – *Ilex* **Ericaceae** – *Gaultheria, Vaccinium* **Grossulariaceae** – *Ribes* **Rosaceae** – *Amelanchier, Aronia, Crataegus, Malus, Physocarpus, Prunus, Rubus, Spiraea* ❖Stems herbaceous: **Malvaceae** – *Malva* **Campanulaceae** – *Campanula* FLOWERS BLUE to PURPLE **Campanulaceae** – *Campanula* **Solanaceae** – *Solanum* FLOWERS PINK to RED **Crassulaceae** – *Hylotelephium* **Ericaceae** – *Vaccinium* **Malvaceae** – *Malva* **Rosaceae** – *Rubus, Spiraea* FLOWERS YELLOW **Asteraceae** – *Mycelis, Solidago* **Malvaceae** – *Tilia* **Ranunculaceae** – *Caltha, Ranunculus* **Scrophulariaceae** – *Verbascum* FLOWERS GREEN **Celastraceae** – *Celastrus*	FLOWERS MOSTLY WHITE ❖Petals <5 mm long: **Apiaceae** – all genera except *Heracleum* **Ranunculaceae** – *Actaea* **Vitaceae** – *Parthenocissus* ❖Petals >5 mm long: **Apiaceae** – *Heracleum* **Asteraceae** – *Achillea* **Malvaceae** – *Malva* **Rosaceae** – *Aruncus, Geum, Rosa, Rubus, Sibbaldiopsis, Sorbaria, Sorbus* FLOWERS BLUE to PURPLE **Ranunculaceae** – *Aquilegia* **Rosaceae** – *Comarum* FLOWERS PINK to RED **Malvaceae** – *Malva* **Ranunculaceae** – *Aquilegia* **Rosaceae** – *Comarum, Rosa* FLOWERS YELLOW ❖Stems with prickles: **Solanaceae** – *Solanum* ❖Stems without prickles: **Anacardiaceae** – *Toxicodendron* **Asteraceae** – *Mycelis* **Oxalidaceae** – *Oxalis* **Ranunculaceae** – *Ranunculus* **Rosaceae** – *Dasiphora, Geum, Potentilla* FLOWERS GREEN **Anacardiaceae** – *Rhus, Toxicodendron*

Continued on the next page

Radially symmetric flowers with 5 petal-like parts

	LEAVES ENTIRE	LEAVES TOOTHED or LOBED	LEAVES DIVIDED
LEAVES OPPOSITE or WHORLED	FLOWERS MOSTLY WHITE ❖Stems woody at least at base: **Adoxaceae** – *Viburnum* **Caprifoliaceae** – *Lonicera, Symphoricarpos* ❖Stems herbaceous: ♦Petals <3 mm long: **Portulacaceae** – *Montia* ♦Petals >3 mm long: **Caryophyllaceae** – all genera except *Dianthus* **Linaceae** – *Linum* **Myrsinaceae** – *Lysimachia* FLOWERS BLUE to PURPLE **Apocynaceae** – *Asclepias* **Gentianaceae** – *Lomatogonium* **Lythraceae** – *Decodon* FLOWERS PINK to RED ❖Stems woody at least at base: **Caprifoliaceae** – *Symphoricarpos* **Ericaceae** – *Kalmia* ❖Stems herbaceous: ♦Stems with milky sap: **Apocynaceae** – *Apocynum, Asclepias* ♦Stems without milky sap: **Caryophyllaceae** – *Dianthus, Saponaria, Spergularia* **Hypericaceae** – *Triadenum* **Lythraceae** – *Decodon, Lythrum* **Myrsinaceae** – *Lysimachia* **Orobanchaceae** – *Agalinis* FLOWERS YELLOW ❖Stems woody at least at base: **Caprifoliaceae** – *Lonicera* **Cistaceae** – *Hudsonia* **Hypericaceae** – *Hypericum* ❖Stems herbaceous: **Myrsinaceae** – *Lysimachia*	FLOWERS MOSTLY WHITE ❖Stems woody at least at base: **Adoxaceae** – *Viburnum* **Ericaceae** – *Chimaphila, Gaultheria* **Sapindaceae** – *Acer* ❖Stems herbaceous: **Asteraceae** – *Eupatorium, Galinsoga* **Lamiaceae** – *Lycopus* FLOWERS BLUE to PURPLE **Verbenaceae** – *Verbena* FLOWERS PINK to RED **Caprifoliaceae** – *Linnaea* **Ericaceae** – *Chimaphila* **Geraniaceae** – *Geranium* **Sapindaceae** – *Acer* FLOWERS YELLOW **Caprifoliaceae** – *Diervilla* **Sapindaceae** – *Acer* FLOWERS GREEN **Sapindaceae** – *Acer*	FLOWERS MOSTLY WHITE **Adoxaceae** – *Sambucus* **Caprifoliaceae** – *Valeriana* **Ranunculaceae** – *Anemone* FLOWERS PINK to RED **Caprifoliaceae** – *Valeriana* **Geraniaceae** – *Geranium*
LEAVES NONE	FLOWERS MOSTLY WHITE **Convolvulaceae** – *Cuscuta* **Ericaceae** – *Hypopitys, Monotropa* **Polygonaceae** – *Polygonum* FLOWERS YELLOW **Ericaceae** – *Hypopitys* **Hypericaceae** – *Hypericum*		

Radially symmetric flowers with 6 petal-like parts

	LEAVES ENTIRE	LEAVES TOOTHED or LOBED	LEAVES DIVIDED
LEAVES BASAL ONLY	FLOWERS MOSTLY WHITE Juncaginaceae – *Triglochin* FLOWERS BLUE to PURPLE Alliaceae – *Allium* Iridaceae – *Iris, Sisyrinchium* FLOWERS PINK to RED Alliaceae – *Allium* FLOWERS YELLOW Liliaceae – *Clintonia* FLOWERS GREEN Juncaceae – *Juncus* FLOWERS BROWN Juncaceae – *Juncus*	FLOWERS YELLOW Ranunculaceae – *Ranunculus*	FLOWERS MOSTLY WHITE Ranunculaceae – *Coptis*
LEAVES ALTERNATE	FLOWERS MOSTLY WHITE Juncaceae – *Luzula* Ruscaceae – *Maianthemum, Polygonatum* FLOWERS BLUE to PURPLE Ericaceae – *Empetrum* Iridaceae – *Iris* FLOWERS PINK to RED Liliaceae – *Streptopus* Nymphaeaceae – *Brasenia* Polygonaceae – *Rumex* FLOWERS YELLOW Asparagaceae – *Asparagus* Asteraceae – *Solidago* Berberidaceae – *Berberis* Colchicaceae – *Uvularia* FLOWERS GREEN Juncaceae – *Juncus, Luzula* Polygonaceae – *Rumex* Ruscaceae – *Polygonatum* FLOWERS BROWN Juncaceae – *Juncus, Luzula*	FLOWERS MOSTLY WHITE Aquifoliaceae – *Ilex* Asteraceae – *Nabalus* FLOWERS PINK to RED Polygonaceae – *Rumex* FLOWERS YELLOW Asteraceae – *Solidago* Berberidaceae – *Berberis* Ranunculaceae – *Caltha* FLOWERS GREEN Polygonaceae – *Rumex*	FLOWERS MOSTLY WHITE Asteraceae – *Achillea, Nabalus* Ranunculaceae – *Actaea* FLOWERS YELLOW Asparagaceae – *Asparagus* Ranunculaceae – *Ranunculus* Resedaceae – *Reseda*
LEAVES OPPOSITE or WHORLED	FLOWERS MOSTLY WHITE Myrsinaceae – *Lysimachia* FLOWERS PINK to RED Lythraceae – *Lythrum* FLOWERS YELLOW Berberidaceae – *Berberis* Liliaceae – *Medeola* FLOWERS ORANGE Liliaceae – *Lilium* FLOWERS GREEN Liliaceae – *Medeola*	FLOWERS YELLOW Asteraceae – *Bidens* Berberidaceae – *Berberis*	

Radially symmetric flowers with 7 or more petal-like parts

	LEAVES ENTIRE	LEAVES TOOTHED or LOBED	LEAVES DIVIDED
LEAVES BASAL ONLY	FLOWERS MOSTLY WHITE Nymphaeaceae – *Nymphaea* FLOWERS YELLOW Asteraceae – *Hieracium* FLOWERS ORANGE Asteraceae – *Hieracium*	FLOWERS MOSTLY WHITE Asteraceae – *Petasites* FLOWERS YELLOW Asteraceae – *Arnoseris, Hieracium, Scorzoneroides, Taraxacum, Tussilago* Ranunculaceae – *Ranunculus*	FLOWERS MOSTLY WHITE Ranunculaceae – *Coptis* FLOWERS YELLOW Asteraceae – *Taraxacum*
LEAVES ALTERNATE	FLOWERS MOSTLY WHITE Asteraceae – *Anaphalis, Doellingeria, Erigeron, Petasites* FLOWERS BLUE to PURPLE Asteraceae – *Arctium, Centaurea, Symphyotrichum* FLOWERS PINK to RED Asteraceae – *Symphyotrichum* FLOWERS YELLOW Asteraceae – *Euthamia, Hieracium, Rudbeckia, Solidago, Tragopogon, Tussilago* Hamamelidaceae – *Hamamelis*	FLOWERS MOSTLY WHITE Aquifoliaceae – *Ilex* Asteraceae – *Achillea, Erigeron, Leucanthemum, Nabalus, Oclemena, Petasites, Solidago, Symphyotrichum* FLOWERS BLUE to PURPLE Asteraceae – *Arctium, Centaurea, Cichorium, Eurybia, Lactuca, Oclemena, Symphyotrichum* FLOWERS PINK to RED Asteraceae – *Oclemena* FLOWERS YELLOW Asteraceae – *Hieracium, Lactuca, Lapsana, Packera, Rudbeckia, Solidago, Sonchus* Hamamelidaceae – *Hamamelis* Ranunculaceae – *Caltha*	FLOWERS MOSTLY WHITE Asteraceae – *Anthemis, Nabalus* Ranunculaceae – *Actaea* FLOWERS BLUE to PURPLE Asteraceae – *Cichorium, Lactuca* FLOWERS YELLOW Asteraceae – *Jacobaea, Lactuca, Lapsana, Sonchus* Ranunculaceae – *Ranunculus*
LEAVES OPPOSITE or WHORLED	FLOWERS MOSTLY WHITE Caryophyllaceae – *Stellaria* Myrsinaceae – *Lysimachia*	FLOWERS YELLOW Asteraceae – *Bidens, Helianthus, Silphium*	
LEAVES NONE	FLOWERS MOSTLY WHITE Asteraceae – *Petasites* FLOWERS YELLOW Asteraceae – *Tussilago*		

Petal-like parts indistinguishable, trees and shrubs, spore-producing plants, and grass-like plants

	LEAVES ENTIRE	LEAVES TOOTHED or LOBED	LEAVES DIVIDED
TREES AND SHRUBS	❖Plant a low shrub: **Cupressaceae** – *Juniperus, Thuja* **Ericaceae** – *Corema, Empetrum* **Myricaceae** – *Morella, Myrica* **Taxaceae** – *Taxus* ❖Plant a tree: **Pinaceae** – *Abies, Larix, Picea, Pinus, Tsuga* **Salicaceae** – *Salix*	❖Plant a low shrub: **Betulaceae** – *Alnus, Carpinus, Corylus, Ostrya* **Myricaceae** – *Comptonia, Morella, Myrica* ❖Plant a tree: **Betulaceae** – *Betula, Carpinus, Ostrya* **Fagaceae** – *Fagus, Quercus* **Pinaceae** – *Larix, Pinus* **Salicaceae** – *Populus, Salix* **Sapindaceae** – *Acer* **Ulmaceae** – *Ulmus*	**Oleaceae** – *Fraxinus*
SPORE-PRODUCING PLANTS	**Equisetaceae** – *Equisetum* **Huperziaceae** – *Huperzia* **Lycopodiaceae** – all genera **Ophioglossaceae** – *Ophioglossum* **Selaginellaceae** – *Selaginella* **Isoëtaceae** – *Isoëtes*	**Polypodiaceae** – *Polypodium*	❖Veins of leaves in a net-like pattern: **Blechnaceae** – *Woodwardia* **Onocleaceae** – *Onoclea* ❖Veins of leaves not in a net-like pattern ♦Leaves dissected into pinnae but not pinnules: **Aspleniaceae** – *Asplenium* **Dryopteridaceae** – *Polystichum* **Osmundaceae** – *Osmunda, Osmundastrum* **Thelypteridaceae** – all genera **Woodsiaceae** – *Deparia, Woodsia* ♦Leaves dissected into pinnules: **Dennstaedtiaceae** – all genera **Dryopteridaceae** – *Dryopteris* **Ophioglossaceae** – *Botrychium* **Osmundaceae** – *Osmunda* **Pteridaceae** – *Adiantum* **Woodsiaceae** – *Athyrium, Cystopteris, Gymnocarpium*
GRASS-LIKE PLANTS	**Cyperaceae** – all genera **Juncaceae** – *Juncus, Luzula* **Juncaginaceae** – *Triglochin* **Poaceae** – all genera **Zosteraceae** – *Zostera*		

Petal-like parts indistinguishable, herbaceous and non-grass-like flowering seed plants

	LEAVES ENTIRE	LEAVES TOOTHED or LOBED	LEAVES DIVIDED
LEAVES BASAL ONLY	FLOWERS MOSTLY WHITE Asteraceae – *Antennaria* Eriocaulaceae – *Eriocaulon* Juncaginaceae – *Triglochin* Plantaginaceae – *Plantago* FLOWERS GREEN Plantaginaceae – *Plantago* FLOWERS BROWN Plantaginaceae – *Plantago*		
LEAVES ALTERNATE	FLOWERS MOSTLY WHITE Asteraceae – *Antennaria, Gnaphalium, Pseudognaphalium* Polygonaceae – *Fallopia* Typhaceae – *Sparganium* FLOWERS BLUE to PURPLE Asteraceae – *Arctium* FLOWERS PINK to RED Cistaceae – *Lechea* Polygalaceae – *Polygala* FLOWERS YELLOW Euphorbiaceae – *Euphorbia* FLOWERS GREEN Amaranthaceae – *Amaranthus, Atriplex, Suaeda* Polygalaceae – *Polygala* Polygonaceae – *Rumex* Potamogetonaceae – *Potamogeton, Stuckenia* Ruppiaceae – *Ruppia* Typhaceae – *Sparganium* FLOWERS BROWN Typhaceae – *Typha*	FLOWERS MOSTLY WHITE Asteraceae – *Erechtites* FLOWERS BLUE to PURPLE Asteraceae – *Arctium* FLOWERS YELLOW Asteraceae – *Senecio* FLOWERS GREEN Amaranthaceae – *Atriplex, Chenopodium* Haloragaceae – *Proserpinaca* Polygonaceae – *Rumex*	FLOWERS MOSTLY WHITE Brassicaceae – *Cardamine* Ranunculaceae – *Actaea, Thalictrum* Vitaceae – *Parthenocissus* FLOWERS BLUE to PURPLE Asteraceae – *Cirsium* FLOWERS PINK to RED Asteraceae – *Artemisia, Cirsium* FLOWERS YELLOW Asteraceae – *Artemisia, Matricaria, Senecio, Tanacetum* FLOWERS GREEN Asteraceae – *Ambrosia* Haloragaceae – *Myriophyllum, Proserpinaca* Vitaceae – *Parthenocissus* FLOWERS BROWN Asteraceae – *Artemisia*
LEAVES OPPOSITE or WHORLED	FLOWERS GREEN Amaranthaceae – *Salicornia* Plantaginaceae – *Callitriche* Potamogetonaceae – *Zannichellia*	FLOWERS MOSTLY WHITE Asteraceae – *Eupatorium* Utricaceae – *Urtica* FLOWERS GREEN Hydrocharitaceae – *Najas* Utricaceae – *Urtica*	FLOWERS YELLOW Asteraceae – *Bidens* FLOWERS GREEN Asteraceae – *Ambrosia* Ceratophyllaceae – *Ceratophyllum* Haloragaceae – *Myriophyllum*
LEAVES NONE	Amaranthaceae – *Salicornia* Santalaceae – *Arceuthobium*		

PLANT FAMILY PHOTOGRAPHS / FAMILIES AND REPRESENTATIVE GENERA

ADOXACEAE – Flowers with 3–5 sepals, 5 petals, 4 or 5 stamens; leaves opposite. p. 54.

Sambucus | *Viburnum* | *Viburnum*

ALISMATACEAE – Aquatic; flowers 3-merous; leaves entire or with basal lobes, either erect or floating; emergent leaves with long petioles; sap milky. p. 57.

Sagittaria

ALLIACEAE – Flowers with 6 tepals, 6 stamens; leaves basal or alternate, venation parallel; leaves and stem with onion odor. p. 59.

Allium

AMARANTHACEAE – Flowers with 4 or 5 sepals, 4 or 5 stamens. p. 59.

Atriplex | *Chenopodium* | *Salicornia* | *Suaeda*

ANACARDIACEAE – Trees, shrubs; flowers with 5 petals, 5 sepals, 5 or 10 stamens; leaves alternate, pinnately compound. p. 66.

Rhus | *Toxicodendron*

APIACEAE – Flowers in compound umbels, with 5 petals, 5 stamens, 2 stigmas; flower stalks usually hollow; petioles generally with inflated bases; aromatic. p. 67.

Angelica | *Aralia* | *Carum* | *Cicuta*

Conioselinum | *Daucus* | *Heracleum* | *Ligusticum* | *Si um*

APOCYNACEAE – Tubular flowers of 5 connate sepals, 5 connate petals, and 5 stamens; leaves opposite; milky latex. p. 74.

Apocynum

Asclepias

AQUIFOLIACEAE – Trees, shrubs; flowers with 4 or 5 sepals, 4–8 petals, 4–6 stamens; leaves alternate. p. 75.

Ilex

Ilex

ARACEAE – Tiny flowers in a dense spike enclosed in a large sheathing bract; leaves alternate; sap milky or watery, aromatic. p. 76.

Arisaema

CWG

Calla

Symplocarpus

ASPARAGACEAE – Flowers inconspicuous, with usually 6 stamens; leaves much reduced. p. 78.

Asparagus

ASPLENIACEAE – Indusia narrow; veins do not reach the margins; petioles at base with 2 vascular bundles. p. 366.

Asplenium

ASTERACEAE – Herbaceous; leaves without stipules; inflorescence a densely packed head of small florets on a flat or rounded receptacle surrounded by a series of bracts in one or more rows; florets of 2 types: disc florets that are tubular and tipped with 5 small teeth, and ray florets that have a petal-like strap. p. 78.

Achillea

Ambrosia

Anaphalis

Antennaria

AH

Anthemis

Arctium

BG

Arnoseris

Artemisia

ASTERACEAE
(continued)

Bidens | *Bidens* | *Centaurea* | *Cichorium*

Cirsium | *Doellingeria* | *Erechtites* | *Erigeron* | *Erigeron*

Eupatorium | *Eurybia* | *Eurybia* | *Euthamia* | *Galinsoga*

Gnaphalium | *Helianthus* | *Hieracium* | *Hieracium* | *Hieracium*

Jacobaea | *Lactuca* | *Lactuca* | *Lapsana* | *Leucanthemum*

Matricaria | *Mycelis* | *Nabalus* | *Oclemena* | *Oclemena*

ASTERACEAE *(continued)*

Packera | *Petasites* | *Pseudognaphalium* | *Rudbeckia*

Scorzoneroides | *Scorzoneroides* | *Senecio* | *Silphium* | *Solidago*

Sonchus | *Sonchus* | *Symphyotrichum* | *Symphyotrichum*

Tanacetum | *Taraxacum* | *Tragopogon* | *Tussilago*

BASLAMINACEAE – Flowers bilaterally symmetric, with a spur; seeds explosively dispersed from a linear capsule. p. 119.

Impatiens

BERBERIDACEAE – Flowers yellow, with 6 sepals and 6 petals; leaves evergreen; inner bark bright yellow. p. 120.

Berberis

BETULACEAE – Trees, shrubs; flowers of separate staminate and carpellate catkins without petals; leaves alternate, simple, toothed. p. 121.

Alnus | *Betula* | *Corylus* | *Ostrya*

BLECHNACEAE – Fronds glossy green, with veins in an interconnected net-like pattern; sori arranged in single, chain-like row. p. 366.

Woodwardia

BORAGINACEAE – Flowers in curved or forked cymes, 5 united petals with 5 adnate stamens, 5 sepals; leaves alternate, simple. p. 125.

Mertensia

Myosotis

BRASSICACEAE – Flowers in a raceme; 4 sepals, 4 petals (narrowed at base and wider toward tip), 4 tall and 2 short stamens; leaves alternate or basal. p. 127.

Alliaria

Barbarea

AH

Boechera

Brassica

Cakile

Capsella

Cardamine

AH

Cardamine

Draba

Erysimum

Hesperis

Lepidium

Lepidium

Raphanus

Sisymbrium

DSC

Subularia

Thlaspi

Thlaspi

CAMPANULACEAE – Flowers bell-shaped or bilaterally symmetric in *Lobelia*; 5-merous, with 5 stamens; leaves alternate, simple; sap milky. p. 138.

Campanula

Lobelia

Lobelia

Lobelia

PLANT FAMILY PHOTOGRAPHS / FAMILIES AND REPRESENTATIVE GENERA

CAPRIFOLIACEAE – Flowers with 5 united petals, 5 small sepals, 5 stamens, an inferior ovary, and long styles; flowers and fruits often in pairs; leaves opposite. p. 141.

Diervilla | *Linnaea* | *Lonicera*

Lonicera | *Lonicera* | *Symphoricarpos* | *Valeriana*

CARYOPHYLLACEAE – Flowers in forked cymes, with 5 sepals and 5 petals; 2–5 styles; leaves opposite, entire. p. 145.

Cerastium | *Dianthus* | *Honckenya* | *Minuartia*

Moehringia | *Sagina* | *Sagina* | *Saponaria*

Silene | *Spergula* | *Spergularia* | *Stellaria*

CELASTRACEAE – Shrubs; flowers with 3–5 sepals and petals, stamens alternating with petals, glandular disk beneath or surrounding the ovary. p. 154.

Celastrus

CERATOPHYLLACEAE – Aquatic; flowers extremely reduced; leaves compound, 2 or 3 times divided. p. 156.

Ceratophyllum

PLANT FAMILY PHOTOGRAPHS / FAMILIES AND REPRESENTATIVE GENERA

CISTACEAE – Flowers with 3 or 5 sepals and petals, petals convolute, quickly falling; leaves often with stellate and glandular hairs. p. 156.

Hudsonia

Lechea

COLCHICACEAE – Flowers with 6 tepals, and 6 stamens; leaves alternate, with parallel veins. p. 157.

Uvularia

CONVOLVULACEAE – Vines; flowers tubular with 5 distinct sepals and 5 connate petals, convolute in bud, fold lines on petals. p. 158.

Calystegia

Cuscuta

Cuscuta

CORNACEAE – Trees, shrubs; colorful bracts look like petals; flowers small, with 4 or 5 petals; leaves opposite or whorled. p. 159.

Chamaepericlymenum

Swida

CRASSULACEAE – Flowers with 4 or 5 sepals, 4 or 5 petals, 4–10 stamens; leaves fleshy. p. 161.

Hylotelephium

Rhodiola

Sedum

CUPRESSACEAE – Trees, shrubs; leaves small, scale-like, aromatic. p. 392.

Juniperus

Juniperus

Thuja

CYPERACEAE – Generally with a triangular stem; leaves in 3 ranks; sheaths closed. p. 402.

Bolboschoenus

Bulbostylis

Carex

Carex

CYPERACEAE
(continued)

Carex | *Carex* | *Carex*

Cladium | *Dulichium* | *Eleocharis* | *Eriophorum*

Rhynchospora | *Schoenoplectus* | *Scirpus* | *Scirpus* | *Trichophorum*

DENNSTAEDTIACEAE – Forming large, tenacious colonies; sori very small, at margin of pinnules. p. 367.

Dennstaedtia | *Pteridium*

DROSERACEAE – Flowers with 5 sepals, 5 petals, 5 stamens; trap insects by sticky hairs. p. 162.

Drosera | *Drosera* | *Drosera*

DRYOPTERIDACEAE – Indusia round to kidney-shaped; teeth on leaf segments often bristle-tipped; petioles with 3–7 vascular bundles at base. p. 368.

Dryopteris | *Polystichum*

ELATINACEAE – Aquatic; petals and sepals usually 4 (2–5); leaves opposite or whorled, simple. p. 163.

Elatine

EQUISETACEAE – Fertile stalks with cone-like spore-producing structures; infertile stalks with whorls of branches at the nodes. p. 371.

Equisetum

Equisetum

ERICACEAE – Flowers bell-shaped, with 4 or 5 connate sepals; leaves without stipules. p. 164.

Andromeda

Arctostaphylos

Calluna

Chamaedaphne

Chimaphila

Corema

Empetrum

Epigaea

Gaultheria

Gaylussacia

Hypopitys

Kalmia

Moneses

Monotropa

Orthilia

Pyrola

Rhododendron

Rhododendron

Vaccinium

Vaccinium

Vaccinium

ERIOCAULACEAE – Flowers with 2 or 3 sepals, 2 or 3 petals, 2–6 stamens; leaves in basal rosette. p. 181.

Eriocaulon

EUPHORBIACEAE – Stem with milky sap. p. 181.

Euphorbia

FABACEAE – Bilaterally symmetric flowers consisting of upper banner petals and lower wings and a keel; leaves often pinnately compound. p. 182.

Amorpha

Amphicarpaea

Genista

Laburnum

Lathyrus

Lotus

Lupinus

Medicago

Melilotus

Robinia

Securigera

Thermopsis

Trifolium

Trifolium

Trifolium

Trifolium

Vicia

Vicia

FAGACEAE – Trees, shrubs; leaves alternate, with straight pinnate veins; fruit a nut partially enclosed in a woody cupule. p. 194.

Fagus

Quercus

Quercus

GENTIANACEAE – Flowers with 4 or 5 sepals, 4 or 5 connate petals, 4 or 5 stamens; leaves opposite. p. 196.

Bartonia | *Bartonia* | *Lomatogonium*

GERANIACEAE – Flowers with 5 sepals, 5 petals, 10 stamens; carpels needle-like. p. 197.

Geranium | *Geranium* | *Geranium*

GROSSULARIACEAE – Flowers with 5 connate sepals, 5 small petals, 5 stamens, 2 styles; leaves palmately lobed; berries with sepals attached. p. 199.

Ribes | *Ribes* | *Ribes*

HALORAGACEAE – Aquatic; flowers greenish; submersed leaves finely dissected. p. 200.

Myriophyllum | *Proserpinaca* | *Proserpinaca*

HAMAMELIDACEAE – Leaves alternate, with deciduous stipules; hairs stellate; fruit a woody capsule. p. 202.

Hamamelis

HUPERZIACEAE – Upright, evergreen; sporophylls (modified leaves) green, unstalked. p. 373.

Huperzia

HYDROCHARITACEAE – Aquatic; flowers with 3 sepals, 3 white petals (or absent), 2 or more stamens. p. 203.

Najas | *Vallisneria*

HYPERICACEAE – Flowers with 2–5 sepals, 4 or 5 petals, numerous stamens; leaves opposite or whorled. p. 204.

Hypericum  | *Hypericum*  | *Hypericum*  | *Triadenum*

IRIDACEAE – Flowers with 3 petals, 3 showy sepals, 3 stamens; capsules 3-chambered; nectaries on partitions of ovaries. p. 210.

Iris  | *Sisyrinchium*

ISOËTACEAE – Aquatic; spore sack located at the base of each leaf; leaves hollow and quill-like. p. 373.

CWG

Isoëtes

JUNCACEAE – Flowers with 6 tepals, 3 or 6 stamens, 3-parted stigma. p. 454.

Juncus  | *Juncus*  | *Juncus*  | *Luzula*

JUNCAGINACEAE – Flowers nonshowy, with 3–6 carpels; leaves basal only; growing in marshes. p. 211.

Triglochin

LAMIACEAE – Bilaterally symmetric flowers with 2 upper and 3 lower lobes; leaves opposite or whorled, often aromatic; stems square. p. 212.

Galeopsis  | *Lycopus*  | *Mentha*  | *Prunella*

Scutellaria  | *Stachys*  | *Teucrium*  | *Thymus*

PLANT FAMILY PHOTOGRAPHS / FAMILIES AND REPRESENTATIVE GENERA

LENTIBULARIACEAE – Aquatic; bilaterally symmetric showy flowers; trapped prey visible in bladders. p. 217.

Utricularia | *Utricularia* | *Utricularia*

LILIACEAE – Flower with 6 tepals; 6 stamens, carpel with a 3-parted stigma; leaves with parallel veins; nectaries at base of tepals. p. 221.

Clintonia | *Lilium* | *Medeola* | *Streptopus*

LINACEAE – Flowers with 5 sepals, 5 petals, 5 or 10 stamens. p. 223.

Linum | *Linum*

LYCOPODIACEAE – Spores in cone-like structures; leaves tiny, with a solitary vein. p. 376.

Dendrolycopodium | *Dendrolycopodium* | *Diphasiastrum* | *Lycopodiella*

Lycopodiella | *Lycopodium* | *Lycopodium* | *Spinulum* | *Spinulum*

LYTHRACEAE – Petals often rugose; leaves opposite or whorled; stem square. p. 224.

Decodon | *Lythrum*

MALVACEAE – Tubular flowers with 3–5 partially connate sepals, and 5 petals; numerous stamens forming a tube surrounding the pistil. p. 225.

Malva  | *Tilia*

MELANTHIACEAE – Flowers with 3 or 4 sepals, 3 or 4 petals, 6–8 stamens; leaves whorled. p. 227.

Trillium

MELASTOMATACEAE – Flowers with 3–5 sepals, 3–5 petals, 6–10 stamens; leaves opposite. p. 228.

Rhexia

MENYANTHACEAE – Aquatic; leaves alternate, divided into 3 leaflets, petioles sheathing. p. 228.

Menyanthes  | *Nymphoides*

MYRICACEAE – Shrubs; leaves alternate; wood and leaves aromatic. p. 229.

Comptonia  | *Morella*  | *Myrica*

MYRSINACEAE – Flowers with 5 sepals connate at base, 5 petals, 5 stamens. p. 231.

Lysimachia  | *Lysimachia*  | *Lysimachia*  | *Lysimachia*

NYMPHAEACEAE – Aquatic; large showy flowers emerge above water surface; leaves large and floating. p. 235.

Brasenia  | *Nuphar*  | *Nymphaea*

CWG

OLEACEAE – Trees, shrubs; flowers with 4 connate sepals, 4 connate petals, 2 distinct short stamens; leaves opposite. p. 236.

Fraxinus

Ligustrum

ONAGRACEAE – Flowers with 4 sepals, 4 petals, 4 or 8 stamens, stigma with 4 lobes. p. 239.

Chamerion

Circaea

Epilobium

Oenothera

ONOCLEACEAE – Fronds with interconnected, net-like veins; spores green. p. 380.

Onoclea

OPHIOGLOSSACEAE – Spores produced on a stalk overtopping the leaf; sporangia thick-walled. p. 380.

Botrychium

ORCHIDACEAE – Bilaterally symmetric flowers; leaves with parallel veins. p. 244.

Arethusa

Calopogon

Corallorhiza

Cypripedium

Epipactis

Goodyera

Listera

Malaxis

Platanthera

Platanthera

Platanthera

Pogonia

Spiranthes

PLANT FAMILY PHOTOGRAPHS / FAMILIES AND REPRESENTATIVE GENERA
OROBANCHACEAE – Parasitic; flowers with 5 sepals, 5 petals, 4 stamens; leaves fleshy. p. 253.
Agalinis
Epifagus
Euphrasia
Euphrasia
Melampyrum
Odontites
Pedicularis
Rhinanthus
OSMUNDACEAE – Fertile leaves brown at maturity; leaves compound; sporangia thin-walled. p. 382.
Osmunda
Osmunda
Osmunastrum
OXALIDACEAE – Flowers with 5 sepals, 5 petals, 10 stamens (outer whorl shorter than inner). p. 257.
Oxalis
Oxalis
PAPAVERACEAE – Showy flowers and petals in multiples of 4, and numerous stamens; stems with milky or yellow sap. p. 258.
Adlumia
Capnoides
Chelidonium
PINACEAE – Trees, leaves needle-like, solitary or in fascicles of 2–5. p. 393.
Abies
Larix
Picea
Pinus

PLANTAGINACEAE – Petals and sepals usually 4 or 5; leaves various. p. 260.

Callitriche | *Chelone* | *Digitalis* | *Linaria*

Nuttallanthus | *Plantago* | *Veronica* | *Veronica* | *Veronicastrum*

PLUMBAGINACEAE – Flowers numerous and small; small leaf-like bracts at base of flowers; leaves alternate, entire. p. 270.

Limonium

POACEAE – Stems generally jointed; each flower subtended by a pair of bracts, the lemma and palea; spikelets subtended by a pair of bracts, the glumes. p. 462.

Agrostis | *Alopecurus* | *Ammophila* | *Anthoxanthum*

Anthoxanthum | *Arrhenatherum* | *Brachyelytrum* | *Bromus* | *Bromus*

Calamagrostis | *Calamagrostis* | *Cinna* | *Dactylis* | *Danthonia*

PLANT FAMILY PHOTOGRAPHS / FAMILIES AND REPRESENTATIVE GENERA
POACEAE
(continued)
Deschampsia
Dichanthelium
Digitaria
Echinochloa
Elymus
Elymus
Festuca
Glyceria
Hordeum
Leersia
Leymus
Lolium
Molinia
Muhlenbergia
Oryzopsis
Panicum
Phalaris
Phleum
Phragmites
Piptatherum
Poa
Puccinellia
Schedonorus
Schizachyrium
Setaria
Spartina
Torreyochloa
Zizania

POLYGALACEAE – Bilaterally symmetric flowers with 3 petals (2 upper and 1 lower), lower keel boat-shaped. p. 270.

Polygala | *Polygala*

POLYGONACEAE – Flowers with 5 or 6 petal-like sepals, 3–9 stamens, 3 styles; swollen nodes; leaves alternate, simple, entire. p. 271.

Fagopyrum | *Fallopia* | *Fallopia* | *Persicaria*

Persicaria | *Persicaria* | *Polygonum* | *Polygonum* | *Polygonum*

Rumex | *Rumex* | *Rumex* | *Rumex*

POLYPODIACEAE – Fronds evergreen, growing in dense colonies on rocks; sori round. p. 383.

Polypodium

PONTEDERIACEAE – Aquatic; flowers with 6 tepals, 6 stamens; leaves alternate, with sheathing bases. p. 283.

Pontederia

PORTULACACEAE – flowers with 2 sepal-like bracts and 5 petals; stems usually red to purple. p. 283.

Montia | *Portulaca*

PLANT FAMILY PHOTOGRAPHS / FAMILIES AND REPRESENTATIVE GENERA

POTAMOGETONACEAE– Aquatic; flowers often 4-parted; inflorescence a spike, without subtending bracts. p. 284.

Potamogeton *Potamogeton*

Potamogeton *Stuckenia* *Zannichellia*

PTERIDACEAE – Fronds clustered together, pinnules fan-shaped, the margins form false indusia. p. 384.

Adiantum

RANUNCULACEAE – Multiple carpels at the center of flowers; leaves alternate or basal. p. 290.

Actaea *Anemone* *Aquilegia*

Aquilegia *Caltha* *Caltha* *Coptis* *Coptis*

Ranunculus *Ranunculus* *Thalictrum*

RESEDACEAE – Flowers with 6 irregularly cleft petals; leaves alternate, with glandular tubercles at the base. p. 298.

CG

Reseda

RHAMNACEAE – Trees, shrubs; flowers with 4 or 5 sepals, 4 or 5 petals, 4 or 5 stamens; capsule 3-parted. p. 298.

Frangula

ROSACEAE – Flowers with 5 sepals, 5 petals, numerous stamens, numerous styles; leaves or leaflets serrate. p. 299.

Amelanchier

Amelanchier

Argentina

Argentina

Aronia

Aruncus

Comarum

Crataegus

AH

Crataegus

Dasiphora

Fragaria

Geum

Geum

Malus

Malus

Malus

Physocarpus

Potentilla

Prunus

Rosa

Rosa

ROSACEAE *(continued)*

Rubus · *Rubus* · *Rubus* · *Rubus*

Sibbaldiopsis · *Sorbaria* · *Sorbaria* · *Sorbus* · *Spiraea*

RUBIACEAE – Flowers with 3–5 connate petals, 4 or 5 stamens; leaves opposite or whorled. p. 330.

Galium · *Galium* · *Houstonia* · *Mitchella*

RUPPIACEAE – Of brackish or saline waters; inflorescence terminal, peduncles often elongate; leaves submersed, sessile. p. 335.

Ruppia

RUSCACEAE – Flowers with 6 tepals, 6 stamens; leaves alternate or basal. p. 335.

Maianthemum · *Polygonatum*

SALICACEAE – Trees, shrubs; staminate and carpellate flowers on separate plants; sepals greatly reduced or absent; petals absent; leaves alternate. p. 338.

Populus · *Salix* · *Salix*

SANTALACEAE – Parasitic; flowers with 3 sepals and 3 stamens. p. 344.

Tanacetum

SAPINDACEAE – Trees, shrubs; leaves palmately lobed; seeds paired, with wings. p. 344.

Acer · *Acer*

SARRACENIACEAE – Insectivorous, found in bogs and marshes; flowers with 4 or 5 sepals, 5 petals; leaves tubular. p. 347.

Sarracenia

SAXIFRAGACEAE – Flowers with 5 distinct sepals, 5 distinct petals, 5 or 10 stamens, 2 styles; leaves without stipules. p. 348.

CG

Chrysosplenium

AH

Micranthes

AH

Mitella

SCHEUCHZERIACEAE – Found in bogs; flowers in racemes, with 6 petals; leaves in 2 ranks; sheaths with ligules. p. 349.

CBH

Scheuchzeria

SCROPHULARIACEAE – Bilaterally symmetric (occasionally nearly radially symmetric) flowers with 2 upper lobes and 3 lower lobes, 4 or 5 connate sepals, 4 or 5 connate petals. p. 350.

AH

Scrophularia

Verbascum

Verbascum

SELAGINELLACEAE – Leaves in 4 ranks along the stem. p. 385.

Selaginella

SOLANACEAE – Flowers with 5 connate sepals, 5 connate petals, 5 stamens; leaves alternate. p. 352.

Solanum

MV

Solanum

TAXACEAE – Shrub; leaves needle-shaped, evergreen; red or green aril berry-like. p. 399.

Taxus

THELYPTERIDACEAE – Fronds pubescent with needle-like, transparent hairs; petioles with 2–7 vascular bundles in cross section at base. p. 385.

Parathelypteris

Phegopteris

Thelypteris

TYPHACEAE – Aquatic; inflorescence a dense spike; leaves narrow, alternate. p. 353.

Sparganium *Typha* *Typha*

ULMACEAE – Leaves asymmetrical at base, alternate. p. 356.

Ulmus

URTICACEAE – Staminate and carpellate flowers separate, in long clusters originating from the leaf axils. p. 357.

Urtica

VERBENACEAE – Flowers with 5 connate sepals, 5 connate petals; leaves opposite or whorled; stem square in cross section. p. 357.

Verbena

VIOLACEAE – Bilaterally symmetric flowers, nodding, with 5 distinct petals; capsules 3-valved. p. 358.

Viola *Viola*

VITACEAE – flowers with 4 or 5 small sepals, petals often connate at tip, 4 or 5 stamens. p. 362.

Parthenocissus

WOODSIACEAE – Fronds with veins not reaching margins of leaf segments; petioles with 2 vascular bundles in cross section at base. p. 387.

Athyrium *Athyrium*

Cystopteris *Deparia* *Gymnocarpium* *Woodsia*

XYRIDACEAE – Flowers with 3 sepals, 3 petals, 3 stamens. p. 362.

Xyris

ZOSTERACEAE – Marine; flowers unisexual; leaves in 2 ranks or opposite. p. 363.

Zostera

Common Elder • *Sambucus nigra*

Small to medium-sized shrub of wet areas, 1–4 m tall. **Flowers** *white, in clusters wider than tall, branched from near the base, blooming July and August.* **Leaves** opposite, pinnately compound; *leaflets 5–11, usually 7,* sharply toothed. **Twigs** *with white pith.* **Fruit** *a purple-black, berry-like drupe, each 5 mm diameter, ripening late summer, edible.*
OCCURRENCE: Occasional; MDI, IAH.
OTHER NAMES: Elderberry, Black Elderberry, *Sambucus canadensis*

Red Elderberry • *Sambucus racemosa*

Small to medium-sized shrub of dry areas, up to 8 m tall. **Flowers** 3–4 mm wide, *creamy white,* often pubescent, *in a pyramid-shaped cluster with a main stalk extending up through the flowers to near the summit, blooming May and June.* **Leaves** opposite, pinnately compound; *leaflets 5–7,* sharply toothed, usually downy on underside, with much variation in shape. **Twigs** often pubescent, *with orange-brown pith* (see middle photo on right). **Fruit** *a bright red, berry-like drupe,* 5 mm wide, *ripening in early summer, inedible.*
OCCURRENCE: Common; MDI, IAH.
NOTES: Leaves, berries, seeds, and bark contain a form of cyanide.
OTHER NAMES: Red-berried Elder, Stinking Elder, Black Elderberry, *Sambucus pubens, Sambucus nigra.*

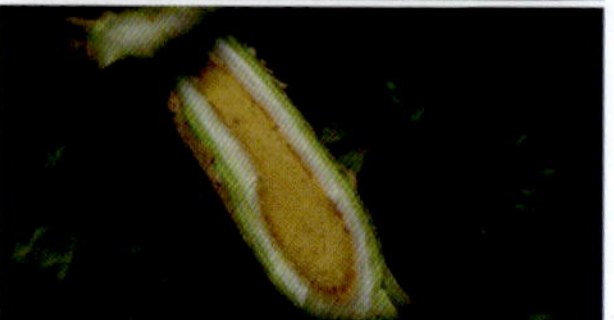

Maple-leaved Viburnum • *Viburnum acerifolium*

Compact shrub of deciduous woodlands, 1–2 m tall. **Flowers** white, in clusters 4–6 cm wide. **Leaves** opposite, *3-lobed*. **Twigs** pubescent with compound hairs branching at the base (stellate). **Fruit** a blue-black, berry-like drupe.
OCCURRENCE: Occasional; MDI.
NOTES: Leaves turn a deep crimson-purple in autumn.
OTHER NAMES: Dockmackie, Arrow-wood

Southern Arrow-wood • *Viburnum dentatum*

Shrub of wet to dry soils, 1–3 m tall. **Flowers** white, *in clusters without hairs*. **Leaves** opposite, *coarsely toothed and prominently veined, their underside dotted with scales*; veins extending to tips of teeth. **Fruit** a blue-black, berry-like drupe.
OCCURRENCE: Rare; MDI, IAH.
OTHER NAMES: Arrow-wood, Smooth Arrow-wood

Hobblebush • *Viburnum lantanoides*

Loosely upright shrub of shady, wet woods, up to 3 m tall. **Flowers** of two types: enlarged, white, sterile flowers, each ~2.5 cm wide, located at the margin of the inflorescence, and smaller, white, fertile flowers in the center of the inflorescence; cyme hairy, sessile. **Leaves** *opposite, finely and sharply toothed, round or egg-shaped*, becoming 10–20 cm long (excluding stalk), with red-brown scaly hairs. **Buds** *large and naked.* **Fruit** a red to black berry-like drupe.
OCCURRENCE: Occasional; MDI, SCH.
OTHER NAMES: Mooseberry, Witch-hobble, Tanglelegs, *Viburnum alnifolium*

Wild-raisin • *Viburnum nudum*

Open shrub of woods and swamps, 1–4 m tall. **Flowers** white, in cymes; peduncles 2.5–5 cm long. **Leaves** opposite, entire or *minutely toothed*, somewhat thick and leathery. **Buds** rusty brown. **Fruit** a blue-black berry-like drupe, sweet.
OCCURRENCE: Common; MDI, IAH, SCH.
NOTES: The small fruits look like raisins. This species is ubiquitous in the northern forest.
OTHER NAMES: Witherod, *Viburnum cassinoides*

Highbush-cranberry • **Viburnum opulus*

Large, erect shrub of wet areas, up to 4 m tall. **Flowers** of two types: enlarged, white, sterile flowers, each 1.5–2.5 cm wide, located at the margin of the inflorescence, and smaller, white, fertile flowers located in the center of the inflorescence. **Leaves** *opposite, deeply 3-lobed*, coarsely toothed. **Buds** red. **Fruit** *a shiny, bright red, berry-like drupe*.
OCCURRENCE: Occasional; MDI, SCH.
NOTES: Ours believed to be all a nonnative variety.
OTHER NAMES: Pimbina, *Viburnum trilobum*

CWG

ALISMATACEAE • ARROWHEAD FAMILY ▼

Large Water-plantain • *Alisma triviale*

Emergent herb of shallow and slow-moving water, 0.1–1 m tall. **Flowers** *white, 3-parted*, 7–13 mm wide; petals much longer than the sepals. **Leaves** basal only, entire.
OCCURRENCE: Rare; IAH.
OTHER NAMES: Northern Water-plantain, *Alisma brevipes*

CBH

AH

AH

Grass-leaved Arrowhead • *Sagittaria graminea*

Submersed to emergent, perennial herb of shallow water, 7–60 cm tall. **Flowers** white, *1–1.5 cm wide,* in erect clusters, *the lowest long-stalked; filaments roughened by tiny hairs or scales.* **Leaves** *simple, unlobed, narrowly lance-shaped.* **Fruit** *an achene 1.5–2 mm long (rarely produced); beak 0.1–0.3 mm long.*

OCCURRENCE: Rare; MDI.

OTHER NAMES: Grass-leaved Sagittaria, Grass-like Arrowleaf

Common Arrowhead • *Sagittaria latifolia*

Emergent, perennial herb of ponds and streams, up to 1.5 m tall. **Flowers** white, *2.5–4 cm wide, with smooth filaments.* **Leaves** variable, *broadly to narrowly sagittate, usually with basal lobes.* **Fruit** *an achene 2.4–4 mm long; beak 0.6–1.8 mm long.*

OCCURRENCE: Occasional; MDI.

OTHER NAMES: Broad-leaved Arrowleaf, Wapato, Duck-potato

Wild Chives • *Allium schoenoprasum*

Perennial herb of shores and headlands, 15–50 cm tall. **Flowers** *pink to light purple, united at base into umbels atop long stems, retaining color when dry.* **Leaves** basal only, erect, round in cross section, hollow, 2–4 mm wide, somewhat grass-like in appearance. **Seeds** black. **Bulbs** 1–several, oblong-ovoid.
OCCURRENCE: Uncommon; MDI, IAH.
OTHER NAMES: *Allium sibiricum*

AMARANTHACEAE • AMARANTH FAMILY ▼

Slender Amaranth • **Amaranthus hybridus*

Weedy, annual herb of fields and waste areas, up to 2 m tall. **Flowers** small, greenish, ~2 mm wide, in terminal and axillary clusters 1–30 cm long, the clusters usually spreading to drooping with many short lateral branches; *tepals of carpellate flowers pointed or bristle-tipped,* 1.5–3 mm long. **Leaves** alternate, entire, usually pubescent beneath, 5–15 cm long. **Stems** tinged with red at base. **Seeds** 1–1.1 mm long and 0.8–0.9 mm wide.
OCCURRENCE: Uncommon; MDI.
OTHER NAMES: Wild-beet, Smooth Pigweed, Green Amaranth

PG

PG

Redroot • **Amaranthus retroflexus*

Annual herb of gardens and waste areas, up to 3 m tall. **Flowers** small, greenish, 2–4 mm wide, in dense terminal clusters up to 20 cm long, the clusters ascending, spiny; *tepals of carpellate flowers rounded or notched at tip*, 2.5–3.5 mm long. **Leaves** alternate, entire, often villous beneath. **Stems** villous above. **Seeds** ~1.2 mm wide.

OCCURRENCE: Common; MDI, IAH.

OTHER NAMES: Green Amaranth, Pigweed, Redroot Pigweed, Rough Pigweed, Redrooted Amaranth

Acadian Atriplex • *Atriplex acadiensis*

Erect to decumbent, annual herb of coastal salt marshes, 20–40 cm tall. **Flowers** in terminal clusters, with leafy bracts only at base of inflorescence; *bracteoles ovate*, more or less rounded at base, with margins united only at base. **Leaves** *often tinged with red*, the lowest on stem 4–7 cm long and 3–5 cm wide, with basal lobes pointing out or forward. **Stems** often tinged with red, *little branched, with opposite branches often of unequal length*. **Seeds** more often brown (2.5–3.5 mm wide) than black (2–2.9 mm wide).

OCCURRENCE: Uncommon; MDI.

OTHER NAMES: Saltgrass Atriplex, Maritime Orache

North-seacoast Atriplex • *Atriplex glabriuscula*

Annual herb of shorelines, 0.3–1 m long. **Flowers** in terminal clusters *with leafy bracts to tip or within 1–2 cm of tip of inflorescence*; bracteoles 5–13 mm long, with margins united almost to middle. **Leaves** variable, lowest on stem triangular, 4–10 cm long and 3–8 cm wide, with basal lobes pointing out or forward. **Stems** usually prostrate, often zigzagging, with profuse branching. **Seeds** mainly larger brown seeds (2.5–3.9 mm wide), the smaller black ones rare.

OCCURRENCE: Uncommon; MDI, IAH, SCH.

OTHER NAMES: Shetland Atriplex, Edmondston's Atriplex, Bracted Orache

Spreading Atriplex • **Atriplex patula*

Erect to decumbent, annual herb of shorelines and rocky outcrops, up to 1.5 m tall. **Flowers** in terminal clusters with leafy bracts only at base of inflorescence; bracteoles 3–7 mm long, triangular, *with margins united almost to the middle.* **Leaves** *tapering to base*, rarely tinged with red, lowest on stem (often falling off by midsummer) 6–12 cm long, thin, with basal lobes pointing forward. **Stems** *with opposite or subopposite branches of equal length.* **Seeds** brown (2.5–3.1 mm wide) or black (1.2–2 mm wide).

OCCURRENCE: Rare; MDI, IAH, SCH.

OTHER NAMES: Spreading Orache, Common Orache, Spearscale, Spearscale Orache

Hastate Atriplex • **Atriplex prostrata*

Erect to decumbent, annual herb of shorelines, 0.1–1 m tall. **Flowers** in terminal clusters with leafy bracts only at base of inflorescence; bracteoles 3–5 mm long, triangular, with united margins only at base. **Leaves** variable, *lowest on stem (often falling off by midsummer) broadly triangular, truncate,* 2–10 cm long and 2–9 cm wide, with basal lobes pointing outward. **Seeds** black (1–1.5 mm wide) or brown (1.5–2.5 mm wide), the black ones often more abundant than brown.
OCCURRENCE: Occasional; MDI, IAH, SCH.
OTHER NAMES: Fat-hen, Hastate Orache, Hastate-leaved Orache, *Atriplex hastata, Atriplex triangularis, Atriplex patula* var. *hastata*

Saltbush Atriplex • *Atriplex subspicata*

Erect, annual herb of shorelines and rocky uplands, 0.3–1.5 m tall. **Flowers** in terminal clusters with leafy bracts only at base of inflorescence; bracteoles 3–7 mm long, broadly triangular, with margins united only at base. **Leaves** variable, lowest on stem (often falling off by midsummer) *linear to lanceolate,* 5–12 cm long and 3–6 cm wide, the uppermost <5 mm wide. **Stems** with few opposite branches. **Seeds** an equal mix of brown (2–3 mm wide) and black (1.5–2 mm wide), *brown ones wider than long.*
OCCURRENCE: Uncommon; MDI.
NOTES: This species is extremely variable; seed shape (wider than long) is a consistent identifying character.
OTHER NAMES: Saline Orache, *Atriplex patula* var. *subspicata, Chenopodium subspicatum*

Lamb's-Quarters • *Chenopodium album*

Annual herb of gardens and waste places, *0.2–2 m tall.* **Flowers** *with mostly 5 tepals*, keeled along the midrib, giving the flower and fruit a star-shaped appearance. **Leaves** white-mealy (farinose) beneath when young, lowest on stem diamond-shaped. **Seeds** an achene *compressed top to bottom*, 0.9–1.5 mm wide and wider than long.

OCCURRENCE: Common; MDI, IAH, SCH.

OTHER NAMES: White Goosefoot, *Chenopodium lanceolatum*

Oak-leaved Goosefoot • *Chenopodium glaucum*

Prostrate to erect, annual herb of gardens and waste places, *5–25 cm tall.* **Flowers** *with mostly 3 or 4 tepals.* **Leaves** oblong to oblong-ovate, 0.5–5 cm long and 3–15 mm wide, glabrous above, densely white-mealy (farinose) on underside. **Seeds** an achene *compressed top-to-bottom although some compressed side-to-side* (longer than wide), 0.5–1 mm wide.

OCCURRENCE: Rare; MDI.

AH

AH

Slender Glasswort • *Salicornia depressa*

Annual herb of salty shores, 5–40 cm tall. **Flowers** *sunken into fleshy stem*; stamens exserted during flowering. **Leaves** opposite and *scale-like*, the stem appearing leafless. **Stems** *jointed*, succulent, 1.5–3 mm wide, *turning red, yellow, or orange in autumn.*
OCCURRENCE: Occasional; MDI, IAH, SCH.
NOTES: Incorrectly referred to in some field guides as *Salicornia europaea*, a species restricted to the old world.
OTHER NAMES: Samphire, Chicken-claws, Common Glasswort

Northern Sea-blite • *Suaeda calceoliformis*

Erect to decumbent, annual herb of beaches. **Flowers** inconspicuous; *sepals unequal at maturity, some with tiny horn-like (corniculate) appendages*; anthers 0.3–0.4 mm long. **Leaves** linear, *acute at tip*, the lowest ~2 cm long. **Stems** *with densely flowered branches ascending*. **Seeds** 0.8–1.7 mm wide.
OCCURRENCE: Rare; MDI.
NOTES: Maine Natural Areas Program ranks this species as threatened in Maine. This species grows on open, sandy areas where there is little competition from other plants.
OTHER NAMES: American Sea-blite, *Suaeda americana*

Southern Sea-blite • *Suaeda linearis*

Erect, annual herb of shorelines, 0.2–0.9 m tall. **Flowers** inconspicuous; *sepals equal in size, keeled at maturity*; anthers ~0.2 mm long. **Leaves** narrowly linear, *acute at tip*, the lowest <4 cm long. **Stems** *much-branched, erect or ascending*. **Seeds** 1–1.8 mm wide.
OCCURRENCE: Uncommon; MDI.
OTHER NAMES: Tall Sea-blite, Annual Sea-blite

White Sea-blite • **Suaeda maritima*

Prostrate to erect, annual herb of shorelines, 5–60 cm tall. **Flowers** nonshowy, green, button-like, 2–3.3 mm wide, growing in leaf axils; *sepals thin, of equal size, rounded or hooded at maturity, without appendages*. **Leaves** alternate, *fleshy*, linear, 1–5 cm long and 0.8–1.7 mm wide, *blunt at tip*, the blade flat above, convex beneath. **Seeds** 1–2.2 mm wide.
OCCURRENCE: Common; MDI, IAH, SCH.
OTHER NAMES: Low Sea-blite, Herbaceous Seepweed, Herbaceous Sea-blite, *Suaeda richii*

Staghorn Sumac • *Rhus hirta*

Deciduous shrub of dry, open areas, 1–10 m tall. **Flowers** densely crowded on previous year's twigs, greenish. **Inflorescence** terminal, pyramid-shaped, 5–20 cm long. **Leaves** *pinnately compound,* with villous petioles and rachis; *leaflets 9–31, serrate, pale beneath,* 5–12 cm long. **Twigs** densely velvety-hairy. **Fruit** *a red, glandular-pubescent drupe.*
OCCURRENCE: Common; MDI, IAH.
OTHER NAMES: Velvet Sumac, Vinegar-tree, *Rhus typhina*

AH

CWG

Common Poison-ivy • *Toxicodendron radicans*

Deciduous, allergenic liana of open woods and rocky outcrops. **Flowers** yellowish green, >25 in axillary panicles. **Leaves** palmately compound; leaflets 3, usually flat and shiny. **Stems** *woody, much-branched, trailing or climbing with clinging aerial roots.* **Fruit** white, slightly hairy or bristly, *pedicellate.*
OCCURRENCE: Rare; MDI.
NOTES: Contact with any part of this plant may cause skin rash. Do not burn brush as inhaled smoke may cause allergic reaction in airways.
OTHER NAMES: Poison-ivy, *Rhus radicans*

AH

Western Poison-ivy • *Toxicodendron rydbergii*

Deciduous, allergenic shrub of open woods and rocky outcrops, 1–3 m tall. **Flowers** greenish or yellowish, <25 in axillary clusters. **Leaves** compound, clustered near stem tip; petioles elongate, glabrous; leaflets 3, shiny, often folding along midrib. **Stems** *woody for lowest 5–60 cm.* **Fruit** white, glabrous, *sessile or nearly so.*
OCCURRENCE: Occasional; MDI, IAH.
OTHER NAMES: *Rhus radicans* var. *rydbergii, Toxicodendron radicans* var. *rydbergii*

APIACEAE • CARROT FAMILY ▼

Seaside Angelica • *Angelica lucida*

Perennial herb of shorelines and fields, 0.5–1.2 m tall. **Flowers** with 5 greenish white petals, in umbels of 20–50. **Leaves** alternate, compound, *the uppermost on petioles with wide, inflated, open sheaths at base* (see lower middle photo), *the sheath shorter than the leaf blade*; leaflets 3–5, dull green, doubly serrate to the base or nearly so, glabrous. **Fruit** rounded, 4–7 mm wide, with corky ribs.
OCCURRENCE: Occasional; MDI, IAH, SCH.
NOTES: Coastal plant growing near beachheads. Compare with *Ligusticum scothicum* (stems purple-tinged, compound leaves purple-tinged at the nodes, shiny leaves, leaves entire in the lower third to half).
OTHER NAMES: Seacoast Angelica, *Coelopleurum lucidum, Coelopleurum actaeifolium*

Bristly Sarsaparilla • *Aralia hispida*

Perennial herb of dry, open woods, 0.2–0.9 m tall. **Flowers** white, with 5 petals, in umbels on long stalks. **Leaves** alternate, bipinnate; leaflets egg-shaped, acute, sharply toothed, up to 10 cm long. **Stems** woody, *armed with sharp bristles at base*. **Fruit** a dark purple berry.
OCCURRENCE: Occasional; MDI, IAH, SCH.
NOTES: This species commonly colonizes burned or otherwise denuded sites.
OTHER NAMES: Dwarf-elder

Wild Sarsaparilla • *Aralia nudicaulis*

Perennial herb of woodlands, 20–40 cm tall. **Flowers** with 4 greenish white petals, borne in 1–3 umbels on a long stalk. **Leaves** *solitary*, long-stalked, divided into 3 groups of 3–5 leaflets. **Stems** smooth, *woody at ground level*. **Fruit** a purple-black berry.
OCCURRENCE: Common; MDI, IAH, SCH.
NOTES: Ubiquitous species of region's forests.

Spikenard • *Aralia racemosa*

Perennial herb of rich soils, up to 3 m tall. **Flowers** with 5 greenish white petals, in numerous umbels. **Leaves** *alternate, with enormous ternately compound leaves up to 80 cm long, the 3 primary divisions pinnately compound*; leaflets to 15 cm long, doubly serrate. **Stems** smooth. **Fruit** a red berry, turning darker with age.

OCCURRENCE: Rare; MDI.

NOTES: Plant of high-pH soils, usually associated with hardwoods.

OTHER NAMES: American Spikenard

Caraway • **Carum carvi*

Biennial herb of fields, roadsides, and waste areas, 0.2–0.8 m tall. **Flowers** with 5 white petals <2 mm long, in umbels with 7–14 primary branches, with narrow bracts beneath umbel. **Leaves** *alternate, very finely divided, the largest with ultimate segments 5–15 mm long and <1 mm wide*. **Stems** glabrous. **Seeds** oblong, with fine ribs, aromatic.

OCCURRENCE: Uncommon; MDI, SCH.

OTHER NAMES: Wild Caraway

Bulb-bearing Water-hemlock • *Cicuta bulbifera*

Perennial herb of wetlands, 0.2–1 m tall. **Flowers** very small, with 5 white petals, in umbels 2–5 cm wide. **Leaves** alternate, divided, *with bulblets often present in axils of upper leaves*; leaflets narrow, 1–7 cm long and <5 mm wide. **Fruit** ovoid, furrowed.

OCCURRENCE: Uncommon; MDI.

NOTES: All parts of plant extremely poisonous.

OTHER NAMES: Bulblet-bearing Water-hemlock, Bulbiferous Water-hemlock

Common Water-hemlock • *Cicuta maculata*

Biennial herb of wetlands, 0.5–2 m tall. **Flowers** with 5 white petals with reflexed margins, in a compound umbel, the lowest rays of umbel 5–6 cm long; sepals 5, triangular. **Leaves** alternate, sharply toothed, divided 2 or 3 times; leaflets >4 cm wide; veins terminating in notches of teeth. **Stems** with a whitish bloom, *usually mottled or striped with purple*, especially at the nodes.

OCCURRENCE: Uncommon; MDI, SCH.

NOTES: Roots and stems extremely poisonous.

OTHER NAMES: Spotted Cowbane, Musquash-root, Spotted Water-hemlock

Hemlock-parsley • *Conioselinum chinense*

Perennial herb of wetlands, up to 1.5 m tall. **Flowers** with 5 white petals, in umbels up to 15 cm wide; sepals absent. **Leaves** alternate, divided with segments deeply lobed, the uppermost on petioles with wide wings. **Stems** *glabrous, unspotted.*

OCCURRENCE: Uncommon; SCH.

OTHER NAMES: Chinese Hemlock-parsley

Queen Anne's Lace • **Daucus carota*

Biennial herb of dry fields and waste areas, 0.4–1 m tall. **Flowers** with 5 white petals; umbels 4–12 cm wide, *with a red or purple flower usually found at center,* bracts under umbel deeply lobed. **Leaves** alternate, finely divided. **Stems** *covered with bristles.*

OCCURRENCE: Common; MDI, IAH.

OTHER NAMES: Wild Carrot, Bird's Nest, Devil's-plague

Giant Hogweed • ***_Heracleum mantegazzianum_**

Perennial or biennial herb, 2–5 m tall. **Flowers** white, *in umbels <50 cm wide with 50–150 primary branches.* **Leaves** alternate, divided, pubescent beneath; *leaflets up to 1.3 m long.* **Stems** up to 10 cm wide.
OCCURRENCE: Rare; MDI.
NOTES: When sap of plant comes in contact with skin and is exposed to sun, it causes skin to burn. This is on the Federal list of noxious weeds.
OTHER NAMES: Giant Cow-parsnip

Scotch Lovage • ***Ligusticum scothicum***

Perennial herb of coastal shorelines, 0.3–0.6 m tall. **Flowers** with 5 white petals, in umbels branched near the top, each umbel with 10–20 rays 2–5 cm long. **Leaves** alternate, divided, shiny, fragrant when crushed, *the uppermost on petioles with narrow, closed sheath at base.* **Stems** *dark red or purple-tinged at base.*
OCCURRENCE: Occasional; MDI, IAH, SCH.
NOTES: Compare with *Angelica lucida* (stem mostly green, compound leaves mostly green at the nodes, dull, leaflets serrate to the base or nearly so).

Burnet-saxifrage • ******Pimpinella saxifraga***

Perennial herb of roadsides, fields, and waste areas, 0.3–1 m tall. **Flowers** white, ~2 mm wide, in compound umbels. **Leaves** *mostly near base of plant, pinnately divided*, the lowest divided into 4–8 pairs of toothed leaflets, the uppermost much reduced. **Fruit** oblong, glabrous, ~2 mm long.
OCCURRENCE: Uncommon; MDI.
OTHER NAMES: Solid-stemmed Burnet-saxifrage

Water-parsnip • ***Sium suave***

Emergent, perennial herb of shallow water and wet banks, 0.3–2 m tall. **Flowers** with 5 white petals equaling the stamens, *in umbels 4–11 cm wide and with 10–25 rays*; pedicels stiffly ascending. **Leaves** alternate, compound; basal leaves submersed, long-petioled, with 5–17 lance-shaped leaflets 3–15 cm long; cauline leaves gradually reduced upward.
OCCURRENCE: Occasional; MDI.

Spreading Dogbane • *Apocynum androsaemifolium*

Perennial herb of dry fields and roadsides, 20–80 cm tall. **Flowers** pink or *pink- and white-striped, bell-shaped*, 5–10 mm long with flaring, recurving lobes. **Leaves** spreading or sometimes drooping on branches. **Stems** 10–50 cm from base to lowest branch. **Fruit** 2 long slender pods (follicles) that split open on 1 side. **Seeds** 2.5–3 mm long.
OCCURRENCE: Common; MDI, IAH, SCH.
NOTES: May be poisonous to livestock. Leaves and stem exude milky juice when torn or broken.
OTHER NAMES: Indian Hemp

Common Milkweed • *Asclepias syriaca*

CWG

Stout, perennial herb, up to 2 m tall. **Flowers** fragrant, pink to red to purple, in terminal umbels, with a showy whorl of 5 hood-like structures with an incurving horn projecting from each hood, the hoods longer than the central disk of the flower; pedicels reflexed, 3–10 cm long. **Leaves** short-stalked, opposite, spreading, oblong or oval, gray-downy beneath, *with transverse veins*. **Fruit** a pair of *pods (follicles) with a warty surface*. **Seeds** *with long, silky hairs*.
OCCURRENCE: Uncommon; MDI, IAH.
NOTES: Leaves and stem exude milky juice when torn or broken. This plant commonly grows in old fields and on roadsides. Preferred food of monarch butterflies.
OTHER NAMES: Silkweed, Silky Milkweed

Inkberry • *Ilex glabra*

Dioecious, evergreen, stoloniferous shrub of wetlands, 0.1–3 m tall. **Staminate flowers** *borne in clusters on long peduncles.* **Carpellate flowers** white, *mostly solitary in leaf axils.* **Leaves** *evergreen, leathery, shiny, with a few obscure teeth near tip*, small, inconspicuous glands that look like dots on underside. **Stems** ashy- or powdery- looking. **Fruit** a black, berry-like drupe.

OCCURRENCE: Rare; IAH.

NOTES: Maine Natural Areas Program ranks this species as endangered in Maine, with only one occurrence. This species is found more commonly in Massachusetts and south.

OTHER NAMES: Evergreen Winterberry, Bitter Gallberry

CWG

Mountain Holly • *Ilex mucronata*

Dioecious shrub, 0.3–3 m tall. **Staminate flowers** with 4 or 5 minute teeth. **Carpellate flowers** occasionally bisexual, *with 4 or 5 white petals*, borne on long peduncles in leaf axils, solitary or few in a cluster. **Leaves** alternate, rounded to oval, *entire throughout*, usually dull above with downy veins beneath, with a short abrupt point (mucro); *petioles purple.* **Buds** *purple.* **Bark** smooth, gray. **Fruit** *a deep red, berry-like drupe ~7 mm wide.*

OCCURRENCE: Occasional; MDI, IAH, SCH.

OTHER NAMES: Catberry, *Nemopanthus mucronatus*

AH

Winterberry • *Ilex verticillata*

Dioecious shrub of wet areas, 1–4 m tall. **Staminate flowers** clustered, *2–10 on short stalks in leaf axils*. **Carpellate flowers** white, 6- to 8-parted, on short stalks. **Leaves** alternate, variable in shape, *with an abrupt point at tip, regularly toothed throughout*. **Bark** *smooth, gray*. **Fruit** *a shiny, bright red, berry-like drupe ~7 mm wide*, conspicuous and persistent into winter.
OCCURRENCE: Common; MDI, IAH, SCH.
NOTES: Winterberry is most noticeable in early winter when leaves are absent and twigs are adorned with bright red berries. Berries are poisonous to humans.
OTHER NAMES: Black Alder, Common Winterberry

Small Jack-in-the-pulpit • *Arisaema triphyllum*

Erect, perennial herb of wet, rich woods, swamps, and bogs, up to 1 m tall. **Flowers** in a club-shaped cluster (spadix) *surrounded by a green- and purple-striped bract (spathe)*. **Leaves** 1 or 2, compound; leaflets 3, green on both sides; veins parallel. **Fruit** a red berry in a dense cluster 1.5–2 cm long.
OCCURRENCE: Uncommon; MDI, IAH, SCH.
OTHER NAMES: Jack-in-the-pulpit, Indian Turnip

Wild Calla • *Calla palustris*

Rhizomatous, perennial herb of wet areas. **Flowers** in a fleshy spike (spadix), the lowest bisexual, 6-parted, greenish, the uppermost often staminate only; *spadix with an adjacent showy, white, persistent bract (spathe).* **Leaves** *simple,* round to heart-shaped; *petioles 5–15 cm long.* **Fruit** a red berry.
OCCURRENCE: Uncommon; MDI.
OTHER NAMES: Water Arum

Eastern Skunk-cabbage • *Symplocarpus foetidus*

Perennial herb of wet swamps and woods, 30–80 cm tall. **Flowers** in a *knob-shaped cluster (spadix) 5–13 cm long,* the spadix nearly enclosed by a bract (spathe) at maturity with a purple to brown inner surface. **Leaves** *simple,* up to 50 cm long, thick, egg-shaped, rounded to heart-shaped at base, *generally present after flowering.* **Fruit** buried in fleshy spadix at maturity.
OCCURRENCE: Uncommon; MDI, IAH.
NOTES: Plant has unpleasant odor, hence the name skunk-cabbage. This species attracts pollinators with its fragrance and by raising the temperature in the spathe 30–40° F above the air temperature.
OTHER NAMES: Skunk-cabbage

Asparagus • **Asparagus officinalis*

Perennial herb from matted rootstock. **Flowers** yellowish, usually with some red at base, arising from leaf axils. **Leaves** small, scale- or thread-like (filiform). **Fruit** a berry turning bright red with maturity.
OCCURRENCE: Uncommon; MDI.
NOTES: Fern-like structures are actually branchlets arising from true leaves. This European plant has escaped from cultivation where shoots are harvested in early spring.
OTHER NAMES: Garden Asparagus

Common Yarrow • **Achillea millefolium*

Perennial herb of fields, roadsides, and shorelines, 0.2–1 m tall. **Flower heads** (capitula) 4–6 mm wide, in a flat-topped capitulescence 6–30 cm wide; *ray florets usually 5, white*, three-toothed at tip of ray; disc florets white. **Leaves** alternate, *finely dissected*, 3–15 cm long and 1–2.5 cm wide, *aromatic*. **Fruit** a flat achene.
OCCURRENCE: Common; MDI, IAH, SCH.
NOTES: Contact with plant can cause a skin rash in sensitive people.
OTHER NAMES: Milfoil, Bloodwort

Sneezeweed • **Achillea ptarmica*

Perennial herb of fields and waste places, 30–60 cm tall. **Flower heads** (capitula) long-peduncled, *12–19 mm wide*, in a loose capitulescence; *ray florets white, 6–15 per head*; disc florets greenish white. **Leaves** alternate, *finely toothed*, sessile, usually glabrous, 3–10 cm long and 2–6 mm wide. **Stems** *with soft, woolly hairs above*. **Fruit** a flat achene.
OCCURRENCE: Rare; MDI.
OTHER NAMES: Pearly Yarrow

Common Ragweed • *Ambrosia artemisiifolia*

Annual, monoecious or dioecious herb of disturbed sites, 0.2–2.5 m tall; **Flower heads** (capitula) in a raceme-like capitulescence 2.5–15 cm long; *staminate heads 2.5–5 mm wide*, with 15–20 small, yellow-green florets; carpellate heads 1–few at base of capitulescence, small, green, *with 4–7 short, erect spines*. **Leaves** opposite below, alternate above, pinnately compound, narrowly to broadly egg-shaped or oval, 2.5–9 cm long. **Fruit** an achene without bristles at the tip.
OCCURRENCE: Common; MDI, IAH, SCH.
NOTES: The wind-dispersed pollen of this plant causes hay-fever in some people.
OTHER NAMES: Roman Wormwood, Hog-weed

Pearly Everlasting • *Anaphalis margaritacea*

Perennial herb of fields and roadsides, 20–90 cm tall. **Flower heads** (capitula) without ray florets, <1 cm wide, numerous in a dense, wide cluster; carpellate heads occasionally with a few staminate florets; involucral bracts pearly white; anthers with a tail-like appendage. **Leaves** alternate, sessile, entire, 5–12 cm long and 0.5–2 cm wide, *variably white to rusty-woolly below*. **Stems** *white-woolly*. **Fruit** an achene with short, rounded bumps.
OCCURRENCE: Occasional; MDI, IAH, SCH.

Small Pussytoes • *Antennaria howellii*

Dioecious, perennial herb of grassy or rocky areas, 5–40 cm tall. **Flower heads** (capitula) white-woolly, in a close, terminal capitulescence; staminate heads (rare) 4–6 mm long; carpellate heads 7–10 mm long; anthers with a tail-like appendage. **Leaves** entire; cauline leaves 5–11, with a flat, thin appendage at tip; *basal leaves glabrous, bright green on upper surface*. **Fruit** a flat achene, 1.2–1.5 mm long, with a single row of bristles at the tip.
OCCURRENCE: Uncommon; MDI.
OTHER NAMES: Howell's Pussytoes, *Antennaria canadensis, Antennaria neodioica*

Field Pussytoes • *Antennaria neglecta*

Stoloniferous, dioecious, perennial herb of grassy or rocky sites, 5–40 cm tall. **Flower heads** (capitula) white-woolly, in a close, terminal capitulescence; staminate heads 4–6 mm long; carpellate heads 1–8, 6.5–9 mm long; involucral bracts purple at base. **Leaves** alternate, entire; cauline leaves 3–8, with a flat, thin appendage at tip; *basal leaves woolly and dull green on upper surface.* **Fruit** a flat achene 1–1.4 mm long, with bristles 6–9 mm long at the tip.
OCCURRENCE: Uncommon; MDI.

Mayweed • **Anthemis cotula*

AH

Annual herb of fields and roadsides, 10–90 cm tall. **Flower heads** (capitula) up to 2.5 cm wide, in a loose capitulescence; ray florets white, 10–16 per head, sterile, the rays 5–11 mm long; disc florets yellow. **Leaves** *alternate, finely dissected, with unpleasant scent.* **Fruit** a knobby, cylindrical to 4-angled achene fused with bristles at the tip.
OCCURRENCE: Uncommon; MDI, SCH.
OTHER NAMES: Stinking Chamomile, Stinking Mayweed, Dog-fennel

AH

Common Burdock • **Arctium minus*

Biennial herb of fields and roadsides, up to 1.3 m tall. **Flower heads** (capitula) 1.5–2.5 cm wide, in a raceme-like capitulescence; ray florets absent; disc florets purplish; *at least some inner involucral bracts with minutely toothed margins below the middle.* **Leaves** alternate, entire or toothed, *heart-shaped at base, woolly beneath,* to 0.5 m long including petioles; *lower petioles usually hollow.* **Fruit** an achene, 4–6 mm long, flat, rugose.
OCCURRENCE: Occasional; MDI.
OTHER NAMES: Lesser Burdock

Dwarf Nipplewort • **Arnoseris minima*

Annual herb of old fields and roadsides, 5–30 cm tall. **Flower heads** (capitula) numerous, 12–18 mm wide; florets all ligulate and fertile, yellow; *peduncles inflated below heads.* **Leaves** coarsely toothed, 0.5–7 cm long and 2–15 mm wide. **Stems** with milky sap. **Fruit** an achene, egg-shaped, 8- to 10-ribbed, 1.5–2 mm long, without bristles at the tip.
OCCURRENCE: Rare; MDI.
OTHER NAMES: Lamb Succory

BG

BG

Beach Wormwood • **Artemisia stelleriana***

Rhizomatous, perennial herb of sea beaches, 20–75 cm tall. **Flower heads** (capitula) *yellow*, 6–7 mm long and 6–9 mm wide; ray florets few or absent. **Leaves** alternate, *white-woolly on both sides*, 3–10 cm long and 1–5 cm wide, with blunt lobes. **Stems** *with matted, woolly hairs*. **Fruit** an achene, narrow at base and rounded above, without bristles at the tip.
OCCURRENCE: Rare; MDI.
OTHER NAMES: Dusty Miller

Common Mugwort • **Artemisia vulgaris*

Rhizomatous, perennial herb of disturbed sites, 0.6–1.5 m tall. **Flower heads** (capitula) crowded, *woolly*, 3–4 mm long and 2–3 mm wide, *in elongate, spike-like branches in a leafy capitulescence*; disc florets reddish brown; ray florets absent. **Leaves** alternate, egg-shaped, *dark green above and white-woolly beneath, aromatic, deeply pinnately compound, with pointed lobes*, 4–12 cm long and 3–7 cm wide. **Fruit** an achene, oval-shaped, without bristles at the tip.
OCCURRENCE: Common; MDI, IAH, SCH.
OTHER NAMES: Mugwort, Common Wormwood

Nodding Bur-Marigold • *Bidens cernua*

Annual herb of shores and marshes, 0.1–1 m tall. **Flower heads** (capitula) few, long-stalked, *nodding at maturity*, 15–25 mm wide; ray florets 6–8 or absent, the yellow rays <17 mm long; disc florets yellow. **Leaves** *unlobed, sessile*, 4–20 cm long and 0.5–4.5 cm wide. **Fruit** an achene 5–8 mm long, the tip with retrorsely barbed awns.
OCCURRENCE: Rare; MDI.
OTHER NAMES: Nodding Beggar-ticks, Bur-marigold

Devil's Beggar-ticks • *Bidens frondosa*

Annual herb of wet soils, 0.1–1.2 m tall. **Flower heads** (capitula) *subtended by 5–10 (usually 8) leaf-like outer involucral bracts* with sparingly ciliate margins toward the base; ray florets golden-yellow if present; disc florets orange; stamens exserted. **Leaves** *opposite, 1–3 times pinnately compound, with 3–5 sharply toothed leaflets*. **Fruit** an achene 5–10 mm long, the tip with 2 retrorsely barbed awns.
OCCURRENCE: Occasional; MDI, IAH, SCH.
OTHER NAMES: Stick-tight, Beggar-ticks, Devil's-pitchfork

Short-fringed Knapweed • **Centaurea nigrescens*

Perennial herb of old fields, 20–80 cm tall. **Flower heads** (capitula) terminal, 2–4.5 cm wide and 1–2 cm tall; disc florets purple, the marginal ones enlarged and ray-like; *middle and outer involucral bracts with black fringes.* **Leaves** alternate, sessile, *pubescent*, entire or toothed, sometimes lobed; cauline leaves gradually reduced upward, becoming sessile.
OCCURRENCE: Uncommon; MDI.

Common Chicory • **Cichorium intybus*

Perennial herb of roadsides and fields, 0.3–1.5 m tall. **Flower heads** (capitula) 2.5–4 cm wide, *opening in morning but closing on overcast days*, clustered on short peduncles from upper leaf axils; ray florets light blue; inner involucral bracts 8–10, longer than the 5 shorter, outer bracts. **Leaves** toothed or pinnately compound, the largest 8–25 cm long and 1–7 cm wide, the uppermost sessile, becoming smaller, and toothed or entire. **Stems** with milky sap. **Fruit** an achene 2–3 mm long.
OCCURRENCE: Uncommon; MDI.
OTHER NAMES: Blue Sailors

AH

Canada Thistle • **Cirsium arvense*

Perennial herb of old fields and sea beaches forming dense colonial mats, 0.3–2 m tall. **Flower heads** (capitula) numerous, 1–2.5 cm long and <2.5 cm wide, in open clusters; disc florets pale pink-purple or white; *outer involucral bracts with weak prickles 0.5–1.5 mm long.* **Leaves** alternate, *green on both sides*, toothed or with shallow lobes, with weak spines 1.5–7 mm long. **Fruit** an achene 2.5–4 mm long, with bristles at the tip.
OCCURRENCE: Common; MDI, IAH.
NOTES: This nonnative species is invasive.
OTHER NAMES: Creeping Thistle

Swamp Thistle • *Cirsium muticum*

Biennial herb of swamps, 0.4–2 m tall. **Flower heads** (capitula) numerous, >3.5 cm long; disc florets deep rose-purple; *involucral bracts blunt at tip, rarely tipped with spines* <0.5 mm long. **Leaves** alternate, *pale beneath*, deeply pinnatifid with entire, lobed, or toothed segments, *with weak spines* <3.5 mm long, the uppermost sessile, not winged. **Fruit** an achene ~5 mm long, with bristles at the tip.
OCCURRENCE: Uncommon; MDI, IAH.

Bull Thistle • **Cirsium vulgare*

Biennial herb of fields and roadsides, 0.5–1.5 m tall. **Flower heads** (capitula) solitary or in loose clusters, 2.5–5 cm long and 2.5–4 cm wide; disc florets purple to pink; *at least the outer involucral bracts tipped with 2–6 mm long spines.* **Leaves** basal only in first year, second-year leaves alternate, *pale and often woolly beneath, the uppermost with spines 0.5–1.5 mm long.* **Stems** *spiny* (see lower right photo). **Fruit** an achene 3–4 mm long, with bristles at the tip.

OCCURRENCE: Common; MDI, IAH, SCH.

OTHER NAMES: Common Thistle, Spear Thistle

Flat-topped Aster • *Doellingeria umbellata*

Rhizomatous, perennial herb of marshes, meadows, and woodlands, 0.4–2.5 m tall. **Flower heads** (capitula) numerous, <2 cm wide, in a flat-topped capitulescence; ray florets 6–14 per head, the rays white, 5–8 mm long; disc florets yellow. **Leaves** entire, sessile, tapering to both ends, 4–16 cm long and 7–35 mm wide, *the uppermost pinnately veined with prominent veins.* **Stems** usually glabrous, especially below capitulescence. **Fruit** *hairy.*

OCCURRENCE: Common; MDI, IAH, SCH.

OTHER NAMES: flat-topped White Aster, Tall White Aster, *Aster umbellatus*

Pilewort • *Erechtites hieraciifolius*

Annual herb of disturbed sites, 0.1–2.5 m tall. **Flower heads** (capitula) numerous, *swollen at base; involucral bracts usually in single row except for a few smaller ones at base.* **Leaves** alternate, up to 20 cm long and 8 cm wide, sharply toothed, sometimes lobed, *with a strong odor.* **Stems** *grooved,* often hairy. **Fruit** an achene, 5-angled, with 10–12 pale ribs, *with fine white hairs at the tip.*

OCCURRENCE: Occasional; MDI, IAH.

OTHER NAMES: American Burnweed, Fireweed

Annual Fleabane • *Erigeron annuus*

Annual or biennial herb of fields and disturbed sites, 0.5–1.5 m tall. **Flower heads** (capitula) forming a many-headed, corymb-like capitulescence; *ray florets 80–125 per head, the rays white, 4–10 mm long and 0.5–1 mm wide*; disc florets yellow. **Leaves** alternate, *numerous, at least the lowest coarsely toothed,* the largest up to 10 cm long. **Stems** *with long, spreading pubescence,* especially mid-stem. **Fruit** a flat achene, with 2 veins.

OCCURRENCE: Occasional; MDI.

OTHER NAMES: Daisy fleabane, Sweet-scabious, White-top

Horse-weed • *Erigeron canadensis*

Annual herb of disturbed sites, 8–80 cm tall. **Flower heads** (capitula) 3–5 mm wide; ray florets 25–40 per head, *the rays erect, narrow, white, 0.5–1 mm long*; disc florets yellow, 4-lobed. **Leaves** alternate, toothed or entire, *the margins with stiff hairs*, the lowest larger than upper leaves. **Stems** usually unbranched until near tip, *with prominent stiff hairs*. **Fruit** a flat achene.
OCCURRENCE: Occasional; MDI.
NOTES: Leaves can cause skin rash in some people.
OTHER NAMES: Canada fleabane, Hog-weed, Butter-weed, *Conyza canadensis*

Lesser Daisy Fleabane • *Erigeron strigosus*

Annual or biennial herb of fields and disturbed sites, 0.3–1 m tall. **Flower heads** (capitula) forming a many-headed corymb-like capitulescence; *ray florets 50–100 per head; rays white or pink, <6 mm long and 0.4–1 mm wide.* **Leaves** alternate, narrow, *entire or with a few small teeth.* **Stems** *with short, usually appressed, pubescence, especially mid-stem.* **Fruit** a flat achene.
OCCURRENCE: Occasional; MDI, SCH.
OTHER NAMES: Rough fleabane, Daisy fleabane, White-top

Boneset • *Eupatorium perfoliatum*

Perennial herb of fresh water wetlands, 0.3–1.5 m tall. **Flower heads** (capitula) in a crowded flat-topped capitulescence; disc florets white, *7–11 per head*; outer involucral bracts less than half as long as inner ones. **Leaves** opposite, 7–20 cm long and 1.5–4.5 cm wide, *rugose above*, pubescent beneath, tapering to the tip, *the bases of adjacent leaves connecting around stem*. **Stems** *with long, spreading hairs*. **Fruit** an achene, 5- to 8-angled, 5- to 8-veined.
OCCURRENCE: Occasional; MDI.
OTHER NAMES: Thoroughwort, Estuary Boneset, Boneset Thoroughwort

Large-leaved Aster • *Eurybia macrophylla*

Rhizomatous, perennial herb of forests and forest edges, 0.2–1.5 m tall. **Flower heads** (capitula) in a corymb-like capitulescence; *peduncles with glands*; ray florets 9–20 per head, light purple, the rays 7–15 mm long; disc florets yellow, becoming darker brown with age; *outer involucral bracts glandular, densely ciliate along the margins*. **Leaves** *not sessile, the lowest heart-shaped at base*, toothed, 4–30 cm long and 3–20 cm wide, the uppermost smaller.
OCCURRENCE: Common; MDI, IAH, SCH.
OTHER NAMES: Big-leaved Aster, Large-leaved Wood-aster, *Aster macrophylla*

Rough-leaved Aster • *Eurybia radula*

Rhizomatous, perennial herb of woodlands and wetlands, 0.1–1.2 m tall. **Flower heads** (capitula) few, 20–40 mm wide, in a leafy-bracted capitulescence; ray florets light purple, 15–40 per head; disc florets yellow; *outer involucral bracts firm, densely ciliate along the margins.* **Leaves** alternate, *sessile, sharply toothed,* with a rough surface, 3–10 cm long and 6–30 mm wide. **Stems** glabrous except below capitulescence.
OCCURRENCE: Occasional; MDI, SCH.
OTHER NAMES: Rough Aster, Low Rough Aster, File-blade Aster, Rough Wood-aster, *Aster radula*

Lance-leaved Goldenrod • *Euthamia graminifolia*

Perennial herb of wetlands, fields, and woodlands, 0.3–1.5 m tall. **Flower heads** (capitula) *in clusters of 2 or more on a peduncle, in a flat-topped capitulescence*; ray florets 7–35 per head, the rays yellow, minute, scarcely spreading; disc florets yellow, 5–10 per head. **Leaves** *numerous,* alternate, entire, 2.5–15 cm long and *3–12 mm wide,* with 3–5 veins, the uppermost with some coarse, stiff hairs. **Fruit** *a short-hairy achene* with white bristles at the tip.
OCCURRENCE: Uncommon; MDI, SCH.
OTHER NAMES: Common Grass-leaved Goldenrod, flat-topped Goldenrod, Common flat-topped Goldenrod, *Solidago graminifolia*

Common Quickweed • **Galinsoga quadriradiata*

Weedy, annual herb of disturbed sites, 10–70 cm tall. **Flower heads** (capitula) ~7 mm wide; ray florets 3–6 per head, the rays white *with 3 teeth on the outer margin*; disc florets yellow. **Leaves** opposite, 2.5–7 cm long and 1.5–5 cm wide, coarsely and sharply toothed. **Stems** often branched, *with coarse, spreading hairs.* **Fruit** a black achene, *4-angled, bristly on inner face.*
OCCURRENCE: Common; MDI, SCH.
OTHER NAMES: Galinsoga, Hairy Galinsoga, Quickweed, Shaggy Soldier, *Galinsoga ciliata*

Low Cudweed • *Gnaphalium uliginosum*

Annual herb of disturbed sites, 4–30 cm tall. **Flower heads** (capitula) *woolly*, white to light brown, 2–4 mm long, *in dense, terminal clusters, often overtopped by leaves*; florets brownish. **Leaves** alternate, entire, *white-woolly beneath.* **Stems** branching, white-woolly. **Fruit** an achene, with bristles in a single row at the tip.
OCCURRENCE: Common; MDI, IAH, SCH.
OTHER NAMES: Mud Cudweed, Brown Cudweed, Marsh Cudweed

Jerusalem Artichoke • *Helianthus tuberosus*

Rhizomatous, tuberous, perennial herb of old fields, 1–3 m tall; **Flower heads** (capitula) numerous, 5–10 cm wide, in a corymb-like capitulescence; ray florets yellow, *8–20 per head, with rays 2.5–4 cm long*; disc florets yellow; involucral bracts with small hairs on the margin. **Leaves** *alternate above, opposite below*, toothed, minutely pubescent beneath; petioles winged. **Stems** hairy. **Fruit** a smooth achene, compressed laterally.
OCCURRENCE: Uncommon; MDI.
OTHER NAMES: Jerusalem Artichoke Sunflower

Orange Hawkweed • **Hieracium aurantiacum*

Perennial herb of fields and woodlands, 10–90 cm tall. **Flower heads** (capitula) ~2 cm wide, in a congested capitulescence; *florets red-orange*, turning purple to deep red when dry; *involucral bracts bristly with blackish gland-tipped hairs*; peduncles with milky sap, *hairy*, occasionally with up to 2 reduced bracts on lower portion. **Leaves** basal only, bristly below, sometimes bristly above, 4–25 cm long and 1–3 cm wide.
OCCURRENCE: Common; MDI, IAH, SCH.
OTHER NAMES: Devil's Paint-brush, Indian Paintbrush, Orange Paintbrush

Field Hawkweed • ***Hieracium caespitosum**

Perennial herb of fields and roadsides, 10–90 cm tall. **Flower heads** (capitula) 5–30 in a compact cluster; *florets yellow; involucral bracts bristly with blackish gland-tipped hairs*; peduncles with milky sap, the lower portion bristly, the upper portion with compound, woolly hairs and black, bland-tipped hairs, occasionally with up to 3 reduced bracts on lower portion. **Leaves** *basal only*, 4–25 cm long and 1–3 cm wide, *entire or with a few small teeth, very hairy to bristly on both sides*. **Fruit** an achene 1.5–2 mm long.
OCCURRENCE: Common; MDI, SCH.
OTHER NAMES: King Devil, Yellow King Devil, Yellow Hawkweed, *Hieracium pratense*

Kalm's Hawkweed • **Hieracium kalmii**

Perennial herb of fields and woodlands, 0.1–1.5 m tall. **Flower heads** (capitula) ~2.5 cm wide, in a loose, flat-topped cluster; ray florets yellow; *peduncles stout, 2–4 cm long, with compound hairs.* **Leaves** alternate, firm to leathery, somewhat clasping at base, often hairy beneath but *without any long, bulbous-based hairs; cauline leaves 25–50,* those of the mid-stem 3–12 cm long and 7–40 mm wide, usually with a few teeth. **Stems** with milky sap, often hairy below but *without long, bulbous-based hairs.* **Fruit** an achene 2.5–3.5 mm long.
OCCURRENCE: Common; MDI.
OTHER NAMES: Canada Hawkweed, *Hieracium canadense*

European Hawkweed • **Hieracium lachenalii*

Perennial herb of fields and roadsides, 0.1–1 m tall. **Flower heads** (capitula) 2.5–4 cm wide, in an open capitulescence; ray florets yellow; peduncles and involucral bracts with gland-tipped hairs. **Leaves** *well developed during flowering, tapering to base, with a few coarse, sharp teeth toward base,* the lowest 2–13 cm long and 1.5–5.5 cm wide; cauline leaves 2–7, reduced, with long hairs, often mottled with red. **Stems** with milky sap, *sparsely bristly with compound hairs.* **Fruit** an achene 2.5–3.5 mm long.
OCCURRENCE: Common; MDI, SCH.
OTHER NAMES: Common Hawkweed, Common Wall Hawkweed, *Hieracium vulgatum*

Wall Hawkweed • **Hieracium murorum*

Perennial herb of disturbed sites, 20–70 cm tall. **Flower heads** (capitula) few, 3–4 cm wide, *with stalked glands,* in an open capitulescence; ray florets yellow; peduncles with milky sap, occasionally with up to 3 leaf-like bracts on lower portion. **Leaves** with long hairs, basal only, oval, *with coarse teeth or lobes, broadly rounded at base.*
OCCURRENCE: Occasional; MDI.
OTHER NAMES: Golden Lungwort

Panicled Hawkweed • *Hieracium paniculatum*

Perennial herb of dry, rocky forests, 0.2–1.5 m tall. **Flower heads** (capitula) numerous, ~13 mm wide, *on long thread-like peduncles*; ray florets yellow. **Leaves** alternate, thin, *with a white bloom beneath*, irregularly toothed, the uppermost 4–12 cm long and 1–2 cm wide; *basal leaves not present during flowering*. **Stems** with milky sap, *solitary, hairy on lower portion with longest hairs >3 mm long*. **Fruit** 1.8–2.5 mm long.
OCCURRENCE: Uncommon; MDI.
OTHER NAMES: Allegheny Hawkweed

AH

AH

Mouse-ear Hawkweed • **Hieracium pilosella*

Stoloniferous, perennial herb of fields and lawns, up to 60 cm tall. **Flower heads** (capitula) *mostly solitary*, rarely 2 or 3 per stem, 2.5–3 cm wide; ray florets yellow; peduncles with milky sap. **Leaves** basal only, *white-woolly beneath when young, bristly above*, 1.5–8 cm long and 5–15 mm wide.
OCCURRENCE: Common; MDI, IAH, SCH.
OTHER NAMES: Mouse-ear

New England Hawkweed • **Hieracium sabaudum***

Weedy, perennial herb of disturbed sites and woodland edges, 0.1–1.5 m tall. **Flower heads** (capitula) on elongate peduncles; capitulescence occupying one-third to two-thirds the height of plant; ray florets yellow; involucral bracts round-tipped, *the outer ones often spreading*. **Leaves** mostly on lower half of stem, usually glabrous above, *with long, bulbous-based hairs beneath; basal leaves not present during flowering*. **Stems** with milky sap, *with long, bulbous-based hairs on lower portion*.
OCCURRENCE: Uncommon; MDI.
OTHER NAMES: Savoy Hawkweed

Rough Hawkweed • ***Hieracium scabrum***

Perennial herb of dry, rocky woods, 0.2–1.5 m tall. **Flower heads** (capitula) on stout peduncles with woolly hairs; *ray florets yellow, 40–100 per head; involucral bracts with stiff, often gland-tipped, hairs*. **Leaves** alternate, *thick*, reduced in size near top of stem, the lowest 4–20 cm long and 1–4.5 cm wide, with hairs <3 mm long on petioles and midribs; *basal leaves not present during flowering*. **Stems** *with hairs >3 mm long on lower portion*, with milky sap. **Fruit** an achene 2–3 mm long.
OCCURRENCE: Uncommon; MDI.
OTHER NAMES: Sticky Hawkweed

Tansy Ragwort • **Jacobaea vulgaris*

Weedy, biennial or short-lived perennial herb of disturbed sites, 0.2–1.3 m tall. **Flower heads** (capitula) 15–25 mm wide, in a terminal umbel-like capitulescence; ray florets yellow, spreading, the rays 4–10 mm long. **Leaves** alternate, usually equally distributed on stem, mostly *2- to 3-times pinnately divided*, 4–23 cm long and 2–11 cm wide, pubescent beneath when young. **Stems** with white, soft, woolly hairs. **Fruit** an achene with minute hairs.
OCCURRENCE: Rare; MDI.
NOTES: Toxic to livestock.
OTHER NAMES: Stinking Willie, Staggerwort, *Senecio jacobaea*

Tall Blue Lettuce • *Lactuca biennis*

Biennial or annual herb of wet forests and openings, *up to 4 m tall.* **Flower heads** (capitula) ~1 cm wide; *ray florets blue to white*, 15–55 per head, the rays 5-toothed. **Leaves** alternate, usually deeply lobed, with coarse teeth, 10–40 cm long and 4–20 cm wide, *with prickles on midrib, often aligned along stem facing the sun.* **Stems** *solitary, with milky sap.* **Fruit** a tapering, thin-edged achene 4–5.5 mm long, with 3 veins on each face and *2 rows of light brown bristles at the tip.*
OCCURRENCE: Uncommon; MDI.

Wild Lettuce • *Lactuca canadensis*

Annual or biennial herb of disturbed sites, fields, and forests, up to 2.5 m tall. **Flower heads** (capitula) numerous, ~6 mm wide and 8–15 mm long, in an open elongate capitulescence; florets yellow. **Leaves** alternate, variable in shape, ranging from nearly entire to deeply lobed, 10–35 cm long and 1.5–12 cm wide, *with prickles on midrib*. **Stems** *with milky sap*. **Fruit** a 1-ribbed, black, flat achene 4.5–6.5 mm long with a beak at least half as long as body, with white bristles at the tip 5–7 mm long.
OCCURRENCE: Uncommon; MDI.
OTHER NAMES: Tall Lettuce, Devil's-weed, Canada Lettuce

AH

Nipplewort • **Lapsana communis*

Annual herb of disturbed sites, fields, and forests, 0.3–1.5 m tall. **Flower heads** (capitula) 1–1.5 cm wide, in a loose panicle-like capitulescence; peduncles hardened; ray florets yellow, 8–15 per head; inner involucral bracts 8, keeled. **Leaves** alternate, thin, entire to lobed, the largest 2.5–10 cm long and 2–7 cm wide, progressively narrowing going up the stem, the lowest with shallow teeth, often with lobes at base. **Stems** slender, branching, with milky sap. **Fruit** an achene 3–5 mm long, narrow, often curving, with 18–30 veins, *without bristles at the tip*.
OCCURRENCE: Occasional; MDI.
OTHER NAMES: Common Nipplewort

AH

Ox-eye Daisy • **Leucanthemum vulgare*

Perennial herb of fields and disturbed sites, 0.2–1 m tall. **Flower heads** (capitula) solitary, long-stalked, 2.5–6.5 cm wide; *ray florets white, 15–35 per head*; disc florets yellow. **Leaves** alternate, 4–15 cm long, usually *lobed or with large teeth, without scent*; cauline leaves gradually reduced upward. **Fruit** a 10-ribbed achene.
OCCURRENCE: Common; MDI, IAH, SCH.
OTHER NAMES: White Daisy, *Chrysanthemum leucanthemum*

Pineapple-weed • **Matricaria discoidea*

Annual herb of roadsides and disturbed sites, 5–40 cm tall. **Flower heads** (capitula) *with a pineapple odor when crushed*; ray florets absent; disc florets yellow, 4-lobed, on a conical receptacle. **Leaves** alternate, 1–5 cm long, 1- to 3-times pinnately compound, *with a pineapple odor when crushed*. **Fruit** an achene with 2–5 veins.
OCCURRENCE: Common; MDI, IAH, SCH.
OTHER NAMES: Rayless Chamomile, Rayless Mayweed, *Matricaria matricarioides*

Wall-lettuce • **Mycelis muralis***

Annual or biennial herb of wet woodlands and disturbed sites, 0.3–1 m tall. **Flower heads** (capitula) <1 cm wide, in an open capitulescence with branches at 90° to the main stem; florets yellow, *5 per head; involucral bracts 5 or fewer.* **Leaves** thin, *pinnately compound, with 3-lobed tip*, the lowest 6–18 cm long and 3–8 cm wide. **Stems** often glaucous, with milky sap. **Fruit** an achene 4–5 mm long, with dark veins and slender beak.
OCCURRENCE: Occasional; MDI.
OTHER NAMES: *Lactuca muralis*

Tall White Lettuce • ***Nabalus altissimus***

Perennial herb of forests, up to 2 m tall. **Flower heads** (capitula) *nodding*, in small axillary and loose terminal clusters; florets white or cream-colored; *inner involucral bracts 4–6*, longer than outer ones. **Leaves** alternate, thin, variable from unlobed to many lobed. **Stems** with milky sap. **Fruit** an achene with bristles at the tip.
OCCURRENCE: Occasional; MDI, SCH.
OTHER NAMES: White Lettuce, *Prenanthes altissima*

Tall Rattlesnake-root • *Nabalus trifoliolatus*

Perennial herb of rocky summits and coastal headlands, 0.6–2 m tall. **Flower heads** (capitula) *nodding*, in small axillary and loose terminal clusters; florets white or cream-colored, *7–18 per head; inner involucral bracts 7–10*, longer than outer ones, with tiny, white, waxy papillae. **Leaves** alternate, highly variable in size and shape, the lowest usually lobed, the uppermost less lobed and smaller. **Stems** stout, glabrous, with milky sap. **Fruit** an achene with white to yellow-brown bristles at the tip.
OCCURRENCE: Common; MDI, IAH, SCH.
OTHER NAMES: Gall-of-the-earth, Three-leaved Rattlesnake-root, *Prenanthes trifoliolata*

Whorled Aster • *Oclemena acuminata*

Rhizomatous, perennial herb of conifer and hardwood forests, 0.2–1 m tall. **Flower heads** (capitula) few to many, 2.5–4 cm wide, in an open capitulescence; ray florets 10–21 per head, the rays white to pinkish; disc florets yellow; *outer involucral bracts with long hairs on the margin.* **Leaves** often sticky beneath, *coarsely toothed* and thin pointed, *the largest on upper stem 1–6 cm wide.* **Stems** *zigzagging.*
OCCURRENCE: Common; MDI, IAH, SCH.
OTHER NAMES: Sharp-leaved Aster, Mountain Aster, Whorled Wood Aster, Sharp-toothed Nodding-aster, *Aster acuminatus*

Bog Aster • *Oclemena nemoralis*

Perennial herb of bogs, 10–90 cm tall. **Flower heads** (capitula) *solitary or few*, 2.5–4 cm wide; ray florets 13–27 per head, light purple or pink, the rays 1.2–1.8 cm long. **Leaves** 30–100, *with rough edges, slightly rolled under*, often with glands and pubescence beneath, *the largest 5–12 mm wide*. **Stems** 1–2 mm wide, *pubescent with slightly sticky hairs*.
OCCURRENCE: Occasional; MDI, IAH, SCH.
OTHER NAMES: Leafy Bog Aster, Bog Nodding-aster, *Aster nemoralis*

New England Groundsel • *Packera schweinitziana*

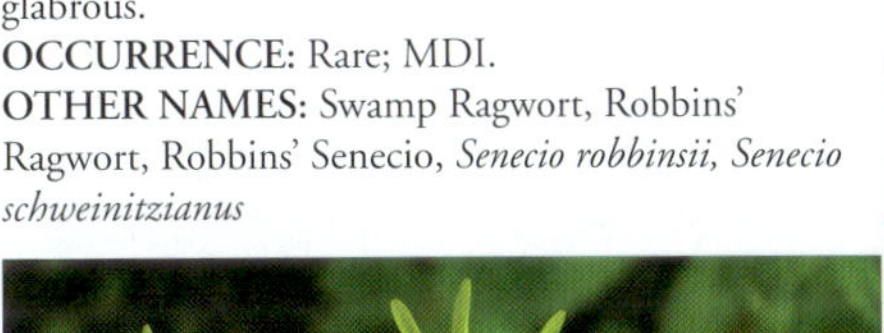

Perennial herb of wet swales and woodlands, 0.3–1 m tall. **Flower heads** (capitula) 12–20 mm wide, on slender peduncles; ray florets yellow, the rays 6–13 mm long. **Leaves** *finely toothed, rounded to heart-shaped at the base*, progressively reduced above, the lowest 2–10 cm long and 1.5–5 cm wide. **Fruit** glabrous.
OCCURRENCE: Rare; MDI.
OTHER NAMES: Swamp Ragwort, Robbins' Ragwort, Robbins' Senecio, *Senecio robbinsii, Senecio schweinitzianus*

Arctic Sweet Coltsfoot • *Petasites frigidus*

Perennial, subdioecious herb of cedar swamps, 0.1–1 m tall. **Flower heads** (capitula) 8–13 mm wide, *appearing before leaves*; ray florets with short whitish rays 2–7 mm long; main stalk of capitulescence scaly, with bracts. **Leaves** basal only, *palmately compound, cleft over halfway to base, white-woolly beneath*, 5–40 cm wide; petioles long. **Fruit** an achene with 5–10 veins and capillary hairs at the tip.
OCCURRENCE: Rare; MDI, IAH.
OTHER NAMES: Northern Sweet-coltsfoot, Sweet Coltsfoot, *Petasites palmatus*

AH

Sweet Everlasting • *Pseudognaphalium obtusifolium*

Weedy, annual herb of disturbed sites and river shores, 0.2–1 m tall. **Flower heads** (capitula) *woolly at base, sweet smelling*; disc florets 75–125 per head; involucral bracts white or tan. **Leaves** alternate, *mildly aromatic when crushed*, sessile, *white-woolly beneath*. **Stems** *with thin, white-woolly pubescence*, sometimes with glands at base. **Fruit** smooth.
OCCURRENCE: Uncommon; MDI.
OTHER NAMES: Catfoot, Fragrant Cudweed, Blunt-leaved Rabbit-tobacco, *Gnaphalium obtusifolium*

AH

AH

Black-eyed Susan • *Rudbeckia hirta*

Biennial or short-lived perennial herb of fields and roadsides, 0.3–1 m tall. **Flower heads** (capitula) solitary, 5–8 cm wide; *ray florets 8–21 per head, yellowish; disc florets dark purple-brown*; involucral bracts long pubescent (see right photo). **Leaves** alternate, entire to finely toothed, *coarsely pubescent*. **Stems** with bristly hairs. **Fruit** 4-angled, smooth.

OCCURRENCE: Occasional; MDI, SCH.

OTHER NAMES: Black-eyed Coneflower, *Rudbeckia serotina*

Fall-dandelion • **Scorzoneroides autumnalis*

Perennial herb of disturbed sites, roadsides, and fields, 10–80 cm tall. **Flower heads** (capitula) ~2.5 cm wide, long-tapering at base into peduncles; ray florets yellow; involucral bracts densely pubescent with black hairs; main stalk of capitulescence slender, *solid*, with few scales, usually branching above. **Leaves** *basal only, deeply pinnately lobed or toothed*, 4–35 cm long and 5–40 mm wide, sometimes pubescent. **Fruit** a narrow, rugose achene 4–7.5 mm long.

OCCURRENCE: Common; MDI, IAH, SCH.

OTHER NAMES: *Leontodon autumnalis*

Woodland Groundsel • **Senecio sylvaticus*

Weedy, annual herb of disturbed sites, 0.1–1 m tall. **Flower heads** (capitula) 7–9 mm long and ~5 mm wide, in a loose capitulescence; *ray florets present*, yellow, the rays <2 mm long; *long, inner involucral bracts without a black tip*. **Leaves** alternate, sticky, mostly pinnately compound, with irregular teeth, 2–12 cm long and 4–40 mm wide. **Stems** with white, soft, woolly hairs.

OCCURRENCE: Occasional; MDI, IAH, SCH.

OTHER NAMES: Wood Groundsel, Woodland Ragwort, Heath Groundsel

Common Groundsel • **Senecio vulgaris*

Weedy, annual herb of disturbed sites, 10–90 cm tall. **Flower heads** (capitula) 4–10 mm long and ~4 mm wide, in a loose capitulescence; *ray florets usually absent; long, inner involucral bracts with a black tip* (see right photo), *short outer bracts usually with a black tip*. **Leaves** alternate, coarsely toothed, often pinnately compound, 2–10 cm long and 5–45 mm wide, the lowest tapering to petiole, the uppermost sessile and clasping. **Stems** with white, soft, woolly hairs.

OCCURRENCE: Occasional; MDI, IAH, SCH.

NOTES: Toxic to livestock.

OTHER NAMES: Grimsel, Common Ragwort

Indian Cup • ***Silphium perfoliatum**

Perennial herb of forests and roadsides, up to 3 m tall. **Flower heads** (capitula) *5–8 cm wide*, in an open capitulescence; *ray florets 17–35 per head, yellow*; disc florets yellow; involucral bracts wide, with ciliate margins. **Leaves** *opposite*, coarsely toothed, *connate at base and forming a cup*. **Stems** square, glabrous. **Fruit** broad, flat, surrounded by a wing.
OCCURRENCE: Rare; MDI.
OTHER NAMES: Cup-plant, Cup-plant Rosinweed

White Goldenrod • ***Solidago bicolor***

Perennial herb of dry, rocky, and sandy sites, 10–90 cm tall. **Flower heads** (capitula) in a spike-like capitulescence; *ray florets white, with 7–9 rays*; disc florets yellow; *outer involucral bracts whitish with green tips*. **Leaves** alternate, the lowest usually toothed, pubescent on both surfaces, the largest 8–20 cm long and 1.5–6 cm wide, *rapidly reduced in size upward*. **Stems** pubescent.
OCCURRENCE: Common; MDI, IAH, SCH.
OTHER NAMES: Silverrod

Canada Goldenrod • *Solidago canadensis*

Perennial herb of uplands and wetlands, up to 2 m tall. **Flower heads** (capitula) *~5 mm wide, arranged on only one side of branch*, forming a pyramid-shaped capitulescence; ray florets yellow, 10–17 per head, with rays 1–3 mm long. **Leaves** alternate, *narrow, sharply toothed, with 2 prominent veins and pubescence parallel to the midrib* (see bottom left photo), the largest 3–15 cm long and 5–22 mm wide, the lowest deciduous at flowering. **Stems** glabrous near base, *pubescent above.*
OCCURRENCE: Common; MDI, IAH, SCH.
OTHER NAMES: Common Goldenrod

AH

Zigzag Goldenrod • *Solidago flexicaulis*

Perennial herb of rich hardwood forests, 0.3–1.2 m tall. **Flower heads** (capitula) in short axillary clusters; ray florets yellow, 3–4 per head; disc florets yellow, 5–9 per head. **Leaves** alternate, sharply toothed, *7–15 cm long and 3–10 cm wide, narrowing abruptly at base to winged petiole, gradually reduced in size upwards.* **Stems** *zigzagging, grooved, pubescent below capitulescence.*
OCCURRENCE: Uncommon; MDI.

Late Goldenrod • *Solidago gigantea*

Rhizomatous, perennial herb of open, wet sites, up to 3 m tall. **Flower heads** (capitula) *arranged on only one side of branch*, forming a pyramid-shaped capitulescence; ray florets yellow, 8–17 per head, with rays 1–3 mm long; disc florets yellow, 6–12 per head. **Leaves** alternate, sharply toothed, sessile, *tapering to both ends*, with 2 prominent veins parallel to the midrib, *the lowest withering before flowering*, the largest 6–17 cm long and 1–4.5 cm wide. **Stems** *glabrous below capitulescence, glaucous.*

OCCURRENCE: Uncommon; MDI.

OTHER NAMES: Smooth Goldenrod

AH

Early Goldenrod • *Solidago juncea*

Perennial herb of dry, open, primarily sandy sites, 0.3–1.2 m tall. **Flower heads** (capitula) in a capitulescence 10–40 cm tall and 3–30 cm wide; ray florets yellow, 7–12 per head, the rays 4–5 mm long; disc florets yellow, ~10 per head; *flowering early, usually in late July*. **Leaves** alternate, *not fleshy*; cauline leaves gradually reduced upward, becoming bract-like; basal and lower leaves with long petioles, *present at flowering, not clasping the stem*. **Stems** *glabrous below capitulescence*, green, branching.

OCCURRENCE: Occasional; MDI.

AH

Gray Goldenrod • *Solidago nemoralis*

Perennial herb of dry, open, primarily sandy sites, 0.1–1.3 m tall. **Flower heads** (capitula) *in one-sided clusters*; ray florets yellow, 5–9 per head; disc florets yellow, 3–6 per head; involucral bracts yellowish, with tiny hairs on edges. **Leaves** alternate, *entire or bluntly toothed, grayish and densely pubescent, the lowest present during flowering*, tapering to a winged petiole. **Stems** *densely pubescent below capitulescence.*
OCCURRENCE: Occasional; MDI, IAH.

Downy Goldenrod • *Solidago puberula*

Perennial herb of open, rocky, or sandy sites, 0.2–1 m tall. **Flower heads** (capitula) in an elongate capitulescence; *ray florets yellow*, 9–16 per head; disc florets yellow, 8–20 per head; involucral bracts narrow, tapering, <0.5 mm wide. **Leaves** alternate, *often minutely pubescent*, the largest 5–15 cm long and 1–3.5 cm wide, *rapidly reduced in size upward.* **Stems** *unbranched, densely pubescent below capitulescence, often purple.*
OCCURRENCE: Common; MDI, IAH, SCH.
OTHER NAMES: Dusty Goldenrod

Rough-stemmed Goldenrod • *Solidago rugosa*

Perennial herb of various habitats, up to 2.3 m tall. **Flower heads** (capitula) *arranged on only one side of branch*; ray florets yellow, 6–11 per head; disc florets yellow, 3–8 per head. **Leaves** alternate, thin, *sharply toothed, pubescent beneath on midrib and veins; cauline leaves elliptic, the lowest deciduous at flowering* and smaller than middle cauline ones. **Stems** *hairy, at least below capitulescence*.
OCCURRENCE: Common; MDI, IAH, SCH.
OTHER NAMES: Common Wrinkle-leaved Goldenrod

Seaside Goldenrod • *Solidago sempervirens*

Perennial herb of salt marshes and coastal headlands, up to 2 m tall. **Flower heads** (capitula) *arranged on only one side of branch*; ray florets yellow, 8–17 per head; disc florets yellow, 12–40 per head. **Leaves** alternate, *entire, fleshy*, 10–40 cm long and 1–6 cm wide, the lowest present during flowering, with wide petioles. **Stems** *glabrous below capitulescence*.
OCCURRENCE: Common; MDI, IAH, SCH.

Rand's Goldenrod • *Solidago simplex*

Perennial herb of rocky or sandy sites, up to 90 cm tall. **Flower heads** (capitula) often resinous, on peduncles 1–10 mm long; ray florets yellow, 7–12 per head; disc florets yellow, 3–10 per head. **Leaves** alternate, usually glabrous, *the lowest sharply toothed, often resinous*; basal leaves with a wide midrib 0.7–1 mm wide. **Stems** pubescent. **Fruit** 2–2.6 mm long *with hairs directed upward.*
OCCURRENCE: Common; MDI, SCH.
OTHER NAMES: *Solidago randii*

Northern Bog Goldenrod • *Solidago uliginosa*

Perennial herb of *bogs*, 0.4–1.5 m tall. **Flower heads** (capitula) usually pubescent, in an capitulescence taller than wide; ray florets yellow, 1–8 per head; disc florets yellow, 4–8 per head. **Leaves** alternate, not fleshy; basal leaves usually finely toothed, with distinct winged petioles; *lowest cauline leaves clasping stem, present during flowering.* **Stems** *glabrous below capitulescence.*
OCCURRENCE: Occasional; MDI, IAH, SCH.
OTHER NAMES: Bog Goldenrod, Swamp Goldenrod

AH

Field Sow-thistle • **Sonchus arvensis*

Weedy, perennial herb of shores, roadsides, and waste areas, 0.4–2 m tall. **Flower heads** (capitula) *2.5–5 cm wide, with yellow glandular hairs at base; florets bright yellow-orange*, 150–235 per head. **Leaves** alternate, with soft spines on the margin, *the uppermost heart-shaped and clasping at base, the lowest deeply lobed*, 6–40 cm long and 2–15 cm wide. **Stems** with milky sap, grooved. **Fruit** an achene, rugose and ribbed, 2.5–3.5 mm long, with copious white hairs at the tip.
OCCURRENCE: Occasional; MDI, SCH.
OTHER NAMES: Perennial Sow-thistle, Creeping Sow-thistle

Spiny-leaved Sow-thistle • **Sonchus asper*

Weedy, annual herb of disturbed sites and sea beaches, 0.3–1.6 m tall. **Flower heads** (capitula) *1.5–2.5 cm wide*, in a loose capitulescence; *florets deep golden-yellow*. **Leaves** alternate, often unlobed, with toothed, spiny margins; *leaf bases round-lobed* (see lower right photo), *clasping the stem*. **Stems** with milky sap. **Fruit** a flat achene, with 6 prominent ribs and copious white hairs at the tip.
OCCURRENCE: Common; MDI, IAH, SCH.
OTHER NAMES: Prickly-leaved Sow-thistle, Spiny-leaf Sow-thistle, Annual Sow-thistle, Prickly Sow-thistle

Annual Sow-thistle • ***Sonchus oleraceus**

Weedy, annual herb of disturbed sites, up to 2 m tall. **Flower heads** (capitula) *1.5–2.5 cm wide*, usually glabrous at base, in a loose capitulescence; *florets pale yellow*. **Leaves** alternate, the lowest deeply lobed and usually with a large, triangular terminal lobe, progressively less divided upward; margins with weak prickles; *leaf bases acutely lobed* (see middle right photo) *and clasping the stem*. **Stems** with milky sap. **Fruit** a slightly flattened achene 2.5–3.5 mm long, with 3–5 faint ribs and copious white hairs at the tip.
OCCURRENCE: Occasional; MDI, IAH.
OTHER NAMES: Common Sow-thistle

Heart-leaved Aster • **Symphyotrichum cordifolium**

Perennial herb of dry, rocky woods, 0.2–1.2 m tall. **Flower heads** (capitula) numerous; ray florets pale blue-violet to rose, 8–20 per head, the rays 5–10 mm long; disc florets yellow to red. **Leaves** alternate, thin, hairy beneath; *basal and lower leaves heart-shaped at base, toothed*.
OCCURRENCE: Occasional; MDI.
OTHER NAMES: Common Blue Heart-leaved Aster, Heart-leaved American Aster, *Aster cordifolius*

Calico Aster • *Symphyotrichum lateriflorum*

Perennial herb of forests and open sites, 0.3–1.2 m tall. **Flower heads** (capitula) small, numerous, *located on only one side of branches*; *ray florets white* or rarely purple, 9–14 per head, the rays 4–6.5 mm long. **Leaves** alternate, the lowest tapering to both ends.
OCCURRENCE: Common; MDI, SCH.
OTHER NAMES: Starved Aster, Goblet Aster, Farewell-summer, Calico American-aster, *Aster lateriflorus*

New England Aster • *Symphyotrichum novae-angliae*

Perennial herb of open sites and forests, 0.3–2 m tall. **Flower heads** (capitula) *densely glandular*, 1–2 cm wide; *ray florets bright purple or pink, 45–100 per head*; involucral bracts usually purplish. **Leaves** alternate, entire, sessile, *clasping*, 3–12 cm long and 6–20 mm wide, pubescent with stiff hairs above, the uppermost sometimes with glands. **Stems** hairy.
OCCURRENCE: Occasional; MDI.
OTHER NAMES: New England American Aster, *Aster novae-angliae*

New York Aster • *Symphyotrichum novi-belgii*

Perennial herb of coastal headlands and saltmarshes, 0.2–1.4 m tall. **Flower heads** (capitula) without glands, numerous, on short peduncles; ray florets light purple, 20–50 per head; involucral bracts long and pointed. **Leaves** alternate, *gradually tapering to and partially clasping the stem*, thick, firm, 4–17 cm long and 4–25 mm wide. **Stems** often wider than 2.5 mm.
OCCURRENCE: Common; MDI, IAH, SCH.
OTHER NAMES: New York American-aster, *Aster novi-belgii*

Purple-stemmed Aster • *Symphyotrichum puniceum*

Perennial herb of marshes and wet ditches, up to 2.5 m tall. **Flower heads** (capitula) few to many in a leafy capitulescence; ray florets light purple to blue, 30–60 per head, the rays 7–18 mm long; disc florets yellow; *involucral bracts of equal length.* **Leaves** alternate, tapering to base, *clasping the stem*, the largest often toothed, 7–16 cm long and 12–40 mm wide. **Stems** *with spreading hairs.*
OCCURRENCE: Occasional; MDI, IAH, SCH.
OTHER NAMES: Bristly Aster, Purple-stemmed American-aster, *Aster puniceus*

Common Tansy • **Tanacetum vulgare*

Weedy, perennial herb of disturbed sites, 0.3–1.5 m tall. **Flower heads** (capitula) 5–15 mm wide, button-like, in a dense, flat-topped capitulescence; ray florets absent; disc florets yellow, tightly packed. **Leaves** alternate, *aromatic*, deeply pinnately compound; leaflets often toothed. **Stems** glabrous, aromatic. **Fruit** usually angled, *dotted with glands*.
OCCURRENCE: Occasional; MDI.
OTHER NAMES: Tansy, Golden-buttons

Common Dandelion • **Taraxacum officinale*

Weedy, perennial herb of lawns, fields, and disturbed sites, 5–50 cm tall. **Flower heads** (capitula) *solitary, 2–5 cm wide; ray florets yellow-orange*; disc florets absent; involucral bracts in 2 series, becoming reflexed; peduncles unbranched, *hollow*, with milky sap. **Leaves** *basal only*, toothed, *deeply pinnately lobed* to occasionally entire, often sparsely pubescent beneath.
OCCURRENCE: Common; MDI, IAH, SCH.

Yellow Goatsbeard • **Tragopogon pratensis*

Biennial herb of fields and disturbed sites, 10–80 cm tall. **Flower heads** (capitula) *solitary, long-stalked, <6 cm wide*, opening only in morning sunshine, closing by noon; ray florets yellow, the rays toothed. **Leaves** alternate, entire, grass-like, *clasping the stem*. **Fruit** a slender achene, widest near the middle, 5- to 10-ribbed with long, white, plumose bristles at the tip.

OCCURRENCE: Uncommon; MDI, SCH.

OTHER NAMES: Showy Goatsbeard, Jack-go-to-bed-at-noon, Meadow Goatsbeard

AH

Coltsfoot • **Tussilago farfara*

Weedy, perennial herb of disturbed sites, 5–50 cm tall. **Flower heads** (capitula) 1.5–3.5 cm wide, appearing in early spring before leaves; ray florets yellow, numerous, small; disc florets yellow; main stalk of capitulescence with alternate scaly bracts. **Leaves** basal only, 5–20 cm long and 5–20 cm wide, white-woolly beneath, *tip hooked*; petioles long.

OCCURRENCE: Uncommon; MDI.

NOTES: This nonnative species is invasive.

Spotted Touch-me-not • *Impatiens capensis*

Annual herb of wet areas, 0.5–1.8 m tall. **Flowers** *2–2.5 mm long, deep yellow to orange with darker red to brown spots*; flower spur 7–10 mm long, strongly curving underneath, projecting forward. **Leaves** *alternate*, short-stalked, egg-shaped, pointed, *with rounded teeth*, pale beneath, fleshy-succulent. **Fruit** *a slender capsule*, exploding when ripe, dispersing the seeds.
OCCURRENCE: Occasional; MDI, IAH, SCH.
NOTES: The flower consists of two lower petals forming the lip, two petals on each side united and appearing as a single petal, and a large upper petal forming a hood.
OTHER NAMES: Orange Touch-me-not, Snapweed, Spotted Jewel-weed

Himalayan Balsam • **Impatiens glandulifera*

Annual herb of wet areas, 0.5–1.8 m tall. **Flowers** *magenta to purple*, otherwise similar in structure to *Impatiens capensis*. **Leaves** *opposite or whorled, sharply serrate*. **Fruit** *an egg-shaped capsule*, exploding when ripe, dispersing the seeds.
OCCURRENCE: Rare; MDI.
NOTES: This nonnative species is invasive and is currently known only from the Bass Harbor area of MDI.

Japanese Barberry • **Berberis thunbergii*

Deciduous, spiny shrub of open areas and roadsides, up to 2 m tall. **Flowers** yellow, solitary or few to a cluster, pendent from horizontal or arching branches. **Leaves** *entire*. **Stems** *with unbranched spines*. **Fruit** a bright red, oval-cylindrical berry.
OCCURRENCE: Occasional; MDI, IAH.
NOTES: This nonnative species is aggressively invasive in natural areas.

European Barberry • **Berberis vulgaris*

Deciduous, spiny shrub of thickets and pastures, up to 3 m tall. **Flowers** yellow, *in pendent axillary clusters of up to 20 flowers*. **Leaves** *bristle-toothed*. **Stems** *with branched spines*. **Fruit** a cylindrical berry, at first yellow, then red when ripe.
OCCURRENCE: Uncommon; MDI.
NOTES: This nonnative species is invasive.
OTHER NAMES: Common Barberry

AH

AH

Speckled Alder • *Alnus incana*

Deciduous shrub of wet areas, up to 3 m tall. **Flowers** of two types: staminate flowers in pendulous catkins, shedding pollen in April before leaves appear, and *carpellate flowers in ovoid catkins.* **Leaves** coarsely double-serrate, widest at or below the middle; *cross-veins (those between parallel secondary veins) conspicuous, extending between secondary veins,* most visible on leaf underside (see middle left photo). **Twigs** with stalked winter buds. **Bark** with white lenticels. **Fruit** cone-like, persisting. **Seeds** winged, 2–3.5 mm long.
OCCURRENCE: Common; MDI, IAH, SCH.
NOTES: *Alnus incana* blooms before *A. viridis.*
OTHER NAMES: *Alnus rugosa*

Mountain Alder • *Alnus viridis*

Deciduous shrub of bogs, rocky shores, and mountains, up to 3 m tall. **Flowers** of two types: staminate flowers in *pendulous catkins, shedding pollen in late May to early June with expansion of leaves,* and carpellate flowers in ovoid catkins, emerging from buds in late spring. **Leaves** with fine, sharp, crowded teeth; *cross-veins (those between parallel secondary veins) not extending all the way between parallel secondary veins,* most visible on leaf underside. **Twigs** with sessile winter buds. **Seeds** winged, 2–3 mm long.
OCCURRENCE: Common; MDI, IAH, SCH.
OTHER NAMES: Green Alder, *Alnus crispa*

Yellow Birch • *Betula alleghaniensis*

Deciduous tree, up to 30 m tall. **Flowers** of two types: staminate flowers in pendulous catkins, and carpellate flowers in shorter, upright catkins. **Leaves** with 8–12 pairs of *distinct, lateral veins*, coarsely and irregularly serrate. **Twigs** pubescent, *with a wintergreen odor and flavor when crushed.* **Bark** *yellowish, exfoliating in thin strips.*
OCCURRENCE: Common; MDI, IAH, SCH.
OTHER NAMES: *Betula lutea*

Mountain Paper Birch • *Betula cordifolia*

Deciduous tree, up to 20 m tall. **Flowers** of two types: staminate flowers in pendulous catkins, and carpellate flowers in shorter, upright catkins. **Leaves** *cordate at base*, pubescent beneath, with 9–12 pairs of lateral veins. **Twigs** glabrous when young. **Bark** *orange-tinged, exfoliating.*
OCCURRENCE: Occasional; MDI, IAH, SCH.
OTHER NAMES: Heartleaf Birch, Mountain White Birch, Heart-leaved Paper Birch

White Birch • *Betula papyrifera*

Deciduous tree, up to 25 m tall. **Flowers** of two types: staminate flowers in pendulous catkins, and carpellate flowers in shorter, upright catkins. **Leaves** with 7–9 pairs of lateral veins, pubescent in vein axils beneath, sharply or doubly serrate, with an acute apex. **Twigs** pubescent when young. **Bark** *white, exfoliating in large sheets.* **Fruit** in catkins 3–5 cm long.
OCCURRENCE: Common; MDI, IAH, SCH.
OTHER NAMES: Canoe Birch, Paper Birch

Gray Birch • *Betula populifolia*

Deciduous tree, up to 10 m tall. **Flowers** of two types: staminate flowers in pendulous catkins, and carpellate flowers in shorter, upright catkins. **Leaves** *triangular, truncate at base,* doubly serrate except at base, mostly with 5–7 pairs of lateral veins, glabrous on underside, *the tip long-acuminate.* **Twigs** ascending at tip, with warty resin glands. **Bark** with dark markings on chalky or ash-white bark that does not exfoliate.
OCCURRENCE: Common; MDI, IAH, SCH.
OTHER NAMES: Fire Birch, Oldfield Birch

AH

CWG

American Hornbeam • *Carpinus caroliniana*

Deciduous small tree or shrub, up to 10 m tall. **Flowers** of two types: staminate flowers in pendulous catkins, and clusters of carpellate flowers among leafy, 3-lobed involucral bracts. **Leaves** oblong to oblong-ovate, sharply and often doubly serrate, with unbranched lateral veins, with dark glands on underside. **Buds** quadrangular in cross section. **Bark** *smooth, light blue-gray*. **Fruit** in catkins, the mature ones 2–5 cm long, nutlets in pairs.
OCCURRENCE: Rare; MDI.
OTHER NAMES: Blue-beech, Musclewood

Beaked Hazelnut • *Corylus cornuta*

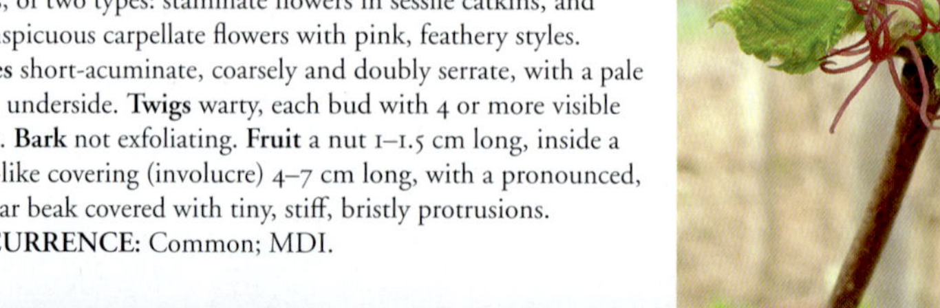

Deciduous shrub, up to 3 m tall. **Flowers** appearing before leaves, of two types: staminate flowers in sessile catkins, and inconspicuous carpellate flowers with pink, feathery styles. **Leaves** short-acuminate, coarsely and doubly serrate, with a pale green underside. **Twigs** warty, each bud with 4 or more visible scales. **Bark** not exfoliating. **Fruit** a nut 1–1.5 cm long, inside a husk-like covering (involucre) 4–7 cm long, with a pronounced, tubular beak covered with tiny, stiff, bristly protrusions.
OCCURRENCE: Common; MDI.

Eastern Hop-hornbeam • *Ostrya virginiana*

Deciduous small tree or shrub, up to 10 m tall. **Flowers** of two types: staminate flowers in pendulous catkins, and cone-like carpellate flowers. **Leaves** oblong or ovate, short-acuminate, sharply and often doubly serrate. **Buds** on winter twigs with longitudinally striate scales. **Bark** furrowed, *exfoliating in vertical strips*. **Fruit** in clusters borne at branch tips, each bract in cluster a closed, inflated sac 1–3 cm long containing a nut.
OCCURRENCE: Occasional; MDI.
OTHER NAMES: American Hop-hornbeam, Ironwood, Leverwood

CWG

BORAGINACEAE • BORAGE FAMILY ▼

Seaside Bluebells • *Mertensia maritima*

Perennial, mat-forming herb of cobble or gravel beaches. **Flowers** tubular, bell-shaped, 4–12 mm long, pink when young, turning pale blue or white with age. **Leaves** *grayish blue, alternate, entire, fleshy, 1–12 cm long, egg-shaped, with a gently pointed tip.*
OCCURRENCE: Rare; MDI, IAH, SCH.
NOTES: Plant of arctic affinity at the southern limit of its range.
OTHER NAMES: Seaside-Lungwort, Oysterleaf, Sea Lungwort

Small Forget-me-not • *Myosotis laxa*

Annual or short-lived perennial herb of wet soils. **Flowers** *<6 mm wide*, blue with a yellow "eye", in a bractless inflorescence; calyx tube longer than style. **Leaves** green, oblong to lance-shaped, 2.5–7.5 mm long. **Stems** *round, not creeping*.
OCCURRENCE: Uncommon; MDI.
OTHER NAMES: Smaller Forget-me-not

True Forget-me-not • **Myosotis scorpioides*

Stoloniferous, perennial herb of wet soils, 30–80 cm tall. **Flowers** blue with a yellow "eye", *6–9 mm wide*, with the style overtopping nutlets and about as long as calyx tube; base of flowering branches with bracts; sepals with few hairs, the lobes usually shorter than tube. **Leaves** green, oblong to lance-shaped, 2.5–7.5 mm long. **Stems** *angled*.
OCCURRENCE: Uncommon; MDI.
OTHER NAMES: Water Scorpion-grass, Large Forget-me-not, Water Forget-me-not

Blue Forget-me-not • **Myosotis stricta*

Annual or winter-annual herb of drier soils, 5–20 cm tall. **Flowers** blue, 1–2 mm wide, with the tube about equaling the calyx, *extending from base of plant to branch tips, the lowest hidden among the leaves*; sepals 3–5 mm long, pubescent. **Leaves** green, pubescent. **Stems** *branching from base*. **Seeds** longer than the style.
OCCURRENCE: Rare; MDI.
OTHER NAMES: Blue Scorpion-grass, *Myosotis micrantha*

BRASSICACEAE • MUSTARD FAMILY ▼

Garlic Mustard • **Alliaria petiolata*

Biennial herb of open areas, up to 1 m tall. **Flowers** *with 4 white petals 4–7 mm long*, clustered at top of stem. **Leaves** *alternate, long-stalked on slender petiole, coarsely toothed, 3–6 cm long, with smell of garlic or onion when crushed.* **Fruit** a narrow silique 2.5–6 cm long, with wide pedicels.
OCCURRENCE: Occasional; MDI.
NOTES: This nonnative species is aggressively invasive in natural areas.
OTHER NAMES: *Alliaria officinalis*

Yellow Rocket • **_*Barbarea vulgaris_**

Perennial or biennial herb of wet woods and open areas, 0.2–1 m tall. **Flowers** *bright yellow*, with 4 petals 5.5–8 mm long; *lower pedicels 3–6 mm long*. **Leaves** of middle and upper stem toothed, occasionally with a few shallow lobes, *the lowest pinnatifid, with a large and rounded terminal lobe and up to 4 pairs of smaller, lateral lobes*. **Fruit** *a silique 1–4 cm long, with a persistent style*; beak 2–3.5 mm long; fruiting pedicel up to 1 mm wide.
OCCURRENCE: Common; MDI, SCH.
OTHER NAMES: Common Winter-cress, Garden Yellow-rocket

Drummond's Rock-cress • ***Boechera stricta***

Biennial herb of ledges and rocky thickets, up to 1 m tall. **Flowers** light purple or yellow, *the petals 5–10 mm long, erect or strongly ascending*; pedicels glabrous. **Leaves** in basal rosettes and sessile along the stem. **Fruit** *a flat silique 4–10 cm long and 1.5–3.3 mm wide.*
OCCURRENCE: Rare; MDI.
NOTES: Known in area covered by this guide from only one site on Mount Desert Island.
OTHER NAMES: Canada Rockcress, *Arabis drummondii*

AH

AH

Indian Mustard • **Brassica juncea*

Annual herb of gardens and waste areas, 0.4–1 m tall. **Flowers** pale yellow, the petals >6 mm long. **Leaves** glabrous, the lowest with a large and rounded terminal lobe and small adjacent lobes, *the uppermost tapering to short petioles or sessile but not clasping.* **Stems** glabrous. **Fruit** *a silique 1.5–5 cm long, erect but not appressed; pedicels 10–15 mm long.*
OCCURRENCE: Uncommon; MDI.
OTHER NAMES: Chinese Mustard, Leaf Mustard

Black Mustard • **Brassica nigra*

Annual herb of open areas, 0.4–1.5 m tall. **Flowers** with 4 yellow petals 7–9 mm long. **Leaves** variable in shape, the lowest with a large and rounded terminal lobe and small adjacent lobes, *the uppermost tapering to a short petiole or sessile but not clasping.* **Stems** hirsute with scattered hairs on the lower portion. **Fruit** *an ascending-appressed silique 1–2.5 cm long, glabrous; pedicels 2–5 mm long.* **Seeds** black.
OCCURRENCE: Occasional; MDI, IAH, SCH.

AH

AH

AH

Field Mustard • ***Brassica rapa**

Annual herb of open areas and waste ground, 0.2–1 m tall. **Flowers** with 4 pale yellow petals 6–11 mm long. **Leaves** sparingly toothed or pinnatifid with 2–4 lateral lobes; *middle and upper leaves sessile and clasping.* **Stems** remotely bristly at least when young, becoming glabrous with age, not thickened at base. **Fruit** a silique 3–7 cm long. **Seeds** dark brown.
OCCURRENCE: Uncommon; MDI.
OTHER NAMES: Rape, Bird's Rape

Sea Rocket • ***Cakile edentula***

Annual herb of saline shorelines, 0.1–1 m tall. **Flowers** *with 4 pale purple petals 5–6 mm wide,* borne on upper portion of stem. **Leaves** alternate, *fleshy, 7–13 cm long, with a tip wider than the base.* **Stems** sprawling, glabrous, much-branched. **Fruit** a silique generally 1–2.5 cm long and <6 mm wide, *constricted around seeds.*
OCCURRENCE: Occasional; MDI, IAH, SCH.
OTHER NAMES: Sea-kale

Shepherd's Purse • **Capsella bursa-pastoris*

Annual or winter-annual herb of gardens and open areas, 10–75 cm tall. **Flowers** *with 4 white petals <3 mm long.* **Leaves** alternate, *the lowest deeply lobed, 5–10 cm long with nearly parallel sides*, deeply toothed or lobed, the uppermost clasping, arrowhead-shaped, entire or with very small teeth and small, ear-shaped appendages at base. **Fruit** *a heart-shaped silique* 6–13 mm wide, flat, indented on top.
OCCURRENCE: Common; MDI, IAH, SCH.
OTHER NAMES: Pick-pocket

Narrowleaf Bitter-cress • **Cardamine impatiens*

Annual or biennial herb of partially open areas, 15–75 cm tall. **Flowers** either lacking petals or with white petals up to 2.5 mm long. **Leaves** *with well developed and prolonged, lanceolate-ciliate auricles at the base* (see lower right photo); basal leaves with 2–4 pairs of leaflets; lower and middle leaves with 6–9 pairs of leaflets. **Fruit** a silique on a spreading to erect pedicel.
OCCURRENCE: Rare; MDI.
NOTES: This nonnative species is aggressively invasive and can colonize undisturbed natural areas. It may have arrived in our area as a contaminant in some birdseed mixes.
OTHER NAMES: Narrow-leaved Bitter-cress

Small-flowered Bitter-cress • *Cardamine parviflora*

Annual or biennial herb of dry ledges and woods, 10–40 cm tall. **Flowers** *with white petals 2–2.5 mm long.* **Leaves** compound; basal leaves with ~5 pairs of leaflets; *cauline leaves 2–4 cm long with 5–8 pairs of linear, entire leaflets.* **Stems** glabrous. **Fruit** *an erect silique 1–2 cm long and <1 mm wide*; pedicels 7–10 mm long.
OCCURRENCE: Uncommon; MDI, IAH.
OTHER NAMES: Dry Land Bitter-cress

Pennsylvania Bitter-cress • *Cardamine pensylvanica*

Biennial or perennial herb of wet woods and swamps, 5–75 cm tall. **Flowers** with white petals 1.5–4 mm long; stamens 6. **Leaves** compound; *basal leaves with 1–6 pairs of leaflets; cauline leaves 4–8 cm long, with elliptic to suborbicular leaflets; petioles glabrous.* **Stems** bristly at base only. **Fruit** *a silique 1–3 cm long, the ripe ones with a persistent, slender style 0.5–2 mm long*; pedicels 2–15 mm long.
OCCURRENCE: Uncommon; MDI.

Cuckoo-flower • ***_Cardamine pratensis_**

Perennial herb of wet, open areas, up to 50 cm tall. **Flowers** *with 4 white or pink petals 8–15 mm long.* **Leaves** *pinnately compound; leaflets in 7–17 pairs, the lowest rounded and stalked, the uppermost sessile.* **Fruit** a silique 2–3 cm long and ~2 mm wide, rarely produced.
OCCURRENCE: Uncommon; MDI.
OTHER NAMES: Lady's Smock, Pink Cuckoo Bitter-cress

Spring Whitlow-grass • ***_Draba verna_**

Annual herb of dry fields and roadsides, 5–15 cm tall. **Flowers** *with deeply notched white petals; blooming in April.* **Leaves** *1–2 cm long, in basal rosettes.* **Fruit** a silique 4–8 mm long.
OCCURRENCE: Occasional; MDI.
OTHER NAMES: Whitlow-grass, Spring Whitlow-mustard

Wormseed-mustard • *Erysimum cheiranthoides*

Annual or biennial herb of open areas and waste places, 0.1–1.3 m tall. **Flowers** *small, with bright yellow petals 3–5.5 mm long*; sepals 2–3.5 mm long; anthers 0.4–0.6 mm long. **Leaves** *scarcely toothed, with wavy margins, finely pubescent with 3-parted hairs.* **Fruit** a silique 1–3 cm long.
OCCURRENCE: Occasional; MDI.
OTHER NAMES: Treacle Mustard, Wormseed Wallflower

AH

Dame's Rocket • **Hesperis matronalis*

Biennial herb of open areas, 0.5–1.3 m tall. **Flowers** *fragrant; with white to pink to purple petals 18–25 mm long.* **Leaves** *of middle stem 5–20 cm long, pubescent, narrowing to base and not clasping; basal leaves absent.* **Stems** *pubescent with simple and branched hairs.* **Fruit** a silique 5–14 cm long.
OCCURRENCE: Occasional; MDI, IAH.
OTHER NAMES: Dame's Violet, Mother-of-the-evening

Field Peppergrass • **Lepidium campestre***

Annual or biennial herb of fields and waste areas, 15–75 cm tall. **Flowers** with 4 white petals 2–2.5 mm long, slightly exceeding sepals; stamens 6. **Leaves** variously lobed, the lowest with petioles, *the uppermost sessile and clasping the stem with ear-shaped appendages.* **Stems** densely short-villous. **Fruit** *a silique 5–6 mm long,* with a densely short-pubescent pedicel.
OCCURRENCE: Uncommon; MDI.
OTHER NAMES: Field-cress, Cow-cress, Field Pepperweed

Wild Peppergrass • ***Lepidium virginicum***

Annual or biennial herb of fields, roadsides, and waste areas, 0.1–1 m tall. **Flowers** white, in numerous, many-flowered racemes; stamens 2 (rarely 4). **Leaves** *of stem lanceolate, ascending, sharply toothed to entire, not clasping;* basal leaves toothed to pinnatifid. **Stems** glabrous or minutely pubescent. **Fruit** *a silique 2.5–4 mm long, notched at tip.*
OCCURRENCE: Uncommon; MDI, SCH.
OTHER NAMES: Poor-man's-pepper, Poor-man's Pepperweed

Wild Radish • **Raphanus raphanistrum*

Annual herb of waste areas, 0.3–1 m tall. **Flowers** *10–20 mm wide, with 4 pale yellow petals.* **Leaves** alternate, *with stiff hairs,* the uppermost not clasping, reduced in size and often entire, the lowest toothed to compound. **Fruit** a silique 2–7 cm long and <6 mm wide, *with constrictions between seeds.*
OCCURRENCE: Occasional; MDI, IAH, SCH.
OTHER NAMES: Jointed Charlock, Noded Charlock

Hedge Mustard • **Sisymbrium officinale*

Annual herb of gardens, fields, and waste areas, up to 0.8 m tall. **Flowers** *with 4 tiny, pale yellow petals up to 4 mm long.* **Leaves** alternate, divided, *the uppermost with 3 spreading lobes;* basal leaves up to 20 cm long, terminal lobe toothed or cut. **Fruit** *a silique up to 1.5 cm long, tightly appressed to stem.*
OCCURRENCE: Uncommon; MDI.
OTHER NAMES: Common Hedge-mustard

Water Awlwort • *Subularia aquatica*

Aquatic, annual herb of *pond and lake margins*, up to 10 cm tall. **Flowers** *white, minute, on a leafless stalk*. **Leaves** *basal only, needle-like, 1–5 cm long, soft*. **Fruit** a silique 2–4 mm long.
OCCURRENCE: Rare; MDI, IAH.
OTHER NAMES: Awlwort, American Water-awlwort

DSC

DSC

Field Penny-cress • **Thlaspi arvense*

Annual herb of fields, roadsides, and waste areas, 10–50 cm tall. **Flowers** *with 4 white petals <4 mm long, twice as long as sepals*. **Leaves** *alternate, sessile, clasping the stem with 2 ear-shaped appendages*; basal leaves unlobed. **Fruit** *a silique 7–20 mm wide at maturity, with a notch at the tip 2–3 mm deep*.
OCCURRENCE: Uncommon; MDI.
OTHER NAMES: Frenchweed, Stinkweed

Marsh Bellflower • *Campanula aparinoides*

Weak-stemmed, perennial herb of swamps and wet meadows, 20–60 cm tall. **Flowers** *white*, sometimes pale blue or with faint blue markings, *0.5–1.2 cm long*, flowering branches spreading. **Leaves** 1.5–4.5 cm long, *linear to narrowly lance-shaped*, entire or minutely toothed, all similar. **Stems** 3-angled, the angles slightly backward-toothed.
OCCURRENCE: Occasional; MDI.
OTHER NAMES: Bedstraw Bellflower

AH

Creeping Bellflower • **Campanula rapunculoides*

Rhizomatous, perennial herb of roadsides and woodland edges, 0.2–1 m tall. **Flowers** *purple-blue, drooping, bell-shaped, 2.5–4 cm long; inflorescence one-sided.* **Leaves** coarse, *often with hairs*, the lowest egg-shaped to oblong, long-stalked with a heart-shaped base, diminishing in size toward top of plant, the uppermost short-stalked or stalkless.
OCCURRENCE: Occasional; MDI.
NOTES: Historically, a cultivated perennial of flower gardens but now has escaped to roadsides and other disturbed areas.
OTHER NAMES: Roving Bellflower, Purple Bell

Harebell • *Campanula rotundifolia*

Slender, perennial herb of cliffs and shorelines, 15–25 cm tall. **Flowers** *deep blue to purple, narrowly bell-shaped, nodding, ~2 cm long.* **Leaves** of two types: the lowest round to heart-shaped, scalloped, *glabrous*, often disappearing by flowering time, the uppermost narrowly linear and often drooping.
OCCURRENCE: Occasional; MDI, IAH, SCH.
NOTES: Often growing upright from rock crevices on cliff faces and on ocean headlands within the spray zone.
OTHER NAMES: Bluebell, Scotch Bellflower

Cardinal flower • *Lobelia cardinalis*

Emergent, perennial herb of wet meadows and shores, 0.5–2 m tall. **Flowers** *deep red or vermilion, showy, 3–4.5 cm long,* with top lip 2-lobed and bottom lip 3-lobed; stamens projecting up and through upper lip of the flower. **Leaves** lanceolate to lance-ovate, irregularly serrate.
OCCURRENCE: Rare; MDI.
NOTES: Showy flower of streambanks and wet meadows, relatively common statewide but documented from only a few sites on Mount Desert Island.
OTHER NAMES: Red Lobelia

Water Lobelia • *Lobelia dortmanna*

Aquatic, perennial herb of ponds and lakes, up to 1 m tall. **Flowers** *violet or white, ~1 cm long, widely spaced along stalk that emerges from water.* **Leaves** in a basal rosette, *narrowly linear, fleshy, hollow, in shallow water.*

OCCURRENCE: Common; MDI, IAH.

OTHER NAMES: Water-gladiole

Indian-tobacco • *Lobelia inflata*

Annual herb of fields, open woods, and roadsides, up to 1 m tall. **Flowers** *light blue, 6–8 mm long.* **Leaves** of middle stem *ovate to oblong,* decreasing in size at top of stem. **Stems** much-branched, hairy. **Fruit** an inflated capsule.

OCCURRENCE: Occasional; MDI, SCH.

OTHER NAMES: Bladder-pod Lobelia

Bush-honeysuckle • *Diervilla lonicera*

Small, deciduous shrub of dry woods and rocky slopes, 0.3–1.2 m tall. **Flowers** *yellow (turning reddish), funnel-shaped*, usually in 3's, with petals 12–20 mm long. **Leaves** serrate, ciliate-margined, sometimes hairy beneath, 5–15 cm long; petioles 3–10 mm long. **Twigs** round in cross section. **Fruit** a slender, 2-valved capsule 8–15 mm long, with many seeds.
OCCURRENCE: Common; MDI, IAH, SCH.
OTHER NAMES: Northern Bush-honeysuckle

Twinflower • *Linnaea borealis*

Low, creeping, evergreen, perennial herb of wet woods, up to 40 cm tall. **Flowers** white with rose-purple markings, funnel-shaped, fragrant, *borne in nodding pairs* from long upright peduncles; petals 10–15 mm long. **Leaves** opposite, leathery, pubescent, 1–2 cm long. **Fruit** 1-seeded, rarely maturing.
OCCURRENCE: Occasional; MDI, IAH, SCH.
NOTES: This species, the only in the genus, was named for celebrated Swedish botanist Linnaeus (1707–1778), who developed the binomial classification system to name plants and animals still used today.
OTHER NAMES: Pink-bells, American Twinflower

American Fly Honeysuckle • *Lonicera canadensis*

Deciduous shrub of wet woods, to 1.5 m tall. **Flowers** *yellow-green or straw-colored, symmetrical or nearly so*, funnel-shaped, ~2 cm long, growing in pairs from leaf axils; style glabrous. **Leaves** opposite, entire, with ciliate margins and petiole. **Twigs** *with solid, white pith*; winter buds with >2 scales. **Fruit** 2 *red-black, cylindrical berries diverging in opposite directions at top of peduncle.*
OCCURRENCE: Uncommon; MDI.
OTHER NAMES: fly Honeysuckle, American Honeysuckle

Japanese Honeysuckle • **Lonicera japonica*

Trailing or climbing liana of various habitats. **Flowers** white or purple-tinged, fading to yellow, fragrant, *in pairs from axils*; petals 2.5–5 cm long with lobes nearly as long or longer than the tube. **Leaves** opposite, *entire, the lowest sometimes lobed.* **Fruit** purple-black, nearly sessile.
OCCURRENCE: Rare; MDI.
NOTES: This nonnative species is aggressively invasive south of this area but has been recorded from only one site on Mount Desert Island.

AH

Morrow's Honeysuckle • **Lonicera morrowii***

Deciduous shrub of various habitats, 1–2 m tall. **Flowers** *growing in pairs from leaf axils*, upper lip with deep sinuses extending nearly to base; petals white, turning yellow with age, *pubescent on outer surface; sepals ciliate but without glands*; style pubescent; peduncles 5–15 mm long, pubescent. **Leaves** opposite, entire, *pubescent beneath*. **Twigs** *pubescent, with hollow, dark pith*. **Fruit** a red or yellow, round berry.
OCCURRENCE: Occasional; MDI, SCH.
NOTES: This nonnative species is extremely invasive and can colonize natural areas, eventually displacing native shrubs. Fruits provide poor nutrition for migrating birds compared with those of native shrubs.

Mountain Fly Honeysuckle • ***Lonicera villosa***

Deciduous shrub of bogs, swamps, and wet thickets, up to 1 m tall. **Flowers** creamy yellow, *radially symmetric*, growing in pairs from leaf axils on ciliate peduncles <1 cm long; bracteoles subtending flowers ciliate, 4–6 mm long; style glabrous. **Leaves** opposite, entire, *leathery, pubescent*. **Twigs** pubescent, *with solid white pith*; winter buds appressed, with 2 scales. **Fruit** *blue-glaucous, fleshy*.
OCCURRENCE: Uncommon; MDI, SCH.
OTHER NAMES: Mountain Honeysuckle

European Fly Honeysuckle • **Lonicera xylosteum*

Deciduous shrub of various habitats, 1–4 m tall. **Flowers** white or yellow, 7–13 mm long, *upper lip with shallow sinuses extending only halfway to the base*; style pubescent; filaments sometimes pubescent on upper half; *sepals glandular-pubescent*. **Leaves** opposite, entire, *pubescent*. **Twigs** *pubescent, hollow*, with dark pith; winter buds with ciliate scales.

OCCURRENCE: Uncommon; MDI.

NOTES: This nonnative species is invasive.

RL

RL

Snowberry • **Symphoricarpos albus*

Deciduous shrub of open areas, up to 2 m tall. **Flowers** with white or pink petals 3–9 mm long and hairy within; style 2–3 mm long; anthers 1–1.5 mm long, nearly as long as filaments. **Leaves** opposite, *entire or with irregular lobes*, 2–3 cm long, usually glabrous beneath. **Twigs** glabrous, pith hollow. **Fruit** *a white berry*, 1–1.5 cm long, with 2 seeds 4–6 mm long.

OCCURRENCE: Uncommon; MDI.

OTHER NAMES: Waxberry, Common Snowberry

Garden Valerian • **Valeriana officinalis*

Perennial herb of woods, fields, and roadsides, 0.5–1.5 m tall. **Flowers** pale pink or white, fragrant, both bisexual and unisexual; stamens 3, distinct; styles slender. **Leaves** opposite, pinnately compound; leaflets 5–25, lanceolate, the margins with hairs bent toward tip. **Stems** hairy. **Fruit** solitary, 1-locular, indehiscent, with conspicuous plumose bristles that unroll after fruiting.
OCCURRENCE: Occasional; MDI.
NOTES: This nonnative species is invasive in natural areas.
OTHER NAMES: Garden Heliotrope, Common Valerian

Field Chickweed • *Cerastium arvense*

Perennial herb of open areas and shorelines, up to 50 cm tall. **Flowers** white, *~1 cm wide*; petals 5, deeply cleft nearly to the middle, *much longer than the sepals.* **Leaves** opposite, linear to narrowly ovate, *mostly 1–5 cm long.*
OCCURRENCE: Occasional; MDI, IAH.

Mouse-ear Chickweed • **Cerastium fontanum***

Short-lived perennial herb of gardens and open areas, up to 65 cm tall. **Flowers** white, *~0.5 cm wide*; petals 5, deeply cleft nearly to the middle, *about as long as the sepals*; stamens 10 (occasionally 5); styles 5. **Leaves** opposite, entire, stalkless, *1–2 cm long and 3–12 mm wide*, densely covered with hairs.
OCCURRENCE: Common; MDI, IAH, SCH.
NOTES: Deep notches in the 5 petals can make flower appear to have 10 petals.
OTHER NAMES: Common Mouse-ear Chickweed, *Cerastium vulgatum*

Deptford Pink • **Dianthus armeria***

AH

Annual or biennial herb of old fields, roadsides, and waste areas, 15–30 cm tall. **Flowers** *dark pink with white splotches*, ~1 cm wide; sepals hairy; styles 2. **Leaves** opposite, narrow to linear, 2–8 mm wide and 2.5–5 cm long, tapering to tip. **Stems** branched.
OCCURRENCE: Uncommon; MDI.

AH

Seabeach Sandwort • *Honckenya peploides*

Rhizomatous, perennial herb of sea beaches, 10–50 cm tall. **Flowers** *inconspicuous, growing deep in axils of upper leaves or terminal*, 7–10 mm wide; petals 5, *white*, paddle-shaped, small; carpellate flowers with petals (rarely >2 mm) shorter than sepals; staminate flowers with petals equal in length to sepals and stamens. **Leaves** opposite, entire, oval, *fleshy*, 0.5–4.5 cm long, *closely spaced and clasping the pale, yellow-green stem*.
OCCURRENCE: Rare; MDI.
NOTES: Plant grows erect and often falls prostrate later in the season. Plant spreads by rhizomes deep in sand and forms dense colonies.
OTHER NAMES: Seaside-sandwort, Sea-chickweed, *Arenaria peploides*

Mountain Sandwort • *Minuartia groenlandica*

Small, mat-forming, perennial herb of mountain summits and rocky outcrops, 5–13 cm tall. **Flowers** white, 1–1.5 cm wide, *borne in clusters of 3–15*; petals 5–10 mm long with small notch at tip; *sepals 3–5.5 mm long*. **Leaves** linear to linear-lanceolate, 0.3–0.8 mm wide. **Stems** *with sterile leafy shoots at base*.
OCCURRENCE: Occasional; MDI, IAH.
NOTES: *Minuartia glabra* (not pictured) is very similar in appearance to *M. groenlandica* except it is an annual, does not form extensive mats, and lacks sterile leafy shoots at the base.
OTHER NAMES: Smooth Sandwort, Mountain Sand-plant, *Arenaria groenlandica*

CWG

Blunt-leaved Sandwort • *Moehringia lateriflora*

Weakly erect, rhizomatous, perennial herb of open areas, 5–40 cm tall. **Flowers** white, 0.5–1.5 cm wide, 1–several in a cluster; *styles 3*; petals *5, entire (not cleft)*; sepals 5, 2–3 mm long. **Leaves** opposite, entire, *oval, with blunt tip*, thin, *1- to 3-veined*, 6–35 mm long and 2–15 mm wide, with underside of midrib pubescent, *not tufted at base*; petiole 0.1–1 mm long.

OCCURRENCE: Common; MDI, IAH, SCH.

NOTES: Delicate plant creeping by extensive, thin rhizomes and forming loose colonies.

OTHER NAMES: Grove-sandwort, Blunt-leaved Grove-sandwort, *Arenaria lateriflora*

Knotted Pearlwort • *Sagina nodosa*

Tiny, perennial herb of rocky crevices, headlands, and shorelines, up to 20 cm tall. **Flowers** *with white petals entire* (or only minutely notched), *about twice as long as sepals*; styles 4 or 5. **Leaves** linear, needle-like, *the uppermost much smaller, appearing like small bumps with smaller leaves growing inside axils of others (axillary fascicles); basal leaves tufted.*

OCCURRENCE: Uncommon; MDI, IAH, SCH.

Birdseye • *Sagina procumbens*

Tufted, perennial herb of open ground and roadsides, up to 10 cm tall. **Flowers** with white petals shorter than sepals or absent; sepals 4 or sometimes 5, 1.5–2.5 mm long; styles 4 or 5, <0.5 mm long. **Leaves** *very narrowly linear, <1 mm wide and 3–15 mm long.*
OCCURRENCE: Occasional; MDI, IAH, SCH.
OTHER NAMES: Bird's-eye Pearlwort

Bouncing Bet • **Saponaria officinalis*

Stout, perennial herb of roadsides and waste areas, 40–80 cm tall. **Flowers** *pink or white*, often in pairs, 2–3 cm wide; *petals with a small notch at tip and an awl-shaped basal appendage.* **Leaves** *oval, with 3–5 prominent ribs.*
OCCURRENCE: Uncommon; MDI.
OTHER NAMES: Common Soapwort

AH

AH

White Campion • **Silene latifolia*

Perennial herb of roadsides and fields, up to 1 m tall. **Flowers** white or pinkish, 2–3 cm wide; *petals deeply cleft up to one quarter of total length; sepals inflated, fine-veined*; styles 5. **Leaves** opposite, entire. **Stems** glabrous on upper portion.
OCCURRENCE: Uncommon; MDI.
NOTES: Blooms early summer into fall.
OTHER NAMES: White Cockle, Evening-lychnis, *Lychnis alba*

Bladder Campion • **Silene vulgaris*

Perennial herb of roadsides, fields, and shorelines, up to 1 m tall. **Flowers** *white, 1–2 cm wide; sepals swollen and bladder-like, prominently veined*; styles 3. **Leaves** opposite, entire. **Stems** with downy hairs on upper portion.
OCCURRENCE: Common; MDI, SCH.
NOTES: Blooms spring into summer.
OTHER NAMES: Maiden's-tears, *Silene cucubalis*

Corn Spurrey • **Spergula arvensis*

Annual herb of gardens and disturbed areas, 10–40 cm tall. **Flowers** white, 4–7 mm wide, in a terminal, forked cyme; styles 5. **Leaves** *linear, blunt, clustered at nodes in 6–8 pairs, appearing whorled.* **Fruit** a 5-valved capsule. **Seeds** rounded, usually narrowly winged on margin.
OCCURRENCE: Occasional; MDI, SCH.
OTHER NAMES: Stickwort

Canada Sand-spurrey • *Spergularia canadensis*

Perennial herb of muddy or sandy tidal areas, up to 25 cm tall. **Flowers** pink; *sepals glabrous; stamens 2–5.* **Leaves** opposite, fleshy, *blunt-tipped,* 6–45 mm long and 0.6–2 mm wide, with secondary axillary tufts; *stipules papery, wider than long.* **Seeds** *0.8–1.4 mm long, brown, often with winged margins.*
OCCURRENCE: Uncommon; MDI.
OTHER NAMES: Northern Sand-spurrey

Saltmarsh Sand-spurrey • **Spergularia marina*

Annual, matted herb of sea beaches and headlands, up to 20 cm tall. **Flowers** *pink*, 6–8 mm wide; petals 5, shorter than or equaling sepals; *sepals 2.5–4.5 mm long in flower and up to 5 mm long in fruit; stamens 2–5.* **Leaves** *opposite, cylindrical, fleshy*, at least some with a short point (mucro) at tip; *stipules pale brown*, papery, *2–4 mm long.* **Seeds** *light brown to reddish brown, usually without wings, 0.5–0.8 mm wide, often with gland-tipped papillae* visible at 30× magnification.
OCCURRENCE: Uncommon; MDI, IAH, SCH.
OTHER NAMES: Lesser Sea-spurrey, *Spergularia salina*

Ruby Sand-spurrey • **Spergularia rubra*

Annual or short-lived perennial herb of dry or sandy soils, 5–30 cm tall. **Flowers** pink, 3–5 mm wide; *sepals with stalked glands; stamens 6–10.* **Leaves** opposite, up to 2. 5 mm long, *flat and not fleshy, with mucronate tip; tufts of smaller leaves growing in leaf axils; stipules silvery,* papery, *long pointed, much longer than wide.* **Seeds** dark brown, wingless, with sculpture-patterned surface, 0.4–0.6 mm long.
OCCURRENCE: Uncommon; MDI, IAH.
OTHER NAMES: Roadside Sand-spurrey, Sand-spurrey, Red Sand-spurrey

Bog Chickweed • *Stellaria alsine*

Annual or biennial herb of wet woods and streambanks, up to 40 cm tall. **Flowers** *with white petals shorter than the sepals*; calyx base funnel-shaped. **Leaves** sessile, glabrous, *oblong, 5–25 mm long.* **Stems** usually square, upright or leaning. **Seeds** *0.5–0.7 mm long*, with pebbled appearance.
OCCURRENCE: Uncommon; IAH.
OTHER NAMES: Bog Stitchwort, Marsh Chickweed

Lesser Stitchwort • **Stellaria graminea*

Weak-stemmed, perennial herb of fields and meadows, 20–50 cm tall. **Flowers** 5–18 mm wide, *many in a terminal cyme*; petals 5 but cleft so deeply that there appear to be 10, *about as long as the sepals*; styles 3. **Leaves** lance-shaped, sessile, *1.5–4 cm long, usually with a fringe of hairs (ciliate) at base.* **Fruit** a pale brown capsule. **Seeds** *0.7–1.2 mm long*, with roughened surface.
OCCURRENCE: Common; MDI, IAH, SCH.
OTHER NAMES: Grass-leaved Stitchwort

Common Chickweed • **Stellaria media*

Weak-stemmed, branched, annual herb common in gardens and disturbed areas, up to 80 cm tall. **Flowers** *small, inconspicuous*; petals 5 but cleft so deeply that there appear to be 10, white, 1–3 mm long; styles 3. **Leaves** cordate, egg-shaped, 0.5–4 cm long, *the lowest with distinct petioles*. **Stems** with 1 or 2 lines of hairs. **Fruit** an ovoid capsule protruding beyond sepals. **Seeds** with a swollen, cap-like structure on one end.
OCCURRENCE: Common; MDI, IAH, SCH.
OTHER NAMES: Common Stitchwort

CELASTRACEAE • BITTERSWEET FAMILY ▼

Asiatic Bittersweet • **Celastrus orbiculatus*

Deciduous, twining liana of various habitats. **Flowers** greenish, *in short axillary clusters*; stamens 5. **Leaves** *alternate, nearly as long as wide*, finely toothed, without tendrils. **Twigs** *round in cross section*. **Fruit** a berry-like, globose capsule, at first green and when ripe, orange to orange-yellow, splitting along the 3 valves, exposing a red, fleshy covering (aril) with 1 or 2 seeds inside each of the 3 chambers (locules).
OCCURRENCE: Occasional; MDI, IAH.
NOTES: This nonnative species is aggressively invasive in natural areas.
OTHER NAMES: Oriental Bittersweet, Asian Bittersweet

CWG

Winged Euonymus • **Euonymus alatus*

Deciduous shrub of woods and streambanks, up to 2.5 m tall. **Flowers** 4-parted, green, bisexual, 6–8 mm wide. **Leaves** opposite, <8 cm long, subsessile, elliptic to obovate, sharply serrulate, *turning bright red to magenta in the fall.* **Twigs** opposite, *with 2–4 conspicuous, longitudinal, corky wings.* **Fruit** a smooth, purple capsule with 2–4 distinct chambers (locules), wrinkling with drying.

OCCURRENCE: Uncommon; MDI.

NOTES: This nonnative species is invasive.

OTHER NAMES: Burning Bush, Winged Spindle-tree

Burning Bush • **Euonymus atropurpureus*

Rhizomatous shrub of wet woods, 2–8 m tall. **Flowers** 4-parted, red, bisexual, 6–8 mm wide, 7–15 in a cyme. **Leaves** opposite, elliptic to lance-ovate, 6–12 cm long, finely toothed, pubescent underneath, turning pale yellow to red in the fall; petioles 1–2 cm long. **Twigs** *quadrangular.* **Fruit** purple, with red aril inside.

OCCURRENCE: Uncommon; MDI.

OTHER NAMES: Wahoo, Eastern Spindle-tree

RL

Prickly Hornwort • *Ceratophyllum echinatum*

Submerged, fresh water, aquatic herb. **Flowers** with styles 5–10 mm long. **Leaves** whorled, forked mostly 3 or 4 times, with end segments hair-like. **Stems** branched dichotomously. **Fruit** an achene *with 4–15 spines*, the spines 2 on the bottom and the remainder on the sides.
OCCURRENCE: Rare; MDI.
NOTES: Often free-floating.
OTHER NAMES: Spiny Hornwort

CBH

DSC

CISTACEAE • ROCK-ROSE FAMILY ▼

Golden-heather • *Hudsonia ericoides*

Low perennial herb of dry, rocky areas, up to 70 cm tall. **Flowers** *bright yellow*, ~1 cm wide; pedicels 5–15 mm long. **Leaves** *gray-green, small, needle-like*, 3–6 mm long, spreading outward, sparsely hairy. **Fruit** a hairy capsule.
OCCURRENCE: Occasional; MDI, IAH, SCH.
OTHER NAMES: Mountain Heather, Pine-barren False Heather

Large-pod Pinweed • *Lechea intermedia*

Slender, erect, perennial herb of dry, open areas, up to 60 cm tall. **Flowers** *small, with 3 inconspicuous, red petals,* rarely open, in a panicle about one-third to one-half the height of plant. **Leaves** green, the uppermost 2–5.3 mm wide; *basal rosettes forming in late summer and persisting through winter.* **Fruit** a capsule with 3 or 5 nerves.

OCCURRENCE: Occasional; MDI, IAH, SCH.

NOTES: Blooms late summer to fall.

OTHER NAMES: Intermediate Pinweed, Pinweed, Round-fruited Pinweed

COLCHICACEAE • BELLWORT FAMILY ▼

Wild Oats • *Uvularia sessilifolia*

Rhizomatous, perennial, spring herb of forests, up to 40 cm tall. **Flowers** *light yellow, 1.5–2.5 cm long, drooping.* **Leaves** alternate, *sessile, pale on the underside.* **Fruit** a triangular capsule.

OCCURRENCE: Uncommon; MDI.

OTHER NAMES: Sessile-leaved Bellwort, Little Merrybells

Hedge Bindweed • *Calystegia sepium*

Perennial, twining herb of islands and shores, up to 3 m long. **Flowers** pink, *funnel-shaped, 5–7 cm long*, with 2 green bracts partly enclosing base. **Leaves** entire, usually square-lobed at base. **Stems** twining or trailing.

OCCURRENCE: Occasional; MDI, IAH, SCH.

NOTES: In our area most commonly at tops of sea beaches.

OTHER NAMES: Wild Morning-glory, Hedge False Bindweed, *Convolvulus sepium*

Common Dodder • *Cuscuta gronovii*

Parasitic, twining, annual herb. **Flowers** *white*, 2–4 mm long, with 5 flaring or widely spreading lobes, *borne in small, dense clusters*. **Leaves** *minute, scale-like*. **Stem** *orange or yellow*, tightly twisting around a variety of host species and absorbing sap through its tiny suckers.
OCCURRENCE: Uncommon; MDI, SCH.
NOTES: This plant has no chlorophyll.
OTHER NAMES: Love Vine, Gronovius' Dodder

CORNACEAE • DOGWOOD FAMILY ▼

Bunchberry • *Chamaepericlymenum canadense*

Herbaceous, perennial herb, 5–30 cm tall. **Flowers** 4-parted, greenish white, in small cymes subtended by *4 petal-like, white, expanded bracts*. **Leaves** in a cluster of 4 or 6 that appear whorled, 2–9 cm long, entire, *with curving, parallel veins*, occasionally with a pair of smaller, opposite leaves below whorl. **Fruit** *a cluster of red drupes* with smooth stones.
OCCURRENCE: Common; MDI, IAH, SCH.
OTHER NAMES: Dwarf Cornel, Canada Bunchberry, Crackerberry, *Cornus canadensis*

Alternate-leaved Dogwood • *Swida alternifolia*

Deciduous shrub or small tree, up to 8 m tall. **Flowers** white, 4-parted, in flat-topped cymes 3–6 cm wide. **Leaves** *alternate*, ovate to oblong or obovate, acuminate, 5–10 cm long, with curving parallel veins; petioles 0.8–6 cm long. **Twigs** green; *branches horizontal*. **Fruit** *a blue drupe on a red pedicel.*

OCCURRENCE: Occasional; MDI.

OTHER NAMES: Pagoda Dogwood, Green Osier, *Cornus alternifolia*

Round-leaved Dogwood • *Swida rugosa*

Deciduous shrub, 1–4 m tall. **Flowers** white, 4-parted, in dense, flat-topped cymes. **Leaves** *opposite*, ovate to suborbicular, entire, 3–13 cm wide, with 7 or 8 pairs of curving, parallel veins, pubescent beneath. **Twigs** *yellow-green, often speckled with red or purple,* with a white pith. **Fruit** a light blue or white drupe.

OCCURRENCE: Uncommon; MDI.

OTHER NAMES: *Cornus rugosa*

Live-forever • **Hylotelephium telephium*

Perennial herb of woods, fields, and ditches, up to 50 cm tall. **Flowers** pink to red, in a dense inflorescence; *stamens shorter than the petals*. **Leaves** *fleshy, 3–8 cm long*, flat, *widened and toothed toward the tip, reduced in size from bottom to top of plant*.
OCCURRENCE: Uncommon; MDI.
OTHER NAMES: Frog's Belly, Garden Orpine, Purple Orpine, *Sedum telephium*

Roseroot • *Rhodiola rosea*

Dioecious, perennial herb of islands, coastal headlands, and shores, 10–30 cm tall. **Staminate flowers** *yellow*, borne on top of stem in branched cluster. **Carpellate flowers** *yellow to red*, borne on top of stem in branched cluster. **Leaves** fleshy, greenish gray-blue, slightly toothed or entire, egg-shaped or ovate. **Fruit** an erect, 1-chambered, dry follicle.
OCCURRENCE: Uncommon; MDI, SCH.
OTHER NAMES: Roseroot Stonecrop, *Sedum rosea*

Golden Carpet • **Sedum acre*

Low-growing, matted, perennial herb, up to 8 cm tall. **Flowers** *yellow*, 4- or 5-parted; petals tapering gradually to a point. **Leaves** alternate, yellow-green, *2–6 mm long, overlapping*, thick and fleshy.
OCCURRENCE: Uncommon; MDI.
OTHER NAMES: Mossy Stonecrop, Wallpepper, Love-entangle

DROSERACEAE • SUNDEW FAMILY ▼

Spatulate-leaved Sundew • *Drosera intermedia*

Low, insectivorous, perennial herb of bogs and swamps, up to 25 cm tall. **Flowers** white, in a one-sided raceme. **Leaves** *spoon-shaped, longer than wide, with red, glandular hairs on the blade.* **Seeds** oblong, red-brown, with papillae.
OCCURRENCE: Occasional; MDI, IAH, SCH.
NOTES: The glandular hairs exude a sticky substance that traps insects.
OTHER NAMES: Narrow-leaved Sundew

Round-leaved Sundew • *Drosera rotundifolia*

Low, insectivorous, perennial herb of bogs and swamps, up to 30 cm tall. **Flowers** white, in a one-sided raceme. **Leaves** *with red, glandular hairs on blades and petioles, the blade round or slightly wider than long.* **Seeds** light brown, spindle-shaped, with striations.
OCCURRENCE: Common; MDI, IAH, SCH.
NOTES: The glandular hairs exude a sticky substance that traps insects.

ELATINACEAE • WATERWORT FAMILY ▼

Small Waterwort • *Elatine minima*

Small, aquatic, annual herb of lakes and ponds, in mats up to 10 cm wide. **Flowers** pinkish, *axillary*, with 2 petals and sepals. **Leaves** tiny, opposite, rounded, 0.7–5 mm long; branchlets ascending, 0.2–5 cm long. **Stems** sometimes rooting at the nodes. **Seeds** *with obtuse cross-ribs that separate round-ended pits.*
OCCURRENCE: Occasional; MDI.
NOTES: These tiny flowering plants grow in small, moss-like mats on pond margins. Seeds are used to distinguish among the 3 species found in Maine; only *E. minima* is documented at ANP.
OTHER NAMES: Waterwort

DSC

CBH

Bog-rosemary • *Andromeda polifolia*

Evergreen shrub of bogs, 0.1–1 m tall. **Flowers** pink or white, bell-shaped; stamens 10; pedicels generally <8 mm long. **Leaves** *blue-green, leathery*, linear to narrowly oblong, 2–5 cm long, *white underneath, with revolute margins*. **Stems** glaucous, ascending. **Fruit** a 5-locular, 5-valved capsule.
OCCURRENCE: Occasional; MDI, IAH.
OTHER NAMES: *Andromeda glaucophylla*

Common Bearberry • *Arctostaphylos uva-ursi*

Evergreen, matted shrub of dry openings and rocky ledges, up to 50 cm tall. **Flowers** white or pink, bell-shaped, <6 mm long and 4–6 mm wide, in terminal racemes; stamens 10; sepals ~1.5 mm long. **Leaves** alternate, entire, 9–30 mm long, tapering to base; petioles short. **Stems** extensively creeping, pubescent, *with papery, exfoliating bark*. **Fruit** a red, mealy drupe, 6–10 mm long.

OCCURRENCE: Occasional; MDI, IAH.

OTHER NAMES: Sandberry, Red Bearberry, Kinnikinick, Mealberry, Hog-cranberry

Scotch Heather • *Calluna vulgaris*

Evergreen shrub of sandy areas, up to 1 m tall. **Flowers** 4-parted, subtended by 3 pairs of sepal-like bracts, *borne in dense, one-sided, spike-like racemes*; sepals petaloid, pink to purple, much exceeding the petals. **Leaves** opposite, *needle-like*. **Fruit** a 4-locular, 4-valved capsule.

OCCURRENCE: Rare; MDI.

NOTES: This plant is known to escape from gardens but has been documented from only one site in Acadia National Park.

OTHER NAMES: Heather, Ling

AH

Leatherleaf • *Chamaedaphne calyculata*

Evergreen shrub of bogs and wetlands, up to 1.5 m tall. **Flowers** bell-shaped, white, *borne in one-sided, leafy racemes at branch tips*; stamens 10; pedicels 2–5 mm long. **Leaves** elliptical, *leathery, dull, with rusty scales on underside*, 1.5–5 cm long; petioles 1–3 mm long. **Fruit** a depressed, 5-locular capsule with many flat, wingless seeds.
OCCURRENCE: Common; MDI, IAH, SCH.
OTHER NAMES: Cassandra

Pipsissewa • *Chimaphila umbellata*

Low, evergreen, woody-based herb of upland woods, 10–30 cm tall. **Flowers** white or pink, *appearing waxy*, 10–15 mm wide, borne in small clusters; stamens 10, with hairy filaments. **Leaves** dark, *shiny*, 3–6 cm long, finely toothed, somewhat whorled or scattered on stem. **Fruit** a capsule that splits from apex down.
OCCURRENCE: Rare; MDI.
OTHER NAMES: Prince's-pine, Noble Prince's-pine

DSC

DSC

Broom-crowberry • *Corema conradii*

Dioecious, evergreen shrub of dry, rocky areas, up to 0.5 m tall. **Flowers** inconspicuous, *borne at branch tips*; stamens 3 or 4, purple to dark red. **Leaves** narrow, needle-like, 3–6 mm long. **Stems** *upright, with distinct swellings at nodes*. **Fruit** a small, dry drupe with 3–5 nutlets.

OCCURRENCE: Uncommon; MDI, IAH, SCH.

OTHER NAMES: Poverty-grass

Black Crowberry • *Empetrum nigrum*

Evergreen, mat-forming shrub of dry, rocky areas, up to 40 cm long. **Flowers** purple, inconspicuous, *borne in leaf axils*; petals 3; sepals 3; stamens 3; styles dark red. **Leaves** narrow, thick, 2.5–8 mm long. **Stems** prostrate, extensively creeping (compare with *Corema conradii*). **Twigs** stipitate-glandular. **Fruit** a black, juicy drupe with 6–9 seed-like nutlets.

OCCURRENCE: Common; MDI, IAH, SCH.

OTHER NAMES: Curlewberry

Trailing-arbutus • *Epigaea repens*

Low, evergreen, trailing shrub of dry openings and wooded edges, 20–40 cm tall. **Flowers** *white or pink*, 8–15 mm long with 5 lobes 6–8 mm long, borne in small clusters, 2–5 cm long, at branch ends; stamens 10. **Leaves** oval, *leathery, hairy*, 2–10 cm long, with a cordate, long-stalked base. **Stems** *trailing, hairy*. **Fruit** pubescent, depressed-globular, a 5-lobed, 5-locular capsule with many seeds.

OCCURRENCE: Uncommon; MDI.

OTHER NAMES: Mayflower

Creeping Snowberry • *Gaultheria hispidula*

Evergreen, mat-forming, woody shrub of wet woods and bogs, up to 20 cm tall. **Flowers** white, 4-parted, 2–3 mm long; stamens 8, with wide, short filaments. **Leaves** 5–10 mm long, *bristly on underside*. **Stems** *trailing or prostrate*, somewhat woody. **Fruit** a white berry, often hidden under leaves and stems, wintergreen-flavored.
OCCURRENCE: Occasional; MDI, IAH, SCH.
OTHER NAMES: Moxieplum, Creeping Spicy-wintergreen

Wintergreen • *Gaultheria procumbens*

Evergreen shrub of woods and open areas, 5–20 cm tall. **Flowers** white, 5-parted, 6–9.5 mm long; pedicels 5–10 mm long; stamens 5, with arching, white, hairy filaments. **Leaves** *shiny, leathery*, toothed, 1.5–5 cm long; petioles 2–5 mm long. **Stems** erect or extensively creeping. **Fruit** a red, wintergreen-flavored berry.
OCCURRENCE: Common; MDI, IAH, SCH.
OTHER NAMES: Checkerberry, Teaberry, Eastern Spicy-wintergreen, Mountain-tea

Black Huckleberry • *Gaylussacia baccata*

Deciduous shrub of woods and thickets, up to 2 m tall. **Flowers** *reddish*, with resin dots on bracts, sepals, and pedicels. **Leaves** elliptic, 2–5 cm long, pale and dull above, *with yellow resin dots on underside* visible with hand lens. **Fruit** black when ripe, without bloom, sweet, with 10 seeds.
OCCURRENCE: Common; MDI, IAH, SCH.

Dwarf Huckleberry • *Gaylussacia bigeloviana*

Deciduous shrub of wet woods, bogs, and thickets, 20–50 cm tall. **Flowers** white or pink, *with stipitate glands on bracts, sepals, and pedicels.* **Leaves** oval, 2–4 cm long, *glossy and stipitate-glandular on top*, with a fleshy, with a distinct point (mucro) at tip. **Fruit** black, glandular, pubescent, with 10 seeds.
OCCURRENCE: Occasional; MDI, IAH.
NOTES: Plant of eastern Maine coastal bogs.
OTHER NAMES: Bog Huckleberry, *Gaylussacia dumosa*

Pine-sap • *Hypopitys monotropa*

Saprophytic or parasitic perennial herb of woodlands, 10–30 cm tall. **Flowers** yellow or white, 3–10 in a drooping raceme, becoming erect at maturity; petals 8–19 mm long; sepals 5 on terminal flowers, 3 or 4 on lower ones; styles 2.4–5 mm long, hirsute; anthers opening along a continuous line into 2 very unequal valves. **Leaves** *not apparent, reduced to scales.* **Stems** *pubescent*, yellow or brown (rarely pink or red).
OCCURRENCE: Uncommon; MDI, IAH.
OTHER NAMES: False Beech-drops, *Monotropa hypopithys*

Sheep Laurel • *Kalmia angustifolia*

Evergreen shrub of dry openings and wetlands, up to 1 m tall. **Flowers** bright pink, 6–12 mm wide, *borne in clusters below stem tips*; anthers 10, pulled back and depressed into petals. **Leaves** entire, 3–5 cm long, in whorls of 3. **Branchlets** *round in cross section.*
OCCURRENCE: Common; MDI, IAH, SCH.
OTHER NAMES: Lambkill, Sheep American-laurel

Bog Laurel • *Kalmia polifolia*

Evergreen shrub of bogs, up to 1 m tall. **Flowers** 5-lobed, pink, 1–2.5 cm wide, *borne in clusters at branch tips.* **Leaves** opposite, 1–4 cm long, *distinctly revolute-margined, white beneath.* **Branchlets** *2-edged.*
OCCURRENCE: Occasional; MDI, IAH, SCH.
OTHER NAMES: Pale Laurel, Bog American-laurel

One-flowered Pyrola • *Moneses uniflora*

Evergreen herb of bogs and mossy woods, 3–14 cm tall. **Flowers** solitary, waxy-looking, white or very light pink, 5-parted, 12–20 mm wide, fragrant, *nodding; styles conspicuous, protruding.* **Leaves** evergreen, finely toothed, veiny, rounded, 1–2 cm long, clustered at ascending apex of creeping, underground shoots; petioles 5–10 mm long. **Fruit** a solitary capsule opening from tip to base.
OCCURRENCE: Uncommon; MDI, IAH, SCH.
OTHER NAMES: One-flowered Shinleaf, Single Delight, One-flowered Wintergreen

Indian-pipe • *Monotropa uniflora*

Saprophytic or parasitic, perennial herb of rich woods, 5–30 cm tall. **Flowers** white, *solitary*, 8–19 mm long, *nodding, becoming upright in fruit*. **Leaves** *reduced to scales*. **Stems** white, rarely pink or red, glabrous, blackening late in season. **Fruit** a woody capsule, often overwintering, the previous year's fruit evident in spring.
OCCURRENCE: Common; MDI, IAH, SCH.
OTHER NAMES: Convulsion-root, Ghost-flower, Corpse-plant, One-flowered Indian-pipe

One-sided Pyrola • *Orthilia secunda*

Evergreen herb of wet woods and bogs, 10–20 cm tall. **Flowers** *pale or mostly white*, ~5 mm long, *in a one-sided raceme*. **Leaves** lustrous, *leathery*, 0.5–4 cm long, the blade longer than the petiole.
OCCURRENCE: Uncommon; MDI.
OTHER NAMES: One-sided Wintergreen, One-sided Shinleaf, *Pyrola secunda*

Round-leaved Pyrola • *Pyrola americana*

Evergreen herb of woodlands, 15–30 cm tall. **Flowers** white, ~12 mm wide, *borne in a spirally arranged raceme*; styles 8–10 mm long, *curving down then upturned at the end*; sepals 3–4 mm long, longer than wide; *bracts below the flowers clasping stem*. **Leaves** *round, dark green, shiny*, thick, the blade usually same length as the petiole.

OCCURRENCE: Occasional; MDI.

OTHER NAMES: Rounded Shinleaf, American Shinleaf, *Pyrola rotundifolia*

AH

AH

AH

Green-flowered Pyrola• *Pyrola chlorantha*

Evergreen herb of dry woods, 10–25 cm tall. **Flowers** green-white, 4–9 mm long, in a spirally arranged raceme of up to 10 flowers. **Leaves** *kidney-shaped*, thick and opaque, 1–4 cm long, on a slender petiole, *the blade usually shorter than petiole*.

OCCURRENCE: Uncommon; MDI.

OTHER NAMES: Green-flowered Shinleaf, *Pyrola virens*

JS

JS

Shinleaf • *Pyrola elliptica*

Evergreen herb of rich woodlands, 15–30 cm tall. **Flowers** white or creamy, rarely pinkish, 5-parted, fragrant, in a spirally arranged raceme of >10 flowers; sepals as wide or wider than long; *bracts below flowers not clasping stem.* **Leaves** basal only, *thin,* opaque, 3–7 cm long, *the blade usually longer than the petiole.*
OCCURRENCE: Occasional; MDI.
OTHER NAMES: Elliptic-leaved Shinleaf

Rhodora • *Rhododendron canadense*

Deciduous shrub of bogs and wet thickets, up to 1 m tall. **Flowers** bilaterally symmetric, *bright magenta, emerging before leaves.* **Leaves** gray-green, 2–5 cm long, alternate, entire, membranaceous, with fine hairs beneath. **Fruit** a capsule 0.7–1.5 cm long.
OCCURRENCE: Common; MDI, IAH, SCH.

Labrador-tea • *Rhododendron groenlandicum*

Evergreen shrub of bogs, up to 1 m tall. **Flowers** 5-parted, white, in terminal clusters; pedicels 1–2 cm long. **Leaves** 2–5 cm long, alternate, entire, with *copious rusty-woolly hairs on underside*. **Fruit** a 5-locular capsule splitting first at the base.
OCCURRENCE: Common; MDI, IAH, SCH.
OTHER NAMES: *Ledum groenlandicum*

Lowbush Blueberry • *Vaccinium angustifolium*

Deciduous shrub of dry open areas, 0.1–1 m tall. **Flowers** *5-parted, bell-shaped, white to pink, 4–7 mm long.* **Leaves** *1–3 cm long, serrulate*, lanceolate. **Fruit** *a sweet and delicious blue berry*, flavor of Maine specimens unparalleled elsewhere in the universe.
OCCURRENCE: Common; MDI, IAH, SCH.
OTHER NAMES: Early Low Blueberry, Late Sweet Blueberry, Low Sweet Blueberry, Common Lowbush Blueberry

Alpine Blueberry • *Vaccinium boreale*

Tiny, deciduous shrub of high-elevation open areas and bogs, <9 cm tall. **Flowers** *white to pink, bell-shaped, 3–4 mm long.* **Leaves** *1–2 cm long and 2–6 mm wide*, lanceolate. **Fruit** *a tiny, blue berry.*

OCCURRENCE: Rare; MDI.

NOTES: Maine Natural Areas Program ranks this species as of special concern in Maine.

OTHER NAMES: Sweet Hurts, Northern Blueberry

Highbush Blueberry • *Vaccinium corymbosum*

Deciduous shrub of wet areas, *0.5–4 m tall.* **Flowers** *white or pink, 5–10 mm long*, in dense clusters. **Leaves** *3–8 cm long and 1.5–4 cm wide*, margins variously toothed. **Bark** *peeling and shredding from base of stem* (see middle photo). **Fruit** a dark blue berry, 3–6 mm wide, sweet.

OCCURRENCE: Occasional; MDI, IAH, SCH.

OTHER NAMES: Swamp Blueberry

Large Cranberry • *Vaccinium macrocarpon*

Woody, evergreen shrub of bogs and wet areas, up to 30 cm tall. **Flowers** white to pink, 5-parted, ~1 cm wide, with petals curled back toward pedicel; *bracteoles emerging above the middle of pedicel, 2–4 mm long, green, leaf-like.* **Leaves** 5–17 mm long and 2–8 mm wide, pale beneath, elliptic-oblong, with flat or slightly revolute margins. **Fruit** a red berry 1–2 cm wide, sour when young but sweeter after several chilly nights.
OCCURRENCE: Common; MDI, IAH, SCH.
NOTES: This is the cranberry of commerce.
OTHER NAMES: American Cranberry

Velvet-leaved Blueberry • *Vaccinium myrtilloides*

Deciduous shrub of wet areas, 0.2–1 m tall. **Flowers** *pale to mostly white, bell-shaped, 4–6.5 mm long.* **Leaves** 1–5 cm long, *pubescent,* elliptic to narrow elliptic, entire. **Stems** and *young branchlets velvety, pilose-hirsute.* **Fruit** a blue berry, 7–10 mm wide.
OCCURRENCE: Occasional; MDI, IAH.
OTHER NAMES: Sourtop Blueberry

Small Cranberry • *Vaccinium oxycoccos*

Woody, evergreen shrub of bogs, up to 30 cm tall. **Flowers** white to pink, 5-parted, with petals curled back toward pedicel; *bracteoles paired at or below the middle of pedicel, 0.5–2 mm long, reddish.* **Leaves** alternate, 2–10 mm long and 1–3 mm wide, ovate to triangular, acute at tip, with revolute margins, *whitish on underside.* **Fruit** a berry, 5–8 mm wide, pale when young, becoming red at maturity.
OCCURRENCE: Common; MDI, IAH, SCH.
OTHER NAMES: Bog Cranberry

Hillside Blueberry • *Vaccinium pallidum*

Small shrub of dry uplands, 25–50 cm tall. **Flowers** white to pink, urn-shaped, 4–8 mm long. **Leaves** ovate, 2.5–5 cm long, *blue-green with whitish cast (glaucous).* **Fruit** a blue-black berry, 5–8 mm wide.
OCCURRENCE: Rare; SCH.

AH

Bog Bilberry • *Vaccinium uliginosum*

Deciduous shrub of rocky barrens and mountain slopes, 2–60 cm tall. **Flowers** *urn-shaped*, white- or pink-tipped, in clusters of 1–4 at tips of branches; pedicels 0.1–7 mm long. **Leaves** *0.5–2.5 cm long, entire, oval, blunt, with conspicuous netted veins*, pale below. **Fruit** a sweet, blue-black berry.
OCCURRENCE: Rare; SCH.
OTHER NAMES: Alpine Bilberry, Bog Blueberry

Mountain Cranberry • *Vaccinium vitis-idaea*

Low, barely woody, evergreen shrub, up to 20 cm tall. **Flowers** 4-parted, bell-shaped, pink to reddish, in short, drooping racemes. **Leaves** *leathery, shiny, 5–18 mm long and 4–9 mm wide, with dark glands beneath*. **Fruit** a red berry.
OCCURRENCE: Common; MDI, IAH, SCH.
NOTES: Known and prized as lingonberries in Scandinavia.
OTHER NAMES: Rock Cranberry, Cowberry, Lingon, Lingberry

Common Pipewort • *Eriocaulon aquaticum*

Submerged to emergent, perennial herb of pond and lake shallows, up to 2 m tall. **Flowers** *white to gray, borne in flat-topped, globular clusters* with blackish bracts below, on a 5- to 7-ridged peduncle. **Leaves** basal only, slender, tapering to tips, 2–8 mm long, *conspicuously septate*. **Seeds** 0.5–0.7 mm long, with dark tip.
OCCURRENCE: Occasional; MDI, IAH.
OTHER NAMES: White-buttons, Pipewort, Duckgrass, Seven-angled Pipewort, *Eriocaulon septangulare*

CWG

EUPHORBIACEAE • SPURGE FAMILY ▼

Cypress Spurge • **Euphorbia cyparissias*

Erect, rhizomatous, perennial herb of roadsides, fields, and cemeteries, 10–50 cm tall. **Flowers** bright yellow-green, in a small terminal cluster, subtended by large yellow bracts. **Leaves** pale green, 1–3 cm long and 0.5–3 mm wide, the uppermost whorled or opposite, the lowest alternate. **Seeds** brown-gray, ~2 mm long, inside a capsule (often undeveloped) 3 mm long.
OCCURRENCE: Uncommon; MDI.
NOTES: Plants have milky latex inside. This species is a nonnative invasive.

False Indigo • **Amorpha fruticosa*

Shrub of wet woods and streambanks, 1–4 m tall. **Flowers** *blue-violet*, <1 cm long, in one or more spike-like racemes 6–20 cm long; sepals triangular; stamens protruding. **Stems** variably pubescent. **Leaves** pinnately compound; leaflets 11–35, ovate, entire, 1–6 cm long, with *glandular dots on underside*. **Fruit** a legume, 5–9 mm long and 2–4.5 mm wide, with 1 or 2 seeds; upper margin of legume usually bulging upward.
OCCURRENCE: Rare; MDI.
OTHER NAMES: Indigo-bush, False Indigo-bush

Hog-peanut • ***Amphicarpaea bracteata***

Annual herb of moist woods, up to 1.5 m tall. **Flowers** purple to white, 12–18 mm long, *in axillary racemes or panicles*. **Leaves** *palmately compound; leaflets 3, entire, ovate*, 2–8 cm long. **Stems** slender, vine-like. **Fruit** a legume, 1.5–3 cm long, with hairs.
OCCURRENCE: Uncommon; MDI.
OTHER NAMES: American Hog-peanut

Dyer's Greenweed • **Genista tinctoria*

Small shrub of dry soils, up to 2 m tall. **Flowers** *yellow, 10–15 mm long, in a terminal, spike-like raceme* 3–6 cm long. **Leaves** simple, alternate, elliptic to *lanceolate*, entire, 1–5 cm long and 3–15 mm wide. **Stems** striate. **Fruit** a flat legume, 1.5–3 cm long and ~5 mm wide, with 2 or more seeds.
OCCURRENCE: Rare; MDI.

Goldenchain Tree • **Laburnum ×watereri*

Tree or shrub of roadsides and edges. **Flowers** yellow, *in showy, pendent racemes* 15–25 cm long. **Leaves** *palmately compound.* **Twigs** round in cross section. **Fruit** a pubescent legume.
OCCURRENCE: Rare; MDI.
OTHER NAMES: Water Laburnum, *Laburnum vossii*

Beach-pea • *Lathyrus japonicus*

Perennial vine of sea beaches, up to 1.5 m tall. **Flowers** purple to blue, 1.2–3 cm long, with 9 of 10 stamens connate. **Leaves** *blue-green, pinnately compound, with simple tendrils*; leaflets fleshy, *blunt*, oblong to obovate, 3–5 cm long and 1.5–2.5 cm wide; *stipules with 2 basal lobes* (see lower right photo). **Stems** *wingless*. **Fruit** a legume, usually 4–6.5 cm long and 8.5–10.5 mm wide.
OCCURRENCE: Common; MDI, IAH, SCH.
OTHER NAMES: Seaside-pea, Beach Vetchling

Marsh Vetchling • *Lathyrus palustris*

Perennial vine of damp shores and meadows, up to 1.5 m tall. **Flowers** purple to blue, 1.2–2 cm long, with 9 of 10 stamens connate. **Leaves** pinnately compound; leaflets linear to elliptic, 2–8 cm long and 3–20 mm wide; *stipules often serrate, with 1 basal lobe* (see lower right photo). **Stems** *often winged*. **Fruit** a legume, usually <8.5 mm wide.
OCCURRENCE: Uncommon; MDI, SCH.
OTHER NAMES: Vetchling, Marsh Pea, Wild-pea

Yellow Vetchling • *Lathyrus pratensis

Highly branched, *rhizomatous*, perennial vine of wet meadows and roadsides, up to 1 m tall. **Flowers** *yellow*, 1.2–1.9 cm long, 2–8 per raceme. **Leaves** bright green, pinnately compound; *stipules arrow- or lance-shaped with 2 basal lobes*, 1–3 cm long. **Stems** wingless, angled. **Fruit** a legume, sometimes pubescent.

OCCURRENCE: Uncommon; MDI, IAH.

OTHER NAMES: Meadow-pea, Meadow Vetchling

WS

WS

Birdsfoot-trefoil • *Lotus corniculatus

Perennial herb of disturbed areas, up to 1 m tall. **Flowers** *yellow*, often marked with red, 10–16 mm long, usually 4–8 per umbel. **Leaves** alternate, pinnately compound; leaflets 5, 5–15 mm long, *the lowest 2 resembling stipules*. **Stems** glabrous. **Fruit** a legume 1.5–3.5 cm long.

OCCURRENCE: Uncommon; MDI, SCH.

OTHER NAMES: Garden Birdsfoot-trefoil

Garden Lupine • **Lupinus polyphyllus***

Perennial herb of fields and roadsides, 0.5–1.3 m tall. **Flowers** bicolored, blue, blue-purple, pink, or white, in *terminal, erect racemes 20–70 cm long*. **Leaves** alternate, *palmately compound, entire*, the lowest with 11–18 leaflets. **Fruit** a legume with 2–several seeds.

OCCURRENCE: Occasional; MDI.

NOTES: Though locally beloved, this species is invasive in the Midwest and has invaded at least one wetland in our area.

OTHER NAMES: Lupine, Blue Lupine

Black Medick • **Medicago lupulina***

Annual or biennial, sprawling herb of disturbed areas, up to 40 cm long. **Flowers** yellow, 2–4 mm long, in globose to *short-cylindric heads of 10–50 flowers*; pollen discharged by explosive trip mechanism. **Leaves** alternate, compound; *leaflets 3, tipped with a short bristle*, serrulate, elliptic to obovate, 1–2 cm long; stipules ovate-lanceolate with a few teeth. **Stems** *pubescent*. **Fruit** a black, 1-seeded, coiled legume 1.5–3 mm long.

OCCURRENCE: Uncommon; MDI.

OTHER NAMES: Nonesuch, Black Clover

CG

Alfalfa • ***Medicago sativa**

Perennial herb of fields and roadsides, 0.5–1 m tall. **Flowers** usually purple to blue, 6–12 mm long, *in axillary heads or short racemes*; pollen discharged by explosive trip mechanism. **Leaves** alternate, compound; leaflets 3, toothed near tip, *middle leaflet turned upward*; stipules lance-ovate, toothed. **Fruit** *a spirally coiled legume with 1–several seeds, green at maturity, with fine hairs.*
OCCURRENCE: Uncommon; MDI.
OTHER NAMES: Lucerne, Purple Medick

CG

Yellow Sweet Clover • ***Melilotus officinalis**

Biennial or annual herb of fields and roadsides, 0.5–3 m tall. **Flowers** yellow, 5–7 mm long, slender, *in spike-like racemes 3–20 cm long*. **Leaves** alternate, compound; leaflets 3, *finely toothed*, obovate to oblong, blunt, 1–2.5 cm long; stipules entire, bristly, with 1 vein. **Fruit** a rugose, *prominently veined*, leathery legume 2.5–5 mm long, with 1 or 2 seeds.
OCCURRENCE: Uncommon; MDI.
NOTES: Plant fragrant when dried.

AH

Bristly Locust • **Robinia hispida*

Stoloniferous shrub or tree of woods, thickets, and slopes, up to 12 m tall. **Flowers** magenta-pink, 5-parted, ~2 cm long, crowded in somewhat erect racemes; *peduncles sticky, glandular.* **Leaves** pinnately compound; leaflets 7–13, *ovate to almost round, bristle-tipped,* glandular bristly. **Twigs** *sticky with warty glands.* **Fruit** a flat, *glandular legume covered with few short, stiff hairs,* several-seeded.
OCCURRENCE: Rare; MDI.
OTHER NAMES: Rose-acacia, Mossy Locust

Black Locust • **Robinia pseudoacacia*

Tree of woods and thickets, up to 25 m tall. **Flowers** white, 5-parted, fragrant, 1.5–2.5 cm long, *in pendulous racemes 10–20 cm long.* **Leaves** pinnately compound; leaflets 7–19, 2–4 cm long, oval or elliptic, rounded at apex; stipules spiny. **Twigs** *with short spines.* **Bark** *of older trees deeply furrowed.* **Fruit** a flat, *wing-margined legume,* 5–10 cm long, with several seeds.
OCCURRENCE: Occasional; MDI.
NOTES: This is a nonnative, invasive species capable of invading natural areas and displacing native plants.
OTHER NAMES: Yellow Locust, False Acacia

Crown-vetch • **Securigera varia*

Perennial herb of roadsides, 0.3–1 m tall. **Flowers** *pink and white, 10–15 mm long,* in dense axillary umbels on long peduncles. **Leaves** alternate, pinnately compound; leaflets 11–25, entire, oblong to obovate, 1–2 cm long. **Fruit** *a 4-angled, leathery legume 2–6 cm long, breaking into 3–7 segments with 1 seed each.*
OCCURRENCE: Uncommon; MDI, IAH.
OTHER NAMES: Axseed, Purple Crown-vetch, *Coronilla varia*

Blue Ridge False Lupine • **Thermopsis villosa*

Perennial herb of roadsides, fields, and open woods, 0.4–1.5 m tall. **Flowers** *yellow, in terminal, elongated racemes.* **Leaves** palmately compound; *leaflets 3, pubescent, diamond-shaped to lanceolate,* 2.5–7.5 cm long; *stipules narrow,* usually shorter than petiole. **Fruit** a narrow legume, somewhat curving, 2–10 cm long.
OCCURRENCE: Rare; MDI.
OTHER NAMES: Piedmont Buckbean, Piedmont False Lupine, Bush-pea

Rabbit-foot Clover • **Trifolium arvense*

Annual herb of roadsides and waste areas, 10–40 cm tall. **Flowers** *grayish pink or grayish white; inflorescence oblong, appearing furry*; peduncles 1–3 cm long. **Leaves** alternate, *trifoliate, with silky hairs*; leaflets finely toothed at tip, 1–2 cm long; petioles 4–10 mm long; *stipules exceeding petioles*. **Stems** soft-hairy, branched. **OCCURRENCE:** Common; MDI, IAH, SCH. **OTHER NAMES:** Stone Clover, Old-field Clover

Hop Clover • **Trifolium aureum*

Biennial or annual herb of fields and roadsides, 20–50 cm tall. **Flowers** yellow, *in short-cylindric, dense heads 1–2 cm long*; peduncles 1–4 cm long. **Leaves** palmately trifoliate; leaflets 1–2 cm long, oblanceolate to obovate-oblong, finely toothed, *the terminal one sessile*; stipules lanceolate, about equal to petioles. **Stems** appressed-hairy. **Fruit** resembling flower head but dry and russet-colored. **OCCURRENCE:** Occasional; MDI, IAH. **OTHER NAMES:** Yellow Clover, Palmate Hop Clover, *Trifolium agrarium*

Low Hop Clover • **Trifolium campestre*

Low-growing, annual herb of fields and roadsides, 10–40 cm tall. **Flowers** yellow, in short-cylindric heads 8–15 mm long; peduncles 1–4 cm long. **Leaves** pinnately trifoliate; leaflets 8–15 mm long, oblong to obovate-oblong, finely toothed, *the terminal one on stalk 1–3 mm long; stipules shorter than petiole.* **Stems** pubescent.
OCCURRENCE: Occasional; MDI, SCH.
OTHER NAMES: Pinnate Hop Clover, *Trifolium procumbens*

Alsike Clover • **Trifolium hybridum*

Perennial herb of roadsides, 25–60 cm tall. **Flowers** *bicolored, white to pink*, sweet smelling, each 7–10 mm long, in *dense heads 2–3.5 cm wide*; peduncles longer than leaves. **Leaves** alternate, trifoliate; leaflets oval to elliptic, finely toothed, rounded or notched at tip; *stipules lance-ovate with free tips* (see middle photo). **Stems** erect, not rooting at nodes. **Fruit** a legume with stipe, with 2–4 seeds.
OCCURRENCE: Uncommon; MDI.
OTHER NAMES: Alsatian Clover

Red Clover • **Trifolium pratense*

Short-lived perennial or biennial herb of fields and roadsides, 15–60 cm tall. **Flowers** *magenta or purple, 10–20 mm long, in globose heads to 3 cm long.* **Leaves** alternate, trifoliate; leaflets blunt, widest near the middle, finely toothed, *often blotched with a white "V"*; stipules oblong, abruptly narrowing to a short bristle. **Stems** appressed-hairy. **Fruit** a legume opening along lid-like structure.
OCCURRENCE: Common; MDI, IAH, SCH.

White Clover • **Trifolium repens*

Creeping, perennial herb of lawns and fields, up to 40 cm tall. **Flowers** *white to pale pink, 7–11 mm long, in rounded heads 1–3 cm wide.* **Leaves** basal only, trifoliate; leaflets elliptic to obovate, rounded with notch at tip; *stipules connate, forming sheath with tips separated.* **Fruit** a legume with 3 or 4 seeds.
OCCURRENCE: Common; MDI, IAH, SCH.

Cow Vetch • **Vicia cracca*

Perennial vine, up to 2 m long. **Flowers** 20–50, blue to purple, 8–15 mm long, *in dense, one-sided racemes*. **Leaves** pinnately compound; *leaflets in 5–11 pairs, linear to narrowly oblong*, 1–3 cm long; stipules entire. **Stems** pubescent, angular, striate. **Fruit** a legume, 2–3 cm long and 5–7 mm wide.
OCCURRENCE: Common; MDI, IAH, SCH.
OTHER NAMES: Tufted Vetch, Bird Vetch, Canada-pea

Narrow-leaved Vetch • **Vicia sativa*

Annual vine of roadsides and waste places, up to 1 m long. **Flowers** purple to pink, 1.2–1.8 cm long, *axillary, usually in pairs*. **Leaves** pinnately compound; leaflets varied, oblong to elliptic to obovate to linear, 1–3.5 cm long; *stipules with a glandular spot beneath, half-sagittate, often sharply serrate* (see left photos). **Fruit** a brown, flat legume 4–8 cm long, with 4–12 seeds.
OCCURRENCE: Uncommon; MDI.
OTHER NAMES: Common Vetch, Spring Vetch

Slender Vetch • **Vicia tetrasperma*

Annual vine of old fields, 10–60 cm long. **Flowers** purple, 3–8 mm long, *solitary or in pairs on peduncles.* **Leaves** pinnately compound; *leaflets in 2–5 pairs, linear, oblong to oblanceolate, or narrowly elliptic*, 1–2 cm long; stipules 2-lobed. **Fruit** *a flat, blunt-tipped legume 1–3 cm long, usually with 4 seeds.*
OCCURRENCE: Uncommon; MDI, SCH.
OTHER NAMES: Four-seeded Vetch

American Beech • ***Fagus grandifolia***

Deciduous tree, up to 30 m tall. **Staminate flowers** in stalked heads, with 8–16 stamens and slender filaments. **Carpellate flowers** in pairs above involucral bracts. **Leaves** *ovate to narrow-ovate*, thin, *distinctly and coarsely serrate*, often remaining on younger trees through winter; petioles 4–12 mm long. **Buds** 8–25 mm long, slender, *sharply pointed.* **Fruit** with 2 triangular nuts in prickly, hardened involucres. **Bark** smooth ash-gray on healthy trees.
OCCURRENCE: Common; MDI, IAH.
NOTES: Most of the trees in our area affected by beech bark disease with dark, warty cankers on bark.

CWG

Bear Oak • *Quercus ilicifolia*

Deciduous small tree of rocky or sandy soils, up to 7 m tall. **Staminate flowers** in slender catkins. **Leaves** 5–12 cm long, *short-triangular or ovate, pointed with bristle-tipped lobes; leaves of fertile branches white-felted beneath*. **Buds** blunt, with loosely imbricated scales. **Fruit** an acorn, often abruptly enlarged above base, 1.2–2 cm long, *the cup covering half to a third of nut*; outer surface of nut and inner surface of cap pubescent.
OCCURRENCE: Rare; MDI.
NOTES: This species is at the northern limit of its range here.
OTHER NAMES: Scrub Oak

Northern Red Oak • *Quercus rubra*

Deciduous tree, up to 30 m tall. **Staminate flowers** in slender catkins. **Leaves** coarsely pinnatifid, pubescent especially when young, on slender petioles; *sinuses shallow; lobes with bristle tips*. **Buds** 5–7 mm long, reddish, pointed. **Fruit** an acorn 1.5–3 cm wide; *cup covering about one-quarter of nut*, with ring of hairs inside around scar. **Bark** hard and furrowed in older trees, sometimes with reddish fissures; inner bark reddish.
OCCURRENCE: Common; MDI, IAH.

Twining Screwstem • *Bartonia paniculata*

Tiny, annual or biennial herb of coastal peatlands, 4–45 cm tall. **Flowers** tiny, ~3 mm long, cream-colored; *stigmas 0.8–1.5 mm long*. **Leaves** *alternate, reduced to tiny scales*. **Fruit** a cylindric capsule.
OCCURRENCE: Rare; IAH, SCH.
NOTES: Maine Natural Areas Program ranks this species as threatened in Maine.
OTHER NAMES: Screwstem

Yellow Screwstem • *Bartonia virginica*

Small, annual or biennial herb of wet mountaintop depressions, 10–40 cm tall. **Flowers** tiny, ~3 mm long, yellow or straw-colored, in a stiff raceme or in a branched cluster; *stigmas (including the basal lobes) 1.5–2.3 mm long*; blooming late summer into fall. **Leaves** *opposite*, reduced to tiny scales. **Fruit** a cylindric capsule.
OCCURRENCE: Uncommon; MDI.
OTHER NAMES: Yellow Bartonia, Virginia Screwstem

AH

AH

AH

Marsh-felwort • *Lomatogonium rotatum*

Annual or biennial herb of bold, rocky shorelines, 5–20 cm tall. **Flowers** *light blue, with deep sinuses, bearing fringed, scale-like appendages at base*; sepals equaling or longer than petals. **Leaves** fleshy, 0.4–3 cm long, the lowest wider than the middle and upper lanceolate ones.
OCCURRENCE: Rare; SCH.
NOTES: Maine Natural Areas Program ranks this species as threatened in Maine. Although it is an annual, it does not begin to bloom until September.

CWG

Bicknell's Cranesbill • *Geranium bicknellii*

Annual or biennial herb of open areas, 15–60 cm tall. **Flowers** *magenta*; petals *2.5–10 mm long*. **Leaves** *deeply and palmately lobed, the divisions deeply toothed*. **Stems** with hairs of unequal length, the hairs sometimes gland-tipped. **Fruit** *with a beak 4–5 mm long*.
OCCURRENCE: Uncommon; SCH.
OTHER NAMES: Bicknell's Wild Geranium, Northern Geranium, Northern Cranesbill

AH

AH

Meadow Cranesbill • **Geranium pratense*

Rhizomatous, perennial herb of fields, 30–80 cm tall. **Flowers** *magenta; petals 12–20 mm long; pedicels and style glandular-hirsute.* **Leaves** *palmately lobed,* the lobes cut into narrow, sharp teeth. **Fruit** with beak 5–10 mm long.
OCCURRENCE: Uncommon; MDI.
OTHER NAMES: Meadow Geranium, Meadow Cranesbill

Herb-robert • **Geranium robertianum*

Annual or biennial herb of rocky woods and shores, up to 60 cm tall. **Flowers** *magenta, 1–2 cm wide.* **Leaves** opposite, *palmately divided; leaflets 3 or 5, often with a reddish tinge, pinnately lobed, middle segment short-stalked.*
OCCURRENCE: Occasional; MDI, IAH, SCH.
OTHER NAMES: Mountain Cranesbill

Skunk Currant • *Ribes glandulosum*

Deciduous shrub of rocky woods and shores, up to 2 m tall. **Flowers** white or mostly white, *in ascending racemes*. **Leaves** alternate, lobed, *palmately veined, with a skunk-like odor when crushed*. **Stems** *smooth*. **Fruit** *a red berry with gland-tipped hairs*.
OCCURRENCE: Uncommon; MDI, SCH.

Bristly Gooseberry • *Ribes hirtellum*

Deciduous shrub of rocky woods and shores, up to 2 m tall. **Flowers** white or mostly white, solitary or in clusters of 2–4. **Leaves** alternate, toothed or lobed, palmately veined. **Stems** *slightly prickly*. **Fruit** *purple-black, glabrous*, not jointed from pedicels.
OCCURRENCE: Occasional; MDI, IAH, SCH.
OTHER NAMES: Smooth Gooseberry, Canada Gooseberry, Hairy-stemmed Gooseberry

Spiny Swamp Currant • *Ribes lacustre*

Deciduous shrub of wet woods and swamps. **Flowers** mostly white with some purple, wide and flat, *in drooping racemes; ovary with gland-tipped hairs.* **Leaves** alternate, deeply lobed, palmately veined. **Stems** *prickly and spiny.* **Fruit** *purple to black berries with gland-tipped hairs.*

OCCURRENCE: Rare; MDI.

OTHER NAMES: Bristly Black Currant, Bristly Currant, Swamp Currant, Bristly Swamp Currant

HALORAGACEAE • WATER-MILFOIL FAMILY ▼

Slender Water-milfoil • *Myriophyllum alterniflorum*

Aquatic, perennial herb of shallow water, up to 1 m tall. **Flowers** 4-lobed, scattered or in pairs on the flowering spike; stamens 4 or 8. **Leaves** opposite or alternate, *pinnately divided, 3–12 mm long.* **Stems** *usually forked.* **Fruit** 1.5–2 mm long.

OCCURRENCE: Rare; MDI.

NOTES: This species is native and is not the aggressively invasive species found elsewhere in Maine.

OTHER NAMES: Alternate-flowered Water-milfoil

AH

DSC

DSC

Leafless Water-milfoil • *Myriophyllum tenellum*

Emergent, perennial herb of shores of granitic ponds and lakes, up to 60 cm tall. **Flowers** 4-lobed; stamens 4 or 8. **Leaves** *reduced to scale-like bumps in emergent leaves, hence looking leafless.* **Stems** *usually simple, unbranched.*
OCCURRENCE: Occasional; MDI, IAH.
NOTES: This species is native and is not the aggressively invasive species found elsewhere in Maine.

CBH

DSC

Mermaid-weed • *Proserpinaca palustris*

AH

Emergent, perennial herb of shallow water, up to 1 m tall. **Flowers** green, tiny, 3-parted, stalkless, growing in leaf axils. **Leaves** alternate, *1.5–6 cm long,* of two types: *above-water leaves sharply toothed, underwater ones divided into 8–14 narrow, paired segments.*
OCCURRENCE: Rare; MDI.
OTHER NAMES: Common Mermaid-weed, Marsh Mermaid-weed

DSC

AH

HALORAGACEAE • WATER-MILFOIL FAMILY

Comb-leaved Mermaid-weed • *Proserpinaca pectinata*

Emergent, perennial herb of coastal bogs, up to 1 m tall. **Flowers** tiny, stalkless, green, 3-parted, growing in leaf axils. **Leaves** alternate, 1–3 cm long, *uniform, divided into 4–9 divisions.*
OCCURRENCE: Rare; MDI.
NOTES: The leaves of this plant look comb-like, suggesting the plant's common name. Maine Natural Areas Program ranks this species as endangered in Maine.

AH

HAMAMELIDACEAE • WITCH-HAZEL FAMILY ▼

Witch-hazel • *Hamamelis virginiana*

Deciduous shrub of dry, rocky woods, up to 5 m tall. **Flowers** yellow; petals 1.5–2 cm long and 1 mm wide, *blooming in small axillary clusters in autumn*; stamens 4; styles 2. **Leaves** toothed, obovate or obovate-oblong, 5–15 cm long, *with asymmetric bases*, rounded or subcordate. **Fruit** *a woody capsule* 1–1.5 cm long, opening across top.
OCCURRENCE: Occasional; MDI, IAH.
OTHER NAMES: American Witch-hazel

Northern Waternymph • *Najas flexilis*

Annual, aquatic herb of lakes and ponds. **Staminate flowers** 2.5–3.2 mm long. **Leaves** *minutely toothed, up to 3 cm long and 0.2–0.6 mm wide, expanded at the base, tapering to the slender blade.* **Fruit** *smooth and glossy*, mostly 2.5–3.7 mm long.
OCCURRENCE: Uncommon; MDI.
OTHER NAMES: Slender Naiad, Bushy Naiad, Wavy Waternymph

CBH

DSC

Slender Waternymph • *Najas gracillima*

Annual, aquatic herb of lakes and ponds. **Staminate flowers** 1–1.5 mm long. **Leaves** minutely toothed, *thread-like, 0.2–0.5 mm wide, with lobed bases.* **Fruit** 2.5–3.5 mm long.
OCCURRENCE: Uncommon; MDI.
OTHER NAMES: Thread-like Naiad

DSC

Tapegrass • *Vallisneria americana*

Dioecious, aquatic, perennial herb of slow-moving water. **Staminate flowers** numerous, minute, 1–1.5 mm wide, on short peduncles. **Carpellate flowers** solitary, white, *carried to the surface of the water on long, often spiraled, peduncles.* **Leaves** *thin, ribbon-like,* up to 2 m long and 1–3 mm wide, *with prominent 3-zoned banding almost their entire width,* all arising from a short basal crown. **Fruit** 5–12 cm long.
OCCURRENCE: Uncommon; MDI.
OTHER NAMES: Water-celery, Wild-celery

DSC

CBH

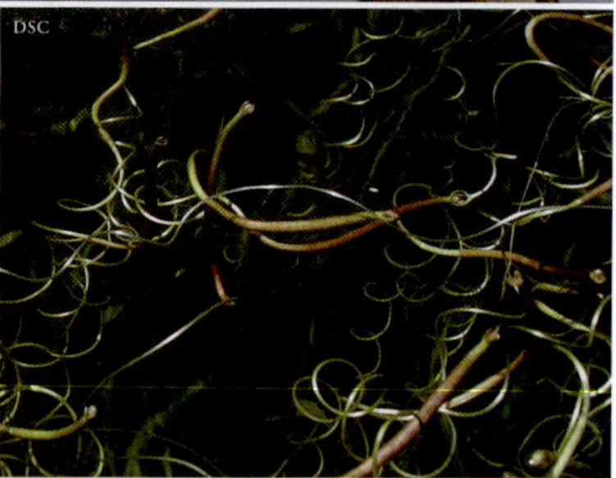
DSC

HYPERICACEAE • ST. JOHN'S-WORT FAMILY ▼

Northern St. John's-wort • *Hypericum boreale*

Rhizomatous, perennial herb of bogs and wet meadows, 10–50 cm tall. **Flowers** yellow, *with many leafy bracts beneath*; petals 2.5–3 mm long; sepals obtuse at tip, *shorter than capsule*; stamens 8–15; styles usually 3. **Leaves** sessile, 3–20 mm long, with 3–5 veins. **Stems** decumbent. **Fruit** a purple, 1-locular capsule, 3–5 mm long. **Seeds** 0.6–0.8 mm long.
OCCURRENCE: Occasional; MDI, IAH.

Canada St. John's-wort • *Hypericum canadense*

Stoloniferous, annual herb of moist ground and low thickets, 10–60 cm tall. **Flowers** yellow, ~6 mm wide, in a terminal inflorescence; petals 2–4 mm long; sepals 4–6 mm long; stamens 12–22. **Leaves** opposite, entire, 1–4 cm long and 1–6 mm wide, with 1 or 3 veins. **Fruit** a conical, 1-locular, red or purplish capsule, 3–6.5 mm long. **Seeds** 0.5 mm long.
OCCURRENCE: Occasional; MDI, IAH, SCH.
OTHER NAMES: Lesser Canada St. John's-wort

Pale St. John's-wort • *Hypericum ellipticum*

Rhizomatous, stoloniferous, perennial herb of marshes and bogs, 20–50 cm tall. **Flowers** bright yellow, 12–20 mm wide, in a few- to many-flowered cyme; petals 5–7 mm long; stamens 20–40; stigmas 3 or 4; styles connate, appearing as a beak at capsule summit. **Leaves** 1.5–3.4 cm long, thin, usually tapering to an almost clasping base. **Stems** obscurely 4-angled. **Fruit** a capsule 5–6 mm long. **Seeds** <1 mm long.
OCCURRENCE: Occasional; MDI.
OTHER NAMES: Elliptic St. John's-wort

Orange-grass • *Hypericum gentianoides*

Annual herb of dry, sandy or rocky soils, 10–50 cm tall. **Flowers** 2–4 mm wide, yellow, *subsessile*; sepals 1.5–2.5 mm long; stamens usually 5–10; styles 3 or 4. **Leaves** appressed to stem, opposite, *minute, scale-like*, 1–4 mm long, 1-veined. **Stems** wiry, thread-like. **Fruit** a capsule 4–7 mm long. **Seeds** 0.4–0.8 mm long.

OCCURRENCE: Occasional; MDI, IAH.

OTHER NAMES: Pineweed, Orange-grass St. John's-wort

Larger Canada St. John's-wort • *Hypericum majus*

Rhizomatous, stoloniferous, perennial herb of swamps and wet areas, 10–75 cm tall. **Flowers** 5–10 mm wide, in nearly naked cymes; petals yellow, 3.5–4 mm long; sepals 4–7 mm long; stamens 14–21; styles 3 or 4. **Leaves** *often ascending*, 1.5–4.5 cm long and 3–15 mm wide, the uppermost with 5–7 veins, *clasping half the stem*. **Fruit** a blunt capsule, 5–7 mm long. **Seeds** 0.5–0.7 mm long.

OCCURRENCE: Uncommon; IAH.

OTHER NAMES: Larger St. John's-wort, Greater Canada St. John's-wort

Dwarf St. John's-wort • *Hypericum mutilum*

Perennial or annual herb of wet fields, swamps, and ditches, 0.1–1 m tall. **Flowers** yellow, 3–4 mm wide; *sepals widest near the middle*, acute at apex; stamens 5–16; styles 3. **Leaves** *pale beneath*, 1–4 cm long, 5-veined. **Fruit** a capsule 2–3.5 mm long. **Seeds** 0.6–0.8 mm long.
OCCURRENCE: Occasional; MDI.

CG

Common St. John's-wort • *Hypericum perforatum*

Stoloniferous, perennial herb of fields, roadsides, and waste areas, 0.3–1 m tall. **Flowers** deep yellow, ~20 mm wide; *petals 5, with black dots along edges*, twice as long as the sepals; sepals pointed, 4–6 mm long. **Leaves** sessile, with many translucent dots. **Stems** with 2 opposite raised ridges. **Seeds** coarsely net-veined, blackish, 1–1.3 mm long.
OCCURRENCE: Common; MDI, IAH, SCH.

Shrubby St. John's-wort • **Hypericum prolificum***

Deciduous, highly branched shrub of low fields, swamps, and thickets, up to 2 m tall. **Flowers** yellow, 1.5–2.5 cm wide; sepals 5–7 mm long, shorter than petals; stamens numerous, yellow. **Leaves** blue-green, the largest 3–7 cm long and 4–18 mm wide. **Stems** *2-edged, flat.* **Fruit** a slender, beaked capsule 7–15 mm long and 3–5 mm wide, containing numerous seeds.
OCCURRENCE: Uncommon; MDI.
NOTES: Blooms in late summer. It has invaded two natural areas in Acadia National Park.
OTHER NAMES: *Hypericum spathulatum*

Spotted St. John's-wort • ***Hypericum punctatum***

Perennial herb of moist fields and roadsides, 0.3–1.3 m tall. **Flowers** pale yellow, *with black lines or spots on petals and sepals*; sepals 2.5–4 mm long. **Leaves** up to 4–6 cm long, *with black dots on underside.* **Fruit** a capsule 3–5 mm long, with elongate oil sacs. **Seeds** <1 mm long.
OCCURRENCE: Occasional; MDI.

Marsh St. John's-wort • *Triadenum fraseri*

Perennial herb of bogs, swamps, and wet woods, 20–75 cm tall. **Flowers** pink, 1–1.5 cm wide; *sepals 2.5–5 mm long when mature, obtuse to rounded at tip*; styles 0.5–2 mm long. **Leaves** blue-green, opposite, up to 5 cm long, with translucent glands. **Fruit** a capsule, tapering abruptly to tip.
OCCURRENCE: Occasional; MDI, IAH, SCH.
OTHER NAMES: Fraser's Marsh St. John's-wort, *Hypericum virginicum* var. *fraseri*

Southern Marsh St. John's-wort • *Triadenum virginicum*

Perennial herb of bogs, swamps, and wet woods, 0.2–1 m tall. **Flowers** pink, 1.5–2 cm wide; *sepals 5–8 mm long when mature, acute to acuminate at tip*; styles 1.8–3 mm long. **Leaves** blue-green, opposite, broadly oblong or egg-shaped, blunt-tipped, 2–7 cm long, with translucent glands. **Fruit** a capsule, tapering gradually to apex.
OCCURRENCE: Occasional; MDI, SCH.
OTHER NAMES: Virginia Marsh St. John's-wort, *Hypericum virginicum*

Arctic Blue Flag • *Iris hookeri*

Perennial herb of rocky headlands and islands, up to 60 cm tall. **Flowers** 6–8 cm wide, blue to purple with some white and yellow at base, with 3 longer outer tepals and *3 minute or absent, bristle-tipped inner tepals.* **Leaves** flat, entire, sword-shaped, up to 1.5 cm wide. **Fruit** a blunt, 3-lobed capsule 2.5–4 cm long. **Seeds** *rounded to pear-shaped.*
OCCURRENCE: Uncommon; MDI, IAH, SCH.
NOTES: This species is difficult to distinguish from *Iris versicolor* when not in flower.
OTHER NAMES: Beachhead Iris, Beach Blue flag, Beachhead flag, *Iris setosa*

Larger Blue Flag • *Iris versicolor*

Perennial herb of fresh water wetlands, wet headlands, and shores, up to 1.5 m tall. **Flowers** ~10 cm wide, blue to purple with some white and yellow at base, with 3 longer, spreading, recurving, outer tepals and *3 distinct, 2–5 cm long, inner tepals.* **Leaves** flat, entire, sword-shaped, 1–3 cm wide, shorter than the flowering stem. **Fruit** a blunt, 3-lobed capsule with a tiny beak, 3.5–5.5 cm long. **Seeds** *shaped like the letter "D", with one straight side.*
OCCURRENCE: Common; MDI, IAH, SCH.
OTHER NAMES: Northern Blue flag, Blue flag, Blue Iris, Poison flag

Common Blue-eyed-grass • *Sisyrinchium montanum*

Perennial herb of meadows, fields, and roadsides, 15–45 cm tall. **Flowers** violet-blue, *6-parted*, overtopped by a pointed bract. **Leaves** very slender and grass-like, the largest 2–3 mm wide and about as long as the flowering stems. **Stems** *distinctly winged, 1.5–3 mm wide*. **Fruit** a round capsule 4–6 mm long, at first green then turning dark.

OCCURRENCE: Common; MDI, IAH, SCH.

OTHER NAMES: Strict Blue-eyed-grass

JUNCAGINACEAE • ARROW-GRASS FAMILY ▼

Seaside Arrow-grass • *Triglochin maritima*

Perennial herb of saltmarshes and shores, up to 1.2 m tall. **Flowers** white, with 6 carpels and 6 feathery stigmas, borne in a narrow spike-like raceme longer than leaves. **Leaves** basal only, slender, grass-like, up to 50 cm long and <6 mm wide. **Fruit** dry, oval-shaped, single-chambered, ~6 mm long, opening by splitting along one side.

OCCURRENCE: Occasional; MDI, IAH, SCH.

NOTES: All parts of plant poisonous.

OTHER NAMES: Common Arrow-grass, Salt-marsh Arrow-grass

Splitlip Hempnettle • **Galeopsis bifida*

Annual herb of fields and disturbed sites, 0.2–1 m tall. **Flowers** magenta, 13–16 mm long, upper lip egg-shaped and arched, *middle lobe of lower lip notched, with 2 narrow swellings near base; sepals with teeth 7.5–11 mm long, spine-tipped.* **Leaves** opposite, coarsely toothed, egg-shaped, *usually wedge-shaped at base*, 3–10 cm long and 1–5 cm wide. **Stems** bristly, soft, swollen below joints, branching. **Fruit** rounded at summit.
OCCURRENCE: Uncommon; IAH.

Brittlestem Hempnettle • **Galeopsis tetrahit*

Annual herb of fields and disturbed sites, 20–75 cm tall. **Flowers** magenta, 15–24 mm long, upper lip egg-shaped and arched, *lower lip without a notch at the tip, with 2 large swellings near base; sepals with teeth 5–8 mm long, spine-tipped.* **Leaves** opposite, coarsely toothed, egg-shaped, *usually rounded at base*, 3–10 cm long and 1–5 cm wide. **Stems** *bristly*, soft, swollen below joints, branching. **Fruit** rounded at summit.
OCCURRENCE: Occasional; MDI, SCH.

Cut-leaved Water-horehound • *Lycopus americanus*

Perennial herb of wetlands, 0.1–1 m tall. **Flowers** small, white, *sessile in leaf axils*; sepals 2–3.3 mm long, *with 5 narrow-triangular lobes 1–2 mm long* and tipped with spines. **Leaves** 3–8 cm long, tapering to base, variably toothed, with glands on underside; basal leaves *pinnately lobed*. **Stems** with low, blunt *angles*, variably pubescent. **Fruit** 1–1.7 mm long and 0.6–1 mm wide, widening upwards.
OCCURRENCE: Occasional; MDI.
OTHER NAMES: Water-horehound, American Water-horehound

Northern Bugleweed • *Lycopus uniflorus*

Tuberous, perennial herb of wetlands, 10–60 cm tall. **Flowers** small, white, sessile in leaf axils; *petals with flaring lobes*; sepals 1–1.4 mm long *with 5 wide-triangular lobes <1 mm long*. **Leaves** 2–11 cm long, tapering to base, with glands on underside; basal leaves coarsely toothed but not lobed. **Stems** becoming glabrous with age. **Fruit** <1.5 mm long, widening upward. **Tubers** *white*.
OCCURRENCE: Occasional; MDI, IAH, SCH.
OTHER NAMES: Northern Water-horehound, Bugleweed

Wild Mint • *Mentha arvensis*

Perennial herb of wetlands, 10–80 cm tall. **Flowers** pink, purple, or white, *densely whorled in axils of leaves; petals 4, the upper lobe widest*; stamens 4, projecting beyond petals; sepals pubescent. **Leaves** toothed, *strongly smelling of mint*, 1.8–8 cm long and 6–40 mm wide, often rounded at base. **Stems** sometimes branched, variably pubescent.

OCCURRENCE: Occasional; MDI.

OTHER NAMES: Field Mint, Common Mint

Self-heal • **Prunella vulgaris*

Perennial herb of disturbed sites, 10–60 cm tall. **Flowers** borne in uninterrupted spikes longer than wide, *blue or purple, upper lip with 3 lobes; lower lip deeply cleft into 2 narrow segments; middle lobe of lower lip fringed.* **Leaves** opposite, <10 cm long, distinctly longer than wide, obscurely toothed. **Stems** sometimes branched, variably pubescent.

OCCURRENCE: Occasional; MDI, IAH, SCH.

OTHER NAMES: Heal-all, Carpenter-weed, Common Self-heal

Marsh Skullcap • *Scutellaria galericulata*

Perennial herb of sea beaches and wet thickets, 0.1–1 m tall. **Flowers** blue to purple, 15–22 mm long, *borne in pairs from axils of leaves; upper lip with small but noticeable crest-like bulge on upper surface*; sepals 3.5–4.5 mm long. **Leaves** toothed, 2–6 cm long and 6–20 mm wide, usually with fine, short hairs beneath; petiole 0.5–4 mm long. **Stems** with downward curving hairs.
OCCURRENCE: Common; MDI, IAH, SCH.
OTHER NAMES: Common Skullcap, Hooded Skullcap, *Scutellaria epilobiifolia*

Mad-dog Skullcap • *Scutellaria lateriflora*

Perennial herb of wet thickets, 15–75 cm tall. **Flowers** light blue, 5–9 mm long, *borne in lateral, elongate inflorescences from leaf axils; upper lip with crest-like bump on top*; sepals 1.5–2.5 mm long. **Leaves** coarsely toothed, thin, 2–8 cm long and 1.5–5 cm wide; petioles 0.5–2.5 cm long. **Stems** with hairs curving upward.
OCCURRENCE: Occasional; MDI.
OTHER NAMES: Blue Skullcap

Marsh Hedge-nettle • *Stachys palustris*

Stoloniferous, perennial herb of disturbed sites and wet meadows, 0.2–1 m tall. **Flowers** magenta with some white, 11–16 mm long, whorled in spikes; *sepals pubescent*. **Leaves** *rank smelling*, 3.5–9 cm long and 1–2 cm wide, pubescent beneath, with rough, stiff hairs above, *with wavy margins*. **Stems** pubescent with long, downward curving, stiff hairs. **Fruit** rounded at summit.
OCCURRENCE: Uncommon; MDI.
OTHER NAMES: Woundwort, Hedge-nettle

American Germander • *Teucrium canadense*

Perennial herb of beach heads and wet meadows, 0.2–1 m tall. **Flowers** pink-purple, 1–2 cm long, whorled in terminal, cylindric spikes; *upper lip apparently absent*; lower lip appearing 5-lobed, middle lobe of lower lip much larger than others; *stamens distinctly pointed upward, protruding from flower base*. **Leaves** toothed, *thick*, 5–12 cm long and 1.5–3 cm wide, with crooked hairs on underside; petioles 5–15 mm long. **Stems** pubescent.
OCCURRENCE: Uncommon; MDI, IAH.
OTHER NAMES: Wood-sage, Canada Germander

Wild Thyme • ***Thymus pulegioides**

Prostrate, perennial herb of lawns and meadows, 0.2–1 m long. **Flowers** pink, *crowded at branch ends*, with 2 distinct lips; upper lip with 3 triangular lobes; lower lip cleft in two. **Leaves** *smelling of thyme when crushed, 5–10 mm long, opposite*, entire, strongly veined. **Stems** *low, branching, forming dense mats*, pubescent on angles.
OCCURRENCE: Uncommon; MDI.
OTHER NAMES: Lemon Thyme

LENTIBULARIACEAE • BLADDERWORT FAMILY ▼

Horned Bladderwort • ***Utricularia cornuta***

Terrestrial, rhizomatous, perennial herb of wet soils, 3–35 cm tall. **Flowers** yellow, ~19 mm long, 1–6 per stem; lower lip 9–16 mm long; *spur at base downward pointing, 5–14 mm long*. **Leaves** round and thread-like, with tiny bladders scattered along branches.
OCCURRENCE: Occasional; MDI, IAH, SCH.
NOTES: This species is neither free-floating nor aquatic like others in this genus but is rooted in wet, often peaty, soil.

Twin-stemmed Bladderwort • *Utricularia geminiscapa*

Aquatic, perennial herb, up to 10 cm tall. **Flowers** yellow, 2–6 per stem; lower lip 6–8 mm long; spur at base sometimes as long as lower lip; *submerged stems occasionally with small, solitary flowers without petals* (see left photo). **Leaves** round, thread-like, *leaf-like branches 1–2 cm long*, progressively narrowing with short-pointed projections near tips.
OCCURRENCE: Occasional; MDI, IAH, SCH.
OTHER NAMES: Mixed Bladderwort

Humped Bladderwort • *Utricularia gibba*

Aquatic, perennial herb, sometimes creeping over wet ground, 2–10 cm tall. **Flowers** yellow, 5–6 mm long, *1–3 per stem*, with upper and lower lip about equal in length, thick; spur at base cone-shaped, about half as long as lower lip; *a prominent raised appendage of lower lip closing the throat.* **Leaves** round and thread-like; leaf-like branches alternate, *divided 2 or 3 times*, progressively narrowing to tip, a few bladders scattered along branches.
OCCURRENCE: Uncommon; MDI.
OTHER NAMES: Creeping Bladderwort

CBH

CG

CG

Flat-leaved Bladderwort • *Utricularia intermedia*

Aquatic, perennial herb of bogs and ponds, 5–30 cm tall. **Flowers** yellow, 2–5 per stem, in a loose raceme 1.2–2 cm high; lower lip 8–12 mm long and longer than upper lip; spur at base nearly as long as the lower lip. **Leaves** with alternate, leaf-like branches; *branch segments flat and of 2 types: branches lacking chlorophyll but with scattered bladders and green branches without bladders.*
OCCURRENCE: Occasional; MDI.
OTHER NAMES: Northern Bladderwort, Intermediate Bladderwort

Common Bladderwort • *Utricularia macrorhiza*

Aquatic, perennial herb of bogs and ponds, 10–20 cm tall. **Flowers** yellow, 9–18 mm long, *6–20 in a loose raceme*; lower lip usually 1–2 cm long; spur at base sometimes as long as the lower lip. **Leaves** round and thread-like, progressively narrowing, *leaf-like branches 1–6 cm long*, alternate, *many bladders scattered along branches*. **Stems** ~0.5 mm wide, *free-floating*.
OCCURRENCE: Occasional; MDI, IAH.
OTHER NAMES: Greater Bladderwort, *Utricularia vulgaris*

AH

Lesser Bladderwort • *Utricularia minor*

Aquatic, perennial herb of shallow water. **Flowers** yellow, sometimes with a purplish tinge on lower lip, 2–9 in a loose raceme; lower lip 4–8 mm long; spur at base about half as long as the lower lip. **Leaves** with leaf-like branches, alternate; *branch segments flat and of one type, green (photosynthetic) with scattered bladders.* **Stems** creeping, forming mats in shallow water.
OCCURRENCE: Rare; MDI.

DSC

CBH

Purple Bladderwort • *Utricularia purpurea*

Aquatic, perennial herb of small ponds. **Flowers** *purple or reddish purple with yellow spot on lower lip*, 1–5, facing upward on peduncles. **Leaves** *with leaf-like branches in whorls of 5–7*, finely dissected, with bladders at branch tips. **Stems** *free-floating.*
OCCURRENCE: Occasional; MDI.
OTHER NAMES: Greater Purple Bladderwort, Spotted Bladderwort, Eastern Purple Bladderwort

DSC

Floating Bladderwort • *Utricularia radiata*

Aquatic, perennial herb of shallow water, up to 25 cm tall. **Flowers** yellow, 1–7 per stem, *on a peduncle held above water by a whorl of inflated branches.* **Leaves** with lower leaf-like branches alternate, round and thread-like, *many times branched, without a main axis*; bladders scattered along branches.
OCCURRENCE: Occasional; MDI.
OTHER NAMES: Inflated Bladderwort, *Utricularia inflata*

LILIACEAE • LILY FAMILY ▼

Bluebead-lily • *Clintonia borealis*

Perennial herb of northern forests, up to 70 cm tall. **Flowers** *light yellow to greenish*, ~2 cm wide, *3 to 6 in a drooping cluster.* **Leaves** *basal only*, oval to lance-shaped, 10–30 cm long, *usually 3 or 4 per plant.* **Fruit** *a blue, bead-like berry.*
OCCURRENCE: Occasional; MDI, SCH.
OTHER NAMES: Bluebead, Yellow Clintonia, Corn-lily, Clintonia, Yellow Bluebead-lily

Wood Lily • *Lilium philadelphicum*

Perennial herb of dry, open woods or mountain ridges, 0.2–1 m tall. **Flowers** erect, *with 6 reddish orange tepals with purple blotches, up to 5 per stem.* **Leaves** lance-shaped, in whorls on the stem, sometimes with bulblets at the base. **Fruit** a capsule, 3–5.5 mm long, broadly rounded at tip.
OCCURRENCE: Uncommon; MDI.
OTHER NAMES: Wild Orange-red Lily

CWG

Indian Cucumber Root • *Medeola virginiana*

Rhizomatous, perennial herb of hardwood or mixed forests, 20–50 m tall. **Flowers** *green to yellow, hanging downward from upper whorl of leaves.* **Leaves** narrowly lance-shaped, borne in 2 whorls: one with 5–9 leaves at the middle stem and another with fewer leaves at top of stem. **Fruit** an erect cluster of dark purple berries.
OCCURRENCE: Uncommon; MDI.

Rosybells • *Streptopus lanceolatus*

Perennial herb of hardwood and mixed forests, 25–60 cm tall. **Flowers** *pink with darker reddish stripes, bell-shaped with 6 recurving tepals.* **Leaves** oval to oblong, *not clasping stalk*, green on underside. **Fruit** *a red berry* hanging from underside of stem.
OCCURRENCE: Uncommon; MDI, SCH.
OTHER NAMES: Rose Twisted-stalk, Rose Mandarin, Lance-leaved Twisted-stalk, *Streptopus roseus*

LINACEAE • FLAX FAMILY ▼

Fairy Flax • **Linum catharticum*

Annual or winter-annual of disturbed sites, 10–30 cm tall. **Flowers** *white with a yellow base; petals 5, 4–8 mm long.* **Leaves** opposite (occasionally alternate on parts of stem), *3–15 mm long*, 2–8 pairs below the flowers, with tufts crowded at the base. **Fruit** a 5-parted capsule 2–3 mm long.
OCCURRENCE: Uncommon; IAH.
OTHER NAMES: White flax

Tiny All-seed • ***Linum radiola**

Tiny, annual herb most often of disturbed areas, 3–10 cm tall. **Flowers** *with 4 white petals, ~1 mm long; stamens 4; styles 4*. **Leaves** opposite, *2–3 mm long*. **Fruit** a capsule splitting into 4 parts, with 4 seeds in each compartment.
OCCURRENCE: Rare; IAH.
OTHER NAMES: All-seed, *Millegrana radiola, Radiola linoides*

Water-willow • ***Decodon verticillatus***

Arching-stemmed shrub of pond and stream shores, 1–3 m tall. **Flowers** pink to purple, *clustered in upper leaf axils*; stamens 8–10. **Leaves** mostly in whorls of 3 or 4. **Stems** *4- to 6-angled, often arching and rooting at the tip*.
OCCURRENCE: Rare; MDI.
OTHER NAMES: Water-oleander

CWG

AH

Purple Loosestrife • **Lythrum salicaria***

Perennial herb of wetlands and shores, 0.5–1.5 m tall. **Flowers** magenta, *in an elongate, dense spike*; petals 5 or 6, *crinkled*, 7–12 mm long; stamens 4–6 or sometimes 12. **Leaves** lance-shaped, 3–10 cm long, opposite or sometimes 3 in a whorl, somewhat clasping the *erect, square stem*, the uppermost often alternate.
OCCURRENCE: Uncommon; MDI.
NOTES: This species is nonnative and extremely invasive. It should never be planted, and existing plants should be removed.
OTHER NAMES: Spiked Loosestrife

MALVACEAE • MALLOW FAMILY ▼

Musk Mallow • **Malva moschata***

Perennial herb of disturbed sites, 0.4–1 m tall. **Flowers** white or pink, 4–5 cm wide, borne in axils of upper leaves; petals with small indentation at tip. **Leaves** *deeply lobed or divided.* **Stems** pubescent with simple hairs.
OCCURRENCE: Uncommon; MDI.

Small-leaved Linden • **Tilia cordata*

Tree of roadsides and other disturbed sites. **Flowers** fragrant, *in an erect inflorescence of 4–15 flowers*; petals 5, cream to yellow. **Leaves** alternate, heart-shaped at the base, toothed, *generally without hairs on upper surface*, occasionally with some red-brown hairs on the veins beneath. **Fruit** *faintly ribbed, 4.5–6.6 mm long.*
OCCURRENCE: Uncommon; MDI.

Big-leaved Linden • **Tilia platyphyllos*

Tree of roadsides and other disturbed sites. **Flowers** fragrant, *in a hanging inflorescence of 2–5 flowers*; petals 5, cream to yellow. **Leaves** alternate, heart-shaped at the base, toothed, *generally with hairs on upper surface*, with red-brown hairs on the veins beneath. **Fruit** *with 5 prominent ribs, 8–10 mm long.*
OCCURRENCE: Uncommon; MDI.
OTHER NAMES: Large-leaved Linden

CG

Nodding Trillium • *Trillium cernuum*

Erect, perennial herb of rich, wet woods, up to 60 cm tall. **Flowers** white, *held below the leaves on a peduncle 0.5–2.5 cm long*; petals 1–2.5 cm long; anthers 3–7 mm long. **Leaves** *sessile* or occasionally with a short petiole.
OCCURRENCE: Rare; MDI.
OTHER NAMES: Birthroot, Nodding Wakerobin

Painted Trillium • *Trillium undulatum*

Erect, perennial herb of wet woods and streambanks. **Flowers** with 3 petals, *white with crimson veins near the base*. **Leaves** *stalked*, tapering to a point, in a whorl of 3 below flower. **Fruit** with 3 lobes.
OCCURRENCE: Uncommon; MDI.
NOTES: Found in early summer.
OTHER NAMES: Painted Wakerobin

Meadow Beauty • *Rhexia virginica*

Perennial herb of damp, sandy or gravelly meadows or shores, 15–60 cm tall. **Flowers** *bright magenta to purple, 4-parted, 2–3 cm wide*; anthers on twisted stalks. **Leaves** oval to oblong, rounded at the base, 2–7 cm long, *strongly 3-veined*, finely and sharply toothed, often with bristles on upper surface. **Stems** simple or branched, distinctly square at base.
OCCURRENCE: Uncommon; MDI.
OTHER NAMES: Deergrass, Wing-stem Meadow Pitcher, Virginia Meadow-beauty

MENYANTHACEAE • BUCKBEAN FAMILY ▼

Bogbean • *Menyanthes trifoliata*

Emergent, perennial herb of peatland margins, 10–50 cm tall. **Flowers** *1.5–3 cm wide*, in erect clusters; *petals white, with prominent white hairs on inner surface*. **Leaves** *compound, with 3 oval leaflets*. **Fruit** a many-seeded capsule. **Seeds** hard, smooth, and shiny.
OCCURRENCE: Uncommon; MDI.
OTHER NAMES: Buckbean

Floating-heart • *Nymphoides cordata*

Aquatic, perennial herb of quiet ponds. **Flowers** white, *~1 cm wide*, with tubers growing near or among the flowers. **Leaves** *simple, heart-shaped, 1.5–5 cm wide, floating*. **Fruit** an oval-shaped capsule 3–5 mm long. **Seeds** smooth.
OCCURRENCE: Occasional; MDI, IAH.
OTHER NAMES: Little floating-heart

MYRICACEAE • WAX-MYRTLE FAMILY ▼

Sweet-fern • *Comptonia peregrina*

Dioecious shrub of dry, disturbed sites, often on bare, mineral soil, up to 1.5 m tall. **Staminate flowers** borne in hanging catkins. **Carpellate flowers** borne in round, bur-like clusters. **Leaves** *pinnately lobed, with a sweet, distinctive smell when crushed*, with stipules. **Fruit** a barrel-shaped, hard, smooth nut, *within a globular bur formed from longer persistent bracts.*
OCCURRENCE: Common; MDI, IAH, SCH.
NOTES: This flowering plant is sometimes mistaken for a fern because of its fern-like leaves.

Northern Bayberry • *Morella caroliniensis*

Shrub of beaches and headlands in both wet and dry soils, 0.3–2 m tall. **Flowers** borne on old wood mostly below leaf bases. **Leaves** *dark and shiny green above,* pale beneath, aromatic, 4–8 cm long, with forward-pointing sharp teeth in upper half. **Twigs** with red, round, bluntly pointed winter buds. **Fruit** an achene, *nearly round,* covered with a *thick layer of blue-white or grayish wax,* at maturity 3.5–4.5 mm wide (see lower middle photo).
OCCURRENCE: Common; MDI, IAH, SCH.
NOTES: Wax on fruit can be used as an additive when making bayberry-scented candles.
OTHER NAMES: Bayberry, Candleberry, Small Bayberry, *Myrica pensylvanica*

Sweet Gale • *Myrica gale*

Shrub of mineral-rich wetlands, 0.3–2 m tall. **Carpellate flowers** borne at the tip of the previous year's twigs. **Leaves** *dull green above,* 2–6 cm long, wider above the middle, *slightly toothed near the tip,* tapering to base. **Twigs** with dark brown, oval, winter buds. **Fruit** *a flat achene covered by 2 conspicuous bracts.*
OCCURRENCE: Common; MDI, IAH, SCH.
OTHER NAMES: Meadow-fern

Starflower • *Lysimachia borealis*

Perennial herb of forests, 10–20 cm tall. **Flowers** *solitary, white, star-shaped,* usually 7-parted, 8–14 mm wide; pedicels 2–5 cm long. **Leaves** *in a solitary whorl at apex of stem,* 4–10 cm long, occasionally with lower scale-like leaves alternating on the stem.
OCCURRENCE: Common; MDI, IAH, SCH.
OTHER NAMES: American Starflower, *Trientalis borealis*

Sea Milkwort • *Lysimachia maritima*

Perennial herb of saline to brackish shores and marshes, 5–40 cm tall. **Flowers** *pink to red,* 5-parted, *axillary.* **Leaves** *opposite, sessile, succulent,* 8–15 mm long and 4–8 mm wide, *bluish green.* **Fruit** a capsule 2.5–4 mm wide with few seeds.
OCCURRENCE: Uncommon; MDI, IAH, SCH.
OTHER NAMES: Saltwort, *Glaux maritima*

Spotted Loosestrife • **Lysimachia punctata***

Perennial herb of old fields and roadsides, up to 1 m tall. **Flowers** yellow, in axillary whorls; *petals 12–16 mm long with stalked glands and a fringe of hairs along the margin*; pedicels 1–2 cm long; sepals 5–10 mm long, green. **Leaves** 5–10 cm long, usually in whorls of 3 or 4, with minute, translucent or colored dots. **Stems** *pubescent*.
OCCURRENCE: Uncommon; MDI.
OTHER NAMES: Large Yellow-loosestrife

Whorled Loosestrife • ***Lysimachia quadrifolia***

Perennial herb of open forests, 0.2–1 m tall. **Flowers** yellow, in axillary whorls; *petals entire*, 6–8 mm long, *with dark lines*; sepals 2–5 mm long. **Leaves** *whorled*, with minute, translucent or colored dots, 3–10 cm long and 1–2.5 cm wide, *hairy beneath*.
OCCURRENCE: Occasional; MDI, IAH, SCH.
OTHER NAMES: Four-leaved Loosestrife, Whorled Yellow-loosestrife

Swamp Candles • *Lysimachia terrestris*

Perennial herb of wetlands, 0.2–1 m tall. **Flowers** *yellow with black or red streaks*, the uppermost subtended by long and narrow leaf-like bracts, in a terminal raceme 5–30 cm long. **Leaves** *usually opposite*, with minute translucent or colored dots, 3.5–10 cm long and 4–16 mm wide, *often with small bulbils emerging from the axils later in the season* (see upper left photo).

OCCURRENCE: Occasional; MDI, IAH, SCH.

OTHER NAMES: Yellow Loosestrife, Swamp Loosestrife, Swamp Yellow Loosestrife

Tufted Loosestrife • *Lysimachia thyrsiflora*

Perennial herb of marshes and bogs, 0.2–1.7 m tall. **Flowers** yellow, *in short, dense, axillary racemes from middle and lower leaves; petals entire, narrow,* 3–5 mm long; *stamens usually longer than petals.* **Leaves** opposite or whorled, with minute colored dots, sometimes pubescent along mid-vein beneath, 5–15 cm long and 1–5.5 cm wide. **Stems** pubescent.
OCCURRENCE: Rare; MDI.
OTHER NAMES: Tufted Yellow-loosestrife

AH

Garden Loosestrife • *_Lysimachia vulgaris_

Perennial herb of disturbed sites and stream margins, up to 1.5 m tall. **Flowers** bright yellow, ~15 mm wide, in terminal panicles; *sepals 3–5 mm long with dark red margins.* **Leaves** opposite or whorled, with minute translucent or colored dots, pubescent beneath, 5–13 cm long and 1.5–4 cm wide. **Stems** pubescent.
OCCURRENCE: Uncommon; MDI.
OTHER NAMES: Garden Yellow-loosestrife

Water-shield • ***Brasenia schreberi***

floating herb of quiet waters. **Flowers** *dull red-purple; petals 12–16 mm long.* **Leaves** *oval,* floating, dark green; *petioles attached to center of blade.*
OCCURRENCE: Occasional; MDI.
NOTES: Underwater portions of plant covered with a gelatinous film (see left photo).
OTHER NAMES: Purple Wen-dock

Yellow Pond Lily • ***Nuphar variegata***

Rhizomatous, perennial herb of lakes and ponds. **Flowers** *yellow, up to 8 cm wide.* **Leaves** floating, *with closed basal cleft;* petioles flat, their upper portion often winged. **Fruit** usually purple.
OCCURRENCE: Occasional; MDI, IAH.
OTHER NAMES: Spatterdock, Cow Lily, Beaver-root, Bobber, Pond-poppy, Bullhead Lily, Yellow Water-lily, Bullhead Pond Lily

Fragrant Water-lily • *Nymphaea odorata*

Aquatic, perennial herb of ponds and lakes. **Flowers** *white*, sometimes pinkish, showy, *7–20 cm wide, strongly fragrant*, with numerous petals tapering to the tip. **Leaves** nearly round, with a narrow cleft, long-stalked, *purplish on underside*. **OCCURRENCE:** Occasional; MDI, IAH. **NOTES:** The tuberous water-lily *Nymphaea odorata* ssp. *tuberosa* grows in Little Long Pond, Seal Harbor, MDI. Its petals are wide at the tip, flowers nearly scentless, and leaves often green on underside.
OTHER NAMES: Sweet-scented Water-lily, Pond-lily, White Water-lily

OLEACEAE • OLIVE FAMILY ▼

White Ash • *Fraxinus americana*

Deciduous tree of rich sites, up to 40 m tall. **Flowers** without petals; sepals *persistent*. **Leaves** opposite, pinnately compound; leaflets 7 (occasionally 5 or 9), without hairs beneath, with stalks 3–15 mm long. **Bark** of mature trunk with distinctive, diamond-patterned ridges. **Twigs** smooth, glabrous; *terminal buds low and rounded, wider than long*. **Fruit** 1–5 cm long, with a long terminal wing. **Seeds** rounded. **OCCURRENCE:** Occasional; MDI, IAH. **NOTES:** This is one of the first species to develop autumn color, and its purplish color is distinctive.

MA

Black Ash • *Fraxinus nigra*

Deciduous tree of swamps, up to 25 m tall. **Flowers** without petals; *sepals deciduous.* **Leaves** opposite, pinnately compound; leaflets 7–11, 11–14 cm long, *toothed, sessile except for the terminal one; hairs generally lacking on underside except where the leaflets meet the rachis.* **Bark** of *mature trunks with soft, corky ridges.* **Twigs** round, smooth, glabrous; *terminal buds dark brown, conical.* **Fruit** winged nearly to base, nearly flat.
OCCURRENCE: Rare; MDI.
NOTES: This is the species used by Native Americans in ash splint baskets.

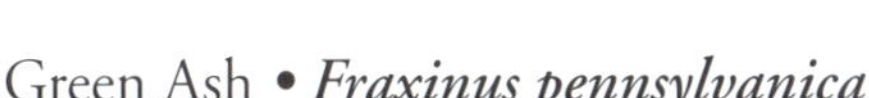

Green Ash • *Fraxinus pennsylvanica*

Deciduous tree of hardwood and mixed forests, up to 25 m tall. **Flowers** without petals; *sepals deciduous.* **Leaves** opposite, pinnately compound; leaflets 7–9, 11–14 cm long, *often hairy on underside,* all on short stalks. **Twigs** round, *pubescent; terminal buds dark brown, conical.* **Fruit** winged almost halfway to base, nearly flat.
OCCURRENCE: Uncommon; MDI.
OTHER NAMES: Red Ash

Amur Privet • ***Ligustrum obtusifolium**

Deciduous shrub, up to 5 m tall. **Flowers** white, in panicles <7 cm long; *lower part of flower tube 5–8 mm long*; anthers ~3 mm long; stigmas 2-lobed. **Leaves** opposite, *pubescent beneath*. **Twigs** *pubescent*. **Fruit** black, berry-like.
OCCURRENCE: Uncommon; IAH.
NOTES: This nonnative species is invasive.
OTHER NAMES: *Ligustrum amurense*

Common Privet • ***Ligustrum vulgare**

Deciduous shrub, up to 5 m tall. **Flowers** white, in panicles 3–6 cm long; *lower part of flower tube 2.5–3 mm long, approximately as long as petal lobes*; anthers 2 mm long; stigmas 2-lobed. **Leaves** opposite, lance-shaped to oblong, *glabrous*, 2.5–5.5 cm long. **Twigs** minutely pubescent or glabrous. **Fruit** black, berry-like.
OCCURRENCE: Uncommon; MDI.
NOTES: This nonnative species is invasive.
OTHER NAMES: Privet, European Privet

Fireweed • *Chamerion angustifolium*

Perennial herb of meadows and fields, commonly becoming established after fire or other disturbance, up to 3 m tall. **Flowers** *magenta, in a crowded, terminal raceme; petals 4, 1–2 cm long*, exceeding the sepals; styles longer than the stamens, with long, soft, straight hairs at base; stigmas 4-cleft. **Leaves** alternate, thin, green above, net-veined beneath, the largest 3–20 cm long, the lowest scale-like. **Stems** glabrous. **Fruit** a capsule 3–8 cm long. **Seeds** 1–3 mm long, with long, downy hairs.
OCCURRENCE: Occasional; MDI, SCH.
OTHER NAMES: Great Willow-herb, Wickup, *Epilobium angustifolium*

Dwarf Enchantress'-nightshade • *Circaea alpina*

Perennial herb of rich forests, 5–25 cm tall. **Flowers** *with 2 white petals, deeply cleft, 1–2.5 mm long*; anthers 0.2–0.3 mm long. **Leaves** *opposite, thin, 2–6 cm long*, sharply and coarsely wavy-margined or toothed; petioles long, slender. **Stems** weak, *unbranched below flowers*. **Fruit** *2–3 mm long and 0.9–1.3 mm wide, bristly with hooked hairs.*
OCCURRENCE: Occasional; MDI, IAH, SCH.
NOTES: Named for Circe, a sorceress in Homer's Odyssey.
OTHER NAMES: Dwarf Enchanter's-nightshade, Small Enchanter's-nightshade, Alpine Enchanter's-nightshade

Northern Willow-herb • ***Epilobium ciliatum***

Perennial herb of wet sites, 0.1–1 m tall. **Flowers** *pale pink, numerous; petals 4, deeply cleft*; sepals with sparse, long, soft, straight hairs; stigmas entire. **Leaves** thin, pale green, with gland-like projections on margins, the uppermost usually alternate, 1–12 cm long and 0.5–3.5 cm wide; petioles 2–10 mm long. **Stems** *4-angled*. **Fruit** a capsule 4–10 cm long. **Seeds** *with a whitish tuft of hair*.
OCCURRENCE: Occasional; MDI, IAH, SCH.
OTHER NAMES: Glandular Willow-herb, American Willow-herb, Seaside Basil, Fringed Willow-herb, *Epilobium glandulosum*

Purple-leaved Willow-herb • ***Epilobium coloratum***

Perennial herb of wet sites, 0.3–1 m tall. **Flowers** pink, numerous; petals 4, 3–5 mm long, cleft; stigmas entire. **Leaves** opposite, long-pointed at tip, *red-veined*, rugose, toothed. **Stems** 4-angled, minutely pubescent above with incurving, pale hairs. **Fruit** a capsule 3–5 cm long. **Seeds** ~1.5 mm long, *blackish with a red-brown tuft of hair*.
OCCURRENCE: Rare; MDI.
OTHER NAMES: Purple-veined Willow-herb, Eastern Willow-herb

CG

Narrow-leaved Willow-herb • *Epilobium leptophyllum*

Perennial herb of wet sites, 0.2–1 m tall. **Flowers** pink; petals 4, 4–6.5 mm long; sepals pubescent. **Leaves** *linear, 1–3 mm wide, pubescent above, with hairs curving in and downward,* margins in-rolled, entire or barely undulate; middle cauline leaves usually alternate. **Stems** *round, minutely pubescent with incurving hairs.* **Fruit** a pubescent capsule. **Seeds** ~1.5 mm long, tapering to a short neck. **OCCURRENCE:** Uncommon; MDI, SCH. **OTHER NAMES:** American Marsh Willow-herb, Bog Willow-herb

Swamp Willow-herb • *Epilobium palustre*

Stoloniferous, perennial herb of bogs and other wetlands, 10–80 cm tall. **Flowers** pink or white; inflorescence nodding in bud; petals 4, 4–8 mm long, deeply notched; sepals sparsely pubescent. **Leaves** 2–7 cm long and 0.2–1.5 cm wide, *with tiny incurving hairs near midrib, otherwise glabrous on top surface*; middle cauline leaves usually opposite. **Stems** round. **Fruit** a capsule 3–9 cm long, on a pedicel 1–5 cm long. **Seeds** 1.5–2 mm long. **OCCURRENCE:** Uncommon; MDI, IAH. **OTHER NAMES:** Marsh Willow-herb

Downy Willow-herb • *Epilobium strictum*

Rhizomatous, stoloniferous, perennial herb of thickets and wet meadows, 0.1–1.5 m tall. **Flowers** pink or white, with 4 notched petals 5–9 mm long. **Leaves** entire or nearly entire, with slightly in-rolled margins, 2–4 cm long and 3–8 mm wide, *with grayish, velvety, short pubescence*; the uppermost alternate. **Stems** with velvety pubescence; *hairs divergent*. **Fruit** a capsule with *velvety pubescence*. **Seeds** ~2 mm long, rounded above to a short neck.
OCCURRENCE: Uncommon; MDI.
OTHER NAMES: Northeast Willow-herb

AH

AH

Common Evening-primrose • *Oenothera biennis*

Biennial or short-lived perennial herb of dry, open, sometimes sandy, soils, up to 2 m tall. **Flowers** *yellow, pubescent with some gland-tipped hairs; petals 4, 1–2.5 cm long; sepals with expanded lobes 1–2.5 cm long*; stamens all the same length, with anthers 3–11 mm long. **Leaves** alternate, thin, unevenly small-toothed, mostly 10–20 cm long. **Stems** green to purple-tinged. **Fruit** *an ascending, cylindric, pubescent capsule 1–4 cm long.*
OCCURRENCE: Uncommon; MDI, SCH.
OTHER NAMES: Evening-primrose, King's-cureall, Yellow Evening-primrose

Southern Sundrops • **Oenothera fruticosa***

Perennial herb of open woods, fields, and roadsides, up to 1 m tall. **Flowers** *yellow, in a compact inflorescence; petals 4, notched, 10–25 mm long*; anthers 4–6 mm long. **Leaves** alternate, entire or nearly so, usually <6 cm long. **Fruit** *a 4-winged or distinctly 4-angled capsule 4–10 mm long*, with straight, stiff, sharp, appressed hairs.
OCCURRENCE: Uncommon; MDI.
OTHER NAMES: Narrow-leaved Evening-primrose

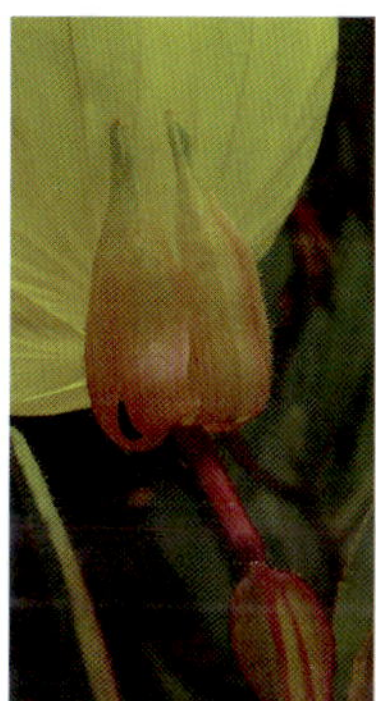

Northern Evening-primrose • ***Oenothera parviflora***

Biennial or short-lived perennial herb of gravelly or sandy soils, 10–80 cm tall. **Flowers** yellow, *opening at night*; petals 4, 1.2–2 cm long; *stamens all the same length*, with anthers 4–7.5 mm long; *sepals with a minute, knob-like appendage just below the tip* (see upper left photo). **Leaves** alternate, thick, stiff, *usually with a red tint*, minutely toothed. **Stems** pubescent above with spreading hairs. **Fruit** a capsule 1.5–4 cm long and 6–10 mm wide. **Seeds** 1.6–2.2 mm long.
OCCURRENCE: Occasional; MDI.
OTHER NAMES: Cross-shaped Evening-primrose, Small-flowered Evening-primrose, *Oenothera cruciata*

Small Sundrops • *Oenothera perennis*

Perennial herb of dry or wet sites, 20–80 cm tall. **Flowers** yellow, scattered, often drooping in bud; petals 4, *3–10 mm long*; sepals with lobes 5–8 mm long; *stamens of 2 lengths*, with anthers 1.2–2.5 mm long. **Leaves** alternate, reduced upward, 1–6 cm long. **Fruit** a 4-winged or quadrangular capsule 4–11 mm long and 3–3.5 mm wide. **OCCURRENCE:** Occasional; MDI, SCH. **OTHER NAMES:** Little Sundrops, Little Evening-primrose

ORCHIDACEAE • ORCHID FAMILY ▼

Dragon's-mouth • *Arethusa bulbosa*

Perennial herb of bogs, 12–25 cm tall. **Flowers** magenta-pink, *one per stem*. **Leaves** folded, grass-like, 0.2–0.4 cm wide, expanding after flowering to 0.3–1.2 cm wide.
OCCURRENCE: Occasional; MDI, IAH, SCH.
OTHER NAMES: Arethusa, Swamp-pink

CWG

CWG

Grass-pink • *Calopogon tuberosus*

Perennial herb of bogs and wet meadows, 12–75 cm tall. **Flowers** *magenta-pink,* ~2.5 cm wide, sessile, *with a yellow crest on top lip, 2–4 per stem,* in a short raceme. **Leaves** 1 or 2 per stem, slender and grass-like, 3–45 cm long and 0.3–4 cm wide, shorter than height of plant.
OCCURRENCE: Occasional; MDI, IAH, SCH.
OTHER NAMES: Tuberous Grass-pink, *Calopogon pulchellus*

Early Coral-root • *Corallorhiza trifida*

Saprophytic, perennial herb of thickets, bogs, and forests, 5–30 cm tall. **Flowers** 2–15 per stalk, yellow-green to brown, the lowest modified petal 3.5–5 mm long; blooming mid-May to mid-June. **Leaves** reduced and scale-like. **Stems** *yellowish, lacking chlorophyll.*
OCCURRENCE: Uncommon; MDI.
OTHER NAMES: Northern Coral-root, Pale Coral-root

Pink Lady's-slipper • *Cypripedium acaule*

Perennial herb of dry woods, 10–55 cm tall. **Flowers** pink, sometimes white, solitary, *the lip, 3–6 cm long, forming an inflated pouch with a cleft in the center.* **Leaves** *basal only, usually* 2, 10–30 cm long and 5–13 cm wide, *creased at veins* forming subtle ridges.
OCCURRENCE: Occasional; MDI, IAH.
OTHER NAMES: Moccasin flower, Stemless Lady's-slipper

Helleborine • **Epipactis helleborine*

Perennial herb of dry or wet sites, 10–80 cm tall. **Flowers** *yellow-green with some pink,* 1–3 cm wide, 15–50 borne in an often one-sided spike. **Leaves** 3–7, *alternate,* 10–18 cm long and 2.5–4 cm wide, egg-shaped or lance-shaped, *clasping the stem.*
OCCURRENCE: Uncommon; MDI.
NOTES: This species is our only nonnative orchid within Acadia National Park. Once established, it can be invasive.
OTHER NAMES: Broad-leaved Helleborine

Downy Rattlesnake-plantain • *Goodyera pubescens*

Rhizomatous, perennial herb of rich woods, often forming dense mats, 15–50 cm tall. **Flowers** white, pubescent, *in a dense, cylindrical, spike-like raceme.* **Leaves** deep green, egg-shaped, 4–10 cm long and 2–4 cm wide, *with distinct, fine, white, netted veins.*
OCCURRENCE: Rare; MDI.

Dwarf Rattlesnake-plantain • *Goodyera repens*

Rhizomatous, perennial herb of coniferous forests and rich woods, often forming dense mats, 5–25 cm tall. **Flowers** white, pubescent, in a distinctly one-sided spike-like raceme; *pouch as deep as long; anthers blunt.* **Leaves** *3–6, basal only, 0.5–2 cm wide and 1–4 cm long, deep green with distinct, netted, white veins,* egg-shaped.
OCCURRENCE: Uncommon; MDI, IAH.
OTHER NAMES: Lesser Rattlesnake-plantain

Checkered Rattlesnake-plantain • *Goodyera tesselata*

Rhizomatous, perennial herb of dry or wet forests and woodlands, often forming dense mats, 12–30 cm tall. **Flowers** white, pubescent, loosely spiraled on a spike-like raceme; *pouch longer than deep; anthers with pointed tips.* **Leaves** basal only, egg-shaped, 2–8 cm long and 1–2.5 cm wide, *dull green with pale white veining.*
OCCURRENCE: Uncommon; IAH.
OTHER NAMES: Alloploid Rattlesnake-plantain

DSC

AH

Heart-leaved Twayblade • *Listera cordata*

Perennial herb of damp, mossy forests, 10–40 cm tall. **Flowers** *purple,* 5–40, in a terminal raceme; *lip 3–5 mm long, deeply cleft, about as long as the petals;* lateral petals 2–2.5 m long. **Leaves** opposite, entire, ~2 cm wide and 1–3 cm long, *with a cordate base.*
OCCURRENCE: Uncommon; MDI.

AH

AH

Green Adder's-mouth • *Malaxis unifolia*

Perennial herb of swamps, bogs, and shores, 8–25 cm tall. **Flowers** *tiny, greenish, many in a compact raceme 2–8 cm long; flower lip 3-toothed at tip*. **Leaves** *solitary*, entire, oval to lance-shaped, *borne at center of stem*, up to 9 cm long and 6 cm wide. **Stems** swollen at the base.
OCCURRENCE: Uncommon; MDI, IAH, SCH.

CWG

Green Woodland Orchis • *Platanthera clavellata*

Perennial herb of wet sands and shores, 10–40 cm tall. **Flowers** bilaterally symmetric, *greenish white, twisted to one side*; spur 7–12 mm long, slender, swollen at the tip, curving. **Leaves** alternate, entire, *with one well developed one at or below the middle of the stem, the others much reduced*.
OCCURRENCE: Uncommon; MDI, IAH, SCH.
OTHER NAMES: Club-spur Orchid, Little Club-spur Orchid, *Habenaria clavellata*

Large Purple-fringed Orchis • *Platanthera grandiflora*

Perennial herb of rich forests and wet meadows, 0.5–1.5 m tall. **Flowers** magenta-pink, in a loose raceme 3–9 cm wide; lip 18–25 mm long, *fringed, with the lobes curving forward*; sepals 6–10 mm long. **Leaves** alternate, entire, *the lowest lance-shaped* to oval, 1.5–7 cm wide and 8–24 cm long, the uppermost much reduced and narrow.

OCCURRENCE: Uncommon; MDI.

OTHER NAMES: Greater Purple-fringed Orchid, *Habenaria fimbriata*

Ragged Orchis • *Platanthera lacera*

Perennial herb of wet woods and meadows, 20–80 cm tall. **Flowers** *greenish white, in a terminal raceme 5–15 cm long; lip deeply 3-lobed and each lobe deeply fringed*. **Leaves** alternate, 3–6, entire, the lowest lance-shaped to oval, 8–24 cm long and 2.5–5 cm wide, the uppermost much reduced and narrow.

OCCURRENCE: Rare; MDI.

OTHER NAMES: Ragged-fringed Orchid, Green-fringed Orchis, *Habenaria lacera*

Small Purple-fringed Orchis • *Platanthera psycodes*

Perennial herb of wet woods, meadows, and shores, 0.3–1 m tall. **Flowers** *magenta-pink, ~2 cm long*, in a loose, terminal raceme 2.5–4 cm wide; *spur 1.2–1.8 cm long, projecting from under the lip*. **Leaves** *2–6, wider near the tip than the middle*, 8–24 cm long and 1.5–7 cm wide.

OCCURRENCE: Uncommon; MDI.

OTHER NAMES: Soldier's-plume, Butterfly Orchid, Smaller Purple-fringed Orchis, Lesser Purple-fringed Orchid, *Habenaria psycodes*

CG

Rose Pogonia • *Pogonia ophioglossoides*

Perennial herb of bogs, 8–35 cm tall. **Flowers** *pink, 1–3, terminal, ~2 cm long, with a yellow bearded lip, subtended by a small leaf-like bract*; sepals and petals approximately equal in size. **Leaves** *solitary*, oblong to lance-shaped, 6–10 cm long and 1–2.5 cm wide, clasping middle of stem, present at flowering time.
OCCURRENCE: Uncommon; MDI, IAH, SCH.
OTHER NAMES: Snakemouth, Beard-flower

Nodding Ladies'-tresses • *Spiranthes cernua*

Perennial herb of open sites, shores, and bogs, 10–50 cm tall. **Flowers** *whitish with green-yellow markings on the top, slightly nodding, in a spiraled spike; blooming late summer and fall.* **Leaves** long and narrow, 3–5, the largest up to 26 cm long and 2 cm wide, *becoming reduced to scale-like near the top of the stem.*
OCCURRENCE: Uncommon; MDI.
OTHER NAMES: Common Ladies'-tresses, Screw-auger

Small-flowered Gerardia • *Agalinis paupercula*

Annual herb of wet, open areas, 5–80 cm tall. **Flowers** *magenta, 1–2 cm wide*, pubescent inside, scattered along stem; sepals with lobes 2–4 mm long; anthers pubescent; pedicels 1–5 mm long. **Leaves** opposite (may be alternate on branches), sessile, 2–4.5 cm long and 1–2.7 mm wide. **Stems** *4-angled*. **Fruit** a capsule, longer than flower tube. **Seeds** 1–1.5 mm long.
OCCURRENCE: Rare; MDI.
OTHER NAMES: Small-flowered Agalinis, *Gerardia paupercula*

Beech-drops • *Epifagus virginiana*

Parasitic or saprophytic herb of dry, beech woodlands, 15–45 cm tall. **Flowers** whitish with purple-brown blotches or stripes, only those toward branch tip opening fully; *pedicels minutely glandular-pubescent on side near stem*. **Leaves** without chlorophyll, alternate, *reduced to scales*, 2–4 mm long. **Stems** *reddish purple to yellow-brown with fine purple lines, persisting to next season*, branching from near the base of plant; upper portion usually glandular-pubescent.
OCCURRENCE: Occasional; MDI, IAH.

Common Eyebright • **Euphrasia nemorosa*

Annual herb of fields and roadsides, 10–45 cm tall. **Flowers** white with purple lines, *5–10 mm long*, with lower lip longer than upper, borne singly in leaf axils; sepals pubescent. **Leaves** opposite (although uppermost may be alternate), pubescent, palmately veined, coarsely toothed. **Stems** with thin, recurving hairs.
OCCURRENCE: Occasional; MDI, IAH, SCH.
OTHER NAMES: *Euphrasia americana*

Rand's Eyebright • *Euphrasia randii*

Annual herb of coastal headlands, 5–40 cm tall. **Flowers** mostly white to magenta to purple, *2.5–4.5 mm long*, strongly 2-lipped, *axillary*. **Leaves** opposite (although uppermost may be alternate), palmately veined, *coarsely toothed with 3–5 rounded teeth on each side*. **Stems** with thin, recurving hairs.
OCCURRENCE: Uncommon; MDI, IAH, SCH.
OTHER NAMES: Nova Scotian Eyebright

Drug Eyebright • ***Euphrasia stricta**

Annual herb of dry, open sites, 15–40 cm tall. **Flowers** white with purple lines, *5–10 mm long*, solitary, axillary, 2-lipped; *sepals with lobes tapering to bristles and overtopping capsule.* **Leaves** opposite (although uppermost may be alternate), palmately veined, *coarsely toothed with large teeth tapering to bristles.* **Stems** with thin, recurving hairs.
OCCURRENCE: Uncommon; SCH.
OTHER NAMES: *Euphrasia rigidula*

Cow-wheat • **Melampyrum lineare**

Annual herb of dry woodlands and forests, 10–30 cm tall. **Flowers** *white with yellow tip*, 1–2 cm long, glabrous, *on short stalks in axils of upper leaves; strongly 2-lipped, the uppermost lip 2-lobed*, the lowest 3-lobed; anthers pubescent. **Leaves** opposite, *the lowest lance-shaped, entire, the uppermost with few pointed teeth at base*; petioles short. **Fruit** a laterally flattened capsule. **Seeds** white, becoming dark with age, 2–4 mm long.
OCCURRENCE: Occasional; MDI, IAH, SCH.
OTHER NAMES: American Cow-wheat

Red Bartsia • *Odontites vernus*

Annual herb of roadsides and disturbed sites, 10–50 cm tall. **Flowers** *rose or pink*, <1 cm long, *pubescent, borne in leafy, spike-like racemes, the lower lip 3-lobed*; anthers pubescent. **Leaves** opposite, lance-shaped, sessile, 1–3 cm long, hairy, with 2 or 3 blunt teeth on each side. **Stems** with downward-pointing hairs.
OCCURRENCE: Uncommon; IAH.
OTHER NAMES: Red False Bartsia, *Odontites serotina*

Wood Betony • *Pedicularis canadensis*

Rhizomatous, perennial herb of dry woods, 15–40 cm tall. **Flowers** *reddish to yellow*, 18–25 mm long, *in dense, terminal, spike-like racemes 3–5 cm long*. **Leaves** alternate, *pinnately lobed over halfway to midrib, thus looking fern-like*. **Stems** hairy above. **Fruit** a capsule, much longer than the sepals.
OCCURRENCE: Rare; MDI.
OTHER NAMES: Common Lousewort, Chickens'-heads, Forest Lousewort

AH

CWG

AH

Yellow Rattle • *Rhinanthus minor*

Parasitic, annual herb of dry, open sites, 10–60 cm tall. **Flowers** *yellow*, 1–2 cm long; *sepals bright green and partially inflated in flower*, later distinctly enlarged and inflated in fruit, becoming dry and tan-brown with age. **Leaves** opposite, toothed, pinnately veined. **Fruit** *a flat capsule with large seeds that rattle inside.*
OCCURRENCE: Occasional; MDI, IAH, SCH.
OTHER NAMES: Common Yellow Rattle, Little Yellow Rattle, *Rhinanthus crista-galli*

OXALIDACEAE • WOOD-SORREL FAMILY ▼

Northern Wood-sorrel • *Oxalis montana*

Creeping, perennial herb of wet, shady forests, 5–15 cm tall. **Flowers** *white with pink veins, ~2 cm wide, 1 per stalk.* **Leaves** *basal only*, compound, with 3 heart-shaped leaflets. **Fruit** a pod splitting down the sides.
OCCURRENCE: Occasional; MDI, IAH, SCH.
OTHER NAMES: Common Wood-sorrel, Northern Wood Sorrel, Wood-shamrock

Yellow Wood-sorrel • *Oxalis stricta*

Erect, rhizomatous, perennial herb of dry, open sites and roadsides, 7–50 cm tall. **Flowers** *yellow, 1–2 cm wide, up to 9 per stalk; petals 5, 4–9 mm long.* **Leaves** compound; leaflets 3, 1–2 cm wide. **Stems** pubescent.
OCCURRENCE: Occasional; MDI, IAH, SCH.
OTHER NAMES: Common Yellow Wood-sorrel

PAPAVERACEAE • POPPY FAMILY ▼

Climbing Fumitory • *Adlumia fungosa*

Twining, *biennial vine*, becoming established after fire or other disturbance. **Flowers** *white to pink or purple*, 1–2 cm long, in clusters drooping from axils; petals 4, fused together forming a heart-shaped oval sac. **Leaves** 3 times pinnately compound; leaflets cut-lobed and delicate; petioles twining and climbing over other vegetation. **Fruit** a few-seeded capsule.
OCCURRENCE: Rare; MDI.
OTHER NAMES: Mountain-fringe, Allegheny Vine, Canary-vine

AH

Pale Corydalis • *Capnoides sempervirens*

Erect, annual or biennial, branched herb of dry, rocky outcrops, 30–80 cm tall. **Flowers** *pink with yellow tips, 10–17 mm long,* bilaterally symmetric, with a basal spur. **Leaves** *finely divided, light green or gray-green.* **Fruit** an erect, thin, cylindrical capsule 3–5 cm long and up to 2 mm wide.
OCCURRENCE: Uncommon; MDI.
OTHER NAMES: Pink Corydalis, Rock-harlequin, Tall Corydalis, *Corydalis sempervirens*

Celandine • **Chelidonium majus*

Biennial herb of wet, disturbed areas, usually near houses, 30–90 cm tall. **Flowers** *yellow,* 20–25 mm wide, with 4 petals and 2 sepals, in small umbels. **Leaves** green with a *white cast,* alternate, pinnately compound; *leaflets irregularly lobed.* **Stems** *with bright yellow or orange latex.*
OCCURRENCE: Uncommon; MDI.
NOTES: All parts of plant poisonous.
OTHER NAMES: Greater Celandine

Greater Water-starwort • *Callitriche heterophylla*

Aquatic herb of muddy ponds, 10–20 cm long. **Flowers** without petals or sepals, with 1 stamen, subtended by a pair of horn-shaped bracteoles, growing singly or in pairs in the leaf axils. **Leaves** opposite, entire, crowded in floating rosettes. **Fruit** 0.9–1.4 mm long and 0.8–1.3 mm wide, *the margins without wings or sharp edges, with pit-like markings not aligned in vertical rows.*

OCCURRENCE: Rare; MDI.

OTHER NAMES: Water-starwort

CG

Vernal Water-starwort • *Callitriche palustris*

Aquatic herb of springs, small streams, and shores, 10–20 cm long. **Flowers** without petals or sepals; subtended by a pair of horn-shaped bracteoles, growing singly or in pairs in leaf axils; stamens 1. **Leaves** *opposite, pale green,* crowded, in *floating rosettes,* entire. **Fruit** 1–1.4 mm long and 0.8–1.2 mm wide, *the margins with wings, with pit-like markings aligned in vertical rows.*

OCCURRENCE: Uncommon; MDI.

White Turtlehead • *Chelone glabra*

Perennial herb of brooks and wet thickets, 0.4–2 m tall. **Flowers** *white*, sometimes with pink, purple, or green-yellow on top, in spikes 3–8 cm long; *lower lip with white or pale yellow hairs*; anthers woolly. **Leaves** opposite, toothed. **Fruit** a capsule 1–1.5 cm long. **Seeds** winged.
OCCURRENCE: Uncommon; MDI.
OTHER NAMES: Balmony

Pink Turtlehead • **Chelone lyonii*

Perennial herb of shores and thickets, up to 1 m tall. **Flowers** *rose-pink to purple*, with 4 long stamens and 1 short stamen; *lower lip with deep yellow hairs*; anthers woolly. **Leaves** opposite, rounded at base, toothed, 3–10 cm wide; petioles 1–4 cm long. **Seeds** winged.
OCCURRENCE: Rare; MDI.

Purple Foxglove • ***Digitalis purpurea**

Biennial herb of dry, mixed woods, 0.5–1.8 m tall. **Flowers** *5-lobed, magenta or white with purple spots inside*, with 2 stigmas; stamens 4, with divergent pollen sacs. **Leaves** *alternate, tapering gradually to base, with rounded teeth on margin, hairy beneath.*
OCCURRENCE: Uncommon; MDI, IAH.
OTHER NAMES: Common Foxglove

Butter-and-eggs • ***Linaria vulgaris**

Perennial herb of roadsides and disturbed sites, 0.3–1 m tall. **Flowers** *yellow with orange palate*, 1.5–3 cm long, in a dense, terminal raceme; *spur straight; upper lip 2-lobed; lower lip 3-parted.* **Leaves** *alternate above*, whorled below, *blue-green*, 3–8 cm long and 2–4 mm wide. **Fruit** a capsule 8–12 mm long. **Seeds** flat, winged.
OCCURRENCE: Occasional; MDI, SCH.
OTHER NAMES: Common Toadflax, Wild Snapdragon, Butter-and-eggs Toadflax

Old Field Toadflax • *Nuttallanthus canadensis*

Annual or biennial herb of dry areas, sandy roadsides, and fields, 10–75 cm tall. **Flowers** *light blue*, 5–11 mm long, *lower lip with 2 short, white ridges*; spur thread-like, 2–9 mm long. **Leaves** 1–3.5 cm long and 1–2.5 mm wide. **Fruit** a capsule 2–4 mm long. **Seeds** angled.
OCCURRENCE: Occasional; MDI, SCH.
OTHER NAMES: Blue Toadflax, *Linaria canadensis*

Many-seeded Plantain • **Plantago intermedia*

Annual or perennial herb of shorelines, 1–50 cm tall. **Flowers** mostly white, in dense spikes usually 5–30 cm long; bracts and sepals keeled. **Leaves** basal only, somewhat fleshy, *usually pubescent on one or both sides*, sometimes toothed, 4–18 cm long and 1.5–11 cm wide; *petioles short*. **Fruit** *a capsule with 14–34 seeds, opening near or slightly below middle, generally below the sepal tips*. **Seeds** 1–1.7 mm long.
OCCURRENCE: Uncommon; MDI.
OTHER NAMES: *Plantago major* var. *intermedia*

AH

AH

English Plantain • ***_Plantago lanceolata_**

Perennial herb of lawns and disturbed sites, 20–80 cm tall. **Flowers** *with slight fragrance*, ~5 mm wide; sepals 3–3.5 mm long. **Leaves** *lance-shaped, with 3–5 veins, 5–40 cm long and 6–40 mm wide*. **Fruit** a capsule 3–4 mm long. **Seeds** *deeply concave on inner face, shiny black*, ~2 mm long.
OCCURRENCE: Uncommon; SCH.
OTHER NAMES: Ribgrass, Buckhorn, Ripplegrass

AH

AH

Common Plantain • ***_Plantago major_**

Annual or perennial herb of roadsides and lawns, 1–50 cm tall. **Flowers** dirty-white, in dense spikes usually 5–30 cm long; bracts and sepals keeled. **Leaves** basal only, somewhat fleshy, sometimes toothed, 4–18 cm long and 1.5–11 cm wide; *petioles long*. **Fruit** *a capsule with 4–13 seeds, opening near or slightly below middle, generally below the sepal tips*. **Seeds** 1–1.7 mm long.
OCCURRENCE: Occasional; MDI, IAH, SCH.
OTHER NAMES: Grand Plantain, White-man's-foot

Seaside Plantain • *Plantago maritima*

Perennial herb of seaside headlands and rocky beaches, up to 40 cm tall. **Flowers** brown, in spikes 0.5–10 cm long; petals 1–1.5 mm long, pubescent on outer surface; stamens pale yellow. **Leaves** 5–20 cm long and 1–12 mm wide, *fleshy, thick, ascending*. **Fruit** a capsule opening near middle, with 2–4 seeds. **Seeds** 2–2.5 mm long, *flat on inner face*.

OCCURRENCE: Occasional; MDI, IAH, SCH.

OTHER NAMES: Goose-tongue, *Plantago juncoides*

Hoary Plantain • **Plantago media*

Perennial herb of lawns and disturbed sites, up to 30 cm tall. **Flowers** *white, fragrant, in dense spikes 2–10 cm long at maturity*; sepals 4, distinct, strongly keeled, 2.2–2.5 mm long. **Leaves** *pubescent on both sides*, 5–20 cm long; *usually growing flat on the ground*. **Fruit** *a thickly elliptic capsule*, 3 mm long. **Seeds** *slightly concave on inner face*, ~2 mm long.

OCCURRENCE: Uncommon; MDI.

AH

AH

Corn Speedwell • ***Veronica arvensis**

Annual herb of dry, disturbed sites, 5–40 cm tall. **Flowers** sessile to short-stalked, *violet-blue; sepals unequal in length.* **Leaves** more or less with long, soft, straight hairs, *the lowest rounded or oval, the uppermost smaller, sessile, lance-shaped.* **Fruit** *a hairy capsule, as long as wide, with style equaling or longer than the lobes of the capsule, with long, soft, straight hairs.*
OCCURRENCE: Rare; MDI.

Bird's-eye Speedwell • ***Veronica chamaedrys**

Perennial herb of fields and disturbed sites, 10–40 cm tall. **Flowers** *blue with a white center,* 8–12 mm wide, in axillary racemes of 10–20; styles 3–5 mm long; *pedicels 5–9 mm long.* **Leaves** thin, egg-shaped, sessile or short-stalked, 1–3 cm long and 8–20 mm wide, *usually with 5–11 rounded teeth per side.* **Stems** often with two opposite rows of long, white hairs.
OCCURRENCE: Occasional; MDI.
OTHER NAMES: Germander Speedwell, Angel's-eye, Bird's-eye

Long-leaved Speedwell • **Veronica longifolia*

Perennial herb of roadsides and thickets, 0.3–1.5 m tall. **Flowers** pale blue, 8–10 mm wide, in a spike-like, terminal raceme subtended by small, leafy bracts; petals partially fused into a tube, the distinct portion 4–5 mm long, the throat with hairs. **Leaves** *opposite or in whorls of three,* 4–10 cm long, with fine, short hairs, sharply toothed; *petioles short.* **Fruit** a pubescent capsule 3 mm long, *half as long as persistent style.*
OCCURRENCE: Uncommon; MDI.
OTHER NAMES: Garden Speedwell

Common Speedwell • **Veronica officinalis*

Mat-forming, perennial herb of dry fields and open woodlands, 10–30 cm tall. **Flowers** *light blue,* 4–8 mm wide, in dense racemes; styles 2.5–4.5 mm long; *pedicels ~2 mm long, shorter than subtending bracts.* **Leaves** *shallowly toothed,* thick, pubescent, 1.5–5 cm long and 0.6–3 cm wide; *petioles short.* **Stems** *hairy, trailing, with ascending tip.* **Fruit** a capsule 4 mm long, *distinctly longer than subtending sepals.*
OCCURRENCE: Common; MDI, IAH.
OTHER NAMES: Gypsyweed, Heath Speedwell

Purslane Speedwell • *Veronica peregrina*

Annual herb of disturbed sites, 10–40 cm tall. **Flowers** *white, ~2 mm wide, on pedicels 1–2 mm long*; styles 0.1–0.3 mm long. **Leaves** *rounded above and tapering to base*, 0.5–3 cm long and 1–8 mm wide. **Stems** *glabrous, fleshy*, with gland-tipped hairs. **Fruit** *a capsule 3–4 mm long with notch at tip*, sometimes with gland-tipped hairs.
OCCURRENCE: Occasional; MDI, SCH.
OTHER NAMES: Neckweed

Marsh Speedwell • *Veronica scutellata*

Weak-stemmed, perennial herb of sandy shores and swamps, 10–70 cm tall. **Flowers** bluish, 6–10 mm wide, in axillary racemes; styles 2–4 mm long; *sepals 4, 2–3.5 mm long and reflexed in fruit, shorter than capsule*; pedicels 6–17 mm long. **Leaves** *sessile, long and narrow to lance-shaped, entire*, 1.5–9 cm long and 1–15 mm wide. **Fruit** *a flat capsule 2.5–4 mm long, wider than long.*
OCCURRENCE: Uncommon; MDI.
OTHER NAMES: Narrow-leaved Speedwell

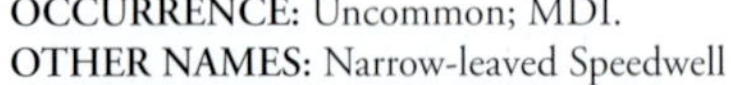

Thyme-leaved Speedwell • *Veronica serpyllifolia*

Perennial herb of lawns and wet woods, 10–30 cm tall. **Flowers** *white or pale blue with darker blue to purple lines*, 2–6 mm wide, in *loose, terminal racemes; rachis and pedicels pubescent.* **Leaves** egg-shaped, 1–2.5 cm long and 5–15 mm wide, the uppermost bract-like. **Stems** with fine, short hairs; *lower branches creeping or prostrate.* **Fruit** a notched capsule 3–4 mm wide, *wider than long, pubescent or with gland-tipped hairs.*
OCCURRENCE: Occasional; MDI.

Culver's Root • **Veronicastrum virginicum*

Perennial herb of rich forests and wet meadows, up to 2 m tall. **Flowers** *white or pinkish, tubular, 7–9 mm wide, in erect, terminal spikes 5–15 cm long.* **Leaves** *in whorls of 3–7*, sharply toothed, lance-shaped; petioles 3–10 mm long. **Fruit** a capsule 4–5 mm long.
OCCURRENCE: Rare; MDI.
OTHER NAMES: Culver's Psychic

Sea-lavender • *Limonium carolinianum*

Perennial herb of *tidal marshes and saline shores*, 15–60 cm tall. **Flowers** *lavender, very small, arranged on one side of branches* in an airy, much-branched cluster. **Leaves** spatula-shaped, with 1 rib, often gently crinkled, mainly in a basal rosette. **OCCURRENCE:** Occasional; MDI, SCH. **OTHER NAMES:** *Limonium nashii*

Fringed Polygala • *Polygala paucifolia*

Rhizomatous, perennial herb of wet forest edges and openings, 7–15 cm tall. **Flowers** *rose-purple*, axillary; *petals 3, all fused into a fringed lower tube 1–2 cm long*; sepals 5, the 3 outer ones tiny and the 2 lateral ones larger and fringed at the tips. **Leaves** *few, alternate, egg-shaped, clustered at stem tips*. **Fruit** a notched, compressed capsule with winged edges. **OCCURRENCE:** Rare; MDI. **OTHER NAMES:** flowering Wintergreen, Gaywings, Bird-on-the-wing, Fringed Milkwort

Purple Milkwort • *Polygala sanguinea*

Perennial herb of wet meadows, 10–40 cm tall. **Flowers** *rose-purple, clustered in dense heads 1–4 cm long and 6–15 mm wide.* **Leaves** *lance-shaped, alternate.*
OCCURRENCE: Uncommon; MDI.
OTHER NAMES: Blood Milkwort

Buckwheat • **Fagopyrum esculentum*

Annual herb of old fields and disturbed sites, 0.2–2 m tall. **Flowers** white or pink, 5-parted. **Leaves** *alternate, arrow-shaped, sometimes with spreading basal lobes, the lowest stalked, the uppermost clasping the stem.* **Stems** pubescent. **Fruit** a 3-angled, brown achene.
OCCURRENCE: Uncommon; MDI.
OTHER NAMES: Garden Buckwheat, *Fagopyrum sagittatum*

Fringed Bindweed • *Fallopia cilinodis*

Perennial vine of dry, open sites, 1–2 m long. **Flowers** white, 1.5–2 mm wide, in a spike-like raceme 4–10 cm long. **Leaves** *heart-shaped to egg-shaped, sharp-pointed*, with long, soft, straight hairs beneath. **Stems** pubescent, often red; *upper nodes with a ring of reflexed bristles* (see lower right photo). **Fruit** *a smooth, black achene 3–4 mm long.*
OCCURRENCE: Occasional; MDI.
OTHER NAMES: Fringed Black-bindweed, *Polygonum cilinode*

Black Bindweed • **Fallopia convolvulus*

Annual vine of old fields and disturbed sites, up to 1 m long. **Flowers** *creamy-white*, in clusters of 3–6. **Leaves** heart-shaped to egg-shaped; *ocreae glabrous*. **Fruit** *a granular, dull black achene.*
OCCURRENCE: Occasional; MDI, SCH.
OTHER NAMES: *Polygonum convolvulus*

Japanese Knotweed • ***Fallopia japonica**

Rhizomatous, perennial herb of roadsides and old home sites, up to 3.5 m tall. **Flowers** *greenish white*, in spike-like racemes; stigmas minute, fringed. **Leaves** 5–15 cm long and 2–12 cm wide, with a truncate base; *ocreae thin*. **Stems** *with hollow internodes*. **Fruit** *a shiny, 3-angled achene*.
OCCURRENCE: Occasional; MDI, IAH.
NOTES: Aggressively invasive! This plant is capable of forming new plants from tiny root fragments only a few cells wide.
OTHER NAMES: fleece-flower, Mexican-bamboo, *Polygonum cuspidatum*

Water Smartweed • **Persicaria amphibia**

Perennial herb of swales, ditches, swamps, and shores. **Flowers** *deep pink to red, 2–3 mm long, in dense terminal racemes* 1–4 cm long and 1–2 cm wide. **Leaves** *pointed at tip*, 5–15 cm long, *glabrous in floating form, hairy in terrestrial form*.
OCCURRENCE: Uncommon; MDI.
OTHER NAMES: Amphibious Bistort, *Polygonum amphibium*

Carey's Knotweed • ***Persicaria careyi***

Annual herb of recently burned or disturbed areas and swamps, 0.1–1.5 m tall. **Flowers** white or pink, in *slender, cylindric, and often drooping racemes* 3–10 cm long; peduncles with stalked glands. **Leaves** *lance-shaped*, rough, with stiff hairs; *ocreae with coarse, spreading, stiff hairs and fringed with bristles.* **Stems** with bristly hairs, the upper portion with stalked glands. **Fruit** *a black, smooth, shiny achene* 1.8–2.4 mm long and 1.5–2 mm wide.
OCCURRENCE: Uncommon; MDI.
OTHER NAMES: Carey's Smartweed, *Polygonum careyi*

Common Smartweed • ****Persicaria hydropiper***

Annual herb of wet, open sites, 20–60 cm tall. **Flowers** white, *4-parted, in a nodding inflorescence; tepals dotted with glands.* **Leaves** *with peppery taste*, up to 9 cm long; ocreae sometimes with stiff, appressed hairs and a fringe of short hairs around the edge. **Stems** often reddish. **Fruit** *a dull, minutely granular, dark brown to black achene* 2.2–3.3 mm long.
OCCURRENCE: Uncommon; MDI.
OTHER NAMES: Water-pepper, Marsh-weed, Water-pepper Smartweed, *Polygonum hydropiper*

AH

AH

Nodding Smartweed • *Persicaria lapathifolia*

Annual herb of swamps, shores, and swales, up to 2.5 m tall. **Flowers** rose or white, 3–4 mm long, *in a dense, nodding inflorescence 1–8 cm long; tepals with an anchor-shaped vein.* **Leaves** variably pubescent, often lance-shaped and sharp pointed. **Fruit** a lens-shaped, shiny achene 1.7–3.2 mm long and 1.5–2.2 mm wide.
OCCURRENCE: Uncommon; MDI, IAH, SCH.
OTHER NAMES: Pale Smartweed, Willow-weed, Dock-leaved Smartweed, *Polygonum lapathifolium*

Lady's-thumb • **Persicaria maculosa*

Annual herb of roadsides and damp, open sites, 0.1–1 m tall. **Flowers** pink or rose, 2–3.5 mm long, *in a cylindric, dense, usually straight, inflorescence 1–4 cm long and 7–12 mm wide.* **Leaves** firm, 3–15 cm long and 5–30 mm wide, *often with a dark central blotch above*; ocreae with minute, straight, stiff, appressed hairs and a fringe of short hairs around the edge. **Stems** nearly glabrous. **Fruit** *a black, smooth, shiny achene* 1.8–3 mm long and 1.4–2.4 mm wide.
OCCURRENCE: Occasional; MDI, SCH.
OTHER NAMES: Heart's-ease, Black Heart, Lady's-thumb Smartweed, *Polygonum persicaria*

Pennsylvania Smartweed • *Persicaria pensylvanica*

Annual herb of sandy roadsides and damp, open sites, 0.2–2 m tall. **Flowers** *numerous, thick, erect, pink to purplish to white*, in spikes 1–6 cm long and 1–1.5 cm wide. **Leaves** lance-shaped, sharp pointed; *ocreae thin, becoming torn.* **Stems** *with gland-tipped hairs on upper portion.* **Fruit** a lens-shaped achene 2.3–3.7 mm wide.
OCCURRENCE: Uncommon; MDI.
OTHER NAMES: Pinkweed, Pink Knotweed, *Polygonum pensylvanicum*

AH

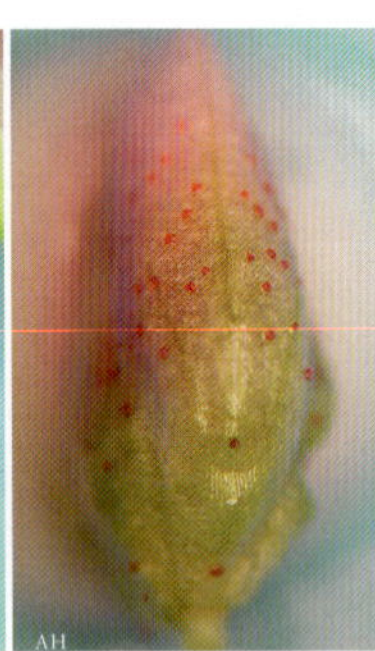
AH

AH AH

Arrow-leaved Tearthumb • *Persicaria sagittata*

Vine-like, annual herb of brackish marshes. **Flowers** pink to white; peduncles glabrous; *styles 3-cleft.* **Leaves** *arrowhead-shaped, with basal lobes directed back*, 3–10 cm long and 0.7–2.8 cm wide. **Stems** *4-angled, with reflexed prickles.* **Fruit** *a 3-angled achene 3–3.5 mm long.*
OCCURRENCE: Occasional; MDI.
OTHER NAMES: Arrow-vine, *Polygonum sagittatum*

Sand Jointweed • *Polygonum articulatum*

Annual herb of dry, sandy sites, 10–60 cm tall. **Flowers** white or pinkish, in an erect, terminal inflorescence; *pedicels strongly reflexed, 2–3 mm long.* **Leaves** *dropping early, 5–20 mm long and 0.5–1 mm wide.* **Fruit** *a 3-angled, smooth achene.*
OCCURRENCE: Uncommon; MDI, SCH.
OTHER NAMES: Nodeweed, Coastal Jointed Knotweed, *Polygonella articulata*

Prostrate Knotweed • **Polygonum aviculare*

Annual herb of disturbed, rarely coastal, sites, up to 10 cm tall. **Flowers** white, occasionally with pink or red tinge; tepals 5, *2.5–4 mm long, the outer 3 flat or folded, the inner 2 same length and width as outer ones.* **Leaves** subtending flowers usually smaller than cauline ones, the largest 1.8–5 cm long and 6–20 mm wide. **Stems** *often prostrate, mat-forming.* **Fruit** an achene 2.2–3.5 mm long, with *2 deeply concave sides, marked with parallel lines of short, rounded bumps or projections.*
OCCURRENCE: Occasional; MDI, SCH.
OTHER NAMES: Common Knotgrass, Doorweed, Dooryard Knotweed, *Polygonum arenastrum*

Box Knotweed • *Polygonum buxiforme*

Annual herb of salt marshes, sand dunes, and shorelines, up to 10 cm tall. **Flowers** white, with pink or red tinge; *tepals 2–3 mm long, outer 3 hood-shaped, wider and often longer than the 2 flat inner ones.* **Leaves** *elliptic, 6–30 mm long and 3–6 mm wide,* those subtending the flowers usually of same length as lower, cauline ones. **Stems** *prostrate, mat-forming.* **Fruit** *an irregularly roughened achene 2–3 mm long.*
OCCURRENCE: Uncommon; MDI.
OTHER NAMES: Prairie Knotweed, *Polygonum aviculare* var. *littorale*

Fowler's Knotweed • *Polygonum fowleri*

Annual herb of sea beaches and salt marshes, up to 50 cm tall. **Flowers** white, with pink or red tinge; *tepals 3–5 mm long, outer 3 hood-shaped, wider and often longer than the 2 flat inner ones.* **Leaves** *elliptic, fleshy, 8–30 mm long and 4–15 mm wide,* those subtending flowers usually of same length as lower, cauline ones. **Stems** *fleshy, ascending.* **Fruit** *a uniformly granular-roughened achene 2.8–4 mm long.*
OCCURRENCE: Uncommon; MDI.

Prolific Knotweed • *Polygonum ramosissimum*

Annual herb of saline or brackish shores and marshes, up to 1 m tall. **Flowers** white, with pink or red tinge; tepals 5, *the outer 3 hood-shaped, wider and often longer than the 2 flat inner ones.* **Leaves** *narrow and long, 8–30 mm long and 4–6 mm wide*, those subtending flowers usually smaller than lower, cauline ones. **Fruit** *a smooth or irregularly roughened achene <2 mm long in early season.*
OCCURRENCE: Rare; SCH.
OTHER NAMES: Yellow-flowered Knotweed, *Polygonum prolificum*

Field Sorrel • **Rumex acetosella*

Rhizomatous, perennial herb of disturbed sites and rock outcrops, 10–50 cm tall. **Flowers** reddish, nodding, on short pedicels. **Leaves** up to 4 cm long and 2–12 mm wide, *with an acid taste; basal lobes spreading or forward pointing.*
OCCURRENCE: Common; MDI, IAH, SCH.
NOTES: An invasive weed with edible leaves.
OTHER NAMES: Sheep Sorrel, Common Sorrel, Red Sorrel, Sheep Dock

Great Water Dock • *Rumex britannica*

Perennial herb of swales, swamps, and shores, 0.8–1.5 m tall. **Flowers** in whorls of 15–25; pedicels 1–4 mm long; *articulation point of pedicels indistinct, not swollen.* **Leaves** entire or with finely rounded teeth along margin. **Fruit** with 3 wing-like tepals; *tubercles 3, distinctly above the base of the associated tepal.*
OCCURRENCE: Occasional; MDI, IAH, SCH.
OTHER NAMES: Water Dock, *Rumex orbiculatus*

Curled Dock • **Rumex crispus*

Perennial herb of old fields, disturbed sites, and beaches, 0.4–1 m tall. **Flowers** in whorls of 10–25; pedicels 4–8 mm long, *with a visibly swollen articulation point.* **Leaves** *with crumpled and crisped margins,* the lowest 1.5–8 cm wide, narrowing to base. **Fruit** with 3 wing-like tepals; *tubercles 1–3, when 3, one distinctly larger than the others, the largest about half as long as associated tepal.*
OCCURRENCE: Occasional; MDI, IAH, SCH.
OTHER NAMES: Yellow Dock, Curly Dock, Sour Dock

Long-leaved Dock • **Rumex longifolius*

Perennial herb of fields, roadsides, and disturbed sites, 0.5–1.2 m tall. **Flowers** in whorls of 10–20; pedicels 4–9 mm long, *with a visibly swollen articulation point.* **Leaves** widest near the middle. **Fruit** with 3 wing-like tepals, *each tepal wider than long; tubercles absent or tiny.*
OCCURRENCE: Uncommon; MDI, SCH.
OTHER NAMES: Yard Dock, *Rumex domesticus*

Bitter Dock • **Rumex obtusifolius*

Perennial herb of fields, roadsides, and disturbed sites, 0.6–1.2 m tall. **Flowers** in slightly remote whorls; pedicels 2.5–8.5 mm long, *with a visibly swollen articulation point.* **Leaves** thin, often with red veins, 10–30 cm long and 5–15 cm wide. **Fruit** with 3 wing-like *tepals with toothed margins, the teeth 0.8–1.5 mm long, visible both in flower and in fruit; tubercles 1, large, often reddish.*
OCCURRENCE: Uncommon; SCH.
OTHER NAMES: Broad-leaved Dock, Blunt-leaved Dock, Red-veined Dock

Seabeach Dock • *Rumex pallidus*

Perennial herb of rocky shorelines, 0.4–1 m tall. **Flowers** in whorls of 10–20; pedicels 4–6 mm long; *articulation point of pedicels indistinct, not swollen.* **Leaves** *glaucous, with leafy tufts usually present in the axils,* not in a basal rosette. **Stems** *usually with lateral branches.* **Fruit** with 3 wing-like tepals; *tubercles 3, wide, white, more than half the width and nearly the length of the associated tepal.*
OCCURRENCE: Uncommon; MDI.
OTHER NAMES: White Dock

Narrow-leaved Dock • *Rumex triangulivalvis*

Perennial herb of brackish sites, 0.4–1 m tall. **Flowers** in whorls of 10–25; pedicels 4–8 mm long; *articulation point of pedicels indistinct, not swollen.* **Leaves** longer than wide, with leafy tufts usually present in the axils, not in a basal rosette. **Stems** *usually with lateral branches.* **Fruit** with 3 wing-like *tepals with an acute apex; tubercles 3, narrow, white, at the base of the midrib, less than half the width and much shorter than the associated tepal.*
OCCURRENCE: Uncommon; SCH.
OTHER NAMES: White Dock, *Rumex salicifolius*

AH

AH

Pickerelweeed • *Pontederia cordata*

Emergent, perennial herb of ponds and coves of shallow lakes and rivers, 0.3–1 m tall. **Flowers** *purple-blue*, in a spike 7–10 cm long, 2-lipped with 3 lobes per lip; stamens *6, with only 3 exserted*. **Leaves** heart-shaped at base, on a long petiole. **Fruit** 1-seeded.
OCCURRENCE: Common; MDI.

PORTULACACEAE • PURSLANE FAMILY ▼

Blinks • *Montia fontana*

Minute, annual herb of coastal headlands and saltmarshes, up to 30 cm tall. **Flowers** with 5 minute, *white- or cream-colored petals* 1.5 mm long. **Leaves** *opposite*, 5–13 mm long, often rooting from the nodes. **Fruit** a *capsule* with 1–3 *shiny, black seeds*.
OCCURRENCE: Rare; IAH, SCH.
NOTES: This plant gets its common name because it is visible for just a few weeks in June and then disappears or "blinks" out. Maine Natural Areas Program ranks this species as of special concern in Maine.
OTHER NAMES: Water-blinks, Water Montia, *Montia lamprosperma*

Common Purslane • ***Portulaca oleracea**

Annual, mat-forming herb of gardens and disturbed sites. **Flowers** 5-parted (occasionally 4 or 6), *yellow*, <1 cm wide, borne singly from leaf clusters; blooming for only a few morning hours. **Leaves** *alternate, fleshy, blunt-tipped*, <2.5 cm long, scattered along the stems and *clustered at branch tips.* **Fruit** a capsule, *opening like a lid from a seam traversing the middle of the fruit.*
OCCURRENCE: Occasional; MDI.

POTAMOGETONACEAE • PONDWEED FAMILY ▼

Bigleaf Pondweed • ***Potamogeton amplifolius***

Perennial, aquatic herb of deeper ponds and lakes. **Flowers** in dense spikes of 9–16 whorls, the spikes 4–8 cm long and 1–1.5 cm wide in fruit. **Floating leaves** with 27–49 veins, 5–10 cm long and 2.5–5 cm wide; petioles 8–20 cm long. **Submersed leaves** *with 23–37 veins, not clasping stem*, entire, with 3–6 rows of prominent clear bands (lacunae) on each side of mid-vein; stipules fibrous. **Stems** round in cross section, 1–3.5 mm wide. **Fruit** beaked, wedge-shaped at base, 3.5–5.5 mm long, with 3 low keels.
OCCURRENCE: Rare; MDI.
OTHER NAMES: Large-leaf Pondweed, Big-leaved Pondweed

Snail-seed Pondweed • *Potamogeton bicupulatus*

Perennial, aquatic herb of slow-moving water. **Flowers** 1–15 in a spike. **Floating leaves** *0.6–2.3 cm long*. **Submersed leaves** 0.1–0.4 mm wide, *with a long-tapering pointed tip*. **Fruit** straw-colored, 1.6–2.2 mm long; *dorsal keel wide and wing-like; lateral keels high, forming a deep cup on each side.* **OCCURRENCE:** Uncommon; MDI.

CBH

AH

Tuckerman's Pondweed • *Potamogeton confervoides*

Perennial, aquatic herb of peaty pools, 10–80 cm long. **Flowers** in spikes 3–12 mm long. **Leaves** *uniform, all submersed, flaccid*, 2–5 cm long and 0.1–0.5 mm wide; *stipules distinct.* **Stems** *thread-like, flaccid, forking repeatedly*. **Fruit** light green, 2.2–3 mm long, *with a sharp, dorsal keel.*
OCCURRENCE: Rare; MDI.
OTHER NAMES: Alga Pondweed, Alga-like Pondweed

CBH

DSC

Ribbonleaf Pondweed • *Potamogeton epihydrus*

Perennial, aquatic herb of ponds and streams, up to 2 m long. **Flowers** numerous, *in spikes 1–4 cm long*. **Floating leaves** 3–8 cm long and 8–35 mm wide, with 9–41 veins, tapering to flat petioles. **Submersed leaves** *with prominent clear bands (lacunae)*. **Stems** compressed. **Fruit** *flat laterally with short beak, pitted on sides*, 2.5–4.5 mm long and 2.5–3.6 mm wide, with dorsal keel 0.2–1.2 mm wide.

OCCURRENCE: Common; MDI, IAH.

OTHER NAMES: Ribbon-leaved Pondweed

AH

Variable Pondweed • *Potamogeton gramineus*

Perennial, aquatic herb of deeper water, 0.3–1.7 m long. **Flowers** *in spikes 1–3 cm long; peduncles 2–30 cm long, wider than stem*. **Floating leaves** 1.5–7 cm long and 8–30 mm wide, *leathery*. **Submersed leaves** 3–10 mm wide, *sessile*, usually with 3–9 veins and *tiny green, short-pointed projections along margin*; petioles 2–15 cm long. **Stems** slender, round in cross section, 0.5–1 mm wide. **Fruit** 1.7–2.8 mm long and 1.4–2.3 mm wide, with a short recurving beak and *sharp dorsal keel with shallowly pitted sides*.

OCCURRENCE: Uncommon; MDI.

OTHER NAMES: Grassy Pondweed

CBH

DSC

Floating Pondweed • *Potamogeton natans*

Perennial, aquatic herb of lakes and slow-flowing streams, 1–2 m long. **Flowers** in spikes 2–5 cm long and 9–12 mm wide. **Floating leaves** 3.2–12 cm long and 2–6.5 cm wide; petioles 1–2.5 mm wide; *blade and petiole separated by a flexible joint of lighter color.* **Submersed leaves** *long and narrow,* 10–40 cm long and 0.8–2 mm wide, *tapering to a blunt tip,* with 3–5 obscure veins; *stipules large.* **Stems** round in cross section, 0.8–2.5 mm wide, *with transverse ridges.* **Fruit** 3–5 mm long and 2.5–3.5 mm wide, *rugose, with short beak.*
OCCURRENCE: Uncommon; MDI.
OTHER NAMES: floating-leaf Pondweed

DSC

Oakes' Pondweed • *Potamogeton oakesianus*

Perennial, aquatic herb of acidic, peaty ponds, up to 1 m long. **Flowers** in spikes 1–3.5 cm long and 7–9 mm wide; peduncles 3–8 cm long, wider than stem. **Floating leaves** 1.5–6 cm long and 1–3 cm wide. **Submersed leaves** 0.3–1 mm wide, flat, delicate, *turning dark on drying; stipules small*; petioles 0.2–1 mm wide. **Stems** round in cross section, 0.4–1 mm wide. **Fruit** 2–3.7 mm long and 1.6–2.4 mm wide, smooth, with acute dorsal keel.
OCCURRENCE: Occasional; MDI.

Perfoliate Pondweed • *Potamogeton perfoliatus*

Perennial, aquatic herb of brackish waters. **Flowers** in spikes 1–4.5 cm long and 8 mm wide; peduncles 1–9 cm long. **Leaves** all submersed, entire, sessile, cordate-clasping at base, delicate, 1–7 cm long and 5–30 mm wide. **Stems** round in cross section. **Fruit** 1.6–3 mm long and 2–2.3 mm wide.
OCCURRENCE: Uncommon; MDI.
OTHER NAMES: Redhead-grass, Clasping-leaved Pondweed

AH

Slender Pondweed • *Potamogeton pusillus*

Perennial, aquatic herb of higher pH waters, up to 1.5 m long. **Flowers** in spikes 5–8 mm long, in a cylindrical inflorescence with 1–4 whorls of flowers; peduncles 5–62 mm long, *thread-like*. **Leaves** *all submersed, long and narrow, 1–7 cm long and 0.2–2.5 mm wide, tapering to a bristle tip*; stipules 0.5–2 cm long, usually *with 2 minute, basal glands*. **Fruit** *rarely found*, 1.5–2.5 mm long.
OCCURRENCE: Occasional; MDI.
OTHER NAMES: Small Pondweed

DSC

Spiral Pondweed • *Potamogeton spirillus*

Perennial, aquatic herb of quiet ponds and lakes, up to 1.5 m long. **Flowers** *1–8 in spikes on recurving peduncles from axils of submersed leaves;* aerial spikes with 4–35 flowers. **Floating leaves** *rounded at tip,* 0.7–3.5 cm long and 2–13 mm wide. **Submersed leaves** *pale green, long and narrow, entire, often curving,* 1.5–8 cm long and 0.5–2 mm wide. **Fruit** 1.3–2.4 mm wide, *green or yellow, with a sharp dorsal keel.*
OCCURRENCE: Occasional; MDI.
OTHER NAMES: Northern Snail-seed Pondweed

AH

CBH

Sago Pondweed • *Stuckenia pectinata*

Submersed, tuberous, aquatic herb of saline, brackish, or higher pH waters, 0.3–1 m long. **Flowers** with 5 stamens and 4 tepals, *in spikes 1–5 cm long on thin flexible peduncles* 3–30 cm long. **Leaves** *long and narrow,* 2–10 cm long and 0.2–1 mm wide, *cross-divided by partitions.* **Fruit** *tiny,* usually 3–4.5 mm long; *styles persistent on the achene, forming a tiny beak.*
OCCURRENCE: Rare; MDI.
OTHER NAMES: Sago False Pondweed, *Potamogeton pectinata*

CG

CG

Horned Pondweed • *Zannichellia palustris*

Perennial, aquatic herb of fresh to brackish water. **Flowers** water pollinated, paired with both staminate and carpellate on an axillary, forked common stalk; *carpellate flowers with a funnel-shaped stigma attached in the middle.* **Leaves** *linear, 0.5 mm wide, 1-nerved, opposite except those at tip of plants appearing to be in whorls of 3 or 4.* **Fruit** ~2.5 mm long, *slightly flat and curving,* warty to toothed on the convex margin, *with a persistent beak-like style.*
OCCURRENCE: Rare, MDI.
NOTES: Maine Natural Areas Program ranks this species as of special concern in Maine.

DSC

DSC

RANUNCULACEAE • CROWFOOT FAMILY ▼

White Baneberry • *Actaea pachypoda*

Perennial herb of rich hardwood forests, 40–80 cm tall. **Flowers** white, with 3–7 petals that narrow abruptly near base, 3–5 mm long; *pedicels stout,* 1–2.5 mm wide. **Leaves** alternate, divided, *glabrous on underside*; leaflets up to 11 cm long. **Fruit** *white, 6–10 mm long, capped by a red stigma.*
OCCURRENCE: Uncommon; MDI.
OTHER NAMES: Doll's Eyes

Red Baneberry • *Actaea rubra*

Perennial herb of acidic forests, 40–80 cm tall. **Flowers** white, in a raceme 3–10 cm long; *pedicels thread-like, 1.3–3 cm long and 0.3–0.7 mm wide, with some long, soft, straight hairs.* **Leaves** alternate, divided, *pubescent with hooked hairs on underside.* **Fruit** *red.*
OCCURRENCE: Uncommon; MDI.
OTHER NAMES: Snakeberry

Wood Anemone • *Anemone quinquefolia*

Rhizomatous, perennial herb of open woodlands and wet clearings, 5–30 cm tall. **Flowers** white, *solitary*. **Leaves** *divided into 3–5 leaflets, whorled, glabrous*. **Stems** glabrous.
OCCURRENCE: Occasional; MDI.
OTHER NAMES: Windflower, Wood Windflower

Wild Columbine • *Aquilegia canadensis*

Perennial herb of rocky woods and outcrops, 0.3–1 m tall. **Flowers** *bright red with yellow, 3–5.3 cm long, nodding; spurs red, 2–2.5 cm long, swollen at the tips*; pedicels 5–10 cm long. **Leaves** *alternate, divided*; leaflets 1–4.5 cm long. **Fruit** a papery, crown-shaped capsule.
OCCURRENCE: Uncommon; MDI.
OTHER NAMES: Canada Columbine, Red Columbine

CWG

European Columbine • ***Aquilegia vulgaris***

Perennial herb of roadsides and fields, up to 2 m tall. **Flowers** *blue, pink, or purple*, 2.5–5.5 cm long; spurs 1.5–2.2 cm long; style beak 0.5–1 cm long; *stamens not protruding from the flower.* **Leaves** alternate, divided; leaflets 1–4.5 cm long. **Fruit** a papery, crown-shaped capsule.
OCCURRENCE: Uncommon; MDI.
OTHER NAMES: Garden Columbine

Marsh Marigold • ***Caltha palustris***

Perennial herb of wet meadows, up to 1 m tall. **Flowers** yellow, 15–50 mm wide, *with 5–9 yellow, petal-like sepals*; true petals absent. **Leaves** *alternate, toothed; cauline leaves gradually reduced upward; basal leaves cordate or kidney-shaped, 4–15 cm wide; petioles up to 20 cm long.* **Stems** *hollow.*
OCCURRENCE: Uncommon; MDI.
OTHER NAMES: Cowslip, King-cup

Goldthread • *Coptis trifolia*

Rhizomatous, perennial herb of wet woods and swamps, up to 13 cm tall. **Flowers** with 5–7 *white, fleshy petals 3–4 mm long,* with nectar in the hollow tip. **Leaves** *evergreen, shiny, basal only,* 1.5–3.5 cm long, *divided, with 3 toothed leaflets.* **Fruit** *stalked, in an umbel-like cluster.* **Rhizomes** *bright yellow, hairy.*
OCCURRENCE: Occasional; MDI, IAH, SCH.
OTHER NAMES: Goldenroot, Yellow Snakeroot, Three-leaved Goldthread, *Coptis groenlandica*

Small-flowered Crowfoot • *Ranunculus abortivus*

AH

Annual or biennial herb of low, rich woods or meadows, 10–50 cm tall. **Flowers** pale yellow, solitary; *petals 5, 2.5–3.5 mm long.* **Leaves** alternate, *deeply lobed or divided; the lowest 1–6 cm wide, kidney-shaped, without deep lobes; cauline leaves gradually reduced upward.*
OCCURRENCE: Rare; MDI.
OTHER NAMES: Kidney-leaved Crowfoot

AH

AH

Tall Buttercup • **Ranunculus acris***

Perennial herb of fields, roadsides, and other disturbed sites, 0.3–1 m tall. **Flowers** *with 5 shiny, yellow petals 5–15 mm long*; sepals about half as long as the petals. **Leaves** alternate, the largest *divided into 3–7 deeply cleft stalkless parts.* **Stems** *usually hairy.*
OCCURRENCE: Common; MDI, IAH, SCH.
NOTES: Fresh plants are problematic for livestock.
OTHER NAMES: Common Buttercup, Meadow Buttercup, Tall Crowfoot

Seaside Crowfoot • *Ranunculus cymbalaria*

Perennial herb of brackish or saline water (very rarely in fresh water), 5–15 cm tall. **Flowers** yellow, few; petals 5 or more, 2.5–5 mm long. **Leaves** *basal only, bluntly toothed,* with blades about as long as wide, *shorter than the petioles.*
OCCURRENCE: Occasional; MDI, IAH, SCH.

Creeping Spearwort • *Ranunculus flammula*

Perennial herb of wet shores, 5–15 cm tall. **Flowers** yellow, solitary; petals 5 or 6, 2.5–5 mm long. **Leaves** *basal only, bluntly toothed*, with blades about as long as wide, *shorter than the petioles.* **Stems** *rooting at nodes.*
OCCURRENCE: Rare; MDI.
OTHER NAMES: Lesser Spearwort, Creeping Crowfoot, *Ranunculus reptans*

Creeping Buttercup • **Ranunculus repens*

Weedy, stoloniferous, perennial herb of wet areas, up to 80 cm tall. **Flowers** yellow, clustered or solitary; petals 5, 5–17 mm long. **Leaves** dark green, usually with light blotches, the lowest divided into leaflets with *terminal leaflet often 3-parted or divided,* 1.5–6 cm long. **Stems** *generally trailing although flowering stems erect, rooting at the nodes.*
OCCURRENCE: Common; MDI, IAH, SCH.
OTHER NAMES: Spot-leaved Crowfoot

Tall Meadow-rue • *Thalictrum pubescens*

Perennial herb of meadows and thickets, up to 3 m tall. **Flowers** generally unisexual; *sepals white*, 2–3.5 mm long; stamens club-shaped; *stigmas often coiled*. **Leaves** alternate, *divided; leaflets 0.5–5.5 cm wide, with 2 or 3 lobes.*

OCCURRENCE: Occasional; MDI, SCH.

OTHER NAMES: King-of-the-meadow, *Thalictrum polygamum*

Yellow Mignonette • ******Reseda lutea***

Matted to erect, biennial or perennial herb of fields and disturbed sites, up to 80 cm tall. **Flowers** *yellow-green, ~6 mm wide, borne in an erect, spike-like, conical raceme; petals 6, the uppermost 2- or 3-lobed, the lowest undivided*; stamens 12–20, bent down. **Leaves** irregularly lobed and deeply divided, with 1–3 lateral segments. **Fruit** a warty capsule, *opening at the top*, with usually 3 apical lobes.
OCCURRENCE: Rare; MDI.
OTHER NAMES: Yellow Upright Mignonette

CG

RHAMNACEAE • BUCKTHORN FAMILY ▼

Alder Buckthorn • ******Frangula alnus***

Deciduous shrub of thickets and disturbed sites, up to 7 m tall. **Flowers** white, *5-parted, 2–8 per inflorescence*; pedicels unequal, 3–10 mm long. **Leaves** entire, alternate, 5–8 cm long, *with few marginal glands near the tip, with lateral veins curving near margin.* **Fruit** red, darkening to nearly black, with 2 or 3 stones. **Twigs** *pubescent*; winter buds hairy.
OCCURRENCE: Occasional; MDI.
NOTES: Aggressively invasive!
OTHER NAMES: European Alder Buckthorn, Glossy False Buckthorn, *Rhamnus frangula*

AH

AH

Downy Shadbush • *Amelan*

One- or *few-stemmed tree or tall shrub* of rich fore... m tall. **Flowers** white, with petals 1–2 cm long. **Leaves** *<50% expanded at flowering time, densely white-woolly on undersides when young, retaining some pubescence at maturity.* **Fruit** a purple-black pome, *dry and tasteless, with a pedicel 8–17 mm long.*

OCCURRENCE: Occasional; MDI.

OTHER NAMES: Downy Serviceberry, Common Shadbush, Bilberry, Wild-pear

AH

Mountain Shadbush • *Amelanchier bartramiana*

Shrub of mountains and some peatlands, up to 2.5 m tall. **Flowers** white, *with 1–4 flowers per cluster; ovary summit conical and hairy.* **Leaves** *wedge-shaped at base,* glabrous at flowering time; *petioles at maturity 2–10 mm long (shorter than other species).* **Fruit** a sweet pome.

OCCURRENCE: Uncommon; MDI.

NOTES: This species *blooms slightly later than others.*

OTHER NAMES: Mountain Serviceberry, Bartram's Shadbush, Mountain Juneberry

AH

Eastern Serviceberry • *Amelanchier canadensis*

Shrub or small tree of thickets and forest edges, up to 8 m tall. **Flowers** white, *with petals 7–10 mm long; ovary summit glabrous; rachis and pedicels densely pubescent.* **Leaves** *densely hairy on undersides, folded when young, retaining some pubescence at maturity, green, with 6–11 teeth per cm.* **Fruit** a juicy pome, *with lower pedicels 5–10 mm long.*
OCCURRENCE: Occasional; MDI, SCH.
OTHER NAMES: Swamp Shadbush, Eastern Shadbush

Intermediate Shadbush • *Amelanchier intermedia*

Shrub or small tree of swamps and thickets, up to 8 m tall. **Flowers** with white petals *9–12 mm long; ovary summit glabrous; rachis and pedicels sparsely pubescent.* **Leaves** *sparsely hairy on undersides when young, often tinged with purple, with 5–7 teeth per cm.* **Fruit** a juicy pome; *lower pedicels 20–35 mm long.*
OCCURRENCE: Occasional; MDI, SCH.
OTHER NAMES: *Amelanchier x intermedia*

AH

AH

Smooth Shadbush • *Amelanchier laevis*

Tree or shrub of forests and forest margins, up to 15 m tall. **Flowers** white, *with petals 12–22 mm long*. **Leaves** at flowering time 50–75% expanded, *nearly glabrous on undersides when young, red- or purple-colored*. **Fruit** *a sweet and juicy pome, with pedicels 25–50 mm long*.
OCCURRENCE: Common; MDI, IAH, SCH.

CWG

Nantucket Shadbush • *Amelanchier nantucketensis*

Colonial shrub with dense stems, of disturbed sites and mountain tops, up to 2 m tall. **Flowers** white, *3–6 mm long, often with reduced, minute petals, or petals bearing pollen*. **Leaves** *folded at flowering time, nearly glabrous on undersides*. **Fruit** a purple-black pome, with pedicels 1–2 cm long.
OCCURRENCE: Rare; MDI.
NOTES: Maine Natural Areas Program ranks this species as threatened in Maine.

AH

CWG

Thicket Shadbush • *Amelanchier spicata*

Colonial, rhizomatous shrub of open and rocky sites, up to 2 m tall. **Flowers** white, with petals 7–22 mm long; *ovary summit hairy in both flower and fruit*. **Leaves** at flowering time *white-woolly, with 6–10 teeth per cm*. **Fruit** a sweet and juicy pome.
OCCURRENCE: Occasional; MDI.
OTHER NAMES: Running Shadbush, Running Serviceberry, Dwarf Shadbush, *Amelanchier stolonifera*

AH

Coastal Silverweed • *Argentina egedii*

Stoloniferous, perennial herb of coastal shores, up to 75 cm tall. **Flowers** *yellow, solitary*. **Leaves** compound, with 7–25 sharply toothed leaflets, *shiny green above, with long, silky hairs on the veins on underside and short, tangled, soft, woolly hairs between the veins*. **Fruit** a flat achene.
OCCURRENCE: Occasional; MDI, IAH, SCH.
OTHER NAMES: Eged's Silverweed, Pacific Silverweed, often misidentified as *Potentilla anserina*

Purple Chokeberry • *Aronia floribunda*

Shrub of mountaintops, exposed areas, and peatlands, 0.3–3 m tall. **Flowers** white, *with 5 petals 4–6 mm long; pedicels sparsely to moderately hairy.* **Leaves** simple, finely and minutely toothed, *with undersides hairy, the upper surface of midrib with a row of dark glands.* **Fruit** *purple.*
OCCURRENCE: Occasional; MDI, SCH.
OTHER NAMES: *Pyrus floribunda, Photinia floribunda*

Black Chokeberry • *Aronia melanocarpa*

Shrub of mountaintops, exposed areas, and peatlands, 0.1–1 m tall. **Flowers** white, *with 5 petals 4–6 mm long; pedicels without or with few hairs.* **Leaves** simple, finely and minutely toothed, *without or with few hairs on underside, the midrib with a row of dark glands on top of leaf.* **Fruit** *black,* 0.4–1 cm wide, *bitter.*
OCCURRENCE: Common; MDI, IAH, SCH.
OTHER NAMES: *Pyrus melanocarpa, Photinia melanocarpa*

Goat's Beard • **Aruncus dioicus*

Perennial herb of fields and forest edges, 1–2 m tall. **Flowers** *white, in feathery branched plumes, with minute petals up to 1 mm long.* **Leaves** *pinnately compound, with sharply toothed, egg-shaped leaflets.* **Fruit** 2 mm long, with a persistent style.
OCCURRENCE: Uncommon; MDI.
NOTES: Native of eastern U.S. from Pennsylvania to Iowa, south. Escaped from cultivation in our region.

Marsh-five-finger • *Comarum palustre*

Perennial herb of bogs, swamps, swales, and shallow water, 20–60 cm tall. **Flowers** *purple to red,* 2–3 cm wide, generally more than one per stalk; *petals shorter than the purple sepals.* **Leaves** *pinnately compound,* with 5–7 sharply toothed, blunt-tipped leaflets.
OCCURRENCE: Rare; MDI.
OTHER NAMES: Marsh-potentilla, Marsh Cinquefoil, *Potentilla palustris*

Cockspur Thorn • *Crataegus crus-galli*

Small tree or large shrub of dry fields and forests, 6–8 m tall. **Flowers** white, *with 1 or 2 styles*. **Leaves** *tapering to base, widest above middle, shiny*, unlobed or only faintly lobed at tip; petioles short, under 1 cm. **Stems** with thorns. **Fruit** a pome with 1 or 2 (sometimes up to 5) nutlets, the nutlets smooth on inner face.
OCCURRENCE: Uncommon; MDI.
OTHER NAMES: Cockspur Hawthorn

AH

AH

Jones' Hawthorn • *Crataegus jonesiae*

Small tree to shrub of rocky sites, up to 7 m tall. **Flowers** white, *19–23 mm wide; sepals entire or with scattered glandular teeth; anthers pink to purple*. **Leaves** *6–9 cm long*, the base with >90 degree angle. **Stems** with thorns. **Fruit** a bright red pome 1–3 cm wide.
OCCURRENCE: Uncommon; MDI.
NOTES: Named for Beatrix Jones Farrand.
OTHER NAMES: Miss Jones' Hawthorn

AH

AH

AH

Keep's Hawthorn • *Crataegus keepii*

Shrub or small tree, 2–5 m tall. **Flowers** white, 1.5–1.9 cm wide, *5–11 in a villous inflorescence*; sepals with toothed margins and glands; *stamens 5–10*, 1.1–1.3 mm long; styles 3 or 4. **Leaves** 3–5.5 cm long during flowering and 4.8–7.8 cm long at maturity. **Branchlets** villous, red-brown. **Stems** with thorns 2.6–7.2 cm long. **Fruit** a pome 1–1.4 cm wide, sparsely villous.
OCCURRENCE: Rare; MDI.
OTHER NAMES: *Crataegus brunetiana*

AH

AH

AH

Long-thorned Hawthorn • *Crataegus macracantha*

Small tree to large shrub of dry, rocky sites, up to 8 m tall. **Flowers** white; *stamens 5–10; anthers 1.2–1.5 mm long; styles 2 or 3*. **Leaves** *lobed, shiny above, somewhat leathery, mostly 3.5–5 cm long; petioles >1 cm long*. **Stems** *with thorns to 7 cm long or longer*. **Fruit** a pome 6–15 mm wide, with 2 or 3 nutlets with depression on inner face.
OCCURRENCE: Rare; MDI.

AH

AH

AH

Variable Thorn • *Crataegus macrosperma*

Small tree to large shrub of rocky thickets, up to 7 m tall. **Flowers** white, with 5–10 stamens, *in a glabrous inflorescence*. **Leaves** *widely rounded or heart-shaped at base*, with distinctly pointed tips and *lateral lobes curving backward*. **Stems** with thorns. **Fruit** a pome, bright red when ripe, juicy.
OCCURRENCE: Uncommon; MDI.
OTHER NAMES: Large-seeded Hawthorn

AH

AH

AH

English Hawthorn • **Crataegus monogyna*

Shrub or small tree of roadsides and forest edges, up to 7 m tall. **Flowers** 9–13 mm wide, *with purple to red anthers and 1 style*. **Leaves** with *3–7 lobes*, the tip rounded, with base wedge-shaped to truncate; *primary veins running to sinuses and tip of lobes*. **Stems** with thorns 7–25 mm long. **Fruit** a pome 5–8 mm wide with *1 nutlet*.
OCCURRENCE: Occasional; MDI.
NOTES: Sometimes used in landscaping.
OTHER NAMES: One-seeded Hawthorn

Shrubby Cinquefoil • ***Dasiphora floribunda***

Shrub of rocky outcrops or rocky shores, 0.2–1 m tall. **Flowers** yellow, 1–3 cm wide, with 5 broad petals. **Leaves** compound; *leaflets 5–7, narrow lance-shaped, covered with silky hairs on both sides giving them a grayish hue*. **Fruit** densely hairy.
OCCURRENCE: Rare; MDI, SCH.
NOTES: This species and a white-flowered form are used widely in landscaping.
OTHER NAMES: Gold-withy, Buckbrush, *Potentilla fruticosa, Pentaphylloides floribunda*

Wild Strawberry • ***Fragaria virginiana***

Stoloniferous, perennial herb of fields, meadows, roadsides, and lawns, up to 40 cm tall. **Flowers** *white, 5-parted, 1–2.5 cm wide*, in clusters usually shorter than the leaves; stamens numerous. **Leaves** basal only, *compound, with 3 leaflets, toothed with terminal tooth usually shorter than adjacent teeth*. **Fruit** round and juicy, with tiny seeds imbedded in surface.
OCCURRENCE: Common; MDI, IAH, SCH.
OTHER NAMES: Thick-leaved Wild Strawberry, Virginia Strawberry

Yellow Avens • *Geum aleppicum*

Stout, perennial herb of wet meadows and swamps, 0.3–1 m tall. **Flowers** *yellow*, with petals 5–10 mm long and 5–9 mm wide. **Leaves** variable in shape; *basal leaves with terminal leaflet wedge-shaped, usually with a deep incision*. **Stems** hairy. **Fruit** *an achene, in an elliptical cluster* of more than 200.
OCCURRENCE: Rare; MDI.

White Avens • *Geum canadense*

Slender, perennial herb of dry woods, meadows, and roadsides, 0.2–1 m tall. **Flowers** *white to creamy yellow, erect; petals 5–9 mm long, about as long or longer than green sepals*. **Leaves** progressively reduced upward, the lowest with long petiole; *terminal leaflet much larger than lateral ones; sometimes lobed or cleft*. **Fruit** *an achene, in a round cluster of 30–160*.
OCCURRENCE: Uncommon; MDI.

AH

AH

AH

Purple Avens • *Geum rivale*

Rhizomatous, perennial herb of wet areas, 0.3–1 m tall. **Flowers** *yellowish with purple veins, nodding*, both petals and sepals erect in fruit. **Leaves** progressively reduced upward, the lowest with 3–5 principal leaflets; *terminal leaflet much larger than others* and sometimes lobed or cleft.
OCCURRENCE: Uncommon; MDI.
OTHER NAMES: Water Avens

Apple • **Malus pumila*

Tall tree of old home sites and fields, up to 15 m tall. **Flowers** *white or light pink, divinely fragrant, 3 cm wide*, with yellow anthers; pedicels hairy. **Leaves** finely toothed, densely hairy when young, retaining hairs beneath on older leaves. **Fruit** *6–12 cm wide, juicy, edible.*
OCCURRENCE: Occasional; MDI, IAH, SCH.
OTHER NAMES: *Pyrus malus, Malus sylvestris*

Siebold's Crabapple • ***_Malus sieboldii_**

Perennial shrub of roadsides and old fields, up to 7 m tall. **Flowers** white, 5-parted, the petals widest below the middle. **Leaves** alternate, *serrate to lobed, 5–8 cm long*, glabrous to pubescent; petioles 6–30 mm long. **Fruit** small, dark red, *up to 1 cm wide*.
OCCURRENCE: Uncommon; MDI.
OTHER NAMES: Sargent's Crabapple, Toringo Crabapple, *Malus sargentii*

Ninebark • ***_Physocarpus opulifolius_**

Shrub of dry woods and margins, 1–3 m tall. **Flowers** *white, 7–10 mm wide*, in large, round, showy clusters. **Leaves** alternate, heart- to wedge-shaped at base, the largest with 3-lobed tips. **Bark** *shredding and peeling with age*. **Fruit** a golden to reddish papery capsule 5–10 mm wide.
OCCURRENCE: Occasional; MDI.
NOTES: Native of southern New England, here escaped from cultivation and invasive.
OTHER NAMES: Atlantic Ninebark

Silvery Cinquefoil • ***Potentilla argentea**

Perennial herb of dry open areas, sandy roadsides, and old fields, 10–50 cm tall. **Flowers** yellow, 7–10 mm wide; petals not much longer than the sepals. **Leaves** *densely hairy and silver beneath; leaflets 5, deeply toothed, with 2–4 tooth-like lobes near tip*; stipules 2, small, toothless. **Stems** woolly.
OCCURRENCE: Occasional; MDI, SCH.
OTHER NAMES: Silver-leaved Cinquefoil, Hoary Cinquefoil

Pennsylvania Cinquefoil • ***Potentilla litoralis***

Perennial herb of dry, rocky sites, 20–80 cm tall. **Flowers** yellow, ~1 cm wide; petals widest above the middle; *styles glandular at base; sepals with dense glands and hairs.* **Leaves** variable, *pinnately compound*; the lowest long-petioled; cauline leaves progressively reduced upward, with shorter petioles. **Stems** *with short, matted, soft, woolly hairs.*
OCCURRENCE: Uncommon; SCH.
OTHER NAMES: *Potentilla pensylvanica*

Rough Cinquefoil • *Potentilla norvegica*

Perennial herb of disturbed sites and old fields, 0.1–0.9 m tall. **Flowers** yellow, 5-parted, ~1 cm wide, *in terminal branched clusters with many per stem*; styles thickened near middle of base; anthers ~0.3 mm long. **Leaves** *green, with long hairs beneath, the uppermost up to 8 cm long with 3 leaflets,* the lowest palmately compound, alternate. **Stems** *branched, stout, and hairy.*
OCCURRENCE: Common; MDI, IAH, SCH.
OTHER NAMES: Strawberry-weed, Norwegian Cinquefoil

Rough-fruited Cinquefoil • **Potentilla recta*

Stout, upright, perennial herb of dry fields and roadsides, 15–80 cm tall. **Flowers** *pale yellow, ~2 cm wide*, with anthers 1–1.5 mm long. **Leaves** palmately compound, *green, with 3–7 lance-shaped, coarsely toothed leaflets.*
OCCURRENCE: Uncommon; MDI.
OTHER NAMES: Sulphur Cinquefoil

AH

Old-field Cinquefoil • *Potentilla simplex*

Rhizomatous, stoloniferous, perennial herb of forests, fields, and thickets, 20–50 cm tall. **Flowers** yellow, 1–1.5 cm wide, *borne singly on leafless stalk from leaf axils, the first usually borne from the axil of the second well developed stem leaf;* style slender, not thickened near middle of base. **Leaves** compound; leaflets 5 or more, the largest 5–7 cm long, toothed from tip to well below the middle, hairy on underside. **Stems** *trailing, slender, often red.*
OCCURRENCE: Common; MDI, IAH, SCH.
OTHER NAMES: Common Cinquefoil, Five-finger

Pin Cherry • *Prunus pensylvanica*

Shrub or small tree of disturbed sites, often becoming established after fire, up to 12 m tall. **Flowers** white, in clusters of 2–5; petals 5–7 mm long; *sepals without glands.* **Leaves** *widest near the base,* narrowly oval to oblong or lance-shaped, mostly without hairs, *with glands on petiole.* **Bark** reddish to brown. **Fruit** *bright red at maturity.*
OCCURRENCE: Common; MDI, IAH, SCH.
OTHER NAMES: Bird Cherry, Fire Cherry

Sand Cherry • *Prunus pumila*

Prostrate or spreading, low shrub of rock outcrops and ledges, up to 3 m tall. **Flowers** white, 2–5 per cluster; sepals with glandular teeth; pedicels 4–12 mm long. **Leaves** 4–10 cm long, *not toothed below the middle*. **Fruit** *black at maturity*.
OCCURRENCE: Rare; MDI.
OTHER NAMES: Dwarf Sand Plum, *Prunus depressa*

AH

Black Cherry • *Prunus serotina*

Tree of hardwood and mixed forests, up to 25 m tall. **Flowers** white, *more than 20 in long racemes*; petals ~4 mm long. **Leaves** *widest at the middle*, finely toothed, *with 15 or more pairs of lateral veins, with red to brown hairs on midrib of leaf underside*. **Bark** *black*. **Fruit** dark purple to *black*, acidic; *sepals persistent in fruit*.
OCCURRENCE: Rare; MDI.
OTHER NAMES: Rum Cherry, Wild Black Cherry

CWG

AH

Choke Cherry • *Prunus virginiana*

Shrub or small tree of forest edges, up to 10 m tall. **Flowers** white, ~12 mm wide, *in dense cylindrical racemes 6–15 cm long*; petals rounded, ~4 mm long. **Leaves** *widest above the middle*, shiny, dark green above, light green on underside, 4–12 cm long and 1.5–4 cm wide, mostly *with 8–11 pairs of lateral veins*, the margins finely and sharply toothed; *petioles with 2 glands near the base of blade*. **Twigs** slender, brown, with *unpleasant odor when scratched*. **Fruit** *dark red to purple*, 6–10 mm diameter, *with poisonous seeds*. **OCCURRENCE:** Common; MDI, IAH, SCH.

Dog Rose • **Rosa canina*

AH

Multistemmed, arching shrub of old home sites, 1–3 m tall. **Flowers** pink to white, 4–5 cm wide; *sepals pinnately cleft; pedicels glabrous*. **Leaves** compound, *glabrous, without glands, with sharp teeth*. **Stems** *armed with stout, hooked prickles 3–8 mm long*. **Fruit** *an achene in a scarlet, ellipsoid to ovoid hip*. **OCCURRENCE:** Occasional; MDI.

AH

AH

Pasture Rose • *Rosa carolina*

Shrub of open, sometimes rocky or dry sites, 20–90 cm tall. **Flowers** pink, *usually solitary*; petals 5, 1.5–2 cm long. **Leaves** dull green or slightly shining, coarsely toothed, the middle teeth ~1 mm long; *stipules with nearly parallel margins, scarcely widening at tip* (see upper right photo). **Stems** *with slender, small-based, straight prickles at nodes; internodal prickles smaller, numerous.*
OCCURRENCE: Occasional; MDI, SCH.
OTHER NAMES: Carolina Rose

Multiflora Rose • *Rosa multiflora*

Shrub of roadsides, forests, and disturbed sites, up to 3 m tall. **Flowers** *white*, 2–4 cm wide, *many in each cluster; styles glabrous, united into a cylinder about as long as stamens, protruding from flower.* **Leaves** compound, with 5–11 leaflets; *stipules fringed and feathery, with glands* (see right photo). **Fruit** in a dull red hip ~5 mm wide.
OCCURRENCE: Uncommon; MDI, SCH.
NOTES: Escaped from cultivation and highly invasive.
OTHER NAMES: Rambler Rose

Bristly Rose • *Rosa nitida*

Shrub of bogs, marshes, and shores, 0.2–1 m tall. **Flowers** pink, 4–7 cm wide. **Leaves** compound, *dark green, shiny*, finely toothed, the middle teeth ~0.5 mm long; *stipules widely spreading to tips.* **Stems** *with slender, small-based, and straight prickles at nodes and internodes.*
OCCURRENCE: Occasional; MDI, IAH, SCH.
OTHER NAMES: Shining Rose, Swamp Rose, Bog Rose, New England Rose

Swamp Rose • *Rosa palustris*

Shrub of wet areas, up to 2.5 m tall. **Flowers** *light pink.* **Leaves** *dull green, sometimes with a gray tone*, finely toothed, the middle teeth ~0.5 mm long; *stipules narrow, barely widening at tip.* **Stems** *with a pair of stout, broad-based, downward curving prickles at most nodes; internodal prickles more slender.*
OCCURRENCE: Uncommon; MDI.

AH

Salt-spray Rose • ******Rosa rugosa*

Shrub of sea beaches and coastal thickets, 1–2 m tall. **Flowers** *pink to magenta-pink, occasionally white*, 8–10 cm wide; *pedicels hairy, with glands.* **Leaves** compound, dark green, *thick, deeply veined on surface*, with 5–9 leaflets. **Stems** *covered with sharp prickles, the young stems densely hairy.* **Fruit** in an orange to dark red, *fleshy hip 2–3 cm wide*, persisting into winter.
OCCURRENCE: Occasional; MDI, IAH, SCH.
NOTES: Rose hips are high in vitamin C. This species was introduced from Asia around 1850.
OTHER NAMES: Rugosa Rose, Japanese Rose, Beach Rose

Red-leaved Rose • ******Rosa setigera*

Shrub of old fields. **Flowers** pinkish, ~6 cm wide. **Leaves** *tinged with red, serrate with fine teeth*, with about 9–11 teeth per cm in upper portion of leaflet. **Stems** *with slender, small-based, straight prickles at the nodes and internodes.*
OCCURRENCE: Uncommon; MDI.
OTHER NAMES: *Rosa rubrifolia*

Scotch Rose • ***Rosa spinosissima**

Shrub of old fields, up to 2 m tall. **Flowers** white to yellow-white to pink, *mostly solitary at branch tips*, 2–4 cm wide. **Leaves** compound; *leaflets 7–11, 5–20 mm long and 5–10 mm wide.* **Stems** *very prickly.* **Fruit** *in a blackish hip with persistent, erect sepals.*
OCCURRENCE: Uncommon; MDI.
OTHER NAMES: Burnet Rose, *Rosa pimpinellifolia*

Virginia Rose • **Rosa virginiana**

Shrub of dry thickets or marshes, up to 2 m tall. **Flowers** pink, with petals 2–3 cm long; sepals elongate, up to 3 cm long. **Leaves** compound, coarsely toothed, the middle teeth ~1 mm long; *leaflets usually 7 or 9, dark green, shiny on top*, 2–6 cm long; *stipules widest at the tip* (see left photo). **Stems** *with a pair of stout, broad-based, curving prickles at most nodes*; internodal prickles more slender.
OCCURRENCE: Common; MDI, IAH, SCH.

Common Blackberry • *Rubus allegheniensis*

Biennial shrub of openings and thickets, 0.5–3 m tall. **Flowers** white, ~2.5 cm wide, with stalked glands, *borne in branched many-flowered clusters 8–20 cm long*; petals longer than sepals. **Leaves** compound, with 3 or more leaflets. **Stems** erect or arched, with stalked glands and stout, broad-based prickles. **Fruit** *juicy, black.*

OCCURRENCE: Occasional; MDI, IAH, SCH.

NOTES: The common blackberry is sometimes separated into many species by experts. The group is also complicated by crosses between species resulting in hybrids with features intermediate between parents.

Smooth Blackberry • *Rubus canadensis*

Biennial shrub of openings and thickets, 0.5–3 m tall. **Flowers** white, *without stalked glands*, up to 25 in clusters 4–17 cm long; petals 1.2–2 cm long and 6–12 mm wide. **Leaves** compound, the petioles without prickles; leaflets 3–5 (sometimes 7), glabrous or nearly so on both surfaces. **Stems** erect to arching, *with no prickles or averaging up to 1 prickle per cm of stem*. **Fruit** round to thimble-shaped, up to 12 mm long, *usually somewhat dry*.

OCCURRENCE: Uncommon; MDI.

OTHER NAMES: Canada Blackberry

AH

Baked-apple Berry • *Rubus chamaemorus*

Dioecious, perennial herb of coastal peatlands, 5–30 cm tall. **Flowers** with white petals 8–18 mm long, longer than sepals. **Leaves** *simple, toothed, 3–9 cm wide, with 5–7 shallow lobes.* **Stems** without prickles. **Fruit** *fleshy, orange or red when mature.*
OCCURRENCE: Rare; MDI.
OTHER NAMES: Cloudberry, Baked-appleberry

Dewdrop • *Rubus dalibarda*

Stoloniferous, perennial herb of wet forests, up to 30 cm tall. **Flowers** with white petals 4–8 mm long, sometimes absent. **Leaves** *simple, unlobed, 3–9 cm wide, margins shallowly scalloped.* **Stems** without prickles.
OCCURRENCE: Occasional; MDI.
NOTES: This species is sometimes confused with *Mitella nuda*, which looks quite similar vegetatively.
OTHER NAMES: Dalibarda, Robin-run-away, False-violet, *Dalibarda repens*

Showy Blackberry • *Rubus elegantulus*

Shrub of open areas and thickets, up to 1 m tall. **Flowers** white; pedicels usually glandular. **Leaves** *divided into 3 or 5 leaflets; petioles as bristly as the stem.* **Stems** with stiff to soft prickles, *not rooting at the tips of branches.*
OCCURRENCE: Uncommon; SCH.

Northern Dewberry • *Rubus flagellaris*

Prostrate, trailing, biennial, vine-like shrub of dry, open areas and thickets, up to 5 m long. **Flowers** *white, ~2.5 cm wide, usually 2–5 in a cluster.* **Leaves** *dull,* compound; leaflets 3–5, egg-shaped, with a broad-rounded to heart-shaped base, widest below the middle. **Stems** *with stout, broad-based prickles on trailing stems.* **Fruit** black, mostly 1–2 cm wide, sweet.
OCCURRENCE: Uncommon; MDI.
OTHER NAMES: Prickly Raspberry, Dewberry, Northern Blackberry

AH

Swamp Dewberry • ***Rubus hispidus***

Trailing or mounding, biennial shrub of open forests, up to 2.5 m long. **Flowers** *white, ~1.5 cm wide.* **Leaves** compound; *leaflets 3, shiny, evergreen*, the terminal one short-stalked, widest above the middle. **Stems** with slender, small-based bristles. **Fruit** reddish black at maturity, *separating from the stalk with the fleshy receptacle.*
OCCURRENCE: Occasional; MDI, IAH, SCH.
OTHER NAMES: Bristly Blackberry

Wild Red Raspberry • ****Rubus idaeus***

Biennial shrub of thickets and disturbed sites, up to 2 m tall. **Flowers** white or greenish white, *bristly or with some stalked glands at base*, 2–5 in a flat-topped cluster; petals shorter than sepals; sepals becoming reflexed at flowering. **Leaves** compound; leaflets 3, *densely hairy and appearing white on undersides.* **Stems** *slightly whitened*, arching but usually not rooting at tip. **Fruit** *red, edible, separating from receptacle.*
OCCURRENCE: Common; MDI, IAH, SCH.
NOTES: Common early plant following coastal forest blowdowns.
OTHER NAMES: Red Raspberry

Purple-flowering Raspberry • *Rubus odoratus*

Biennial shrub of thickets and forest edges, 1–2 m tall. **Flowers** *pink to purple-pink, showy, with petals 1.5–2.5 cm long*. **Leaves** 10–20 cm wide, with 3–5 lobes. **Stems** *without prickles*; many parts of plant covered with short, dark, glandular hairs. **Fruit** wide, short-hemispherical, not edible, dry.
OCCURRENCE: Uncommon; MDI.
OTHER NAMES: flowering Raspberry

Dwarf Raspberry • *Rubus pubescens*

Perennial herb of wet forests and thickets, 10–40 cm tall. **Flowers** white or pale pink; petals 4–8 mm long and 1.5–3 mm wide; *sepals reflexed*. **Leaves** compound, *with central leaflet egg-shaped to diamond-shaped, tapering to pointed base and tip*. **Stems** *without prickles, not woody*, with erect, leafy branches. **Fruit** dark red, 1–2 cm wide, juicy, *difficult to separate from receptacle*.
OCCURRENCE: Occasional; MDI.
OTHER NAMES: Swamp Red Raspberry

Blanchard's Dewberry • ******Rubus recurvicaulis***

Biennial, vine-like shrub of dry, open sites, up to 5 m long. **Flowers** white, 2–8 in a cluster; *pedicels hairy, 5–40 mm long*, generally ascending to spreading. **Leaves** *without hairs on the lower surface*. **Stems** *with stout, broad-based prickles*. **Fruit** black, mostly 1–2 cm wide, sweet.
OCCURRENCE: Uncommon; MDI.
OTHER NAMES: Arching Dewberry, Arching Blackberry

Three-toothed Cinquefoil • ***Sibbaldiopsis tridentata***

Creeping, woody-based, perennial herb of exposed headlands, mountains, and rock outcrops, 2–10 cm tall. **Flowers** *white*, ~1 cm wide, *in branched clusters*. **Leaves** compound, light to dark green; *leaflets 3, with a 3-toothed tip, evergreen*. **Fruit** hairy.
OCCURRENCE: Common; MDI, IAH, SCH.
OTHER NAMES: *Potentilla tridentata*

False Spiraea • **Sorbaria sorbifolia*

Erect shrub forming dense colonies along forest edges and roadsides, up to 2 m tall. **Flowers** *numerous, small, white, in a long, terminal panicle*; petals 2.5–3 mm long. **Leaves** *pinnately compound; leaflets 13–21, 3–7 cm long, doubly toothed.*
OCCURRENCE: Uncommon; MDI.

American Mountain-ash • *Sorbus americana*

Shrub or small tree of coastal forests and mountaintops, up to 8 m tall. **Flowers** white, *with petals 3–4 mm long, in an inflorescence with at most a few long, soft, shaggy hairs.* **Leaves** divided; *leaflets with at most with a few long, soft, shaggy hairs above.* **Twigs** glabrous or sparsely hairy; *bud scales with a sparse, marginal fringe of hairs, sticky.* **Fruit** 4–7 mm wide, *red*, often remaining on tree late in winter.
OCCURRENCE: Occasional; MDI, IAH, SCH.
OTHER NAMES: *Pyrus americana*

European Mountain-ash • **Sorbus aucuparia***

Small tree of varous habitats, up to 10 m tall. **Flowers** white, *in an inflorescence with dense, long, soft, shaggy hairs.* **Leaves** divided; leaflets 3–5 cm long, *with long, soft, shaggy hairs above.* **Twigs** and bud scales *with dense, long, soft, shaggy hairs* (see upper right photo); *bud scales not sticky.* **Fruit** ~10 mm wide, *orange.*
OCCURRENCE: Occasional; MDI, SCH.
OTHER NAMES: *Pyrus aucuparia*

Showy Mountain-ash • *Sorbus decora*

Shrub or small tree of coastal forests and mountaintops, up to 8 m tall. **Flowers** white, *with petals 4–5 mm long, in an inflorescence at most with a few long, soft, shaggy hairs.* **Leaves** divided; *leaflets at most with a few long, soft, shaggy hairs above.* **Twigs** glabrous or sparsely hairy; *bud scales with a marginal fringe of hairs* (see upper right photo), *sticky.* **Fruit** 7–10 mm wide, often remaining on tree late in winter.
OCCURRENCE: Occasional; MDI, IAH.
OTHER NAMES: *Pyrus decora*

Meadowsweet • *Spiraea alba*

Shrub of wetlands and coastal thickets, 0.3–1.2 m tall. **Flowers** *white or pink-tinged*, 4–7 mm wide, in a terminal panicle 5–10 cm long. **Leaves** alternate, coarsely toothed, egg-shaped to broadly lance-shaped, 3–7 cm long; *underside green, glabrous*. **Twigs** *reddish to purple-brown, without hairs*.
OCCURRENCE: Common; MDI, IAH, SCH.
OTHER NAMES: Narrow-leaved Meadowsweet, White Meadowsweet, *Spiraea latifolia*

Steeple-bush • *Spiraea tomentosa*

Shrub of wetlands, 0.3–1.2 m tall. **Flowers** *pink, 3–4 mm wide, in elongate, slim, terminal cluster*. **Leaves** alternate, *rugose, white-woolly on underside*. **Twigs** *white-woolly*.
OCCURRENCE: Occasional; MDI, IAH, SCH.
NOTES: This species gets its common name from the flower cluster looking like a church steeple.
OTHER NAMES: Rosy Meadowsweet

Spring Cleavers • *Galium aparine*

Annual herb of wet woods and thickets, up to 1 m tall. **Flowers** white, 1.5–2.8 mm wide, 1–3 on a pedicel. **Leaves** entire, 2.5–7 cm long, narrow, with bristle-tipped hairs bent toward base, *the lowest in whorls of 6 or 8.* **Stems** *weak, reclining, square, with tiny, downward-pointing, stiff hairs.* **Fruit** *bristly,* 1.5–5 mm wide.
OCCURRENCE: Occasional; MDI, SCH.
NOTES: Very clingy, knots up your shoelaces!
OTHER NAMES: Cleavers, Goose-grass, Scratch Bedstraw

Rough Bedstraw • *Galium asprellum*

Perennial herb of wet wood and thickets, 0.5–1 m tall. **Flowers** white, in terminal cymes. **Leaves** entire, 8–20 mm long and 2–6 mm wide, *prickly, retrorsely scabrous on margins, the lowest in whorls of 6.* **Stems** square, weak, *with downward-pointing prickles,* branched, with matted basal offshoots. **Fruit** smooth, <2 mm long.
OCCURRENCE: Occasional; MDI.

Marsh Bedstraw • *Galium palustre*

Perennial herb of swales, wet thickets, and swamp margins, 25–50 cm tall. **Flowers** white, 2.5–4 mm wide, 5 or more in terminal cymes branching 3 or more times; *pedicels strongly divergent*. **Leaves** *in whorls of 2 to 4*, entire, 1.2–1.5 cm long, *blunt at tip, thin*. **Stems** square, weak, branched. **Fruit** smooth, to 2 mm wide. **OCCURRENCE:** Occasional; MDI.

Southern Three-lobed Bedstraw • *Galium tinctorium*

Perennial herb of swales, wet thickets, and swamp margins. **Flowers** white, *1–1.8 mm wide; pedicels glabrous.* **Leaves** *in whorls of 4–6,* 5.5–22 mm long, entire, blunt at tip; principal leaves with 1 vein, firm. **Stems** weak, square, branching. **Fruit** smooth, 1–2 mm long.
OCCURRENCE: Uncommon; MDI, IAH, SCH.
OTHER NAMES: Clayton's Bedstraw, Dyer's Bedstraw, Small Bedstraw, Stiff Three-petaled Bedstraw

AH

Northern Three-lobed Bedstraw • *Galium trifidum*

Perennial herb of swamps and bogs. **Flowers** *solitary, greenish white, usually with 3 blunt petals* 0.5 mm long; *peduncles 5–30 mm long, usually 3 at each node with 1 or 3 flowers each, arching in fruit.* **Leaves** *in whorls of 4, entire,* 7–20 mm long, narrow, the lowest with 1 vein. **Stems** weak, square, *with matted basal offshoots.* **Fruit** smooth, to 2 mm wide.
OCCURRENCE: Occasional; MDI, IAH, SCH.
OTHER NAMES: Three-petaled Bedstraw, Dyer's Cleavers

Sweet-scented Bedstraw • *Galium triflorum*

Perennial herb of wet forests and thickets, [illegible] m long. **Flowers** *sweet-scented,* greenish white, 2–3 mm wide. **Leaves** *usually in whorls of 6, entire;* hairs on midvein beneath bent toward base, *hairs on margin bent toward tip.* **Stems** square, weak, *often with stiff hairs.* **Fruit** *bristly,* to 2.5 mm long.
OCCURRENCE: Uncommon; SCH.
OTHER NAMES: Fragrant Bedstraw

Yellow Bedstraw • **Galium verum*

Perennial herb of fields and disturbed sites, up to 1 m tall. **Flowers** *bright yellow,* in dense panicles, *blackened when dry.* **Leaves** usually in whorls of 8 or more, 1.5–4 cm long and 0.5–3 mm wide, entire, pubescent on lower surface, the lowest with 1 vein. **Stems** *square, stiff.* **Fruit** smooth.
OCCURRENCE: Occasional; MDI.
OTHER NAMES: Our-lady's Bedstraw

Bluets • *Houstonia caerulea*

Perennial herb of lawns, fields, and forest openings, 5–20 cm tall. **Flowers** *pale blue with yellow "eye"*, on slender, erect peduncles 1.5–7 cm long. **Leaves** opposite, entire, *mostly basal*, 5–15 mm long. **Stems** *delicate*. **Fruit** *a flat capsule 2.5–4 mm wide, with globular seeds with cavity on inner face.*
OCCURRENCE: Common; MDI, IAH, SCH.
OTHER NAMES: Quaker Ladies, Innocence, Little Bluet

Partridge-berry • *Mitchella repens*

Trailing, perennial herb of dry and wet forests, 10–30 cm long. **Flowers** *white, in terminal pairs, fragrant*, 10–14 mm wide; petals with long, soft, shaggy hairs above. **Leaves** *evergreen, opposite, entire, round to egg-shaped*, 1–2 cm long, *with white mid-vein*. **Stems** *creeping, forming mats, rooting at the nodes*. **Fruit** a solitary, fleshy, red drupe 5–8 mm wide, resulting from the union of the paired flowers, retaining the sepals lobes of both flowers.
OCCURRENCE: Occasional; MDI, IAH, SCH.

Ditch-grass • *Ruppia maritima*

Submersed, aquatic herb of saline to brackish pools and ditches, up to 75 cm long. **Flowers** with 2 stamens, no sepals or petals, in spikes at first enclosed in sheathing leaf base; *peduncles often spirally twisted.* **Leaves** 2–10 cm long and ~0.5 mm wide, with a solitary midvein. **Fruit** 1.5–3 mm long, long-stalked.
OCCURRENCE: Uncommon; MDI.
OTHER NAMES: Sea-grass, Beaked Ditch-grass

RUSCACEAE • MAYFLOWER FAMILY ▼

Canada Mayflower • *Maianthemum canadense*

Perennial herb of woods, 5–15 cm tall. **Flowers** small, white, in a short raceme. **Leaves** light green, *heart-shaped at base, 2 or 3 per plant.* **Fruit** a red, speckled berry.
OCCURRENCE: Common; MDI, IAH, SCH.
OTHER NAMES: Wild Lily-of-the-valley, False Lily-of-the-valley

False Solomon's Seal • *Maianthemum racemosum*

Perennial herb of rich woods and clearings, 0.3–1 m tall. **Flowers** white, *in a panicle 7–17 cm long.* **Leaves** oblong, *7–15 mm long.* **Stems** *zigzagging, often arching.* **Fruit** a green berry, becoming light red with maturity.
OCCURRENCE: Uncommon; MDI, SCH.
OTHER NAMES: Feathery False Solomon's Seal, False Spikenard, *Smilacina racemosa*

Star-flowered False Solomon's Seal • *Maianthemum stellatum*

Perennial herb, 30–75 cm tall. **Flowers** white, *in an unbranched cluster 2–4.5 cm long.* **Leaves** *4 or more, narrowly lance-shaped.* **Fruit** a green to red berry *striped with black.*
OCCURRENCE: Rare; MDI.
OTHER NAMES: Star-flowered Solomon's Seal, Star-like False Solomon's Seal, *Smilacina stellata*

Three-leaved False Solomon's Seal • *Maianthemum trifolium*

Perennial herb of bogs and forested wetlands, 5–20 cm tall. **Flowers** small, white, in slender *unbranched clusters*. **Leaves** *usually 3*, sometimes 2 or 4, clasping stem, *lance-shaped to elliptical, ascending*. **Fruit** a green berry, turning dull red.
OCCURRENCE: Occasional; MDI, IAH, SCH.
OTHER NAMES: Three-leaved Solomon's Seal, *Smilacina trifolia*

Hairy Solomon's Seal • *Polygonatum pubescens*

Perennial herb of moist woods and thickets, 0.3–1 m tall. **Flowers** white or greenish, *bell-shaped, 7–15 mm long, solitary or paired, drooping from stem*. **Leaves** broadly lance-shaped, *with 3–9 pubescent veins on underside*. **Stems** unbranched, arching, slender. **Fruit** a dark blue to black berry.
OCCURRENCE: Uncommon; MDI, IAH.
OTHER NAMES: Solomon's Seal

AH

White Poplar • ***Populus alba**

Deciduous tree of old home sites and fields, up to 30 m tall. **Flowers** on drooping catkins, appearing before leaves; scales toothed. **Leaves** lobed or coarsely and irregularly toothed, *with tangled, white-woolly hairs beneath; petioles pubescent.* **Buds** *with tangled, white-woolly hairs.* **Bark** whitish gray, smooth in upper trunk. **Fruit** on pedicels 1–2 mm long.
OCCURRENCE: Occasional; MDI.
OTHER NAMES: Silver Poplar

Balsam Poplar • **Populus balsamifera**

Deciduous tree of rich, wet sites, up to 30 m tall. **Flowers** in drooping catkins appearing before leaves; scales of catkins with a marginal fringe of long hairs; stamens 20–30; pedicels <2.5 mm long. **Leaves** egg-shaped, finely and regularly toothed, *shiny above and streaked with orange resin beneath.* **Buds** *large, sticky, shiny, with a sweet fragrance.* **Bark** furrowed, upper trunk smooth. **Fruit** 5–8 mm long.
OCCURRENCE: Uncommon; MDI, SCH.
NOTES: The resin-coated leaves make the tree fragrant on sunny, dry days. This is the Biblical Balm of Gilead.

CWG

Big-toothed Aspen • *Populus grandidentata*

Deciduous tree of rocky soils, up to 30 m tall. **Flowers** in drooping catkins appearing before leaves; scales of catkins with 5–7 lobes. **Leaves** with fine, matted, soft, woolly hairs beneath when young, 4–12 cm long, *not shiny above, coarsely toothed with teeth 1.5–6 mm deep*. **Buds** *with white hairs, dull, not sticky*. **Bark** greenish gray, smooth, darkening and furrowing with age; branches smooth. **Fruit** slenderly conic, 3–5 mm long, on pedicels 1–2 mm long.
OCCURRENCE: Common; MDI, IAH.
OTHER NAMES: Large-toothed Aspen, Poplar, Big-toothed Poplar

Trembling Aspen • *Populus tremuloides*

Deciduous tree of dry, rocky soils, up to 20 m tall. **Flowers** in drooping catkins appearing before leaves; scales of catkins with 3–5 lobes. **Leaves** glabrous, 2–10 cm long, *round, finely toothed, shiny above*. **Buds** *shiny, terminal, not sticky, without hairs*, <1 cm long. **Bark** grayish green, smooth, darkening and furrowing with age, branches smooth. **Fruit** slenderly conic.
OCCURRENCE: Common; MDI, IAH, SCH.
NOTES: Although seed is produced, most reproduction is clonal via underground shoots.
OTHER NAMES: Quaking Aspen, Quaking Poplar

Long-beaked Willow • *Salix bebbiana*

Deciduous shrub or tree of wet thickets and swales, up to 10 m tall. **Staminate catkins** appearing before leaves, with a stipe 3–6 mm long. **Carpellate catkins** 1–6 cm long, *expanding with leaves; bracts yellowish to red at tip.* **Leaves** 1.5–3 cm wide, *net-veined, the veins impressed above*, white-pubescent beneath; *margins entire, undulate, or bluntly toothed*, not revolute. **Twigs** *pubescent, red.* **Fruit** 5–12 mm long, with a long beak, *pubescent.*
OCCURRENCE: Common; MDI.
OTHER NAMES: Bebb's Willow

Pussy Willow • *Salix discolor*

Deciduous shrub of wet thickets, swamps, and swales, 2–7 m tall. **Staminate catkins** 2–4 cm long; filaments pubescent near base; anthers 0.5–1 mm long. **Carpellate catkins** *4–10 cm long, expanding before leaves; styles 0.2–0.4 mm long*; bracts brown to black at tip. **Leaves** alternate, the blades 4–10 cm long and 1.5–5 cm wide, white-pubescent beneath, *the veins not impressed above; margins entire, undulate, or bluntly toothed*, not revolute. **Twigs** hairy when young, becoming glabrous, *yellowish.* **Buds** <1 cm long. **Fruit** lance-shaped, *beaked, pubescent, 5–12 mm long*, on stipes 1–4.5 mm long.
OCCURRENCE: Common; MDI, SCH.

AH

Red-tipped Willow • *Salix eriocephala*

Deciduous shrub or tree of wetlands and shores, 0.2–4 m tall. **Staminate catkins** with wavy or curly scales; anthers 0.4–0.6 mm long. **Carpellate catkins** 2–5 cm long, expanding with or after leaves; styles 0.3–0.6 mm long; bracts brown to black at tip. **Leaves** *sharply and uniformly toothed*, green or white beneath, heart-shaped to rounded at base, *the youngest red*, the blades 7–15 cm long and 1.5–4 cm wide; *petioles without dark glands at apex; stipules large.* **Twigs** *yellowish, flaky*; branchlets flexible at base. **Fruit** *4–6 mm long, glabrous.*
OCCURRENCE: Uncommon; MDI.
OTHER NAMES: Heart-leaved Willow

Prairie Willow • *Salix humilis*

Deciduous upright shrub of dry areas, sandy flats, and slopes, 0.3–3 m tall. **Staminate catkins** 1–2 cm long; anthers 0.4–0.6 mm long. **Carpellate catkins** *15–32 mm long; expanding before leaves; styles 0.2–0.4 mm long*; bracts brown to black at tip. **Leaves** with white, wavy hairs beneath, the blades 3–10 cm long and 1–2.5 cm wide; margins entire, undulate, or bluntly toothed, *revolute*; petioles 3–7 mm long; stipules present on older leaves. **Twigs** often pubescent, flexible. **Fruit** *5–12 mm long, pubescent; capsule with a beak twice as long as plump base.*
OCCURRENCE: Uncommon; MDI, IAH, SCH.
OTHER NAMES: Small Pussy Willow, Upland Willow

Shining Willow • *Salix lucida*

Deciduous shrub or tree of swales, swamps, and shores, up to 4 m tall. **Staminate catkins** 2–5 cm long. **Carpellate catkins** 2–5 cm long; expanding with or after leaves; *bracts yellowish to red at tip*; styles 0.3–0.8 mm long. **Leaves** *sharply and uniformly toothed*, narrow to rounded at base, *green beneath*, the blades 5–17 cm long and 1.5–4 cm wide; petioles 5–15 mm long, *with dark glands at tip*; *stipules present on emerging leaves*. **Buds** blunt and shiny. **Fruit** *glabrous*, 4–7.5 mm long, with rugose beak, opening early.

OCCURRENCE: Uncommon; SCH.

AH

AH

Slender Willow • *Salix petiolaris*

Deciduous shrub of meadows and swales, 0.3–4 m tall. **Staminate catkins** 1–3.5 cm long; filaments hairy near base. **Carpellate catkins** 1–3.5 cm long, *expanding with or after leaves*; bracts brown to black at tip; styles 0–0.5 mm long. **Leaves** whitish beneath, *sharply toothed, sometimes entire at base*, the blades 2.5–7 cm long and 0.3–2 cm wide; expanding leaves with red-brown hairs, *mature ones quickly turning glabrous; stipules absent*. **Twigs** *flexible at base*. **Fruit** *5–9 mm long, pubescent with straight, silky hairs, beaked*.

OCCURRENCE: Occasional; MDI.

OTHER NAMES: Meadow Willow, *Salix gracilis*

AH

AH

Balsam Willow • *Salix pyrifolia*

Deciduous shrub or tree of thickets and forest edges, up to 4 m tall. **Staminate catkins** 2–8 mm long; stamens 2. **Carpellate catkins** 1–3 cm long, expanding with or after leaves; *bracts yellowish to red at tip*; styles 0.3–0.5 mm long. **Leaves** sharply or bluntly toothed, thin, *glabrous, whitened beneath*, the margins not revolute, the blades 4–13 cm long and 2–5 cm wide, net-veined beneath, *with balsamic fragrance especially when dried*; petioles 0.8–2 cm long. **Twigs** *becoming red, glabrous, and shiny*. **Fruit** *7–8 mm long, glabrous*, on stipes 1.8–3.5 mm long, subtended by scales.
OCCURRENCE: Uncommon; MDI.

AH

AH

Silky Willow • *Salix sericea*

Deciduous shrub or tree of thickets and wetland edges, up to 4 m tall. **Staminate catkins** 1–3.5 cm long. **Carpellate catkins** 2–4.5 cm long, with stipe 0.6–2.7 mm long; styles 0.1–0.6 mm long; *bracts brown to black at tip*. **Leaves** *sharply and uniformly toothed to base*, glaucous and silky beneath, *darkening on drying*, the blades 4–15 cm long and 1–4 cm wide; *expanding leaves without red-brown hairs; stipules present*. **Twigs** *brittle at base*, pubescent at nodes. **Fruit** *2.5–4 mm long, short-beaked or blunt at tip, pubescent*.
OCCURRENCE: Occasional; MDI, SCH.

AH

AH

AH AH

Dwarf Mistletoe • *Arceuthobium pusillum*

Minute shrublet, parasitic on white and black spruce branches (rarely larch and white pine), up to 2 cm tall. **Flowers** *borne singly in axils; staminate flowers usually 3-parted; carpellate flowers 2-parted.* **Leaves** *scale-like on rectangular branches.* **Stems** olive-green, rust, or purple. **Fruit** a drupe, olive to brown, 2–3.5 mm long.
OCCURRENCE: Occasional; MDI, IAH, SCH.
NOTES: Dwarf mistletoe is the cause of "witches brooms", the dense, abnormal growths seen on spruces in the park.
OTHER NAMES: Small Mistletoe, Eastern Dwarf Mistletoe

Amur Maple • **Acer ginnala*

Deciduous tree or shrub of dry, rocky woods, up to 9 m tall. **Flowers** *appearing after leaf emergence*, white, glabrous, fragrant, *in drooping, long-peduncled panicles.* **Leaves** *lobed*, green below, rounded at base, the central lobe dominant. **Buds** sessile, covered with imbricate scales. **Fruit** a samara 2–3 cm long, with wings nearly parallel.
OCCURRENCE: Uncommon; MDI, IAH.
NOTES: This nonnative species is invasive.

Striped Maple • *Acer pensylvanicum*

Deciduous tree in understory of mixed forests, up to 9 m tall. **Flowers** appearing after leaf emergence, *bright yellow*, glabrous, *in slender, drooping racemes*. **Leaves** with 3 lobes, *pale green and pubescent below*, the largest 15–20 cm long, *finely and sharply toothed*. **Bark** *green or red-brown, with slender white stripes*. **Fruit** a samara 2–3.3 cm long, ribless over seeds.
OCCURRENCE: Common; MDI, IAH, SCH.
OTHER NAMES: Moosewood, Goose-foot Maple

Norway Maple • **Acer platanoides*

Deciduous tree of mixed forests, up to 20 m tall. **Flowers** *yellow-green*, appearing before leaf emergence, with petals 4–7 mm long, glabrous, *in erect corymbs*. **Leaves** *dark green*, with 5–7 lobes, *the notches between lobes rounded, sparsely toothed; petioles with a milky sap*. **Fruit** a samara 3.5–5.5 cm long, *with divergent wings*.
OCCURRENCE: Occasional; MDI, IAH.
NOTES: This species is a prolific seeder and is aggressively invasive in natural areas.

CWG

Red Maple • *Acer rubrum*

Deciduous tree of upland and wetland forests and woodlands, up to 20 m tall. **Flowers** *red or yellow-red*, appearing before leaf emergence, in rounded clusters on short pedicels that elongate at maturity; nectar disk present. **Leaves** with 3–5 lobes, *the notches between lobes V-shaped, pale beneath*, irregularly doubly toothed, those on reproductive branches 3–10 cm wide. **Buds** sessile, with imbricate scales. **Fruit** a samara 1.5–5 cm long, the seed-bearing base 5–9 mm long.

OCCURRENCE: Common; MDI, IAH, SCH.

OTHER NAMES: Scarlet Maple, Soft Maple, Swamp Maple

Sugar Maple • *Acer saccharum*

CWG

Deciduous tree of deep, rich soils, up to 25 m tall. **Flowers** *greenish yellow, appearing during leaf emergence*; pedicels drooping, pubescent. **Leaves** with 3–5 lobes, *the notches between the lobes rounded, sparsely toothed, pale green beneath*. **Buds** brown, pointed at apex. **Fruit** a samara 2.5–4 cm long, the seed-bearing base 8–12 mm long.

OCCURRENCE: Uncommon; MDI.

OTHER NAMES: Hard Maple, Rock Maple

CWG

Mountain Maple • *Acer spicatum*

Deciduous shrub of cool, wet forests, up to 10 m tall. **Flowers** *yellow-green*, appearing after leaf emergence, pubescent, *in slender erect panicles*. **Leaves** 7.5–12.5 cm long, with 3 (sometimes 5) lobes, *coarsely toothed, with sunken veins on the upper surface*. **Twigs** pubescent. **Buds** stalked, with 2 pubescent scales. **Fruit** a samara 1.5–2.5 cm long, strongly ribbed over seeds.
OCCURRENCE: Occasional; MDI, IAH, SCH.

SARRACENIACEAE • PITCHER-PLANT FAMILY ▼

Pitcher-plant • *Sarracenia purpurea*

Perennial herb of bogs, up to 75 cm tall. **Flowers** *deep red, ~5 cm wide, nodding*. **Leaves** *funnel-shaped, the margins connate, forming a water-holding structure*, with purple veins and downward pointing hairs.
OCCURRENCE: Occasional; MDI, IAH, SCH.
NOTES: This insectivorous plant lures insects and other small organisms into leafy pitchers, where some eventually drown and decompose; the plant absorbs nutrients from this liquid.

Golden-saxifrage • *Chrysosplenium americanum*

Low, mat-forming, creeping herb of stream beds and wet sites. **Flowers** *yellow, sometimes greenish, 4–parted*, borne at tips of branches. **Leaves** opposite, obscurely toothed, *<2.5 cm long*.
OCCURRENCE: Occasional; MDI.
OTHER NAMES: Water Carpet, Water-mat

Early Saxifrage • *Micranthes virginiensis*

Perennial herb of wet, rocky ledges and outcrops, 5–40 cm tall. **Flowers** *white, 5–parted, in branched clusters blooming in early spring*. **Leaves** egg-shaped to oval, narrowing at the base, often with a reddish hue, somewhat fleshy, *1–7 cm long*.
OCCURRENCE: Uncommon; MDI.
OTHER NAMES: Early Small-flowered Saxifrage, *Saxifraga virginiensis*

Naked Miterwort • *Mitella nuda*

Rhizomatous, perennial herb of cool, wet forests (particularly cedar swamps), up to 18 cm tall. **Flowers** *greenish, 5–parted*, few per plant, *with fringed petals*. **Leaves** light green, heart-shaped, with blunt teeth.
OCCURRENCE: Uncommon; MDI.
OTHER NAMES: Naked Bishop's-cap

AH

SCHEUCHZERIACEAE • SCHEUCHZERIA FAMILY ▼

Podgrass • *Scheuchzeria palustris*

Perennial, (sometimes aquatic) herb of bogs and peaty pondshores, 20–40 cm tall. **Flowers** *yellow-green*, in a terminal raceme 3–10 cm long, with tepals 2–3 mm long. **Leaves** alternate, erect, 5–30 cm long and 1–3 mm wide, with a pore at the tip, the lowest clustered at base. **Stems** zigzagging, with hairs at nodes. **Fruit** 5–8 mm long, with 1 or 2 seeds 3–4 mm long.
OCCURRENCE: Uncommon; MDI.
OTHER NAMES: Scheuchzeria

CG

CBH

Hare Figwort • *Scrophularia lanceolata*

Perennial herb of thickets and forest edges, up to 2 m tall. **Flowers** lustrous, 5–10 mm long, *brownish with a yellow-green lower lobe*, in a terminal, branched inflorescence 10–30 cm long. **Leaves** opposite, *coarsely toothed*, 8–20 cm long, with a winged petiole 1.5–3 cm long. **Stems** 4-angled. **Seeds** 6–10 mm long.
OCCURRENCE: Uncommon; MDI.
OTHER NAMES: American Figwort, Lance-leaved Figwort

AH

AH

Woodland Figwort • **Scrophularia nodosa*

Perennial herb of rocky thickets and forest edges, up to 3 m tall. **Flowers** in a stiff, terminal panicle. **Leaves** opposite, *bluntly toothed*, acute at tip; *petioles winged, much shorter than the blade*. **Stems** 4-angled, *with thin lines on acute angles*.
OCCURRENCE: Rare; MDI.

Moth Mullein • **Verbascum blattaria*

Biennial herb of old fields and disturbed sites, 0.6–1.5 m tall. **Flowers** yellow, with purple tinge on back, 5-parted, 2–3 cm wide, in loose racemes; *sepals glandular-hairy*. **Leaves** *alternate, with glandular hairs*. **Stems** *with glandular hairs*. **Seeds** longitudinally ridged.
OCCURRENCE: Uncommon; MDI, SCH.

Common Mullein • **Verbascum thapsus*

Biennial herb of old fields, beaches, and disturbed sites, up to 2.6 m tall. **Flowers** yellow, 5-parted, 1–2.8 cm wide. **Leaves** alternate, up to 30 cm long, *woolly on both sides with branched hairs*. **Stems** *woolly with branched hairs*. **Seeds** longitudinally ridged; capsules pubescent.
OCCURRENCE: Occasional; MDI, IAH, SCH.
OTHER NAMES: flannel-plant

Bittersweet Nightshade • **Solanum dulcamara*

Woody to herbaceous, perennial vine of wet forests, ditches, shorelines, and disturbed sites, 1–3 m long. **Flowers** *purple to blue, 5-parted,* 1–1.5 cm wide, with reflexed petals; stamens yellow, clustered, up to 8 mm long; peduncles 1.5–4 cm long. **Leaves** alternate, stalked, divided into 3 leaflets or deeply lobed with larger terminal segment and small basal lobes, or sometimes entire, *with simple hairs.* **Stems** *smooth, without prickles or spines.* **Fruit** *oval, shiny, red at maturity.*
OCCURRENCE: Occasional; MDI, IAH, SCH.
NOTES: This nonnative species is invasive. All parts of plant poisonous!
OTHER NAMES: Climbing Nightshade

Buffalo Bur • **Solanum rostratum*

Weedy, annual herb of disturbed sites. **Flowers** *yellow; anthers of two lengths, the lowest longer and larger.* **Leaves** deeply divided, with branched hairs. **Stems** *with numerous yellow prickles.* **Fruit** *a round berry enclosed in a persistent covering.*
OCCURRENCE: Rare; MDI.
OTHER NAMES: Horned Nightshade

MV

MV

Lesser Bur-reed • *Sparganium americanum*

Erect, perennial herb of muddy or peaty shores. **Flowers** in a bur-like inflorescence, *spikes and lateral branches emerging from leaf axils.* **Leaves** long and slender. **Fruit** in spikes 1.5–2.5 cm wide; *beak of mature fruit circular in cross section and only slightly curving.*
OCCURRENCE: Occasional; MDI, IAH.
OTHER NAMES: American Bur-reed

Narrow-leaved Bur-reed • *Sparganium angustifolium*

Slender, submersed, perennial herb of deep or shallow water and wet shores. **Flowers** in a bur-like inflorescence, *some or all of the sessile carpellate spikes of the main axis or the pedicel bases of the lateral branches borne above the axil of leaves or bracts, the staminate portion of flowering stalk 1–4 cm long and contiguous.* **Leaves** long and slender, usually *flaccid and floating, up to 1.2 m long.* **Fruit** *a red-based achene, with a beak shorter than the achene body,* the beak 1.5–2 mm long.
OCCURRENCE: Occasional; MDI, IAH.

Green-fruited Bur-reed • *Sparganium emersum*

Erect, perennial herb of peaty, shallow water. **Flowers** in a bur-like inflorescence, *the staminate portion* of flowering stalk *4–10 cm long*. **Leaves** long and slender, *usually emergent and erect*. **Fruit** *an achene with a green base, the beak nearly as long as achene body*, the beak 2–4.5 mm long.
OCCURRENCE: Uncommon; MDI.
OTHER NAMES: Simple-stemmed Bur-reed, *Sparganium erectum, Sparganium chlorocarpum*

Floating Bur-reed • *Sparganium fluctuans*

Aquatic, perennial herb of cold lakes and ponds. **Flowers** in a bur-like inflorescence, with 2 or more spikes of staminate flowers; *tepals inserted on the basal half of the spike*. **Leaves** long and slender. **Fruit** *an achene with a flat, strongly curving beak >1.5 mm long*.
OCCURRENCE: Occasional; MDI.

DSC

DSC

Small-fruited Bur-reed • *Sparganium natans*

Very slender, submersed to emergent, perennial herb of shallow water. **Flowers** in a bur-like inflorescence, *with 1 spike of staminate flowers.* **Leaves** long and slender. **Fruit** *in spikes 5–12 mm wide; achene beak 0.5–1.5 mm long.*

OCCURRENCE: Uncommon; MDI.

OTHER NAMES: Arctic Bur-reed, *Sparganium minimum*

CBH

DSC

Narrow-leaved Cat-tail • *Typha angustifolia*

Perennial herb of coastal marshes, up to 1.5 m tall. **Flowers** *in a spike with carpellate flowers at the base and staminate flowers at the top with a space of >5 mm between them.* **Leaves** *5–11 mm wide.* **Fruit** 1-chambered, dry, wind-dispersed.

OCCURRENCE: Rare; MDI.

Broad-leaved Cat-tail • *Typha latifolia*

Perennial herb of marshes and shallow water, up to 2.5 m tall. **Flowers** *in a spike with carpellate flowers at the base and staminate flowers at the top and without space between them.* **Leaves** long, lance-shaped, *10–23 mm wide.* **Fruit** 1-chambered, dry, wind-dispersed.
OCCURRENCE: Occasional; MDI, IAH, SCH.
OTHER NAMES: Common Cat-tail

ULMACEAE • ELM FAMILY ▼

American Elm • *Ulmus americana*

Deciduous tree of rich, wet soils, up to 40 m tall. **Flowers** *in loose, drooping fascicles emerging before leaves, on unequal, long pedicels.* **Leaves** alternate, *coarsely double-toothed,* 5–15 cm long, *abruptly pointed.* **Bark** alternating in pale and dark layers. **Fruit** 9–14 mm long, *winged on all sides, with a hairy margin.*
OCCURRENCE: Rare; MDI.
OTHER NAMES: White Elm

Stinging Nettle • **Urtica dioica*

Perennial herb of coastal meado
to 2.5 m tall. **Flowers** very smal
petals; *staminate and carpellate*
slender, spreading or drooping cl
opposite, egg-shaped, with a h
toothed, *with stinging hairs us*
surfaces; stipules erect, 5–15 m
conspicuous, bulbous-based stin
OCCURRENCE: Occasiona
NOTES: Native of Eurasia; t
the pain their stinging hairs inflict whe
touched.

VERBENACEAE • VERVAIN FAMILY ▼

Blue Vervain • *Verbena hastata*

Perennial herb of damp thickets, wet meadows, shores, swales, and swamps, 0.5–1.5 m tall. **Flowers** *blue to purple, small, on branched, erect, narrow spikes.* **Leaves** lance-shaped, coarsely toothed, 5–18 cm long, the lowest sometimes lobed, *on a short stalk.* **Fruit** a *nutlet* 2 mm long.
OCCURRENCE: Uncommon; MDI.
OTHER NAMES: Simpler's-joy, Common Vervain

Sand Violet • *Viola adunca*

Perennial, tufted herb of rocky slopes, gravelly soil, and woods, 2–8 cm tall. **Flowers** pale blue to violet; *lower petal glabrous; sepals without hairs, narrow, lance-shaped.* **Leaves** variable, often with pubescence; *petioles distinctly winged* and often pubescent; *stipules fringe-toothed.* **Fruit** green to tan, 4–5 mm long. **Seeds** dark brown to olive-black, 1.5–2 mm long and 0.8–1 mm wide.
OCCURRENCE: Rare; MDI.
OTHER NAMES: Hooked Violet, Early Blue Violet, Hook-spurred Violet

AH

AH

Sweet White Violet • *Viola blanda*

Rhizomatous, perennial herb of rich woods, cool, wet slopes, and shaded ravines, 3–11 cm tall. **Flowers** white; lowest petal glabrous, *with purple to brown lines near base*; sepals without hairs. **Leaves** often wider than long, *with sparse to dense pubescence on one or both surfaces*; petioles usually longer than blade; stipules distinct. **Rhizomes** prostrate to ascending, *1–3 mm wide.* **Fruit** purple to purple-brown, 4–6 mm long. **Seeds** light to dark brown, 1.6–2.1 mm long and 1–1.3 mm wide.
OCCURRENCE: Uncommon; MDI, SCH.
OTHER NAMES: Large-leaved White Violet

AH

AH

AH

Marsh Blue Violet • *Viola cucullata*

Tufted, rhizomatous, perennial herb of bogs, swamps, and wet meadows, 4–20 cm tall. **Flowers** *light violet with white center*, rarely white with a purple border; *lower petal glabrous; lateral petals pubescent with hairs <1 mm long and knob-shaped at tip*. **Leaves** *unlobed, cordate at base, toothed*. **Rhizomes** *4–6 mm wide*. **Fruit** green, 10–15 mm long. **Seeds** dark brown to reddish or greenish black, 1.2–1.7 mm long and 0.8–1.2 mm wide.
OCCURRENCE: Occasional; MDI, IAH.
OTHER NAMES: Blue Marsh Violet

Lance-leaved Violet • *Viola lanceolata*

Rhizomatous, perennial herb of wet, sandy to peaty soil of open areas, 2–17 cm tall. **Flowers** white; lower petal glabrous, with purple to brown lines near base; lateral petals glabrous. **Leaves** glabrous, much longer than wide, *widest at the middle of the blade*, round-toothed with a minute red-brown to black gland at tip of each tooth. **Rhizomes** 1–2 mm wide. **Fruit** green, 5–8 mm long. **Seeds** brown to olive-black, 1.4–1.5 mm long and 0.9–1 mm wide.
OCCURRENCE: Occasional; MDI, IAH, SCH.
OTHER NAMES: Straw-leaved Violet

Northern White Violet • *Viola pallens*

Rhizomatous, perennial herb of wet springy meadows, thickets, woods, and shallow water, 2–9 cm tall. **Flowers** white *with purple veins on lower 3 petals*; lower petal glabrous. **Leaves** *glabrous*, rounded at apex; petioles glabrous or pubescent, usually green. **Rhizomes** prostrate to ascending, 1–2 mm wide. **Fruit** green, often with orange dots, 4–6 mm long. **Seeds** brown to nearly black, 1–1.4 mm long and 0.7–0.8 mm wide.
OCCURRENCE: Occasional; MDI, IAH, SCH.
OTHER NAMES: Small White Violet, Wild White Violet, Smooth White Violet, *Viola macloskeyi*

Primrose-leaved Violet • *Viola primulifolia*

Rhizomatous, perennial herb of wet to dry streambanks, shores, meadows, and thin woods, 5–25 cm tall. **Flowers** white; lower petal glabrous, with purple to brown lines near base. **Leaves** glabrous, much longer than wide, *widest at the base*, round-toothed with a minute red gland at tip of each tooth. **Rhizomes** 1–2 mm wide. **Fruit** green, often with orange dots, 5–8 mm long. **Seeds** red-brown to olive black, 1.5–1.7 mm long and 0.9–1.1 mm wide.
OCCURRENCE: Rare; MDI.

AH

Arrow-leaved Violet • *Viola sagittata*

Rhizomatous, perennial herb of wet to dry woods, clearings, meadows, and fields, 3–20 cm tall. **Flowers** *violet-purple; lower petal pubescent; lateral petals pubescent with hairs >1 mm long and tapering to tip*. **Leaves** glabrous to pubescent, much longer than wide, *with linear to triangular lobes at base*. **Rhizomes** *4–6 mm wide*. **Fruit** green, 6–10 mm long. **Seeds** gray or sometimes olive-black with red-brown spots, 1.3–1.8 mm long and 0.8–1.2 mm wide.
OCCURRENCE: Uncommon; MDI.
OTHER NAMES: Fringed Violet, Arrowhead Violet

Woolly Blue Violet • *Viola sororia*

Rhizomatous, perennial herb of woods, clearings, meadows, or slopes, 3–25 cm tall. **Flowers** *light violet* or rarely white; *lower petal pubescent; lateral petals pubescent with hairs >1 mm long and tapering to tip*. **Leaves** pubescent, *unlobed, cordate at base, toothed*; petioles ascending, usually pubescent. **Rhizomes** 4–6 mm wide. **Fruit** green with purple, 6–10 mm long. **Seeds** light yellow-brown to dark gray-brown, 1.5–2.5 mm long and 0.8–1.5 mm wide.
OCCURRENCE: Occasional; MDI, IAH, SCH.

CWG

Virginia Creeper • *Parthenocissus quinquefolia*

Perennial trailing or sometimes climbing liana. **Flowers** *very small, white to greenish, 25–200 in branching clusters.* **Leaves** *palmately compound, with 5 coarsely toothed leaflets; tips of tendrils with a disc-like foot that attaches to walls, tree trunks, etc., allowing the plant to climb.* **Fruit** a dark blue to black berry 5–7 mm wide.
OCCURRENCE: Uncommon; MDI.
OTHER NAMES: Woodbine

XYRIDACEAE • YELLOW-EYED-GRASS FAMILY ▼

Carolina Yellow-eyed-grass • *Xyris difformis*

Perennial herb of sometimes inundated peaty and sandy shores, 35–80 cm tall. **Flowers** yellow, 3-parted, in spikes 5–15 mm long; *floral scales 5–8 mm long, with a well-defined, green, central area.* **Leaves** grass-like, erect, *3–15 mm wide.* **Seeds** *0.5 mm long.*
OCCURRENCE: Rare; MDI.
OTHER NAMES: Yellow-eyed Grass, Bog Yellow-eyed-grass, *Xyris caroliniana*

Northern Yellow-eyed-grass • *Xyris montana*

Perennial herb of sometimes inundated peaty and sandy shores, 5–30 cm tall. **Flowers** yellow, 3-parted, in spikes <1 cm long; *floral scales 3–4.5 mm long, lacking a well-defined, green, central region.* **Leaves** grass-like, erect, *0.8–2.5 mm wide.* **Seeds** *nearly 1 mm long.*
OCCURRENCE: Occasional; MDI.
OTHER NAMES: Yellow-eyed-grass

ZOSTERACEAE • EEL-GRASS FAMILY ▼

Eel-grass • *Zostera marina*

Submerged, perennial, *marine herb of shallow water.* **Flowers** alternating staminate and carpellate in each row on the flowering spike, the spikes 2–8 cm long. **Leaves** long, linear, *parallel-veined.*
OCCURRENCE: Occasional; MDI, IAH, SCH.
OTHER NAMES: Sea-wrack, Grass-wrack

CWG

Maidenhair Spleenwort • *Asplenium trichomanes*

Rhizomatous, perennial herb of shaded rocky areas, up to 20 cm tall. **Fronds** with blades divided into pinnae (pinnate), long and narrow, *tapering at both ends*; fertile fronds erect, otherwise similar to the prostrate sterile fronds; pinnae small and rounded, smaller toward blade tip, toothed, slightly stalked. **Stipes** dark, purplish brown, brittle. **Sori** 2–4 pairs per pinna; indusia narrow, attached to one side of vein.
OCCURRENCE: Rare; MDI.

BLECHNACEAE • CHAIN FERN FAMILY ▼

Virginia Chain Fern • *Woodwardia virginica*

Perennial herb of wetlands, up to 1.5 m tall. **Fronds** with blades divided into deeply lobed pinnae (pinnate-pinnatifid), widest near the middle; *pinnae with veins netted along midrib*. **Stipes** *swollen at base, at least twice as long as blade*. **Sori** elongate, in rows on either side of midrib; indusia inconspicuous.
OCCURRENCE: Uncommon; MDI.

Hay-scented Fern • *Dennstaedtia punctilobula*

Perennial herb of spruce-fir forests and old fields, 0.4–1.3 m tall. **Fronds** with blades divided into pinnae and further divided into lobed pinnules (bipinnate-pinnatifid), *with glandular hairs, sharp pointed, with the tips drooping*; pinnae with soft hairs on both surfaces. **Stipes** slightly hairy, glandular, dark brown or black near base. **Sori** small, *at margins, in cup-shaped indusia.*
OCCURRENCE: Common; MDI, IAH, SCH.
OTHER NAMES: Boulder Fern

AH

Bracken Fern • *Pteridium aquilinum*

Perennial herb of forests, meadows, uplands, and wetlands, up to 1 m tall. **Fronds** with blades divided into pinnae and further divided into lobed pinnules (bipinnate-pinnatifid) or pinnulets (tripinnate), *broadly triangular*; pinnae longer than wide, *distinctly stalked.* **Stipes** about as long as blade, *grooved.* **Sori** along pinnule margins, *rare.*
OCCURRENCE: Common; MDI, IAH, SCH.
NOTES: This fern is among the most widely distributed plants on earth, growing on all continents except Antarctica.
OTHER NAMES: Hogbrake

Mountain Wood Fern • *Dryopteris campyloptera*

Perennial herb typically of hardwood forests, up to 1 m tall. **Fronds** with blades divided into pinnae and further divided into lobed pinnules (bipinnate-pinnatifid) or pinnulets (tripinnate); pinnules with bristles on teeth; *innermost lower pinnule of basal pinnae 2 times the width and 3–5 times the length of offset upper pinnule and longer than or equal to adjacent pinnule.* **Stipes** *with tan scales without central dark stripe.* **Sori** round, numerous, located between midvein and margin; indusia kidney-shaped.
OCCURRENCE: Occasional; MDI, IAH, SCH.
OTHER NAMES: Spreading Wood Fern, *Dryopteris spinulosa* var. *americana*

Spinulose Wood Fern • *Dryopteris carthusiana*

Widely distributed fern of hardwood and conifer forests, up to 80 cm tall. **Fronds** with blades divided into pinnae and further divided into lobed pinnules (bipinnate-pinnatifid) or pinnulets (tripinnate); pinnules with bristles on teeth; *innermost lower pinnule of basal pinnae not much wider and 2 times the length of offset upper pinnule and longer than or equal to adjacent pinnule.* **Stipes** with pale brown scales. **Sori** *small,* located between midvein and margin of pinnules; indusia kidney-shaped.
OCCURRENCE: Common; MDI, IAH, SCH.
OTHER NAMES: Toothed Wood Fern, *Dryopteris spinulosa*

Crested Wood Fern • *Dryopteris cristata*

Perennial herb of forested wetlands, up to 70 cm long. **Fronds** with blades divided into deeply lobed pinnae (pinnate-pinnatifid); *with narrow, parallel-sided blades; lowest pinnae widely spaced, blunt.* **Stipes** with abundant light brown scales. **Sori** round, numerous, located between midvein and margin; indusia kidney-shaped.

OCCURRENCE: Occasional; MDI.

NOTES: This species hybridizes with several others, producing plants intermediate between the parents, making them difficult to identify.

Fragrant Wood Fern • *Dryopteris fragrans*

Perennial herb of cliffs and seaside headlands, up to 40 cm tall. **Fronds** with blades divided into pinnae and further divided into lobed pinnules (bipinnate-pinnatifid); narrowing at both ends, *with abundant aromatic glands*, with *dried fronds persisting at base*; pinnae crowded, with rounded teeth. **Stipes** short, with shining, reddish scales. **Sori** round, numerous, large, located between midvein and margin; indusia kidney-shaped, *with glands on margin.*

OCCURRENCE: Rare; SCH.

AH

AH

Glandular Wood Fern • *Dryopteris intermedia*

Perennial herb of forests, up to 90 cm tall. **Fronds** with blades divided into pinnae and further divided into lobed pinnules (bipinnate-pinnatifid) or pinnulets (tripinnate); *with glandular hairs on rachis; innermost lower pinnule of basal pinnae shorter than or equal to adjacent pinnule.* **Stipes** with scales mostly at base. **Sori** round, small, located between midvein and margin; indusia kidney-shaped.
OCCURRENCE: Common; MDI.
OTHER NAMES: Evergreen Wood Fern, Fancy Wood Fern, *Dryopteris spinulosa* var. *intermedia*

Marginal Wood Fern • *Dryopteris marginalis*

Perennial herb of rocky slopes, up to 1.3 m tall. **Fronds** with blades divided into deeply lobed pinnae (pinnate-pinnatifid) or divided into pinnules (bipinnate); arching; *pinnae entire.* **Stipes** stout, brittle, with many long scales mostly at base. **Sori** *prominent on margins of pinnae*; indusia kidney-shaped, without glands.
OCCURRENCE: Common; MDI, IAH.

Christmas Fern • *Polystichum acrostichoides*

Perennial herb of shady areas, up to 1 m tall. **Fronds** with blades divided into pinnae (pinnate), leathery, smooth on upper surface and scaly below; pinnae shiny green, with bristle-toothed edges, *with a basal lobe*. **Stipes** *short, scaly, stout*. **Sori** *completely covering lower surface of distal pinnae when mature*; indusia round, attached at center.
OCCURRENCE: Occasional; MDI, IAH.

EQUISETACEAE • HORSETAIL FAMILY ▼

Field Horsetail • *Equisetum arvense*

Perennial herb of wet meadows, roadsides, and woods, 0.1–1 m tall. **Stems** dimorphic; *fertile stems leafless, with strobili 2.5–4 cm long*, emerging in spring and producing spores mid-April to May, withering soon after; sterile stems green, hollow, grooved, emerging later than fertile stems. **Branches** whorled, *not rebranching*. **Leaves** tiny, whorled, fused into a sheath around each node.
OCCURRENCE: Occasional; MDI, IAH, SCH.
OTHER NAMES: Common Horsetail, Common Field Horsetail

Water Horsetail • *Equisetum fluviatile*

Perennial herb of wetlands and shallow fresh water, 0.4–1.2 m tall. **Stems** with fertile and sterile stems alike, hollow, thin-walled, 2.5–9 mm wide; strobili appearing in summer, 1–2 cm long. **Branches** up to 15 cm long, often absent. **Leaves** tiny, whorled, fused into a sheath around each node.
OCCURRENCE: Uncommon; MDI.
OTHER NAMES: River Horsetail, Pipes

Woodland Horsetail • *Equisetum sylvaticum*

Perennial herb of wet roadsides, forests, fields, wetlands, and thickets, 25–70 cm tall. **Stems** dimorphic; *fertile stems pale, branching and looking like sterile stems after spores discharge, with strobili 1.5–3 cm long, falling off after pollen production*; sterile stems brownish to green, hollow. **Branches** *often rebranching*. **Leaves** tiny, whorled, fused into a sheath around each node.
OCCURRENCE: Common; MDI, IAH, SCH.
OTHER NAMES: Wood Horsetail

CWG

Mountain Firmoss • *Huperzia appressa*

Diminutive, evergreen herb of exposed, rocky sites, 6–10 cm tall. **Sporangia** on upper portion of stem. **Leaves** *green to yellow-green, 2–6 mm long, pointed, entire, with parallel margins.* **Stems** *clustered.*
OCCURRENCE: Rare; MDI, IAH.
NOTES: Maine Natural Areas Program ranks this species as of special concern in Maine.
OTHER NAMES: *Huperzia appalachiana, Lycopodium selago* var. *appressum*

CWG

ISOËTACEAE • QUILLWORT FAMILY ▼

Acadian Quillwort • *Isoëtes acadiensis*

CWG

Small, aquatic, perennial herb of lakes and slow-moving streams. **Megaspores** *with smooth girdle and smooth, rounded ridges* (see lower right photo), produced at the leaf bases. **Leaves** slender, unbranched, pliant, *curling at tips*, flattening into a spoon-like shape at base (see left photo).
OCCURRENCE: Rare; MDI.
NOTES: Maine Natural Areas Program ranks this species as of special concern in Maine.

DSC

DSC

Spiny-spored Quillwort • *Isoëtes echinospora*

Small, aquatic, perennial herb of lakes and slow-moving streams. **Megaspores** *covered with small spines,* produced at the leaf bases. **Leaves** slender, unbranched, flattening into a spoon-like shape at base.
OCCURRENCE: Occasional; MDI, IAH.
OTHER NAMES: *Isoëtes muricata*

DSC

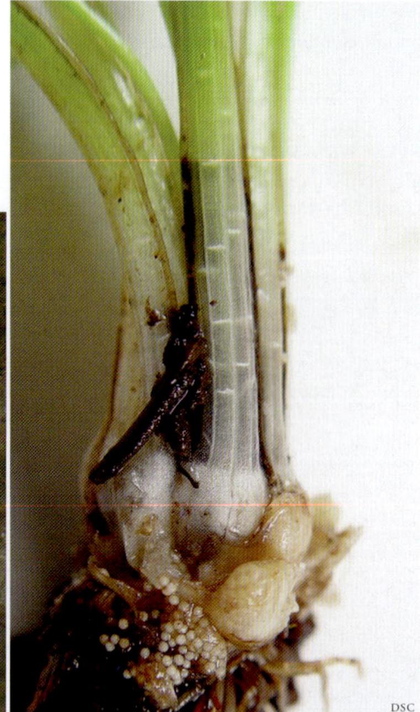

DSC

Deep-water Quillwort • *Isoëtes lacustris*

Small, aquatic, perennial herb of lakes and slow-moving streams, *often in water 1–3 m deep.* **Megaspores** *0.5–0.8 mm wide, with an evident girdle,* produced at the leaf bases. **Leaves** dark green, slender, unbranched, flattening into a spoon-like shape at base.
OCCURRENCE: Uncommon; MDI.
OTHER NAMES: Lake Quillwort, *Isoëtes macrospora*

AH

Prototype Quillwort • ***Isoëtes prototypus***

Small, aquatic, perennial herb of cold, clear lakes, submerged in water to 1 m deep. **Megaspores** *<6 mm wide, with the girdle only vaguely evident,* produced at the leaf bases. **Leaves** slender, unbranched, *rigid, straight,* flattening into a spoon-like shape at base.

OCCURRENCE: Rare; MDI.

NOTES: Maine Natural Areas Program ranks this species as threatened in Maine.

Tuckerman's Quillwort • ***Isoëtes tuckermanii***

Small, aquatic, perennial herb of lakes and slow-moving streams, usually in water <1 m deep. **Megaspores** *with honeycomb-like ridges on the rounded side,* produced at the leaf bases. **Leaves** slender, unbranched, *soft, curling at tip,* flattening into a spoon-like shape at base.

OCCURRENCE: Occasional; MDI, IAH.

Prickly Tree Clubmoss • *Dendrolycopodium dendroideum*

Perennial herb of dry forests, 12–30 cm tall. **Strobili** *sessile*, 1–7 per stem, ~4 cm long. **Leaves** *equal in size*, pointed at tip, *spreading on the main stem below the branches; in alternating pseudowhorls of 2 upper, 2 lower, and 2 lateral untwisted leaves.* **Lateral branches** *round in cross section.* **Upright stems** *prickly to the touch.*
OCCURRENCE: Occasional; MDI.
OTHER NAMES: *Lycopodium dendroideum, Lycopodium obscurum* var. *dendroideum, Lycopodium obscurum* var. *hybridum*

Flat-branched Tree Clubmoss • *Dendrolycopodium obscurum*

Perennial herb of forests and shrubby areas, up to 21 cm tall. **Strobili** *sessile*, 1–6 per stem, ~4 cm long. **Leaves** *unequal in size*, pointed at tip, *tightly appressed on the main stem below the branches; in alternating pseudowhorls of 1 upper (appressed), 1 lower (much smaller than others), and 4 lateral (twisted, not keeled) leaves.* **Lateral branches** *flat in cross section.* **Upright stems** *not prickly to the touch.*
OCCURRENCE: Occasional; MDI, IAH.
OTHER NAMES: *Lycopodium obscurum*

Southern Ground-cedar • *Diphasiastrum digitatum*

Perennial herb of dry soils, 15–50 cm tall. **Strobili** 2–4 per stalk, *2–4 cm long, on long stalks.* **Leaves** *unequal in size; in alternating pseudowhorls of 1 upper (appressed), 1 lower (much smaller than others), and 2 lateral (keeled, spreading at tips) leaves.* **Lateral branches** *flat in cross section.* **Upright stems** *branching up to 3 times.*
OCCURRENCE: Uncommon; MDI.
OTHER NAMES: *Diphasium flabelliforme, Lycopodium complanatum* var. *flabelliforme, Lycopodium digitatum, Lycopodium flabelliforme*

AH

Blue Gound-cedar • *Diphasiastrum tristachyum*

Perennial herb of dry, upland forests, 15–35 cm tall. **Strobili** 3 or 4 per stalk, *10–24 mm long, on long stalks.* **Leaves** *unequal in size; in alternating pseudowhorls of 1 upper (appressed, same size as lower), 1 lower (same size as upper), and 2 lateral (keeled, twice the size of upper and lower ones) leaves.* **Lateral branches** *4-angled in cross section.* **Upright stems** *branching 4–7 times.*
OCCURRENCE: Uncommon; MDI.
OTHER NAMES: *Diphasium tristachyum, Lycopodium chamaecyparissus, Lycopodium tristachyum*

AH

AH

Northern Bog Clubmoss • *Lycopodiella inundata*

Perennial herb of bogs, <10 cm tall. **Strobili** *1 per stalk, bushy*, 1–7 cm long. **Leaves** narrow, ascending or spreading, *seldom toothed*. **Upright stems** *solitary, unbranched, upright*.
OCCURRENCE: Uncommon; MDI, IAH.
OTHER NAMES: *Lepidotis inundata, Lycopodium inundatum*

Common Clubmoss • *Lycopodium clavatum*

Perennial herb of dry fields and open woods, 10–25 cm tall. **Strobili** *1–5 per stalk (commonly more than 2)*, ~8 cm long, *on long, branched stalks*. **Leaves** 4–6 mm long, *with a long colorless hair at tip*. **Lateral branches** *round in cross section*. **Upright stems** bristly, *with 2 or 3 spreading to ascending branches*.
OCCURRENCE: Occasional; MDI.

One-cone Clubmoss • *Lycopodium lagopus*

Perennial herb of fields and open woods, 10–25 cm tall. **Strobili** *1 or rarely 2 per stalk*, ~8 cm long. **Leaves** 3–5 mm long, *with a long colorless hair at tip*. **Lateral branches** *round in cross section*. **Upright stems** bristly, *with 2 or 3 upright branches*.
OCCURRENCE: Uncommon; MDI.
OTHER NAMES: *Lycopodium clavatum* var. *lagopus, Lycopodium clavatum* var. *megastachyon, Lycopodium clavatum* var. *monostachyon*

AH

AH

Interrupted Clubmoss • *Spinulum annotinum*

Perennial herb of coniferous forests, ~15 cm tall. **Strobili** *usually 1 per upright stem*, 1.5–4 cm long, *sessile*. **Leaves** 5–10 mm long, *with a minute bristle at tip*. **Lateral branches** *round in cross section*. **Upright stems** *branching near base*.
OCCURRENCE: Uncommon; MDI, IAH, SCH.
OTHER NAMES: *Lycopodium annotinum*

Sensitive Fern • *Onoclea sensibilis*

Rhizomatous, perennial herb of open and forested wetlands, up to 1.3 m tall. **Fertile fronds** *erect, appearing as clusters of green beads, becoming brown and persisting through the winter.* **Sterile fronds** with blade lobed but not fully cut to the rachis (pinnatifid), green, triangular, *with netted veins* (see left photo); *pinnae untoothed.* **Stipes** longer than blade, yellowish.
OCCURRENCE: Common; MDI, IAH, SCH.

OPHIOGLOSSACEAE • ADDER'S-TONGUE FAMILY ▼

Moonwort • *Botrychium lunaria*

Diminutive perennial herb of open areas, 3–25 cm tall. **Sporophores** branched, with sporangia on the surface, erect in bud, *0.5–7 cm long.* **Sterile blades** *1–9 cm long and 0.7–3.6 cm wide, glabrous, bright green,* succulent, *divided into 6–9 pairs of fan-shaped pinnae.*
OCCURRENCE: Rare; MDI.
NOTES: Maine Natural Areas Program ranks this species as endangered in Maine. It requires high-pH soils and is often associated with shell middens.
OTHER NAMES: Common Moonwort

Rattlesnake-fern • *Botrychium virginianum*

Perennial herb of shaded woods, 5–75 cm tall. **Sporophores** branched, with sporangia on the surface, *6–15 cm long*. **Sterile blades** divided, *7–20 cm long and 10–30 cm wide, sparingly pilose, more or less 3-parted.*
OCCURRENCE: Rare; MDI.
OTHER NAMES: Common Grapefern

AH

Northern Adder's-tongue • *Ophioglossum pusillum*

Perennial herb of open fields and marshes, 7–35 cm tall. **Sporophores** *1–5 cm long and 2.5–4 mm wide, with 2 rows of sporangia embedded in tip, with copious sulphur-yellow spores*. **Sterile blades** *unlobed*, widest at the middle, 4–8 cm long and 1–4 cm wide.
OCCURRENCE: Rare; MDI.
OTHER NAMES: Northern Adder's-tongue Fern, *Ophioglossum vulgatum*

AH

AH

CWG

Interrupted Fern • *Osmunda claytoniana*

Tall, perennial herb of woodlands and wetlands, up to 1.5 m tall. **Fertile fronds** with blades divided into deeply lobed pinnae (pinnate-pinnatifid), taller than sterile fronds, *with 2–5 pairs of fertile pinnae midway on the rachis.* **Sterile fronds** pinnate-pinnatifid, widest at the middle; *pinnae with few or no tufts of hairs at base.* **Sori** absent; sporangia short-stalked. **Stipes** smooth, green, *hairy early, becoming glabrous.*
OCCURRENCE: Common; MDI, IAH, SCH.
NOTES: Fiddleheads from this species carcinogenic.

Royal Fern • *Osmunda regalis*

Tall, perennial herb, primarily of wetlands, up to 1.5 m tall. **Fertile fronds** with blades divided into pinnae and further divided into pinnules (bipinnate), similar to sterile fronds, *with fertile pinnae at branch tips.* **Sterile fronds** *bipinnate.* **Sori** absent; sporangia short-stalked. **Stipes** smooth, reddish at base.
OCCURRENCE: Occasional; MDI, IAH.
NOTES: Fiddleheads from this species carcinogenic.
OTHER NAMES: flowering Fern

CWG

Cinnamon Fern • *Osmundastrum cinnamomeum*

Perennial herb of woodlands and wetlands, up to 1.5 m tall. **Fertile fronds** *cinnamon-colored at maturity, narrow, without expanded pinnae*. **Sterile fronds** with blades divided into deeply lobed pinnae (pinnate-pinnatifid); *pinnae with tufts of white-brown hairs at base*. **Sori** absent; sporangia large, short-stalked. **Stipes** slightly shorter than blade, smooth, green, *with at least some with long hairs*.
OCCURRENCE: Common; MDI, IAH, SCH.
NOTES: Fiddleheads from this species carcinogenic.
OTHER NAMES: *Osmunda cinnamomea*

POLYPODIACEAE • POLYPODY FAMILY ▼

Appalachian Polypody • *Polypodium appalachianum*

Rhizomatous, perennial herb of rocks and cliffs, up to 40 cm tall. **Fronds** with blade lobed but not fully cut to rachis (pinnatifid), *widest just above base, lobes with narrow tips*. **Stipes** slender, round, light green. **Sori** round, prominent; indusia absent.
OCCURRENCE: Uncommon; MDI.

Rock Polypody • *Polypodium virginianum*

Fern of rocks and cliffs, usually under forest canopy, *evergreen*, up to 40 cm tall. **Fronds** with blade lobed but not fully cut to rachis (pinnatifid), *widest near middle, lobes with blunt tips*. **Stipes** slender, round, light green. **Sori** round, prominent; indusia absent.
OCCURRENCE: Occasional; MDI, IAH, SCH.
OTHER NAMES: Common Polypody, Polypody Fern

PTERIDACEAE • MAIDENHAIR-FERN FAMILY ▼

Northern Maidenhair-fern • *Adiantum pedatum*

Perennial herb of rich hardwood forests, up to 75 cm tall. **Fronds** *divided at summit into 2 spreading rachises; pinnae elongated, smooth, divided into 12–35 pinnules; pinnules alternate, fan-shaped, 12–22 mm long and 5–9 mm wide*; sterile and fertile fronds similar. **Stipes** long and smooth, with scales at base, *black or purplish brown*. **Sori** *elongate; indusia formed from reflexed margin of pinnules.*
OCCURRENCE: Uncommon; MDI.

Meadow Spikemoss • *Selaginella rupestris*

Perennial herb of exposed rocky areas, up to 6 cm tall. **Strobili** *at ends of branches, 4-angled.* **Leaves** *<5 mm long, appressed, spirally arranged, bristle-tipped.* **Stems** much branched, creeping.
OCCURRENCE: Rare; MDI.
OTHER NAMES: Creeping Spikemoss, Rock Spikemoss, Ledge Spikemoss

THELYPTERIDACEAE • MARSH FERN FAMILY ▼

New York Fern • *Parathelypteris noveboracensis*

Perennial herb of open and forested sites, up to 70 cm tall. **Fronds** with blades divided into deeply lobed pinnae (pinnate-pinnatifid), *tapering to base and tip; lowest pinnae often minute.* **Stipes** *shorter than the blade, often darkened.* Sori few, round, small, near margins; indusia <1 mm wide, pale, with long hairs.
OCCURRENCE: Common; MDI, IAH, SCH.
OTHER NAMES: *Dryopteris noveboracensis, Thelypteris noveboracensis*

AH

Long Beech Fern • *Phegopteris connectilis*

Perennial herb of wet woods, up to 50 cm tall. **Fronds** with blades divided into deeply lobed pinnae (pinnate-pinnatifid), *triangular*, often hairy; *lowest pinnae distinctly angled down*. **Stipes** hairy, scaly. **Sori** small and round, near margins; *indusia absent*.
OCCURRENCE: Occasional; MDI, IAH, SCH.
OTHER NAMES: *Dryopteris phegopteris*

Marsh Fern • *Thelypteris palustris*

Perennial herb of open and forested wetlands, up to 1 m tall. **Fronds** with blades divided into deeply lobed pinnae (pinnate-pinnatifid), without glands, pale green, *often twisted*; pinnae with forked veins, *margins of fertile segments revolute*. **Stipes** *longer than blade*. **Sori** numerous, round, near midvein; indusia often hairy.
OCCURRENCE: Occasional; MDI, IAH, SCH.
OTHER NAMES: *Dryopteris thelypteris*

Lady Fern • *Athyrium angustum*

Perennial herb of wet woods and wetlands, up to 1 m tall. **Fronds** with blades divided into pinnae and further divided into 12–20 lobed pinnules (bipinnate-pinnatifid), *usually drooping at tip, in circular clusters*; blades broadest near middle; *pinnules with toothed margins*; sterile and fertile fronds similar. **Stipes** *smooth, with dark brown scales, without glandular hairs.* **Sori** *elongate, usually arched (eyebrow-shaped)*; indusia attached along one side, hairy.
OCCURRENCE: Occasional; MDI, IAH, SCH.
OTHER NAMES: Narrow Lady Fern, *Athyrium filix-femina*

Fragile Fern • *Cystopteris fragilis*

Perennial herb of rocky forests and cliffs, up to 40 cm long. **Fronds** with blades divided into pinnae and further divided into variously lobed and toothed pinnules (bipinnate-pinnatifid), widest just below middle; pinnae at right angles to rachis, *lowest widely spaced*; sterile and fertile fronds similar. **Stipes** *brittle*, smooth, dark, with few scales near base. **Sori** scattered on veins; indusia round, thin, attached on one side of sori, without glandular hairs.
OCCURRENCE: Rare; MDI, IAH, SCH.
OTHER NAMES: Brittle Fern, Brittle Bladder-fern

AH

Silver Spleenwort • *Deparia acrostichoides*

Perennial herb of rich hardwood forests, up to 1.2 m tall. **Fronds** with blades divided into deeply lobed pinnae (pinnate-pinnatifid); hairy along veins, tapering at both ends, *with lowest pair of pinnae downward pointing*; fertile fronds taller and more erect than sterile ones. **Stipes** *short, dark red-brown and swollen at base*, with long, white hairs and light brown scales. **Sori** parallel to the veinlets of the pinnae.

OCCURRENCE: Rare; MDI.

OTHER NAMES: Silver Glade Fern, *Athyrium thelypteroides*

AH
AH

AH

Oak Fern • *Gymnocarpium dryopteris*

Perennial herb of upland and wetland forests, up to 50 cm tall. **Fronds** with blades divided into pinnae and further divided into lobed pinnules (bipinnate-pinnatifid); *broadly triangular; lower pinnae at right angles to stipe and almost parallel to ground*; upper surface without glandular hairs. **Stipes** *longer than blade, dark at base.* **Sori** small, rounded, located near margin, *without indusia.*

OCCURRENCE: Occasional; MDI, IAH, SCH.

OTHER NAMES: Northern Oak Fern

Rusty Cliff Fern • *Woodsia ilvensis*

Perennial herb of dry, exposed rocks and cliffs, up to 30 cm tall. **Fronds** with blades divided into deeply lobed pinnae (pinnate-pinnatifid); *with abundant brown hairs and scales*; pinnae with veins that do not extend to the margins. **Stipes** stout, brittle, hairy. **Sori** round, numerous; *indusia multilobed, with filamentous segments.*
OCCURRENCE: Uncommon; MDI.
OTHER NAMES: Rusty Woodsia, Cliff Fern

AH

Ground Juniper • *Juniperus communis*

Low, evergreen shrub of dry fields, and shores, sometimes forming extensive mats on coastal headlands. **Leaves** needle-like, *blue-green with white or yellowish central stripe*, whorled, often in groups of 3, *tapering to a sharp point.* **Seed cones** fleshy, resembling a berry, *borne in axils of branches.*
OCCURRENCE: Common; MDI, IAH, SCH.
OTHER NAMES: Common Juniper

Bar Harbor Juniper • *Juniperus horizontalis*

Prostrate, evergreen shrub of exposed coastal headlands. **Leaves** *scale-like on mature branches and needle-like on young branches, blue-green,* opposite, *appressed.* **Seed cones** fleshy, resembling a berry, *borne on branch tips.*
OCCURRENCE: Occasional; MDI, IAH, SCH.
OTHER NAMES: Creeping Juniper

Northern White-cedar • *Thuja occidentalis*

Upright, evergreen tree or shrub of wet slopes and woods, up to 20 m tall. **Leaves** *deep green*, scale-like, *keeled and overlapping*; *branchlets flat*. **Bark** shredding, light reddish brown. **Seed cones** *leathery-woody, erect*, with winged seeds inside the larger, middle scales.
OCCURRENCE: Common; MDI, IAH, SCH.
NOTES: A favorite food of deer. Although usually thought of as a wetland species, this tree forms extensive woodlands on the rocky slopes on some of the mountains in Acadia National Park.
OTHER NAMES: Eastern White-cedar, Arbor Vitae

PINACEAE • PINE FAMILY ▼

Balsam Fir • *Abies balsamea*

Evergreen tree of uplands and wetlands, up to 25 m tall. **Leaves** *a flat needle with whitened lower surface and prominent midrib*, 1–3.2 cm long, sessile, *leaving circular scar*. **Twigs** pubescent to glabrous. **Bark** thin, with resin-filled blisters. **Seed cones** erect, 3–8.5 cm long, on upper sides of branches, violet-magenta when young, becoming brown.
OCCURRENCE: Common; MDI, IAH, SCH.

American Larch • *Larix laricina*

Deciduous tree or shrub of wetlands, up to 20 m tall. **Leaves** *soft, needle-like*, 1–2.5 cm long, in circular clusters on short, woody spurs on older branches or scattered spirally on younger branches, *turning vibrant yellow in autumn*. **Twigs** with many spurs. **Bark** thin and scaly. **Seed cones** ovoid, upright, 1.2–2 cm long.
OCCURRENCE: Occasional; MDI, IAH, SCH.
NOTES: This is our only deciduous conifer; the wood is resistant to decay and is often used in construction of docks and wharves.
OTHER NAMES: Hackmatack, The Larch, Tamarack, Black Larch

White Spruce • *Picea glauca*

Evergreen tree of maritime, spruce-fir forests and old fields, up to 30 m tall. **Leaves** needle-like, *whitened*, 12–19 mm long, stiff, *with an odor of cat urine when crushed*. **Twigs** whitened to orange-brown, glaucous, glabrous. **Bark** thin and scaly, the inner bark whitish. **Seed cones** 3–5 cm long, *longer than wide*, with entire margin on thin scales.
OCCURRENCE: Common; MDI, IAH, SCH.
OTHER NAMES: Cat Spruce

Black Spruce • *Picea mariana*

Evergreen tree or shrub of wetlands, up to 25 m tall. **Leaves** needle-like, 6–15 mm long, blunt, *dull bluish green*. **Twigs** *with glandular pubescence*. **Bark** thin, scaly, *the inner bark yellowish*. **Seed cones** 1.5–3 cm long, remaining attached after opening, often clustered near top of tree, *with brittle scales with ragged margins*.
OCCURRENCE: Occasional; MDI, IAH, SCH.
OTHER NAMES: Bog Spruce

Red Spruce • *Picea rubens*

Evergreen tree of inland and coastal forests, up to 30 m tall. **Leaves** needle-like, 6–15 mm long, stiff, with a sharp point, *shiny, yellowish green*. **Twigs** *pubescent*. **Bark** thin, scaly, the inner bark yellowish. **Seed cones** 1.5–3 cm long, *almost round when open*, remaining attached after opening, often clustered near top of tree, *with scales entire or barely toothed*.
OCCURRENCE: Common; MDI, IAH, SCH.

Jack Pine • *Pinus banksiana*

Evergreen tree or shrub, up to 20 m tall. **Leaves** needle-like, *in fascicles of 2, 2–4 cm long, the pairs widely forking*. **Bark** thin, with narrow, scaly ridges. **Seed cones** 3–5 cm long, usually remaining closed.
OCCURRENCE: Occasional; MDI, SCH.
NOTES: at the southern limit of its range in our area, restricted to a few stands here, the largest on the Schoodic Peninsula
OTHER NAMES: Scrub Pine, Gray Pine

CWG

Red Pine • *Pinus resinosa*

Evergreen tree of deep, sandy soils, up to 25 m tall. **Leaves** needle-like, *in fascicles of 2, 7–16 cm long*, with marginal resin ducts, *brittle, snapping when bent*. **Bark** *reddish, with wide, flat scales*. **Seed cones** 4–6 cm long, nearly stalkless, opening and shedding from tree soon after maturity.
OCCURRENCE: Occasional; MDI, IAH, SCH.

CWG

Pitch Pine • *Pinus rigida*

Evergreen tree of granite outcrops, up to 15 m tall. **Leaves** needle-like, *in fascicles of 3, 3.5–14 cm long, often twisted.* **Bark** rough, furrowed. **Seed cones** 3–7 cm long, often clustered, persistent.
OCCURRENCE: Occasional; MDI, IAH, SCH.

White Pine • *Pinus strobus*

Evergreen tree of forests and fields, up to 40 m tall. **Leaves** needle-like, *in fascicles of 5, 6–13 cm long.* **Bark** smooth in young trees, becoming rough, thick, and furrowed with age. **Seed cones** much longer than wide, up to 20 cm long, with long stalk.
OCCURRENCE: Common; MDI, IAH, SCH.
NOTES: White pine is very fast-growing and even 20-year-old trees can be large.
OTHER NAMES: Eastern White Pine

Scotch Pine • **Pinus sylvestris***

Evergreen tree, up to 20 m tall. **Leaves** needle-like, *in fascicles of 2, twisted, blue-green, 3–7 cm long*. **Bark** thin, scaly, reddish brown, older trees often shedding plates of bark. **Seed cones** 3–6 cm long, with a short stalk.
OCCURRENCE: Uncommon; MDI.

Eastern Hemlock • ***Tsuga canadensis***

Evergreen tree, of cool, wet sites, often growing as a monoculture or with yellow birch and sugar maple, up to 25 m tall. **Leaves** needle-like, 8–13 mm long, blunt-tipped, flat, with *2 white lines on underside, with a short petiole*. **Bark** coarse, the inner bark rose-colored. **Seed cones** 1.5–2.5 cm long, with suborbicular scales, pendent from ends of twigs.
OCCURRENCE: Occasional; MDI, IAH.

American Yew • *Taxus canadensis*

Evergreen shrub of forests, up to 2 m tall. **Leaves** *linear, flat, green on underside.* **Stems** diffuse. **Seeds** naked, surrounded by a red, juicy, cup-shaped aril.
OCCURRENCE: Rare; MDI.
OTHER NAMES: Canada Yew, Ground-hemlock

Saltmarsh Bulrush • *Bolboschoenus maritimus*

Rhizomatous, perennial herb of coastal marshes and shores, 0.5–1.5 m tall. **Spikelets** 2–40, *sessile*, 7–40 mm long and 4–10 mm wide, *usually densely clustered near the top of the stem, with many long, leafy, subtending bracts.* **Leaves** 2–12 mm wide. **Achenes** *with bristles reaching beyond the top.* **Tubers** *large, bulbous.*
OCCURRENCE: Occasional; MDI, IAH, SCH.
NOTES: *A very coarse, stocky-looking plant.*
OTHER NAMES: Alkali Bulrush, Bayonet-grass, Saltmarsh Tuber-bulrush, *Scirpus maritimus, Scirpus paludosus*

Tufted Hair-sedge • *Bulbostylis capillaris*

Densely tufted, annual herb of dry, open areas, 30–40 cm tall. **Spikelets** relatively large, *purplish to black.* **Leaves** very fine and mostly basal, minutely hairy, *turning a bright coppery orange in the fall.* **Achenes** *triangular, with a tiny bump (tubercle) at the top.* **Stems** *short, stiff, hair-like.*
OCCURRENCE: Common; MDI, SCH.
OTHER NAMES: Vagabond, Hair Sedge

Swarthy Sedge • *Carex adusta*

Tufted, short-lived, perennial herb of disturbed roadsides, blueberry barrens, dry woods, and fields, 14–30 cm tall. **Spikelets** 5–8, *stiffly erect*, very dense, *greenish brown to gold*, with staminate flowers at base. **Leaves** *with tips U- or V-shaped.* **Perigynia** erect to spreading; subtending *scales equal to or exceeding the perigynium, reddish brown with pale centers.* **Achenes** widest at top to elliptic.
OCCURRENCE: Rare; MDI, IAH.
NOTES: Section *Ovales.*
OTHER NAMES: Burnt Sedge, Lesser Brown Sedge

CWG

MA

Emmons' Sedge • *Carex albicans*

Tufted, perennial herb of forests and open areas, 5–50 cm tall. **Spikelets** *sessile; inflorescence 8–30 mm long.* **Leaves** *0.5–2.5 mm wide; usually shorter than the inflorescence; ligules wider than long.* **Perigynia** 2.3–3.2 mm long and 0.7–1.1 mm wide; beak 0.5–0.9 mm long.
OCCURRENCE: Uncommon; MDI.
NOTES: Section *Acrocystis.*
OTHER NAMES: White-tinged Sedge, *Carex emmonsii, Carex artitecta*

Yellow-fruited Sedge • *Carex annectens*

Perennial herb of wet meadows, ditches, shores, and marshes, 0.7–1 m tall. **Spikelets** *stiff, clustered in a head 2–10 cm long*, with staminate flowers at base. **Leaves** *firm; top of inner leaf sheath square to slightly convex; basal sheaths without blades*. **Perigynia** broadly ovate, 2.5–3.5 mm long and 1.6–2.4 mm wide, *with a prominent notched beak, much shorter than the body*. **Stems** *stout, scabrous, clustered, much taller than the firm leaves*.

OCCURRENCE: Uncommon; MDI.

NOTES: Section *Multiflorae*. Looks very much like *Carex vulpinoidea*.

OTHER NAMES: *Carex brachyglossa*

Appalachian Sedge • *Carex appalachica*

Tufted, perennial herb of open woods and thickets, 20–60 cm tall. **Spikelets** 3–6, *green, the faces not veined*, with staminate flowers at summit. **Leaves** 0.9–1.5 mm wide; sheaths tight, green, *the fronts transparent*. **Perigynia** *with styles coiled more than once*. **Achenes** egg-shaped or wider at the top.

OCCURRENCE: Uncommon; MDI.

NOTES: Section *Phaestoglochin*.

AH

Drooping Wood Sedge • *Carex arctata*

Densely tufted, perennial herb of wet woods, borders, thickets, meadows, and clearings, 0.2–1 m tall. **Terminal spikelet** mostly staminate, *with at least a few carpellate flowers.* **Carpellate spikelets** 2–5, the uppermost close together, *the lowest remote, drooping.* **Leaves** flat, 3–10 mm wide, *reddish purple at base, with rough edges.* **Perigynia** green, *often red-dotted, with 2 ribs,* loosely covering the achene, *stalked, 3-angled, abruptly narrowing to a short beak.* **Stems** *obtusely angled.*
OCCURRENCE: Common; MDI.
NOTES: Section *Hymenochlaenae.*
OTHER NAMES: Compressed Sedge, Drooping Woodland Sedge

Silvery-flowered Sedge • *Carex argyrantha*

Densely tufted, perennial herb of dry woods, openings, and banks, up to 1 m tall. **Spikelets** *arching or drooping, pale silver, separated from one another, with a few densely bunched near the tip, with staminate flowers at base.* **Leaves** loose, *pale green or whitened,* ~5 mm wide. **Perigynia** *and associated pale scales equal in length.* **Achenes** flat.
OCCURRENCE: Uncommon; MDI, IAH.
NOTES: Section *Ovales.* A tall, very silvery-colored sedge with arching stems. This is the only *Ovales* sedge besides *Carex adusta* with pale scales as long as perigynia.
OTHER NAMES: Hay Sedge

Eastern Sedge • *Carex atlantica*

Tufted, perennial herb of open or forested wetlands, 0.1–1.1 m tall. **Spikelets** *3–8 per stem, in a cluster 1.8–4.5 cm long*, with staminate flowers at base. **Leaves** *0.5–4 mm wide*. **Perigynia** *strongly spreading, plump, spongy at base, egg-shaped to widely heart-shaped triangular, strongly nerved on both faces*, just slightly longer than wide, *tapering to a short, forked beak*.
OCCURRENCE: Uncommon; MDI, IAH.
NOTES: Section *Stellulatae*.
OTHER NAMES: Atlantic Sedge, Prickly Bog Sedge

Golden-fruited Sedge • *Carex aurea*

Rhizomatous, perennial herb of wet meadows and clearings, 5–40 cm tall. **Terminal spikelet** *staminate, occasionally with a few carpellate flowers at tip*. **Carpellate spikelets** loosely flowered, with spreading perigynia. **Leaves** pale green, 1.4–3 mm wide, delicate, arching. **Perigynia** *plump, fleshy, gold-brown to orange when mature*.
OCCURRENCE: Rare; MDI.
NOTES: Section *Bicolores*.
OTHER NAMES: Golden Sedge

Brownish Sedge • *Carex brunnescens*

Tufted, perennial herb of bogs, wet woods, headlands, and summits, 30–90 cm tall. **Spikelets** subglobose to ellipsoid, *with 5 to 10 loosely flowered spikelets, with staminate flowers at base.* **Leaves** *firm, erect, nearly hair-like, 1–2.5 mm wide, rough.* **Perigynia** loosely spreading when mature, green to pale brown, *tapering to a very short beak, toothed at base of distinct beak.* **Stems** *very fine.*
OCCURRENCE: Occasional; MDI, IAH, SCH.
NOTES: Section *Glareosae.*

Brown Hay Sedge • *Carex buxbaumii*

Perennial herb of ledges and shores, 0.2–1 m tall. **Terminal spikelet** *carpellate above or staminate throughout, top-shaped.* **Carpellate spikelets** *2–5, sessile or on short stalks.* **Leaves** *narrow, 1.5–4 mm wide, pale green and whitened, sharply keeled, the old sheaths becoming shredded.* **Perigynia** lens-shaped; *subtending scales purple-black, often with long awns at the tip and a green midrib.* **Stems** sharply angled, solitary or several together.

OCCURRENCE: Rare; MDI, SCH.

NOTES: Section *Racemosae*. Found within the salt-spray zone on Schoodic Peninsula.

OTHER NAMES: Brown Sedge, Brown Bog Sedge

Silvery Sedge • *Carex canescens*

Tufted, perennial herb of bogs, swamps, and shallow water, 15–90 cm tall. **Staminate spikelets** terminal. **Carpellate spikelets** oblong-ovoid to cylindric, close together or remote; inflorescence 0.6–15 cm long. **Leaves** *whitened*. **Perigynia** 2.3–3 mm long, often toothed near the summit. **Stems** *mostly overtopping the soft, pale leaves*.

OCCURRENCE: Occasional; MDI, IAH, SCH.

NOTES: Section *Glareosae*.

OTHER NAMES: Hoary Sedge

Fibrous-rooted Sedge • *Carex communis*

Perennial herb of clearings and forested areas, 10–60 cm tall. **Staminate spikelets** terminal, 3–16 mm long. **Carpellate spikes** 2–5. **Leaves** flat, 3–7 mm wide, densely tufted; *bases purple, rarely forming fibers.* **Perigynia** 2.5–4 mm long, *the body sub-globose to thick ellipsoid, the base spongy-thickened.* **Stems** *sharply angled, mostly overtopping the leaves,* densely tufted.
OCCURRENCE: Common; MDI, IAH, SCH.
NOTES: Section *Acrocystis.*

Field Sedge • *Carex conoidea*

Perennial herb of wet shores and grassy areas, 10–75 cm tall. **Staminate spikelets** *terminal,* 1–2 cm long, *long stemmed.* **Carpellate spikelets** 2–4, *with rough peduncles.* **Leaves** green, the largest 2.3–3.9 mm wide. **Perigynia** 17- to 25-veined; *subtending scales 2.4–4.7 mm long and 1.4–2.1 mm wide, with green midrib, shorter than the perigynium.* **Stems** densely tufted.
OCCURRENCE: Uncommon; MDI.
NOTES: Section *Griseae.*
OTHER NAMES: Conical Sedge, Open-field Sedge, *Carex katahdinensis*

Crawford's Sedge • *Carex crawfordii*

Tufted, perennial herb of wet meadows, shores, and swamps, 20–85 cm tall. **Spikelets** *5–12, dark, densely clustered at top of the stem*; staminate flowers at base. **Leaves** *shorter than the stems, the largest 1–4 mm wide, with 2 blades per stem.*
OCCURRENCE: Occasional; MDI.
NOTES: Section *Ovales.*

Long-haired Sedge • *Carex crinita*

Densely tufted, perennial herb of wet woods, thickets, and swales, 0.4–1.3 m tall. **Carpellate spikelets** 2–5, the lowest 3.5–11.5 cm long and 4.2–6.8 mm wide. **Leaves** 14–50 cm long and 3.3–10.3 mm wide; sheaths smooth, not rough to the touch. **Perigynia** green; subtending scales with a long awn at the tip.
OCCURRENCE: Occasional; MDI, SCH.
NOTES: Section *Phacocystis.* May be confused with *Carex gynandra* that has rough basal sheaths.
OTHER NAMES: Fringed Sedge, Drooping Sedge

Hidden-scaled Sedge • *Carex cryptolepis*

Tufted, perennial herb of wet, calcareous meadows and shores, 10–80 cm tall. **Staminate spikes** terminal, 12–21 mm long. **Carpellate spikes** *clustered at the top of stem, greenish, mostly ellipsoid to sub-cylindric, with long, leafy, subtending bracts.* **Leaves** *flat, soft, stiffish.* **Perigynia** recurving; *subtending scales hidden, same color as the perigynia.* **Stems** slender, *sharply angled at summit.*
OCCURRENCE: Occasional; MDI.
NOTES: Section *Ceratocystis.*
OTHER NAMES: Greenish Sedge, Northeastern Sedge, *Carex flava* var. *fertilis*

Clustered Sedge • *Carex cumulata*

Tufted, perennial herb of rocky or sandy soils, 15–90 cm tall. **Spikelets** *3–30 in a compact to loose head,* thick-cylindric to ellipsoid, with staminate flowers at base. **Leaves** *thick, firm; sheaths loose.* **Stems** coarse, stiffly erect.
OCCURRENCE: Common; MDI, IAH.
NOTES: Section *Ovales.*
OTHER NAMES: Dense Sedge

White-edged Sedge • *Carex debilis*

Tufted, perennial herb of wet woods, thickets, meadows, clearings, and shores, 0.2–1 m tall. **Staminate spikelets** *terminal*, 15–50 mm long. **Carpellate spikelets** 2–5, *pendulous, often overtopped by leafy bracts*. **Leaves** 2–4 mm wide, *thin, slender, lax*. **Achenes** stalked.
OCCURRENCE: Common; MDI, IAH, SCH.
NOTES: Section *Hymenochlaenae*.
OTHER NAMES: Weak Sedge

Northern Sedge • *Carex deflexa*

Loosely to densely tufted, short-rhizomatous, perennial herb of wet clearings, slopes, open woods, and swamps, 0.1–1.2 m tall. **Staminate spikelets** *terminal*, 2–5 mm long. **Carpellate spikes** *1–4, overlapping*. **Perigynia** *green, stalked*, 2–3 mm long, the body ovoid or pear-shaped, *2-ribbed, with fine, short hairs, abruptly contracted to a minutely bidentate beak*; subtending scales shorter than the perigynium. **Leaves** soft, thin, 1–3 mm wide, overtopping the spikelets. **Stems** slender, purple-tinged at base.
OCCURRENCE: Uncommon; IAH.
NOTES: Section *Acrocystis*.
OTHER NAMES: Depressed Sedge

Round-fruit Short-scale Sedge • *Carex deweyana*

Densely tufted, perennial herb of rich, open woods, 0.2–1.2 m tall. **Spikelets** 2–7, 3- to 12-flowered, *the lowest very remote*, egg-shaped or ovoid-cylindric; *heads flexuous, subtended by a long bract*, with staminate flowers at base. **Leaves** 2–5 mm wide, *very lax, whitened*. **Perigynia** *about half as long as the beak, exceeding the egg-shaped, pointed, pale scale.*
OCCURRENCE: Uncommon; MDI.
NOTES: Section *Deweyanae.*
OTHER NAMES: Dewey's Sedge

AH

Two-seeded Sedge • *Carex disperma*

Loosely tufted, rhizomatous, perennial herb of bogs, wet woods, clearings, and thickets, 50–60 cm tall. **Spikelets** *1–3, with staminate flowers at summit.* **Leaves** *soft, flat, and weak.* **Perigynia** 1–3 per spikelet, *scattered on the stem, rounded at the summit to a minute beak.* **Stems** *very fine.*
OCCURRENCE: Occasional; MDI, IAH, SCH.
NOTES: Section *Dispermae*
OTHER NAMES: Soft-leaved Sedge, Fine-leaved Sedge

Star Sedge • *Carex echinata*

Densely tufted, perennial herb of bogs, swamps, wet meadows, and ditches, 10–50 cm tall. **Spikelets** *mostly carpellate, with staminate flowers at base.* **Leaves** *firm, ascending, flat.* **Perigynia** spreading at maturity; *beak 1–1.6 mm long; subtending scales pale, blunt, half as long as the perigynia.* **Stems** mostly overtopping the leaves.
OCCURRENCE: Occasional; MDI, IAH, SCH.
NOTES: Section *Stellulatae.*
OTHER NAMES: Bur Sedge, Prickly Sedge

Coast Sedge • *Carex exilis*

Densely tufted, perennial herb of *Sphagnum* bogs and wet soils, 5–70 cm tall. **Spikelets** *solitary, either all carpellate, all staminate, or carpellate on top.* **Leaves** *wiry, involute.* **Perigynia** *soon divergent,* ~3 mm long, *with slightly toothed margins.* **Stems** *subrigid, mostly overtopped by stiff leaves.*
OCCURRENCE: Occasional; MDI, IAH, SCH.
NOTES: Section *Stellulatae.*

Yellow-green Sedge • *Carex flava*

Tufted, perennial herb of fens, meadows, swales, and shores, 10–80 cm tall. **Staminate spikelets** terminal, sessile to short-stalked. **Carpellate spikelets** 2–6, close together, the lowest remote. **Leaves** *yellow-green, flat*, 1.5–6 mm wide. **Perigynia** somewhat inflated over the achene, *the lowest spreading downward at maturity.* **Stems** sharply angled at the summit.
OCCURRENCE: Uncommon; MDI.
NOTES: Section *Ceratocystis*. Similar to *Carex cryptolepis* but with dark brown scales.
OTHER NAMES: Yellowish Sedge

Copper Sedge • *Carex foenea*

Densely tufted, rhizomatous, short-lived, perennial herb of dry woodlands, slopes, and ledges, 0.2–1.2 m tall. **Spikelets** *5–7, widely spaced*, forming a loose head, with staminate flowers at base. **Leaves** *3–6 per stem; sheaths white-transparent or green and white mottled.* **Perigynia** erect-ascending, green or brown, with white or brown beaks; *subtending scales longer than the perigynia, covering the beaks, reddish brown with a green or brown midstripe.*
OCCURRENCE: Uncommon; MDI.
NOTES: Section *Ovales*. Similar to *Carex argyrantha* but with 5–7 widely spaced spikelets.
OTHER NAMES: Dry-spike Sedge, Straw Sedge

Northern Long Sedge • *Carex folliculata*

Tufted, perennial herb of wet thickets, swamps, and swales, 0.3–1.2 m tall. **Staminate spikelets** terminal. **Carpellate spikelets** 2–4, *widely separated, with few perigynia per spikelet,* the lowest stalked. **Leaves** *2.5–10 mm wide, shiny, bright green.* **Stems** *very coarse and sagging to the ground at maturity,* reaching far beyond the leaves.
OCCURRENCE: Occasional; MDI, IAH, SCH.
NOTES: Section *Rostrales.*
OTHER NAMES: Long Sedge

Graceful Sedge • *Carex gracillima*

Tufted, perennial herb of woods, thickets, and meadows, 0.2–1 m tall; **Terminal spikelet** *with carpellate flowers at summit and staminate flowers at base.* **Carpellate spikelets** 2–4. **Leaves** *membranaceous, rarely as tall as stems,* deep green, *purplish at base, glabrous.* **Perigynia** ascending, green, slenderly ellipsoid, obtusely angled, *beakless.* **Stems** slender, diffuse to erect, glabrous.
OCCURRENCE: Common; MDI.
NOTES: Section *Hymenochlaenae.*

Nodding Sedge • *Carex gynandra*

Densely tufted, perennial herb of wet woods, clearings, and ditches, 0.5–1.4 m tall. **Spikelets** *large, long-drooping, with very long, protruding awns.* **Leaves** 12–55 cm long and 4–11 mm wide; *sheaths upwardly rough.* **Perigynia** not invaginated.
OCCURRENCE: Common; MDI, IAH.
NOTES: Section *Phacocystis.* May be confused with *Carex crinita* (smooth basal sheaths).
OTHER NAMES: *Carex crinita* var. *gynandra*

Marsh Straw Sedge • *Carex hormathodes*

Densely tufted, perennial herb of coastal areas and edges of tidal marshes, 20–50 cm tall. **Spikelets** 3–9, 6–15 mm long and 4–8 mm wide; *heads usually nodding.* **Leaves** *3–5 per stem,* 14–25 cm long and 1–3 mm wide. **Perigynia** reddish brown, lance-ovate, gradually tapering to an appressed, ascending beak. **Stems** slender, loosely ascending to spreading.
OCCURRENCE: Occasional; MDI, IAH, SCH.
NOTES: Section *Ovales.*

Houghton's Sedge • *Carex houghtoniana*

Rhizomatous, stoloniferous, perennial herb of dry clearings, banks, and roadsides, 15–90 cm tall. **Staminate spikelets** *terminal.* **Carpellate spikelets** 1–3, *unstalked except the lowest on a short stalk, cylindric to egg-shaped.* **Leaves** flat, *often with involute margins,* 2–8 mm wide. **Perigynia** *hairy.* **Stems** *1–few, stiff, rough, sharp-angled.*
OCCURRENCE: Uncommon; MDI, IAH.
NOTES: Section *Paludosae.*

Inland Sedge • *Carex interior*

Tufted, perennial herb of wet areas, 15–50 cm tall. **Spikelets** *2–7, sessile, with staminate flowers at base.* **Leaves** flat, or rolled and roundish in cross section. **Perigynia** 2–3.3 mm long and 1–2 mm wide, olive-green, becoming brown, plump and firm, egg-shaped to triangular, nerveless, *with a wide, short, notched beak.* **Stems** *firm, slender, sharply angled,* overtopping the leaves.
OCCURRENCE: Rare; IAH.
NOTES: Section *Stellulatae.*

AH

Bladder Sedge • *Carex intumescens*

Solitary or tufted, perennial herb of wet meadows, alluvial woods, and swales, 30–80 cm tall. **Carpellate spikelets** subglobose, *1.5–3 cm wide; subtended by lax, leafy bracts.* **Leaves** 2.5–8 mm wide, *soft, lax, dark green.* **Perigynia** *strongly inflated and nerved, loosely spreading.* **Achenes** *3-sided to ellipsoid, widest near the middle, 4–5.5 mm long, with flat to slightly concave sides.* **Stems** stout.
OCCURRENCE: Occasional; MDI, IAH.
NOTES: Section *Luplulinae.*
OTHER NAMES: Swollen Sedge, Greater Bladder Sedge

Lake Bank Sedge • *Carex lacustris*

Rhizomatous, perennial herb of swamps, marshes, ditches, and shallow water, 0.6–1.3 m tall. **Carpellate spikelets** short-oblong to elongate, *2–10 cm long.* **Leaves** bluish green, *often with white partitions; margins saw-edged; sheaths splitting into shreds; ligules very long.* **Perigynia** 5.5–7 mm long, lance-ovoid, with many light nerves; *tapering to a thick beak with erect to arching teeth.* **Stems** *sharply angled.*
OCCURRENCE: Occasional; MDI, IAH.
NOTES: Section *Paludosae.*
OTHER NAMES: Lake Sedge, Lake-side Sedge

DSC

DSC

Slender Sedge • *Carex lasiocarpa*

Rhizomatous, stoloniferous, perennial herb of bogs, swales, and shallow water, 0.3–1.2 m tall. **Staminate spikelets** *1–3, on a rough pedicel.* **Carpellate spikelets** 1–3, ascending. **Leaves** light green, *very slender, rolled in except at base.* **Perigynia** oblong-ovoid, 4–6 mm long, *hairy; beak with sharp teeth.* **Stems** quill-like at base, slender, *obtusely angled*, smooth, *reddish purple at base.*

OCCURRENCE: Common; MDI, IAH.

NOTES: Section *Paludosae.*

OTHER NAMES: Woolly-fruited Sedge

Loose-flowered Sedge • *Carex laxiflora*

Tufted, perennial herb of rich woods, 20–60 cm tall. **Staminate spikelets** terminal. **Carpellate spikelets** 3 or 4 per stem, scattered. **Leaves** 3.5–10 mm wide, ascending; *basal sheaths light brown.* **Perigynia** 3–20 per spikelet, widest at top, *with a spongy stalk and a slightly oblique, curving tip.* **Stems** *wingless,* 0.7–2 mm wide.

OCCURRENCE: Uncommon; MDI.

NOTES: Section *Laxiflorae.*

OTHER NAMES: Broad Loose-flowered Sedge

DSC

AH

Lenticular Sedge • *Carex lenticularis*

Densely tufted, perennial herb of meadows, swales, and wet shores, 10–60 cm tall. **Terminal spikelet** entirely staminate or with carpellate flowers at base. **Carpellate spikelets** 3–8. **Leaves** *very narrow, 1–3 mm wide, erect, sharply angled.* **Perigynia** lance-ovate to sub-orbicular, *brown-nerved, 1.8–3.5 mm long, short-stalked.* **Achenes** *lens-shaped.* **Stems** *slender, erect, sharply angled,* in dense tussocks.
OCCURRENCE: Uncommon; MDI.
NOTES: Section *Phacocystis.*
OTHER NAMES: Lake Shore Sedge

Bristle-stalked Sedge • *Carex leptalea*

Densely tufted, rhizomatous, perennial herb of wet woods, swales, and fens, 10–70 cm tall. **Spikelets** *1 per stem,* staminate at summit, linear-oblong. **Leaves** *very lax, soft green, shorter than stem.* **Perigynia** closely appressed, oblong, *narrow, blunt, beakless, 2.5–3.5 mm long; subtending scales pale brown with green midrib, shorter than the perigynia.* **Stems** *hair-like, 0.5–1.3 mm wide, obtusely angled, flaccid.*
OCCURRENCE: Uncommon; MDI.
NOTES: Section *Leptocephalae.*
OTHER NAMES: Bristly-stalk Sedge

Ribless Woodland Sedge • *Carex leptonervia*

Tufted, perennial herb of wet woods, thickets, and clearings, 12–45 cm tall. **Staminate spikelets** *terminal, usually hidden among top-most carpellate spikelets.* **Carpellate spikelets** crowded at summit, the lowest remote, linear-cylindric, 1–3 cm long and 3–4 mm wide; *subtending bracts overtopping the inflorescence.* **Leaves** 3–10 mm wide. **Perigynia** erect, 2.5–4 mm long and 1–1.5 mm wide, *nerveless or nearly so, tapering to a long, slender beak, as long as the slender stalk.* **Stems** *rough.*
OCCURRENCE: Uncommon; MDI.
NOTES: Section *Laxiflorae.*
OTHER NAMES: Two-edged Sedge, Nerveless Woodland Sedge

AH

AH

Mud Sedge • *Carex limosa*

Solitary or clustered, perennial herb of bogs and pond margins, 15–60 cm tall. **Staminate spikelets** *terminal,* 1–3 cm long, on *long stalks.* **Carpellate spikelets** 1–3, *the lowest on long drooping stalks.* **Leaves** blue-green with whitish wash. **Perigynia** 2.5–4 mm long; subtending scales *brownish.* **Stems** from old rootstocks, slender, *sharply angled, rough above.*
OCCURRENCE: Uncommon; MDI, SCH.
NOTES: Section *Limosae.*

DSC

DSC

Forest Sedge • *Carex lucorum*

Tufted, perennial herb of dry woods, thickets, and barrens, 10–40 cm tall. **Staminate spikelets** terminal, 8–23 mm long. **Carpellate spikelets** 1–4, globose or ovoid. **Leaves** *with reddish bases and persistent tufts of fibers, forming dense leafy tufts.* **Perigynia** 2.5–4 mm long, *hairy; subtending scales dark, reddish purple to brown.* **Stems** slender, erect, *sharply rough-angled.*
OCCURRENCE: Common; MDI, IAH.
NOTES: Section *Acrocystis.*
OTHER NAMES: Blue-ridge Sedge, *Carex pensylvanica* var. *distans*

DSC

Bottle-brush Sedge • *Carex lurida*

Tufted, perennial herb of swamps, swales, wet meadows, and woods, 0.2–1 m tall. **Staminate spikelets** terminal, 1–7 cm long. **Carpellate spikelets** 1–4, 1–7.5 cm long and 1.4–2 cm wide, *densely flowered; subtending leafy bracts taller than the inflorescence.* **Leaves** *partitioned*, flat, 4–7 mm wide; *ligules triangular, much longer than wide.* **Perigynia** *numerous, in many rows, 6–9 mm long, somewhat inflated, pale, smooth, shiny, strongly ~10-nerved.* **Stems** obtusely 3-angled, *purplish at base.*
OCCURRENCE: Occasional; MDI, IAH, SCH.
NOTES: Section *Vesicariae.*
OTHER NAMES: Sallow Sedge

Mackenzie's Sedge • *Carex mackenziei*

Tufted, perennial herb of saline to brackish marshes and shores, 10–45 cm long. **Spikelets** *2–6, scattered, with staminate flowers at base.* **Leaves** yellow-green with whitish bloom, *soft, flat, narrow, 1–2.5 mm wide.* **Perigynia** *faintly nerved,* 2.5–3 mm long, wide, *abruptly tapering to base, closely covered by obtuse scales.* **Stems** smooth, soft, very fine, mostly overtopping the leaves.
OCCURRENCE: Rare; SCH.
NOTES: Section *Glareosae.*

Bog Sedge • *Carex magellanica*

Densely tufted, perennial herb of wetlands, 20–70 cm tall. **Spikelets** mostly drooping on thin stalks, usually with staminate flowers at base. **Leaves** flat, green, 1–3 mm wide; *lowest bract longer than inflorescence.* **Perigynia** broadly ovate, *with minute projections; subtending scales longer than the perigynium.* **Stems** loosely clustered in small tufts, *acutely angled at summit.*
OCCURRENCE: Occasional; MDI, IAH, SCH.
NOTES: Section *Limosae.*
OTHER NAMES: Boreal Bog Sedge, Stunted Sedge, *Carex paupercula* var. *irrigua*

Fernald's Sedge • *Carex merritt-fernaldii*

Densely tufted, perennial herb of dry banks and roadsides, 0.3–1 m tall. **Spikelets** 7–15 mm long and 5–9 mm wide, 4–10 per inflorescence, arching or nodding. **Leaves** *3–6 per culm, 1.5–3 mm wide.* **Perigynia** *3.3–5 mm long and 2.3–3.5 mm wide; subtending scales greenish to yellowish, shorter than tip of perigynia.*
OCCURRENCE: Rare; MDI.
NOTES: Section *Ovales.*
OTHER NAMES: Merritt Fernald's Sedge

Smooth Black Sedge • *Carex nigra*

Loosely tufted, perennial herb of wet meadows and edges of saltmarshes, 50–60 cm tall. **Staminate spikelets** terminal, more or less stalked. **Carpellate spikelets** 1.2–4.2 cm long and 3–5 mm wide; *lowest bract subtending inflorescence subequal to uppermost spikelet.* **Leaves** blue-green with whitish bloom; *basal sheaths red-brown.* **Perigynia** appressed, *minutely granular, brown-nerved; subtending scales dark purple-brown or black with a green midrib.* **Stems** *sharply angled.*
OCCURRENCE: Occasional; MDI, IAH, SCH.
NOTES: Section *Phacocystis*
OTHER NAMES: Goodenough's Sedge

Larger Straw Sedge • *Carex normalis*

Densely tufted, perennial herb of open woods, thickets, and swales, up to 1.5 m tall. **Spikelets** pale green, 3–10, with staminate flowers at base; *inflorescence straight*, subcylindric to lance-shaped, 1.5–4 cm long. **Leaves** 3.5–6.5 mm wide, with loose, mottled sheaths. **Perigynia** pale green, becoming straw-colored, narrowly ovate, 3–4 mm long; *beak soon spreading or slightly recurving, giving spikelets a prickly look.*
OCCURRENCE: Uncommon; MDI.
NOTES: Section *Ovales*.
OTHER NAMES: Greater Straw Sedge

AH

New England Sedge • *Carex novae-angliae*

Densely tufted, perennial herb of wet woods and slopes, 5–40 cm tall. **Carpellate spikelets** 1–3, *remote, short-stalked.* **Leaves** *soft, pale green, 0.7–1.5 mm wide.* **Perigynia** thin, *pale, 2–2.5 mm long, minutely hairy, with a yellowish base.* **Perigynia** translucent. **Stems** *weak, very slender, triangular, hardly rising above the leaves.*
OCCURRENCE: Common; MDI, IAH.
NOTES: Section *Acrocystis.*

Few-seeded Sedge • *Carex oligosperma*

Turf-forming, perennial herb of bogs, swamps, wet meadows, and shallow water, 0.4–1 m tall. **Staminate spikelets** *terminal*. **Carpellate spikelets** *1–3, widely separated, unstalked*, ovoid to short-cylindric, each spikelet with 3–15 flowers. **Leaves** pale green, stiff, involute, 1–3 mm wide; *ligules much longer than wide*. **Perigynia** ovoid, scarcely inflated, *compressed, shiny, 4–7 mm long*, abruptly narrowing to a smooth beak. **Achenes** *3-sided*, egg-shaped, 2–3 mm long; *styles persistent, coiled*. **Stems** *slender, purplish at base*.
OCCURRENCE: Uncommon; MDI, SCH.
NOTES: Section *Vesicariae*.

Bead-like Sedge • *Carex ormostachya*

Tufted, perennial herb of rich woods and clearings, 25–50 cm tall. **Staminate spikelets** terminal, *conspicuous*, often stalked. **Carpellate spikelets** *scattered, linear-cylindric*, the largest 1–4 cm long. **Leaves** green, those of both sterile and fertile shoots 1–5 mm wide; basal sheaths purple. **Perigynia** *broadly ovoid, less than twice as long as wide*, 2.5–3.5 mm long, *strongly ribbed, rounded above to an abrupt, short beak*. **Stems** *roughened on the angles*.
OCCURRENCE: Rare; MDI.
NOTES: Section *Laxiflorae*.
OTHER NAMES: Necklace Spike Sedge, *Carex laxiflora* var. *ormostachya*

DSC

DSC

Chaffy Sedge • *Carex paleacea*

Solitary or clustered, rhizomatous, perennial herb of brackish to saline marshes and shores, 30–80 cm tall. **Staminate spikelets** *terminal*, 1 or 2, 2–4 cm long. **Carpellate spikelets** 2–4, *stout-cylindric, 2–5 cm long and 5–8 mm wide, drooping*; bracts leaf-like, without sheaths. **Leaves** 3–8 mm wide. **Perigynia** *biconvex to flat on one side*, whitish green, firm, elliptic, 2.2–3.5 mm long; *subtending scales shorter than the perigynia, with brown sides, the conspicuous pale midvein prolonged into a rough, flat awn up to 1 cm long*. **Achenes** flat, *strongly constricted on one side near the middle*.
OCCURRENCE: Occasional; MDI, IAH, SCH.
NOTES: Section *Phacocystis*
OTHER NAMES: Scaly Sedge

Pale Sedge • *Carex pallescens*

Tufted, perennial herb of wet woods, thickets, and meadows, 20–50 cm tall. **Staminate spikelets** terminal, stalked. **Carpellate spikelets** *2–4, shiny, densely flowered, short-cylindric*, 8–15 mm long, *the lowest short-stalked, the upper subsessile; lower bracts exceeding the inflorescence*. **Leaves** 2–4 mm wide, *soft-hairy, especially on the lower surface and sheaths*. **Perigynia** ascending, ellipsoid, 2.1–2.8 mm long, *nearly round in cross section*, obscurely finely nerved, *beakless*. **Achenes** *concavely 3-sided*.
OCCURRENCE: Common; MDI, IAH.
NOTES: Section *Porocystis*.

Few-flowered Sedge • *Carex pauciflora*

Solitary or clustered, long-rhizomatous, perennial herb of bogs and fens, 10–60 cm tall. **Spikelets** *solitary, with staminate flowers at summit.* **Leaves** 1–2 mm wide, *shorter than the inflorescence; lower sheaths without blades.* **Perigynia** *1–6, soon reflexed, slender and long-tapering; subtending scales shorter than perigynia.*
OCCURRENCE: Occasional; MDI.
NOTES: Section *Leucoglochin.*

Necklace Sedge • *Carex projecta*

Densely tufted, perennial herb of damp woods, thickets, meadows, and shores, 0.5–1 m tall. **Spikelets** subglobose to wider at the top, 5–8 mm long, distinct, with staminate flowers at base; inflorescence flexuous, 3–5 cm long. **Leaves** *2–7 mm wide; sheaths ventrally green.* **Perigynia** *winged, the wings narrowing at the bottom, 15–30 per spikelet, dull brown, 3–5 mm long.* **Stems** stout.
OCCURRENCE: Occasional; MDI, IAH.
NOTES: Section *Ovales.*
OTHER NAMES: Spreading Sedge

Cyperus Sedge • *Carex pseudocyperus*

Loosely tufted, perennial herb of swamps, bogs, and slow-moving shallow water, 0.3–1 m tall. **Terminal spikelet** all staminate, staminate on top, or carpellate on top. **Carpellate spikelets** *2–7, densely flowered, loose and nodding on slender stalks*; lowest bract much surpassing the inflorescence. **Leaves** 5–15 mm wide. **Perigynia** reflexed, 4.2–6.2 mm long, *firm-textured, stalked,* slenderly ovoid, *gradually tapering to a long, stiff beak with straight, parallel teeth; subtending scales with long awns as long as or longer than the perigynia.*
OCCURRENCE: Uncommon; MDI.
NOTES: Section *Vesicariae.* The beaks and scales are sharp enough to stick into fingers when touched and can be painful!
OTHER NAMES: Cyperus-like Sedge, Hop Sedge

Eastern Star Sedge • *Carex radiata*

Densely tufted, perennial herb of wet woods, thickets, and pond shores, 20–80 cm tall. **Spikelets** 4–7, staminate at summit, unstalked; subtending bracts very thin. **Leaves** elongate, the largest 1.3–1.9 mm wide. **Perigynia** 1–20 per spikelet, light green, widely spreading at maturity, *flat on one side, lance-ovate, 2.6–3.8 mm long, spongy at base, tapering to a 2-toothed beak; subtending scales persistent, shorter than the perigynia,* rounded to acute, seldom short-awned.
OCCURRENCE: Rare; MDI, SCH.
NOTES: Section *Phaestoglochin.*

Rough Sedge • *Carex scabrata*

Densely tufted, rhizomatous, perennial herb of wet woods, meadows, and swamps, 40–90 cm tall. **Staminate spikelet** 2–4 cm long. **Carpellate spikelets** 3–several, cylindric, 2–4 cm long, erect, the lowest long-stalked, the upper subsessile. **Leaves** *very rough, 4–8 mm wide, those of the sterile shoots to 14 mm wide.* **Perigynia** egg-shaped, obtusely 3-angled, 3.2–4.4 mm long, minutely scabrous, conspicuously 2-ribbed, abruptly narrowing to a somewhat out-curving beak. **Achenes** *concavely 3-sided.*
OCCURRENCE: Uncommon; MDI.
NOTES: Section *Anomalae.*
OTHER NAMES: Eastern Rough Sedge

Pointed Broom Sedge • *Carex scoparia*

Densely tufted, perennial herb of a wide variety of habitats, 0.2–1 m tall. **Spikelets** 3–10, 7–16 mm long and 3–13 mm wide, with staminate flowers at the base; inflorescence usually arching or nodding. **Leaves** 3–5 per fertile stem. **Perigynia** *wing-margined, serrulate, lanceolate, very flat, much wider than the achene.*
OCCURRENCE: Common; MDI, IAH, SCH.
NOTES: Section *Ovales.* A very variable species; hang tough!

Seabeach Sedge • *Carex silicea*

Densely tufted, perennial herb of coastal rocks, sand, and sandy soil, 30–80 cm tall. **Spikelets** *3–10, tapering to both ends, usually well separated, 7–10 mm long, densely flowered*, with staminate flowers at base. **Leaves** *2–4 mm wide, equaling or shorter than the culms, bluish to whitish green; base of leaves with auricles* (see left photo). **Perigynia** mostly appressed, flat, ovate, *sharply nerved on top; subtending scales as long as perigynia but distinctly narrower*. **Stems** *stiff*.
OCCURRENCE: Rare; MDI, IAH, SCH.
NOTES: Section *Ovales*.

Awl-fruited Sedge • *Carex stipata*

Tufted, perennial herb of wet areas, 0.3–1 m tall. **Spikelets** numerous, *small, few-flowered, sessile*, with staminate flowers at summit, *clustered into a dense, compound inflorescence* 3–10 cm long and 1–3 cm wide; *bracts often hair-like, extending beyond the inflorescence*. **Leaves** *coarse, often elongate, thin, fragile; sheaths prolonged beyond base of blade*. **Perigynia** *widely spreading, making the heads look prickly; subtending scales shorter than the perigynia*. **Stems** *stout, triangular*.
OCCURRENCE: Common; MDI, IAH, SCH.
NOTES: Section *Vulpinae*.
OTHER NAMES: Stalk-grain Sedge

Tussock Sedge • *Carex stricta*

Densely tufted, perennial herb of swales and swamps, 0.4–1.4 m tall. **Staminate spikelets** terminal. **Carpellate spikelets** 2–4, overlapping, erect, linear-cylindric, sessile or nearly so. **Leaves** *the largest 3–6 mm wide, M-shaped in cross section*. **Perigynia** nearly flat, ovate, 1.6–3.4 mm long, 2-ribbed, *tapering to a minute beak; subtending scales reddish brown or purple-brown with a conspicuous pale midrib*. **Achenes** lens-shaped. **Stems** *rough on angles, lax*, usually surpassing leaves.

OCCURRENCE: Occasional; MDI, IAH.

NOTES: Section *Phacocystis*.

OTHER NAMES: Stiff Sedge

Quill Sedge • *Carex tenera*

Densely tufted, perennial herb of wet woodlands, thickets, and meadows, 20–90 cm tall. **Spikelets** 4–8 in an interrupted inflorescence 1.5–5 cm long, *with staminate flowers at base*. **Leaves** 1.5–2.5 mm wide. **Perigynia** *wing-margined, 2.8–4 mm long and 1.4–1.9 mm wide*. **Achenes** *1.3–2.1 mm long and 0.9–1.3 mm wide*. **Stems** slender.

OCCURRENCE: Occasional; MDI, IAH.

NOTES: Section *Ovales*.

Deep Green Sedge • *Carex tonsa*

Densely tufted, rhizomatous, perennial herb of dry open areas, oak-pine forests, and roadsides, 10–60 cm tall. **Staminate spikelets** *terminal, sessile or short-stalked, on leafy stems.* **Carpellate spikelets** *borne on short to elongate penduncles, sometimes hidden among the leaves.* **Leaves** 1–5 mm wide. **Perigynia** 3.2–4.7 mm long, with a beak 0.9–1.7 mm long; *subtending scales equal to or slightly exceeding the perigynia.*
OCCURRENCE: Occasional; MDI, IAH.
NOTES: Section *Acrocystis.*
OTHER NAMES: Shaved Sedge, Glabrous-fruited Sedge

Twisted Sedge • *Carex torta*

Densely tufted, rhizomatous, perennial herb of streambanks and shallow water, 20–70 cm tall. **Staminate spikelets** terminal. **Carpellate spikelets** 3–6, much overlapping, linear-cylindric, 3–8 cm long, *the lowest short-stalked and drooping; lowest leaf-like bracts usually shorter than the inflorescence.* **Leaves** 3–5 mm wide, *M-shaped in cross section, the lowest reduced to bladeless sheaths.* **Perigynia** ovate, 2.5–4.2 mm long, half as wide, *2-ribbed,* otherwise nerveless, *gradually tapering to a minute, bent or twisted beak; subtending scales as long as perigynia, with a wide greenish midstripe with blackish or deep brown-purple sides.* **Stems** *stout.*
OCCURRENCE: Uncommon; MDI.
NOTES: Section *Phacocystis.*

AH

Three-seeded Sedge • *Carex trisperma*

Loosely tufted, short-rhizomatous, perennial herb of bogs and wet woods, 20–70 cm tall. **Spikelets** 1–3, sessile, 1–4 cm apart; *lowest spikelet subtended by a thin bract 2–4 cm long.* **Leaves** soft, lax, flat or folded, 1–2 mm wide. **Perigynia** oval, finely many-nerved; beak slender, smooth, notched, ~0.5 mm long; subtending scales ovate, clear, with a green center. **Stems** very slender and weak.

OCCURRENCE: Common; MDI, IAH, SCH.

NOTES: Section *Glareosae. Carex billingsii* (not pictured but uncommon in the ANP region) is very similar in appearance to *C. trisperma* except the leaves are involute and <0.8 mm wide.

Umbel-like Sedge • *Carex umbellata*

Densely tufted to mat-forming, perennial herb of dry, open areas, 5–10 cm tall. **Staminate spikelets** terminal. **Carpellate spikelets** with 1–12 perigynia; *subtending bract of the carpellate spikelet scale-like and shorter than the staminate spikelet.* **Leaves** 1–5 mm wide; *sheaths shredding.* **Perigynia** green, 2.5–4 mm long, finely hairy to glabrous. **Stems** *much surpassed and often concealed by the leaves.*

OCCURRENCE: Rare; MDI.

NOTES: Section *Acrocystis*

OTHER NAMES: Parasol Sedge

AH

AH

Beaked Sedge • *Carex utriculata*

Perennial herb of swamps, wet meadows, ditches, and pond margins, 0.5–1.2 m tall. **Staminate spikelets** *terminal, several, 2–7 cm long.* **Carpellate spikelets** *2–10 cm long and 1–1.5 cm wide; the lowest bract subtending the spikelets longer than the inflorescence.* **Leaves** *flat, yellow-green, glabrous above,* the largest 5–12 mm wide. **Perigynia** densely clustered, *inflated, strongly nerved, 4–7 mm long, abruptly tapering to a smooth beak 1–2 mm long with short teeth; subtending scales short-awed.* **Achenes** *with a persistent bony style, strongly contorted at maturity.* **Stems** coarse, *bluntly 3-angled, spongy-based.*
OCCURRENCE: Occasional; MDI, IAH.
NOTES: Section *Vesicariae.*
OTHER NAMES: Bottle-shaped Sedge, Swollen-beaked Sedge, *Carex rostrata* var. *utriculata*

Salt Marsh Sedge • *Carex vacillans*

Rhizomatous, perennial herb of saline to brackish shores and marshes, 16–60 cm tall. **Staminate spikelets** terminal. **Carpellate spikelets** ascending, erect. **Leaves** 2.8–4 mm wide. **Perigynia** *conspicuously nerved, densely long-papillose; subtending scales red-brown to blackish, awned.* **Achenes** *dull, weakly to somewhat indented.* **Stems** *acutely angled.*
OCCURRENCE: Rare; MDI, SCH.
NOTES: Section *Phacocystis.* Maine Natural Areas Program ranks this species as endangered in Maine.
OTHER NAMES: Swinging Sedge

AH

Inflated Sedge • *Carex vesicaria*

Densely tufted, perennial herb of wet meadows, streambanks, pond shores, bogs, and swamps, 0.3–1 m tall. **Staminate spikelets** terminal, sometimes with some carpellate flowers beneath, 2–7 cm long. **Carpellate spikelets** several, *erect or nearly so, the lowest 2–7 cm long and 1–1.5 cm wide.* **Leaves** flat, 3–8 mm wide. **Perigynia** *ascending, in 6–8 rows, 5–8 mm long and 2–3 mm wide, strongly 10- to 20-ribbed, inflated below,* gradually tapering to a poorly defined beak with short teeth; *subtending scales scarcely awned.* **Stems** slender, *sharply 3-angled, strongly scabrous above.*
OCCURRENCE: Occasional; MDI.
NOTES: Section *Vesicariae.*
OTHER NAMES: Lesser Bladder Sedge

Little Green Sedge • *Carex viridula*

Densely tufted, perennial herb of boggy shores and springy, often calcareous, areas, 10–40 cm tall. **Staminate spikelets** terminal, 7–21 mm long, sessile or short-stalked. **Carpellate spikelets** *2–4, short, stout, 5–15 mm long, crowded near the summit; lowest bracts exceeding the inflorescence.* **Leaves** flat to channeled, *often equaling or surpassing the stems,* mostly 1–3 mm wide. **Perigynia** 2.2–3.3 mm long, *spreading, the lowest often reflexed,* pale green to yellowish, egg-shaped; subtending scales shorter than the perigynia.
OCCURRENCE: Occasional; MDI, IAH, SCH.
NOTES: Section *Ceratocystis.*

Fox Sedge • *Carex vulpinoidea*

Densely tufted, perennial herb of marshes, wet meadows, shores, and low areas, 0.3–1 m tall. **Spikelets** densely aggregated and overlapping into an irregular or interrupted inflorescence 5–10 cm long and up to 1.5 cm wide. **Leaves** scattered along lower portion of the stem, flat, ~5 mm wide; *sheaths sparsely red-dotted along lower portion.* **Perigynia** flat, *light brown or greenish, 2–3.5 mm long, the body narrowly ovate to round-ovate, nerveless, serrulate-margined; subtending scales with a firm midrib extending beyond as a greenish awn.*
OCCURRENCE: Uncommon; MDI.
NOTES: Section *Multiflorae.*
OTHER NAMES: Common Fox Sedge

Wiegand's Sedge • *Carex wiegandii*

Densely tufted, perennial herb of *Sphagnum* bogs, wet thickets, and shores, 0.1–1 m tall. **Spikelets** 4–6, *4.5–8 mm long,* sessile, with carpellate flowers on top, *in an inflorescence 1–3 cm long.* **Leaves** 3–8, *all in the basal third of the stem, shorter than the inflorescence, folded, 2–5 mm wide, scabrous above.* **Perigynia** 5–25 per spikelet, *the lowest spreading to reflexed,* green to reddish brown, broadly ovate, spongy-thickened at the base, *2.5–3.7 mm long; subtending scales reddish brown with a green midrib and clear edges.* **Stems** smooth to slightly scabrous above.
OCCURRENCE: Rare; MDI, SCH.
NOTES: Section *Stellulatae.* This species has the widest leaves of any of the members of its section.

Twig Rush • *Cladium mariscoides*

Solitary or clustered, perennial herb of fresh or brackish swamps, marshes, and shores, up to 1 m tall. **Spikelets** lance-shaped, becoming ovoid, 3–5 mm long; inflorescence slender, 5–10 cm long. **Leaves** 1–3 mm wide, *channeled near the base, becoming round in cross section near the tip* (see left photo), glabrous or nearly so. **Achenes** *conspicuously pointed*, dull brown, 2.5–3.5 mm long. **Stems** stiff, solitary or a few together, slender.
OCCURRENCE: Uncommon; MDI, IAH, SCH.
OTHER NAMES: Smooth Saw-grass, Smooth Saw-sedge

Three-way Sedge • *Dulichium arundinaceum*

Solitary or clustered herb of swamps, marshes, and margins of ponds and streams, up to 1 m tall. **Spikelets** 10–25 mm long; inflorescence 1–3 cm long. **Leaves** *numerous, diverging from the stem at 120-degree angle from each other; blades 5–15 cm long and 2.5–8 mm wide.* **Achenes** *short-stalked*, 2.5–3 mm long; *bristles 6–9.* **Stems** erect, *hollow, jointed.*
OCCURRENCE: Occasional; MDI, IAH.

Needle Spike-rush • *Eleocharis acicularis*

Densely tufted, perennial herb of wetlands and muddy shores, 3–12 cm tall. **Spikelets** 2.5–7 mm long, *scarcely wider than the stem*, 3- to 15-flowered; *scales 1.5–2.2 mm long, with a greenish midrib; styles 3-branched.* **Achenes** white to pale gray, *longitudinally 8- to 18-ribbed with very fine, numerous straight cross ridges*; perianth bristles mostly 4; *tubercle clearly differentiated from and joined to the achene, usually of different color and texture.* **Stems** extremely thin, *up to 0.3 mm wide.*
OCCURRENCE: Occasional; MDI, SCH.
OTHER NAMES: Needle Spikesedge

Bright Green Spike-rush • *Eleocharis flavescens*

Densely tufted, rhizomatous, perennial herb of wet areas, 3–15 cm tall. **Spikelets** ovoid, 2–7 mm long, *with fewer than 20 flowers*; floral scales ovate or elliptic, obtuse or subacute, with brown sides; styles usually 2. **Leaves** *with pale sheaths, prolonged into a loose, white, rough tip.* **Achenes** *flat*, 1 mm long; *tubercle pale, short-conic above a swollen base; perianth bristles white or pale green.* **Stems** widely spreading.
OCCURRENCE: Rare; MDI.
OTHER NAMES: Yellow Spikesedge

Blunt Spike-rush • *Eleocharis obtusa*

Densely tufted, annual herb of wet soil, sometimes intertidal, 3–50 cm tall. **Spikelets** broadly ovoid, 5–13 mm long and 3–4 mm wide; *floral scales light brown*, 1.5–2.5 mm long and 1–1.5 mm wide; *stamens usually 3*. **Leaves** *with sheaths obtuse to acute*, with a prominent tooth at the apex up to 0.3 mm long. **Achenes** 0.9–1.2 mm long; perianth bristles 6 or 7, stout, *exceeding the tubercle*.
OCCURRENCE: Occasional; MDI, IAH.
OTHER NAMES: Blunt Spikesedge

Creeping Spike-rush • *Eleocharis palustris*

Rhizomatous, perennial herb of shores and wetlands, 0.1–1 m tall. **Spikelets** 5–40 mm long, light to dark brown to chestnut; *lower floral scale, if solitary, encircling the base of the spikelet, the upper, fertile ones 2–4.5 mm long*. **Achenes** flat, yellow to medium brown, 1–2 mm long, *very finely roughened; tubercle 0.4–0.7 mm long, constricted at base; perianth bristles 4, retrorsely barbed, barely longer than the achene*. **Stems** scattered or in small clusters.
OCCURRENCE: Uncommon; MDI.
OTHER NAMES: Common Spike-rush, Small's Spike-rush, Common Spikesedge

Low Spike-rush • *Eleocharis parvula*

Rhizomatous, mat-forming, perennial herb of saline shores and marshes, 2–6 cm tall. **Spikelets** 1–3 mm long, floral scales green or pale brown. **Leaves** *with summit of sheaths without a prominent tooth at the apex.* **Achenes** *3-angled, 0.9–1.3 mm long including the short tubercle.* **Stems** very fine. **Tubers** *tiny.*
OCCURRENCE: Uncommon; SCH.
NOTES: Often found in nonflowering patches.
OTHER NAMES: Dwarf Spike-rush, Little-headed Spikesedge

Robbin's Spike-rush • *Eleocharis robbinsii*

Rhizomatous, perennial herb of muddy soil, shallow, still, or slow-moving water, up to 1 m tall. **Spikelets** *gradually tapering to a slender point, about as wide as the top of the stem.* **Achenes** compressed to 3-angled, *brown, 2–3 mm long, constricted to an urn-shaped neck, marked with vertical rows of transversely elongate cells; tubercle dark.* **Stems** 3-angled, often producing many elongate, hair-like, sterile, floating stems.
OCCURRENCE: Occasional; MDI.
OTHER NAMES: Robbin's Spikesedge

Slender Spike-rush • *Eleocharis tenuis*

Rhizomatous, perennial herb of various habitats, 5–70 cm tall. **Spikelets** 3–10 mm long, 10- to 30-flowered; *floral scales ovate, obtuse to acute, dark, rough-margined, 2–3 mm long.* **Achenes** *unequally 3-angled, distinctly roughened, usually yellow*, 0.6–1.3 mm long; *perianth bristles reduced or wanting.* **Stems** slender, 4- to 8-angled; sheaths conspicuously reddened at base.
OCCURRENCE: Uncommon; MDI, IAH, SCH.
OTHER NAMES: Slender Spikesedge

Saltmarsh Spike-rush • *Eleocharis uniglumis*

Mat-forming, perennial herb of brackish to saline habitats, 10–60 cm tall. **Spikelets** 5–10 mm long and 2–3 mm wide, dark brown, *with only one empty glume at the base of the spikelet.* **Leaves** *with sheaths red-purple at base, not splitting.* **Achenes** dark yellow to dark brown, 1.3–1.8 mm long. **Stems** slender, creeping.
OCCURRENCE: Occasional; MDI, IAH, SCH.
OTHER NAMES: Slender Spike-rush, One-glumed Spikesedge, *Eleocharis halophila*

AH

White Cotton-grass • *Eriophorum angustifolium*

Perennial herb of wetlands, up to 1 m tall. **Spikelets** 3–several, spreading or drooping on slender, roughened stalks to 5 cm long, with 2 or 3 unequal, leafy bracts beneath inflorescence; *floral scales tawny to drab or blackish green, with a slender midvein not extending to the clear tip*. **Leaves** *2–8 mm wide, flat at least basally; sheaths with a dark border at the top*. **Achenes** blackish, narrow, 2–3 mm long; *perianth bristles white*.
OCCURRENCE: Occasional; MDI, IAH, SCH.
NOTES: Leaves often tinged reddish, especially in the summer.
OTHER NAMES: Tall Cotton-grass, Thin-scale Cotton-grass, Common Cotton-grass, Tall Cottonsedge

Conifer Cotton-grass • *Eriophorum tenellum*

Rhizomatous, perennial herb of wetlands, 30–80 cm tall. **Spikelets** *3–6, 1 or 2 on scabrous stalks up to 5 cm long, with erect, leafy bracts below inflorescence; floral scales straw-colored to reddish brown, ovate, obtuse or rounded*. **Leaves** more or less flat, 1–2 mm wide, *channeled, the uppermost equaling or longer than its sheath*. **Achenes** *brown*, narrowly obovate-oblong; *perianth bristles dingy white*. **Stems** arising singly, obtusely 3-angled, slightly roughened above.
OCCURRENCE: Occasional; MDI, SCH.
OTHER NAMES: Five-nerve Cotton-grass, Few-nerved Cottonsedge

AH

Tussock Cotton-grass • ***Eriophorum vaginatum***

Densely tufted, perennial herb of wetlands and alpine bogs, 10–60 cm long. **Spikelets** *solitary, 10–20 mm long in flower, up to 50 mm long in fruit.* **Leaves** filiform, ~1 mm wide; *sheaths below middle of stem.* **Achenes** distinctly obovate, 2.5–3.5 mm long, slightly over half as wide; *perianth bristles bright white.*
OCCURRENCE: Occasional; MDI, IAH, SCH.
OTHER NAMES: Harestail Cotton-grass, Tussock Cottonsedge, *Eriophorum spissum*

Tawny Cotton-grass • ***Eriophorum virginicum***

Solitary or clustered, perennial herb of wetlands, 0.4–1.2 m tall. **Spikelets** *several on short, unequal stalks, forming a crowded cluster; bracts beneath inflorescence 2, unequal, the longest surpassing the head; floral scales thin, coppery to brown, sharp, 3- to 7-nerved.* **Leaves** flat, elongate, 2–4 mm wide. **Achenes** 3–3.5 mm long; *perianth bristles tawny.* **Stems** stiff.
OCCURRENCE: Occasional; MDI, IAH, SCH.
OTHER NAMES: Tawny Cottonsedge

White Beak-rush • *Rhynchospora alba*

Densely tufted, perennial herb of bogs and fens, up to 70 cm tall. **Spikelets** *4–5 mm long, clustered, the upper barely overtopped by its bracts, the lateral ones remote and long-stalked.* **Leaves** 0.5–2.5 mm wide. **Achenes** *flat to pear-shaped, 1.2–2 mm long, contracted at base, brownish green with very faint, transverse, brown lines*; perianth bristles 8–14, stout, flat, *about equaling the awl-shaped tubercle.* **Stems** overtopping leaves.
OCCURRENCE: Occasional; MDI, IAH, SCH.
OTHER NAMES: White Beaksedge

Small-headed Beak-rush • *Rhynchospora capitellata*

Densely tufted, perennial herb of bogs, damp shores, and ledges, 30–80 cm tall. **Spikelets** 2–several, loosely top-shaped or hemispheric, chestnut-colored. **Leaves** flat, 1.5–3.5 mm wide. **Achenes** plump, pear-shaped to obovate, 1.2–1.8 mm long, *uniformly dark brown*; perianth bristles *6*, retrorsely barbed, 1.2–1.8 mm long, *about equaling or a little shorter than the tubercle; tubercle 0.8–1.6 mm long, much widened at the base.*
OCCURRENCE: Rare; MDI.
OTHER NAMES: Brownish Beaksedge

Brown Beak-rush • *Rhynchospora fusca*

Rhizomatous, stoloniferous, perennial herb of bogs, marshes, springy areas, and wet sands, 10–50 cm tall. **Spikelets** 4–7 mm long, *dark brown*. **Leaves** *very slender, rolled in, mostly shorter than the stems.* **Achenes** triangular-obovate to pear-shaped, 1.1–1.4 mm long, light brown; *perianth bristles 5 or 6, upwardly barbed.*
OCCURRENCE: Uncommon; MDI.
OTHER NAMES: Brown Beaksedge

CBH

Hardstem Bulrush • *Schoenoplectus acutus*

Rhizomatous, perennial herb of shores of ponds and streams, 1–3 m tall. **Spikelets** 8–15 mm long, *nearly all sessile, in small clusters.* **Leaves** *few, near the base, with prominent, well developed sheath and short, poorly developed blades; floral scales mostly 3.5–4 mm long, thin, with numerous short, linear, reddish, soft brown stripes on a pale gray-white background, longer than the achene.* **Achenes** 2.2–2.5 mm long, more or less completely hidden by the floral scales. **Stems** *stout, erect, round, very firm, with numerous internal partitions* (see lower right photo).
OCCURRENCE: Uncommon; MDI.
OTHER NAMES: Great Bulrush, Hard-stemmed Bulrush, *Scirpus acutus*

Common Three-square • *Schoenoplectus pungens*

Rhizomatous, perennial herb of fresh to saline shores and marshes, 0.2–1.5 m tall. **Spikelets** 1–6, *mostly sessile, in a compact cluster*, the largest 7–20 mm long; *floral scales thin, rough, with a firm, brown midrib sticking beyond the apical notch as a short awn; subtended by a prominent, sharply pointed, green bract appearing as a continuation of the stem.* **Leaves** several near the base, barely passing mid-stem, *channeled above and folded.* **Achenes** 2.2–2.3 mm long including the tiny, sharp tip; *perianth bristles 4–6, often unequal, retrorsely barbed, barely exceeding the achene if at all.* **Stems** *3-angled, with flat to slightly concave or convex sides.*
OCCURRENCE: Occasional; MDI.
OTHER NAMES: Chair-maker's-rush, Three-square, Three-square Bulrush, *Scirpus americanus*

Water Bulrush • *Schoenoplectus subterminalis*

Aquatic, perennial herb of shallow, quiet water and bogs, up to 1 m tall. **Spikelets** *1 per stem, light brown, ovoid to cylindric, 7–12 mm long; floral scales thin, almost translucent.* **Leaves** *numerous, hair-like,* arising from near the base, *trailing just below the surface.* **Achenes** brown, 3-angled, 2.5–3.8 mm long including the beak; *perianth bristles usually shorter than the achene.* **Stems** slender, sub-round, emergent or floating.
OCCURRENCE: Occasional; MDI.
OTHER NAMES: Swaying Bulrush, Water Club-rush, Water Bulrush, *Scirpus subterminalis*

Soft-stemmed Bulrush • *Schoenoplectus tabernaemontani*

Perennial herb of fresh to brackish marshes and shores, up to 2.5 m tall. **Spikelets** *3–17 mm long, shiny, reddish brown; floral scales 2–3.5 mm long, brown or tawny, the awn tip straight; inflorescence loose, with long, lax, sometimes drooping rays.* **Achenes** 1.8–2.3 mm long, *not fully concealed by the scales.* **Stems** *soft, easily crushed between the fingers, with few, large internal partitions* (see left photo).
OCCURRENCE: Occasional; MDI, SCH.
NOTES: Similar to *Schoenoplectus acutus* but smaller and more slender.
OTHER NAMES: *Scirpus validus*

Black-girdled Wool-grass • *Scirpus atrocinctus*

Densely tufted, short-rhizomatous, perennial herb of meadows and swamps, 0.3–1.8 m tall. **Spikelets** *individually stalked.* **Leaves** 4–7 per stem, 3–6 mm wide. **Achenes** *with perianth bristles smooth, contorted, and much exceeding the scales, making the head appear woolly; ripening late June to early July.* **Stems** 1–4 mm wide.
OCCURRENCE: Occasional; MDI, IAH, SCH.
OTHER NAMES: Black-girdled Woolsedge

Black Bulrush • *Scirpus atrovirens*

Densely tufted, perennial herb of wetlands and shores. **Spikelets** ovoid to short-cylindric, *3–5 mm long, densely crowded in subglobose bunches; inflorescence loose or sometimes compact, often with axillary bulblets; floral scales brownish to blackish.* **Leaves** up to 18 mm wide, mostly on lower half of stem. **Achenes** very pale to white, compressed, 3-angled, 0.8–1.2 mm long; perianth bristles smooth, usually 6, *shorter to slightly longer than the achene, exceeding the floral scales.*

OCCURRENCE: Occasional; MDI, IAH, SCH.

NOTES: This species is found in wetter habitats than *Scirpus hattorianus,* with which it is most likely to be confused.

OTHER NAMES: Dark-green Bulrush

DSC

DSC

Common Wool-grass • *Scirpus cyperinus*

Densely tufted, short-rhizomatous, perennial herb of bogs, marshes, swamps, and wet meadows, up to 2 m tall. **Spikelets** *grouped together in 2s or 3s.* **Leaves** 3–10 mm wide. **Achenes** pale; *perianth bristles 6, smooth, long, contorted, greatly exceeding the scales, giving the head a woolly look, ripening in August.*

OCCURRENCE: Common; MDI, IAH, SCH.

OTHER NAMES: Wool-grass, Common Woolsedge

Mosquito Bulrush • *Scirpus hattorianus*

Densely tufted, short-rhizomatous, perennial herb of wet meadows, marshes, and ditches, up to 1.8 m tall. **Spikelets** *2–3.5 mm long*. **Leaves** green, 2–10 mm wide. **Achenes** 0.1–1.1 mm long; *longer perianth bristles shorter than to equaling the length of the achene*.
OCCURRENCE: Occasional; MDI, IAH, SCH.
OTHER NAMES: *Scirpus atrovirens* var. *georgianus*

AH

Red-tinged Bulrush • *Scirpus microcarpus*

Perennial herb of marshes, wet meadows, and low thickets, 0.6–1.5 m tall. **Spikelets** 4–6 mm long, *very numerous, sessile, in small, stalked clusters in a compound terminal cyme, subtended by several leaf-like, unequal, long, sheathless bracts; floral scales numerous, 1–2 mm long, largely blackish to greenish black with a midrib that may stick out beyond the tip; styles 2*. **Leaves** several, flat, 8–15 mm wide, *with red sheaths*. **Achenes** pale, 1–1.2 mm long including the tiny pointed tip; *perianth bristles 4–6, slender, minutely retrorsely barbed, slightly surpassing the achene*. **Stems** coarse, arising singly or a few together, obscurely 3-angled.
OCCURRENCE: Occasional; MDI, IAH, SCH.
OTHER NAMES: Barber-pole Bulrush, *Scirpus rubrotinctus*

Stalked Bulrush • *Scirpus pedicellatus*

Tufted, perennial herb of wet thickets and meadows, up to 1.5 m tall. **Spikelets** *individually stalked, 3–9 mm long and 2–3 mm wide.* **Achenes** whitish, *maturing in midsummer; perianth bristles woolly.*
OCCURRENCE: Uncommon; MDI.
OTHER NAMES: Pedicellate Wool-grass, Stalked Woolsedge

Alpine Bulrush • *Trichophorum alpinum*

Short-rhizomatous, perennial herb of swales, wet thickets, meadows, and shores, 10–40 cm tall. **Spikelets** *1 per stem, terminal, brown.* **Achenes** with 6 white, flat, perianth *bristles 1–3 cm long at maturity, clearly surpassing the spikelet.* **Stems** *triangular in cross section, scabrous on the angles.*
OCCURRENCE: Uncommon; MDI, SCH.
OTHER NAMES: Alpine Club-rush, Alpine Leafless-bulrush, Alpine Club-sedge, *Scirpus hudsonianus*

Tufted Club-rush • *Trichophorum cespitosum*

Densely tufted, short-rhizomatous, perennial herb of bogs and alpine areas, 5–45 cm tall. **Spikelets** 3.3–7 mm long. **Achenes** *with 3–6 brown perianth bristles ~2 mm long, hidden by the scales.* **Stems** *round in cross section, smooth.*
OCCURRENCE: Occasional; MDI, IAH, SCH.
OTHER NAMES: Deer's Hair, Deer Grass, Tufted Clubsedge, *Scirpus cespitosus*

JUNCACEAE • RUSH FAMILY ▼

Sharp-fruited Rush • *Juncus acuminatus*

Tufted, perennial herb of damp meadows, shores, and wet woods, 0.3–1 m tall. **Flowers** numerous at tip of pedicels, *with 3 stamens*; tepals lance-shaped, sharp-pointed, as long as the capsule. **Leaves** usually 2 per stem, round in cross section, with internal partitions, the lowest shorter than the inflorescence. **Fruit** *a light brown capsule.* **Seeds** *0.3–0.7 mm long, pointed at ends, without tails.*
OCCURRENCE: Occasional; MDI, IAH, SCH.

AH

AH

Jointed Rush • *Juncus articulatus*

Loosely tufted, rhizomatous, perennial herb of bogs, wet meadows, ditches, and shores, 10–60 cm tall. **Flowers** numerous at tip of peduncles, *with 6 stamens.* **Leaves** round in cross section, 2–15 cm long and 0.7–1.5 mm wide, with internal partitions, the lowest shorter than the inflorescence. **Fruit** *dark-brown, longer than the tepals.* **Seeds** *0.3–0.7 mm long, pointed at ends, without tails.*

OCCURRENCE: Uncommon; MDI.

OTHER NAMES: Noded Rush, Joint-leaved Rush

Wire Rush • *Juncus balticus*

Long-rhizomatous, perennial herb of brackish to fresh water shores, 40–80 cm tall. **Inflorescence** *subtended by a solitary bract appearing as a continuation of stem.* **Flowers** *with 6 stamens.* **Leaves** with bladeless sheaths. **Stems** *slender, round in cross section, with a smooth, unfurrowed surface.*

OCCURRENCE: Occasional; MDI, IAH, SCH.

OTHER NAMES: Baltic Rush, Arctic Rush, *Juncus arcticus*

Short-tailed Rush • *Juncus brevicaudatus*

Densely tufted, perennial herb of marshes, wet meadows, and shores, 10–50 cm long. **Flowers** numerous from tip of peduncles. **Leaves** round in cross section, 1–2 mm wide, with internal partitions. **Fruit** 3-sided, much exceeding the tepals. **Seeds** *0.7–1.2 mm long including the white tail; tail less than one-quarter the length of the seed, often arising from only one end.*
OCCURRENCE: Occasional; MDI, IAH, SCH.
OTHER NAMES: Narrow-panicled Rush

Toad Rush • *Juncus bufonius*

Simple or branched, annual herb of wet, open areas, and coastal shores, up to 30 cm tall. **Inflorescence** *over one-third of total plant height.* **Flowers** *solitary on pedicels*; tepals slender with a greenish mid-stripe. **Leaves** very fine, flat or channeled on the upper surface, without internal partitions; sheaths without auricles.
OCCURRENCE: Common; MDI, IAH, SCH.

Canada Rush • *Juncus canadensis*

Tufted, perennial herb of swamps, marshes, wet shores, and ditches, 0.4–1 m tall. **Flowers** numerous at tip of pedicels. **Leaves** round in cross section, ~1 mm wide, with internal partitions. **Fruit** 3-sided, 3.3–4.5 mm long, *abruptly narrowing to a short beak.* **Seeds** *spindle-shaped, 1.1–1.9 mm long including the white tails at each end, each tail over half as long as seed body.*
OCCURRENCE: Occasional; MDI, IAH, SCH.
OTHER NAMES: Canadian Rush

Forked Rush • *Juncus dichotomus*

Densely tufted, short-rhizomatous, perennial herb of dry to wet soils. **Inflorescence** *less than one-quarter total plant height*; subtended by 2 or more bracts. **Flowers** solitary on pedicels, with greenish brown and lustrous tepals. **Leaves** very fine, without internal partitions, *reaching beyond mid-point of the stem*; auricles cartilaginous, <1 mm long; *inner sheaths purple-tinged.* **Fruit** *highly lustrous.*
OCCURRENCE: Uncommon; MDI.

DSC

DSC

Soft Rush • *Juncus effusus*

Densely tufted, perennial herb of swamps, thickets, and pool margins, up to 1.4 m tall. **Inflorescence** *subtended by a solitary bract appearing as a continuation of stem, many-flowered.* **Flowers** with 3 stamens; tepals 2–2.5 mm long, tan. **Leaves** *bladeless, basal sheaths up to 20 cm long, mostly reddish brown.* **Stems** *tall, round, smooth.*
OCCURRENCE: Occasional; MDI, IAH.
OTHER NAMES: Common Rush, Smooth Rush, Taper Rush, Common Soft Rush

Black-grass • *Juncus gerardii*

Tufted, rhizomatous, perennial herb of saline to brackish marshes, 20–60 cm tall. **Inflorescence** less than one-quarter total plant height, subtended by 2 or more bracts, *many-flowered.* **Flowers** solitary on pedicels; *tepals brownish, with green midstripe, narrowing to an obtuse, incurving tip; stamens 6.* **Leaves** *without internal partitions, some borne on upper half of stem; sheaths entire at summit.* **Fruit** 2.4–3.3 mm long, *about the same height as the tepals.* **Seeds** 0.5 mm long, *longitudinally ribbed.*
OCCURRENCE: Occasional; MDI, IAH, SCH.
OTHER NAMES: Saltmarsh Rush

Bayonet Rush • *Juncus militaris*

Tufted, stout-rhizomatous, perennial herb of shallow water and wet shores, up to 1 m tall. **Inflorescence** subtended by 2 or more bracts. **Flowers** numerous at tip of pedicels. **Leaves** round in cross section, without internal partitions, *of two types: lower cauline leaves 3–6 mm wide at the middle, taller than the inflorescence; leaves on the rhizome, submerged, very thin.* **Fruit** 3-sided, 2.4–3.5 mm long, *with a sharp beak.* **Seeds** 0.3–0.7 mm long, pointed at ends, without tails.
OCCURRENCE: Occasional; MDI, IAH.
OTHER NAMES: Noded Bog Rush

Brown-fruited Rush • *Juncus pelocarpus*

Rhizomatous, perennial herb of damp shores and boggy areas, 10–50 cm tall. **Inflorescence** subtended by 2 or more bracts, *much-branched, 5–15 cm long, the branches bearing numerous solitary or paired flowers, often with numerous vegetative bulbils.* **Leaves** *round in cross section, with obscure internal partitions.* **Fruit** 2.4–3.1 mm, *gradually tapering to a beak.* **Seeds** 0.3–0.7 mm long, pointed at the ends, without tails.
OCCURRENCE: Occasional; MDI.

AH

Lopsided Rush • *Juncus secundus*

Loosely tufted, perennial herb of ledges and rocky forests, 30–60 cm tall. **Inflorescence** less than one-quarter total height of plant, subtended by 2 or more bracts; *branches of the inflorescence ascending*, commonly incurving above. **Flowers** solitary on pedicels, with 6 anthers. **Leaves** on only lower portion of stem, *not reaching middle of stem*, flat or involute, without internal partitions; *auricles <1 mm long, pale, membranous, rounded at the summit.*
OCCURRENCE: Rare; MDI.
NOTES: Maine Natural Areas Program ranks this species as threatened in Maine.

Path Rush • *Juncus tenuis*

Tufted, perennial herb of fields, roadsides, and open areas, 10–80 cm tall. **Inflorescence** less than one-quarter total plant height, subtended by 2 or more bracts 1–10 cm long, *the bracts often surpassing the inflorescence but not appearing as a continuation of the stem.* **Flowers** solitary on pedicels. **Leaves** on only lower portion of stem, flat, becoming involute, 1–1.5 mm wide, without internal partitions; *auricles 1–5 mm long*; sheaths with white margins.
OCCURRENCE: Occasional; MDI, IAH, SCH.
OTHER NAMES: Slender Rush, Poverty Rush, Yard Rush

Hairy Woodrush • *Luzula acuminata*

Loosely tufted, perennial herb of woods and open areas, 10–40 cm tall. **Flowers** *solitary or rarely paired at ends of branches on drooping or curving pedicels*; tepals 2.5–4.5 mm long, with scarious margins. **Leaves** 2–4, dark green, often persistently hairy on margins, 5–12 mm wide, with a blunt, callous tip. **Fruit** a capsule, exceeding tepals, 3.2–4.5 mm long. **Seeds** with pale appendages nearly as long as the seed.
OCCURRENCE: Uncommon; MDI, IAH.
OTHER NAMES: Pointed Woodrush, Hairy Woodrush

Forest Woodrush • **Luzula luzuloides*

Loosely tufted, perennial herb of open woods, roadsides, and lawns, 45–70 cm tall. **Inflorescence** *a terminal cluster.* **Flowers** *with inner tepals white with some pink, 3–3.8 mm long.* **Leaves** *dark, lustrous green, tapering to a long point.* **Fruit** red-brown, about equaling the outer tepals. **Seeds** 0.1–1.3 mm long, *with a pale ridge along one side.*
OCCURRENCE: Uncommon; MDI.
NOTES: Aggressively invasive!
OTHER NAMES: Oak-forest Woodrush

Common Woodrush • *Luzula multiflora*

Densely tufted, perennial herb of open woods, fields, and meadows, 20–40 cm tall. **Inflorescence** a terminal cluster; *peduncles strongly ascending, sometimes branched.* **Flowers** with tepals lance-shaped; tepals brown to dark brown, *the outermost just equaling or slightly longer than the inner ones.* **Leaves** *flat except near the callous, pointed tip* (see left photo). **Fruit** *shorter than the tepals, yellowish green, dull.*
OCCURRENCE: Occasional; MDI, IAH, SCH.

AH

POACEAE • GRASS FAMILY ▼

Velvet Bentgrass • *Agrostis canina*

Tufted, stoloniferous, perennial herb of fields and meadows, 20–70 cm tall. **Inflorescence** a panicle 5–20 cm long, longer than wide; branches of panicle rough, bearing flowers in both far and near portions. **Spikelets** *1-flowered*, 1–1.8 mm long. **Florets** *with unnerved, minute paleas, less than one-third as long as lemmas; lemmas with a bent awn 1.3–6 mm long, produced near the middle of the lemma.* **Leaves** flat, 4–6 cm long and 1–3 mm wide, not crowded toward the base.
OCCURRENCE: Uncommon; MDI.
OTHER NAMES: Brown Bentgrass, Dog Bentgrass

Rhode Island Bentgrass • **Agrostis capillaris*

Loosely tufted, rhizomatous, sod-forming, perennial herb of pastures and roadsides, 20–60 cm tall. **Inflorescence** *a panicle 4–20 cm long, permanently open, with smooth branches and pedicels, not drooping, the lower half of panicle branches without spikelets.* **Spikelets** *1-flowered,* 2–3 mm long, *usually bronze or purple-tinged; callus minutely bearded.* **Florets** with paleas half to two-thirds as long as lemmas; lemmas 1.5–2.5 mm long, rarely short-awned. **Leaves** 1–5 mm wide; auricles absent; ligules wider than long, mostly 0.5–2 mm long. **Stems** smooth.
OCCURRENCE: Occasional; MDI, IAH.
OTHER NAMES: Fine Bentgrass, *Agrostis tenuis*

Black Bentgrass • **Agrostis gigantea*

Rhizomatous, perennial herb of wet areas and along shores, up to 1 m tall. **Inflorescence** a panicle 10–20 cm long, *not drooping, with widely spreading unequal branches,* at least some of the panicle branches with spikelets toward the base; panicle branches and pedicels scabrous. **Spikelets** 1-flowered, 2–3.5 mm long; callus minutely bearded; anthers 0.8–1.5 mm long. **Florets** with paleas half to two-thirds as long as lemmas. **Leaves** 3–8 mm wide; *upper ligules 2.5–6 mm long, longer than wide.*
OCCURRENCE: Common; MDI, IAH, SCH.
OTHER NAMES: Redtop, Redtop Bentgrass

DSC

Autumn Bentgrass • *Agrostis perennans*

Tufted, perennial herb of dry areas and open woods, 0.5–1 m tall. **Inflorescence** *a panicle, longer than wide*, smooth or scabrous; *panicle branches forking near or below the middle, soon spreading*. **Spikelets** 1-flowered, 1.8–2.8 mm long; *glumes subequal*, scabrous on the midvein. **Florets** with lemmas 1.3–2 mm long, mostly awnless; *paleas minute*. **Leaves** flat, 2–6 mm wide, the uppermost >5 cm long.
OCCURRENCE: Occasional; IAH.
OTHER NAMES: Upland Bentgrass

Ticklegrass • *Agrostis scabra*

Densely tufted, perennial herb of wet or dry areas, 30–80 cm tall. **Inflorescence** a panicle 10–30 cm long, *diffuse, zigzagging, often red-purple; panicle branches abundantly scabrous*, usually forking beyond the middle. **Spikelets** borne near the branch tips, 1-flowered, 1.2–3.2 mm long. **Florets** *with reddish tinge; lemmas lacking a tuft of hairs at the base; callus short-bearded*; paleas <0.3 mm long; anthers 0.3–0.6 mm long. **Leaves** numerous, fine, short, *originating below middle of stem*, 1–3 mm wide; auricles absent; ligules 1–3 mm long. **Stems** *rough*.
OCCURRENCE: Occasional; MDI, IAH, SCH.
OTHER NAMES: Hairgrass, fly-away Grass, Rough Bentgrass

Creeping Bentgrass • **Agrostis stolonifera***

Stoloniferous, perennial herb of wet areas, 20–50 cm tall. **Inflorescence** a panicle, not drooping, *opening during anthesis and closing after flowering*. **Spikelets** 1-flowered. **Florets** greenish to reddish; *lemmas lacking a tuft of hairs at the base*. **Leaves** <3 mm wide; ligules 2–6 mm long. **Stems** *prostrate at base, rooting at the nodes*.
OCCURRENCE: Occasional; MDI, IAH, SCH.
OTHER NAMES: Carpet Bentgrass, *Agrostis alba*

Meadow Foxtail • **Alopecurus pratensis***

Perennial herb of wet fields, meadows, and open areas, 40–80 cm tall. **Inflorescence** *a spike-like panicle, 2–8 cm long and 5–10 mm wide, cylindrical*. **Spikelets** 1-flowered, 4–6.5 mm long; glumes 4–5.5 mm long. **Florets** *with lemmas not bearded at the base, with awn attached below the middle*. **Leaves** flat, up to 10 mm wide; *ligules membranaceous*. **Stems** erect.
OCCURRENCE: Occasional; MDI.
OTHER NAMES: Field Meadow Foxtail

Beach Grass • *Ammophila breviligulata*

Perennial herb of sandy shores and dunes. **Inflorescence** *a spike-like panicle, flattened from side to side,* thickened in the middle, 10–40 cm long, *base often partially enclosed in the upper leaf sheath.* **Spikelets** 1-flowered. **Florets** *with lemmas with a tuft of hairs at the base; callus hairs 1–3 mm long.* **Leaves** *dark green, shiny, rough on upper surface,* 4–8 mm wide when flat; ligules 1–3 mm long; *sheaths with summit always tinged with red.*
OCCURRENCE: Uncommon; MDI.
NOTES: Compare with *Leymus mollis* (leaf sheath not tinged in red; leaves dull green and wide).
OTHER NAMES: American Beach Grass

Sweet Grass • *Anthoxanthum nitens*

Tufted, perennial herb of meadows, shores, swales, and bog margins, 30–60 cm tall. **Inflorescence** *an open panicle 5–10 cm long.* **Spikelets** *with 3 florets;* glumes 4–6 mm long. **Florets** *with awnless lemmas.* **Leaves** *sweetly scented.*
OCCURRENCE: Uncommon; MDI, SCH.
OTHER NAMES: Indian Grass, Vanilla Grass, Vanilla Sweet Grass, *Hierochloe odorata*

Sweet Vernal Grass • ******Anthoxanthum odoratum***

Tufted, perennial herb of fields, roadsides, and waste areas, 30–70 cm tall. **Inflorescence** *a spike-like panicle, narrow, sweet-scented, asymmetrical, 2–9 cm long.* **Spikelets** 3-flowered; *glumes wide, sharp-pointed, longer than lemmas, upper one much longer than the lower one.* **Florets** *with lemmas awned from a notched tip,* the awn of the lower, sterile lemma straight. **Leaves** *mostly basal,* flat, hairy toward base, 2–7 mm wide; *auricles ~1 mm long, hairy;* ligules 1–3 mm long. **Stems** glabrous.
OCCURRENCE: Common; MDI, IAH, SCH.
OTHER NAMES: Large Sweet Grass

Tall Oatgrass • ******Arrhenatherum elatius***

Tufted, short-lived, perennial herb of wet fields, roadsides, and waste areas, up to 2 m tall. **Inflorescence** *a densely congested panicle, shining, slender, 10–30 cm long, with short, bunched branches.* **Spikelets** *each with 1 bisexual floret and 1 staminate floret.* **Florets** *with awn of lower lemma 10–20 mm long, bent near the middle;* awn of upper lemma 0–6 mm long. **Leaves** scabrous, 4–8 mm wide.
OCCURRENCE: Uncommon; MDI.

AH

AH

Tucker Northern Short-husk • *Brachyelytrum aristosum*

Erect, short-rhizomatous, perennial herb of forests, 0.5–1 m tall. **Inflorescence** a panicle. **Spikelets** few, appressed; lower glume none or up to 0.8 mm long, the upper *awl-shaped,* 1–4 mm long. **Florets** *with lemmas 6–10 mm long and scabrous on the nerves, the awn 12–25 mm long.* **Leaves** scabrous or hairy, *ciliate-margined, septate* (see left photo).

OCCURRENCE: Occasional; MDI, IAH.

OTHER NAMES: Northern Long-awned Wood Grass, *Brachyelytrum erectum, Brachyelytrum septentrionale*

AH

Fringed Bromegrass • *Bromus ciliatus*

Tufted, perennial herb of wet forests, thickets, slopes, and shores, 0.6–1.2 m tall. **Inflorescence** 10–20 cm long, open, *with slender, often flexuous, drooping or spreading branches up to 15 cm long.* **Spikelets** *drooping, 4- to 10-flowered*; glumes glabrous, the lower 1-veined, 5–8 mm long, the upper 3-veined, 7–10 mm long, *often with a short awn.* **Florets** *with lemmas 10–13 mm long, long-hairy near the margins, with awns, 3–5 mm long.* **Leaves** 4–10 mm wide, glabrous to sparsely hairy; sheaths hairy (see middle photo); *ligules 0.3–1 mm long.*

OCCURRENCE: Common; MDI, SCH.

OTHER NAMES: Fringed Brome

Smooth Bromegrass • **Bromus inermis*

Solitary, rhizomatous, perennial herb of fields and roadsides, 0.5–1 m tall. **Inflorescence** 10–20 cm long, open during flowering, *later contracted, with 4–10 branches per node.* **Spikelets** 15–30 mm long and ~3 mm wide, 7- to 11-flowered; *lower glume 4–8 mm long, 1-veined, the upper 7–10 mm long and 3-veined.* **Florets** with lemmas 10–12 mm long, 3- or 5-veined, *without awns.* **Leaves** 5–15 mm wide, *both the blades and sheaths glabrous; ligules 0.5–1 mm long.*

OCCURRENCE: Occasional; MDI.

OTHER NAMES: Awnless Bromegrass, Hungarian Bromegrass, Smooth Brome

AH

Junegrass • **Bromus tectorum*

Annual herb of roadsides and waste areas, 20–70 cm tall. **Inflorescence** *10–20 cm long, often nodding.* **Spikelets** 3- to 8-flowered, mostly drooping; glumes awl-shaped, the lower 5–7 mm long, the upper 8–11 mm long. **Florets** *with lemmas 8–12 mm long, hairy, toothed at tips, 5- to 7-veined, with awns 10–17 mm long.* **Leaves** *soft-hairy; ligules 1–2.5 mm long*; auricles absent. **Stems** with fine, downward-pointing hairs.

OCCURRENCE: Uncommon; MDI.

OTHER NAMES: Downy Chess, Downy Brome, Cheat Brome

AH

Canada Bluejoint • *Calamagrostis canadensis*

Rhizomatous, perennial herb of wet meadows, swamps, and bogs, 0.5–1.5 m tall. **Inflorescence** somewhat nodding, 8–25 cm long, the longer branches 2–8 cm long. **Spikelets** 2–6 mm long. **Florets** *with awn of lemma delicate, erect, straight or nearly so, inserted near the middle; callus-hairs abundant, nearly as long as the lemma.* **Leaves** *scabrous on both sides, flat, 4–8 mm wide, bluish green*; ligules 3–8 mm long; sheaths glabrous. **Stems** often branched above, *with 5 or more leaves.*
OCCURRENCE: Common; MDI, IAH, SCH.
OTHER NAMES: Bluejoint, Blue-node, Canada Reed Grass

Pickering's Bluejoint • *Calamagrostis pickeringii*

Rhizomatous, perennial herb of bogs, wet shores, and open woods, 20–70 cm tall. **Inflorescence** *contracted, 4–15 cm long.* **Florets** *with scabrous lemmas 2.6–3.7 mm long, awn of lemma inserted ~1 mm above base, twisted below, bent near the middle, about equaling the lemma; callus hairs one-quarter the length of lemma.* **Leaves** flat, 3–7 mm wide, tapering to the base, *scabrous beneath, glabrous above; ligules 2–5 mm long.* **Stems** *with 2 or 3 leaves.*
OCCURRENCE: Rare; IAH, SCH.
NOTES: Maine Natural Areas Program ranks this species as threatened in Maine.
OTHER NAMES: Pickering's Reed Bentgrass, Pickering's Blue-node, Pickering's Reed Grass

New England Northern Reedgrass • *Calamagrostis stricta*

Rhizomatous, perennial herb of wet meadows and damp woods, up to 1 m tall. **Inflorescence** 5–15 cm long. **Florets** *with copious callus hairs, half to nearly as long as the lemma; lemmas with a straight awn inserted near the middle.* **Leaves** *involute*, 2–6 mm wide when flat, *shiny green above, glaucous below.* **Stems** with 2 or 3 leaves.
OCCURRENCE: Rare; MDI.
NOTES: Maine Natural Areas Program ranks this species as endangered in Maine.
OTHER NAMES: Slim-stem Reedgrass, *Calamagrostis inexpansa*

Drooping Woodreed • *Cinna latifolia*

Solitary or clustered, perennial herb of wet woods, thickets, and clearings, 1–1.5 m tall. **Inflorescence** *lax and open, drooping, pale green, somewhat shiny.* **Spikelets** *1-flowered.* **Florets** with awn of lemma up to 1.5 mm long. **Leaves** up to 15 mm wide; *ligules colorless.*
OCCURRENCE: Uncommon; MDI.
OTHER NAMES: Wide-leaved Cinna, Slender Wood-reed

Orchard Grass • ******Dactylis glomerata***

Tufted, perennial herb of wet fields, roadsides, and waste areas, 0.5–1.2 m tall. **Inflorescence** *open, the branches and main axis bearing numerous short-stalked spikelets in dense, 1-sided clusters.* **Spikelets** 3- to 6-flowered. **Florets** with lemmas 5–8 mm long, usually ciliate on the keel. **Leaves** elongate, 3–8 mm wide; *sheaths compressed; ligules membranaceous* (see lower right photo).
OCCURRENCE: Occasional; MDI, IAH, SCH.
OTHER NAMES: Cook's-foot Grass

Wild Oatgrass • ***Danthonia compressa***

Densely tufted, perennial herb of wooded areas, 10–60 cm tall. **Inflorescence** *lax, 5–10 cm long; branches filiform, the lowest with 2 or 3 spikelets.* **Florets** with lemmas 4.5–8 mm long; *upper tooth of lemma 2–4 mm long; awn of lemma 5.5–8 mm long.* **Leaves** *mostly basal, usually flat, 2–4 mm wide and up to 20 cm long; ligules with a white band of hairs; sheaths glabrous.* **Stems** very slender, flat, overtopping the leaves.
OCCURRENCE: Rare; MDI, IAH.
NOTES: Generally found in more wooded and less open sites than *Danthonia spicata.*
OTHER NAMES: flattened Oatgrass

AH

Poverty Oatgrass • *Danthonia spicata*

Perennial herb of open areas, 20–60 cm tall. **Inflorescence** *a spike-like raceme 2–5 cm long.* **Florets** *with upper tooth of lemma 0.5–2 mm long.* **Leaves** *curly, usually involute, 0.8–2 mm wide* and <12 cm long; *ligules with a white band of hairs* (see middle photo).

OCCURRENCE: Common; MDI, IAH, SCH.

NOTES: Generally found in drier, more sterile habitats than *Danthonia compressa.*

OTHER NAMES: Common Wild Oatgrass

Tufted Hairgrass • *Deschampsia cespitosa*

Densely tufted, perennial herb of shores, thickets, fields, and roadsides, 0.3–1.2 m tall. **Inflorescence** *open or contracted*; lower branches in bundles of 2–5. **Spikelets** purplish or silvery, 2.3–5.7 mm long, *2-flowered.* **Florets** *with lemmas usually truncate; awn of lemma attached below the middle, straight or nearly so, shorter than to barely exceeding the lemma.* **Leaves** *mostly below middle of stem*, flat or folded, 1–5 mm wide; *ligules often elongate, 3–12 mm long.*

OCCURRENCE: Occasional; MDI, SCH.

Wavy Hairgrass • *Deschampsia flexuosa*

Densely tufted, perennial herb of rocky forests, cliffs, and subalpine areas, 0.3–1 m tall. **Inflorescence** loose and open, *somewhat nodding*. **Spikelets** *2-flowered*. **Florets** *with awn of lemma arising near the base; awn bent below the middle, the outer half divergent, surpassing the lemma by 1–3 mm*. **Leaves** *mostly near the base, involute*, 1–2 mm wide; ligules 1–2.5 mm long. **Stems** overtopping the leaves.
OCCURRENCE: Common; MDI, IAH, SCH.
OTHER NAMES: Common Hairgrass

Woolly Panic Grass • *Dichanthelium acuminatum*

Perennial herb of dry to wet, areas, 10–80 cm tall. **Spikelets** usually <2 mm long. **Leaves** usually <1 cm wide; basal leaves wider than cauline ones, often not crowded; *ligules with a band of hairs 2–5 mm long, conspicuously protruding from the sheath*.
OCCURRENCE: Occasional; MDI, IAH, SCH.
OTHER NAMES: Hairy Rosette-panicgrass, *Panicum lanuginosum, Panicum spretum, Panicum acuminatum*

Northern Panic Grass • *Dichanthelium boreale*

Tufted, perennial herb of thickets, fields, meadows, shores, and streambanks, 40–70 cm tall. **Inflorescence** *a panicle with ascending branches.* **Spikelets** pubescent, 1.5–2.3 mm long. **Leaves** narrow, not crowded, *rounded or cordate-auriculate ("eared") at base.*
OCCURRENCE: Uncommon; MDI, IAH.
OTHER NAMES: Northern Rosette-panicgrass, *Panicum boreale*

Starved Panic Grass • *Dichanthelium depauperatum*

Densely tufted, perennial herb of open woods and shores, 15–40 cm tall. **Inflorescence** *spear-shaped or narrowly ellipsoid.* **Leaves** elongate-linear, *forming dense tussocks; sheaths copiously hairy.* **Stems** straight or arching, simple or forking below in the fall, naked or with 1–3 erect leaves.
OCCURRENCE: Occasional; MDI.
OTHER NAMES: Starved Rosette-panicgrass, *Panicum depauperatum*

AH

Smooth Crabgrass • *Digitaria ischaemum*

Tufted, annual herb of cultivated and waste areas, 2–40 cm tall. **Inflorescence** with 2–6 racemes 4–10 cm long. **Spikelets** 1–2.3 mm long, becoming dark brown to purplish black; *lower glume absent or minute, the upper over half as long as entire spikelet.* **Leaves** smooth, *glabrous except for a few long hairs at junction of the blade and sheath; ligules 2–3 mm long.*
OCCURRENCE: Occasional; MDI, SCH.
OTHER NAMES: Small Crabgrass

Northern Crabgrass • *Digitaria sanguinalis*

Branched, annual herb of cultivated areas, lawns, fields, and waste areas, 0.3–1.2 m tall. **Inflorescence** with 3–6 racemes 5–15 cm long; main axis 1 mm wide, *broadly winged.* **Spikelets** *with lower glume 0.2–0.4 mm long, the upper glume less than half as long as entire spikelet.* **Leaves** 4–10 cm long and 5–10 mm wide, *pubescent, the hairs enlarged at base; ligules <2 mm long.*
OCCURRENCE: Uncommon; MDI.
OTHER NAMES: Large Crabgrass, Hairy Crabgrass

Barnyard Grass • **Echinochloa crus-galli*

Annual herb of cultivated ground and waste areas, 0.1–1 m tall. **Inflorescence** 10–25 cm long, erect, with usually 15–25 appressed or spreading branches 2–4 cm long; *main axis and branches of the inflorescence stout, often pubescent, the hairs enlarged at base.* **Florets** with lower lemmas usually awned. **Leaves** 5–30 mm wide; sheaths glabrous; auricles and ligules absent. **Stems** *decumbent at base, reddish.*
OCCURRENCE: Occasional; MDI, SCH.
OTHER NAMES: Cockspur Grass

Quack Grass • **Elymus repens*

Long-rhizomatous, perennial herb of shores and waste areas, 0.5–1 m tall. **Inflorescence** *an erect spike 8–17 cm long; middle internodes 4–7 mm long; rachis joints flat on one side and rounded on the other.* **Spikelets** 10–18 mm long, *3- to 8-flowered, disarticulating below the glumes.* **Leaves** *mostly flat, 3–10 mm wide, usually with scattered hairs above, with numerous slender veins*; auricles and ligules present. **Stems** green or sometimes glaucous, *hollow below inflorescence at flowering.*
OCCURRENCE: Common; MDI, IAH, SCH.
NOTES: Rhizomes can suppress growth of other plants.
OTHER NAMES: Quick Grass, Witch Grass, *Agropyron repens*

Slender Wheatgrass • *Elymus trachycaulus*

Tufted, perennial herb of various habitats, 0.3–1 m tall. **Inflorescence** a compact spike 4–15 cm long. **Spikelets** *mostly solitary, 9–16 mm long, overlapping, 3- to 5-flowered, readily disintegrating at maturity, disarticulating above the glumes.* **Leaves** usually flat, 2–6 mm wide, scabrous at least on the upper surface; auricles short or none.
OCCURRENCE: Uncommon; MDI, IAH, SCH.
OTHER NAMES: Wheatgrass, *Agropyron trachycaulum*

Virginia Wild Rye • *Elymus virginicus*

Tufted, perennial herb of wet woods, thickets, meadows, and shores, 0.5–1 m tall. **Inflorescence** *a rigidly erect spike, 4–10 cm long, the base often included in the summit of the more or less inflated, uppermost sheath.* **Spikelets** *mostly paired, 2- to 4-flowered, disarticulating below the glumes.* **Florets** *with lemmas small, 6–9 mm long, 5-veined, with a long straight awn up to 3.5 cm long.* **Leaves** mostly 6–10 per culm, flat, 4–10 mm wide, scabrous on both sides; auricles up to 1 mm long.
OCCURRENCE: Occasional; MDI, IAH, SCH.
OTHER NAMES: Virginia Lyme Grass, Terrel Grass, Common Eastern Wild-rye

Hair Fescue • ***Festuca filiformis**

Densely tufted, perennial herb of mixed forests, lawns, and waste areas, 10–60 cm tall. **Inflorescence** *an erect spike.* **Florets** *with lemmas awnless or with a tiny, pointed tip.* **Leaves** *involute, scabrous, delicately wiry-capillary; basal sheaths usually glabrous, not shredding, white-brown to light brown.*
OCCURRENCE: Common; MDI, IAH, SCH.
OTHER NAMES: Fine-leaved Sheep Fescue, *Festuca capillata*

Sheep Fescue • ***Festuca ovina**

Densely tufted, perennial herb of fields and roadsides, 15–30 cm tall. **Inflorescence** *usually opening and spreading,* if narrow, the spikelets not densely crowded. **Spikelets** 5–7 mm long. **Florets** with lemmas 3–4 mm long and *awned from the tip*; anthers 2–2.5 mm long. **Leaves** 0.3–0.7 mm wide with obscure ribs; *sheaths open to the base.*
OCCURRENCE: Common; MDI.

Red Fescue • *Festuca rubra*

Loosely tufted, perennial herb of disturbed soils and shorelines, 7–90 cm tall. **Spikelets** small, often reddish purple or glaucous green. **Florets** with lemmas 5–7 mm long with an awn 1–3 mm long, emerging from the tip. **Leaves** *folded to involute, 0.7–2 mm wide, glabrous, without auricles*; ligules <0.5 mm long; *lower sheaths closed and reddish purple when young, turning into loose, reddish brown fibers with age* (see left photo). **Stems** *decumbent*.
OCCURRENCE: Occasional; MDI, IAH, SCH.

AH

Northern Mannagrass • *Glyceria borealis*

Perennial herb of shallow water and wet areas, up to 1 m tall. **Spikelets** *10–20 mm long*. **Florets** *with lemmas blunt, glabrous between the veins; paleas exceeding lemmas*. **Leaves** *limp, floating, with a pubescent, nonwettable surface when growing in water*. **Stems** weak, decumbent.
OCCURRENCE: Uncommon; MDI.
OTHER NAMES: Small floating Mannagrass

Rattlesnake Mannagrass • *Glyceria canadensis*

Solitary to tufted, perennial herb of wetlands and cedar swamps, 0.3–1 m tall. **Inflorescence** *an open panicle.* **Spikelets** *3–5 mm wide, ovoid, on spreading, undulate pedicels often longer than the spikelets.* **Florets** *with lemmas distinctly pointed, exceeding the paleas.* **Leaves** firm, 2–10 mm wide, *somewhat scabrous.*
OCCURRENCE: Occasional; MDI, IAH, SCH.
OTHER NAMES: Rattlesnake Grass

American Mannagrass • *Glyceria grandis*

Clustered, perennial herb of wet meadows, streamsides, marshes, and shallow water, 1–1.5 m tall. **Inflorescence** *an open panicle.* **Spikelets** *4–6 mm long, with purplish florets; glumes acute.* **Florets** *with lemmas clearly 7-nerved.* **Leaves** *6–15 mm wide.*
OCCURRENCE: Uncommon; MDI, IAH.
OTHER NAMES: Reed Meadowgrass

Flaccid Mannagrass • *Glyceria laxa*

Solitary to tufted, perennial herb of bogs and swamps, 0.3–1 m tall. **Inflorescence** *an open panicle*. **Spikelets** *4–5 mm long, with 2–5 florets*. **Florets** *with lemmas obtuse at the apex*, shorter than or equal to the paleas. **Leaves** firm, 2–10 mm wide, *somewhat scabrous*.
OCCURRENCE: Uncommon; MDI.

DSC

DSC

Coastal Mannagrass • *Glyceria obtusa*

Perennial herb of wet woods, bogs, and shallow water, 0.1–1.3 m tall. **Inflorescence** *thick-cylindric to ellipsoid*. **Spikelets** 4–7 mm long. **Leaves** *firm, erect, 2–8 mm wide, 7–9 per stem*; ligules 0.5–0.9 mm long.
OCCURRENCE: Occasional; MDI.
OTHER NAMES: Atlantic Mannagrass

Fowl Mannagrass • *Glyceria striata*

Tufted, perennial herb of wet woods, stream margins, marshes, and swamps, 0.3–1.5 m tall. **Inflorescence** *a lax, open panicle.* **Spikelets** 1.5–2.5 mm long; *glumes obtuse, greenish purple, minute.* **Florets** *with lemmas strongly 7-nerved.* **Leaves** flat, 2–10 mm wide; *sheaths scabrous,* closed nearly to the summit.
OCCURRENCE: Occasional; MDI, IAH, SCH.
OTHER NAMES: Fowl Meadowgrass

Foxtail Barley • *Hordeum jubatum*

Tufted, perennial herb of fields, meadows, and roadsides, 30–70 cm tall. **Inflorescence** *nodding.* **Spikelets** with glumes 2.5–15 cm long including awns. **Florets** *with awns of lemma 1–6 cm long.* **Leaves** <5 mm wide, *scabrous.*
OCCURRENCE: Uncommon; MDI.
OTHER NAMES: Squirrel-tail Grass, flicker-tail Grass

CWG

Rice Cutgrass • *Leersia oryzoides*

Long-rhizomatous, perennial herb of wet meadows, ditches, and shores, up to 1.5 m tall. **Inflorescence** *a panicle 10–20 cm long, diffusely branched.* **Spikelets** 1-flowered, 3.8–6 mm long. **Florets** with pilose lemmas. **Leaves** *elongate, very harsh-scabrous on margins* (see left photo), *6–15 mm wide.* **Stems** ascending to sprawling, decumbent, rooting at the nodes.
OCCURRENCE: Rare; MDI, IAH.

Sea Lymegrass • *Leymus mollis*

Long-rhizomatous, perennial herb of dunes and sandy beaches, 0.5–1.5 m tall. **Inflorescence** *a dense, stiff spike 10–30 cm long.* **Spikelets** *usually in pairs, each 3- to 7-flowered.* **Florets** *with awnless lemmas.* **Leaves** dull green; sheaths not tinged red at summit. **Stems** *coarse, glaucous.*
OCCURRENCE: Occasional; MDI, IAH, SCH.
NOTES: Compare with *Ammophila breviligulata* (summit of leaf sheath always tinged with red; leaves shiny and narrower).
OTHER NAMES: American Dunegrass, Strand Wheat, American Lyme Grass, *Elymus arenarius*

Perennial Ryegrass • ***Lolium perenne**

Short-lived, perennial herb of fields, roadsides, and waste areas, 30–60 cm long. **Inflorescence** a spike. **Spikelets** with 5–10 florets; *glumes shorter than the spikelet.* **Leaves** *usually <4 mm wide, folded in bud.*
OCCURRENCE: Uncommon; MDI, SCH.
OTHER NAMES: Common Darnel, Ryegrass

Moorgrass • ***Molinia caerulea**

Densely cespitose, perennial herb of fields, meadows, and roadsides, 0.3–2 m tall. **Inflorescence** a spike-like panicle, on a long stem, *turning a beautiful reddish blue at flowering.* **Spikelets** 1- to 5-flowered. **Leaves** *rigid, elongate, the lowest in a firm clump*; cauline leaves few; *ligules a tuft of hairs.* **Stems** *overtowering the basal clump of leaves.*
OCCURRENCE: Rare; IAH, SCH.
OTHER NAMES: Purple Moorgrass

Marsh Muhly • *Muhlenbergia glomerata*

Rhizomatous, perennial herb of wet meadows, shores, and bogs, 0.3–1 m tall. **Inflorescence** *a long-stemmed, purplish green panicle.* **Leaves** *firm, erect, scabrous,* 7–15 cm long. **Stems** simple or with few erect basal branches, *stiffly erect; nodes and stems fuzzy.*
OCCURRENCE: Occasional; MDI.
OTHER NAMES: Spiked Muhly

AH

Bog Muhly • *Muhlenbergia uniflora*

Tufted, perennial herb of wet fields, meadows, shores, and bogs, 5–45 cm tall. **Inflorescence** *a long-stemmed, openly diffuse panicle.* **Spikelets** *purple, on pedicels much longer than the spikelets; glumes subequal, blunt, much shorter than the lemma.* **Leaves** flat, 1–2 mm wide, mostly basal. **Stems** *loosely matted, delicate,* arising from axils of the old, depressed culm.
OCCURRENCE: Occasional; MDI, IAH, SCH.
OTHER NAMES: One-flowered Dropseed

AH

Rough-leaved Ricegrass • *Oryzopsis asperifolia*

Loosely tufted, perennial herb of woods and thickets, 20–70 cm tall. **Inflorescence** *a contracted panicle 5–12 cm long.* **Spikelets** 6–8 mm long excluding awns. **Florets** *with lemmas sparsely pubescent, with awns 5–10 mm long.* **Leaves** flat, 4–15 mm wide, *the lowest evergreen, erect, scabrous, especially on the bluish green undersurface*; uppermost bladeless or with a tiny blade <1 cm long; sheaths crowded at the base. **Stems** *erect or bending at the lowest node.*

OCCURRENCE: Common; MDI, IAH.

NOTES: Seeds look like grains of rice, hence the common name "ricegrass".

OTHER NAMES: Rough Mountain-rice, White-grained Mountain Ricegrass

Witch Panicgrass • *Panicum capillare*

Annual herb of fields and gardens, 20–80 cm tall. **Inflorescence** *a very large and diffuse panicle, often purple.* **Spikelets** *lance-ovoid, short-pointed, 2–3 mm long, mostly on long stalks.* **Leaves** 0.3–2 cm wide, *copiously papillose-bristly.* **Stems** *stout,* with basal branches.

OCCURRENCE: Uncommon; MDI, SCH.

Fall Panicgrass • *Panicum dichotomiflorum*

Annual herb of cultivated ground, shores, waste areas, up to 1 m tall. **Inflorescence** a panicle. **Spikelets** *with lower glume less than half as long as the upper one.* **Leaves** narrowly lanceolate, *20–50 cm long and 0.3–2.5 cm wide,* without hairs on compressed sheath; *ligules a long band of hairs* (see photo). **Stems** *succulent, divergently branching from base, nodes bent, often zigzagging.*
OCCURRENCE: Rare; MDI.
OTHER NAMES: Forked Rosette-panicgrass

Reed Canarygrass • *Phalaris arundinacea*

Rhizomatous, perennial herb of meadows, shores, and marshes, 0.6–2 m tall. **Inflorescence** *a spike-like panicle, 0.5–20 cm long.* **Spikelets** *lanceolate, 4–6 mm long.* **Florets** *with pale, sterile lemmas with minute, hairy scales.* **Leaves** *flat, elongate, 0.6–2 cm wide.*
OCCURRENCE: Occasional; MDI.

Common Timothy • ***Phleum pratense**

Solitary or clumped, perennial herb of fields and roadsides, up to 1 m tall. **Inflorescence** *cylindrical, stiff, bristly, 5–10 cm long and 5–8 mm wide, very dense and spike-like, longer than wide.* **Spikelets** 1-flowered, flat; *glumes awned, the awns 0.7–1.5 mm long.* **Leaves** tapering to a sharp point, *flat, 8–23 cm long and 4–8 mm wide, glabrous, the margins rough especially toward the base;* ligules 2–3 mm long. **Stems** whitish, *producing a swollen bulb at base* (see lower left photo).
OCCURRENCE: Common; MDI, IAH, SCH.

Common Reed • **Phragmites australis**

Long-rhizomatous, perennial herb of wetlands, ditches, and brackish marshes, 1.4–4 m tall. **Inflorescence** *a tawny panicle, purplish green when young,* 15–40 cm long; *branches ascending and densely flowered.* **Leaves** *15–60 cm long and 1–6 cm wide, flat.*
OCCURRENCE: Rare; MDI, SCH.
NOTES: Aggressively invasive!
OTHER NAMES: Cane Grass, *Phragmites communis*

Canada Mountain Ricegrass • *Piptatherum canadense*

Loosely tufted, erect, perennial herb of woods, slopes, and blueberry barrens, 20–90 cm tall. **Inflorescence** *a loose panicle 8–15 cm long,* the slender branches opposite and loosely ascending. **Spikelets** ~4 mm long excluding awns; glumes slightly exceeding the pubescent lemma, *the awns 6–10 mm long.* **Leaves** rolled in on the edges and very fine, *the lowest about half the length of the culm.*

OCCURRENCE: Rare; MDI.

NOTES: Maine Natural Areas Program ranks this species as of special concern in Maine.

OTHER NAMES: *Oryzopsis canadensis*

AH

Slender Mountain Ricegrass • *Piptatherum pungens*

Densely tufted, perennial herb of rocky or sandy woods, 15–60 cm tall. **Inflorescence** *a panicle 3–8 cm long, branches erect or ascending.* **Spikelets** 3–4 mm long excluding the awns; *glumes subequal, obtuse, obscurely 5-nerved.* **Florets** with lemmas usually as long as the glumes, *awns 0.5–2 mm long.* **Leaves** in dense tussocks, the blades rolled in on the edges, very fine; *sheaths usually crowded at the base.*

OCCURRENCE: Uncommon; MDI.

NOTES: Seeds look like grains of rice, hence a common name "ricegrass".

OTHER NAMES: Short-awned Mountain Ricegrass, *Oryzopsis pungens*

AH

Annual Bluegrass • **Poa annua*

Tufted, annual herb of fields, cultivated ground, lawns, and waste areas, up to 50 cm tall. **Inflorescence** *a pyramid-shaped panicle, 1–8 cm long.* **Spikelets** crowded, 3- to 6-flowered, 3–7 mm long. **Florets** *with lemmas distinctly 5-nerved and not cobwebby at base.* **Leaves** *1–4 mm wide, very soft, the tips boat-shaped; sheaths loose and glabrous.* **Stems** *often rooting at lower nodes and forming large mats.*
OCCURRENCE: Occasional; MDI, SCH.
OTHER NAMES: Low Speargrass, Dwarf Meadow Grass

Canada Bluegrass • **Poa compressa*

Rhizomatous, perennial herb of dry soil, 20–70 cm tall. **Inflorescence** *compact and narrow,* 2–8 cm long, branches usually paired. **Spikelets** *small, 2- to many-flowered; glumes shorter than first floret.* **Florets** *with cobwebby hairs at base*; lemmas usually keeled on back, with veins converging at tip. **Leaves** 2–4 mm wide; ligules mostly 1–2 mm long. **Stems** *strongly flattened above.*
OCCURRENCE: Occasional; MDI, IAH, SCH.
OTHER NAMES: Wiregrass, flat-stemmed Bluegrass

Wood Bluegrass • ***Poa nemoralis**

Tufted, perennial herb of various habitats, 0.1–1 m tall. **Inflorescence** *an open, lax panicle.* **Spikelets** 3–6.5 mm long, loosely dispersed on panicle branches; *glumes narrowly spear-shaped, long-acuminate, straight.* **Florets** *with lemmas with few cobwebby hairs at base.* **Leaves** 1–3 mm wide, *deep green*, in dense clumps; *ligules squared off*, 0.5–1 mm long.
OCCURRENCE: Common; MDI.
NOTES: Aggressively invasive!
OTHER NAMES: Wood Meadow Grass

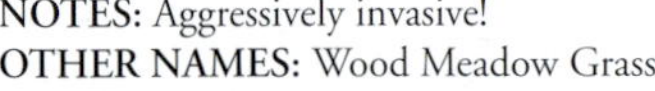

Swamp Meadowgrass • **Poa palustris**

Loosely tufted, perennial herb of wet thickets, meadows, shores, and roadsides, 0.5–1.5 m tall. **Inflorescence** *an open, loose panicle*, many-flowered, 10–30 cm long, with spreading branches; lower branches in whorls of 3–5. **Spikelets** small, 2- to many-flowered; *glumes shorter than first floret.* **Florets** *with cobwebby hairs at base; lemmas 2.5 mm long*, usually keeled on back with veins converging at tip. **Leaves** flat or folded, *usually ~6, 1.5–6 mm wide, with boat-shaped tips*; auricles absent; ligules 2–5 mm long. **Stems** *stout, usually curving and purplish at base.*
OCCURRENCE: Uncommon; MDI, IAH.

Kentucky Bluegrass • **Poa pratensis***

Tufted, long-rhizomatous, perennial herb of fields, meadows, shores, and lawns, 5–80 cm tall. **Inflorescence** *an open, pyramid-shaped panicle, usually with 3–5 branches at each joint.* **Spikelets** 2- to many-flowered; glumes shorter than first floret. **Florets** *with basal, cobwebby hairs; lemmas ~3.5 mm long,* usually keeled on back with veins that converge at tip. **Leaves** *2–5 mm wide, numerous, with distinct boat-shaped tips,* without auricles; ligules 1–3 mm long. **Stems** glabrous. **OCCURRENCE:** Common; MDI, IAH, SCH.

Tundra Alkali Grass • ***Puccinellia pumila***

Densely tufted, perennial herb of saline shores, 5–45 cm tall. **Inflorescence** *a panicle 2–18 cm long, with smooth, ascending, spreading, sometimes reflexed branches.* **Spikelets** 4–7 mm long. **Leaves** *flat, soft.*
OCCURRENCE: Occasional; MDI, IAH, SCH.
OTHER NAMES: *Puccinellia paupercula, Puccinellia tenella*

Meadow Fescue • **Schedonorus pratensis*

Loosely tufted, perennial herb of fields and meadows, 0.5–1.2 m tall. **Inflorescence** *a panicle, contracting after blooming.* **Spikelets** *8–12 mm long.* **Florets** with lemmas oblong-lanceolate, *the scarious tip acute, awnless.* **Leaves** 4–10 mm wide, *scabrous above.*
OCCURRENCE: Uncommon; MDI, IAH, SCH.
OTHER NAMES: Tall Fescue, Meadow Rye Grass, *Festuca elatior, Lolium pratense*

Broom Beardgrass • *Schizachyrium scoparium*

Loosely or densely tufted, perennial herb of sandy soils and rocky shores, 0.5–1.5 m tall. **Inflorescence** *simple, with stalked flowers on an elongate raceme 3–7 cm long.* **Florets** *with awns twisted at base.* **Leaves** 3–6 mm wide; *sheaths glabrous or hairy, green or whitened.* **Stems** *stiff, hard, forming vase-like clusters,* the upper half more or less branching; *nodes often purplish bluish.*
OCCURRENCE: Occasional; MDI.
OTHER NAMES: Little Bluestem, *Andropogon scoparius*

Yellow Foxtail • **Setaria pumila*

Tufted, annual herb of cultivated ground, roadsides, and waste areas, 1–1.2 m tall. **Inflorescence** *a dense, spike-like panicle* 1.5–12 cm long and 0.9–1.4 cm wide, *yellowish, with 4–12 bristles below each spikelet, the bristles reddish at the tips.* **Spikelets** *green, 3–3.5 mm long.* **Leaves** *with loosely spiraling blades and keeled sheaths.* **Stems** *compressed, often tufted, bent at base or erect.*
OCCURRENCE: Uncommon; MDI.
OTHER NAMES: Pigeon Grass, *Setaria glauca*

Green Foxtail • **Setaria viridis*

Annual herb of gardens, fields, roadsides, and waste areas, 1–1.2 m tall. **Inflorescence** *dense, a spike-like panicle 1.5–15 cm long and 1–2.3 cm wide, with 1–3 bristles below each spikelet; axis of panicle hairy but not rough.* **Leaves** without hairs on upper surface, 5–15 mm wide. **Stems** *compressed, often tufted.*
OCCURRENCE: Occasional; MDI.
OTHER NAMES: Green Bristlegrass, Bottle Grass

Smooth Cordgrass • ***Spartina alterniflora***

Long-rhizomatous, perennial herb of saltmarshes and coastal shores, up to 2.5 m tall. **Inflorescence** a spike with spikelets arranged on one side of the rachis, 2–15 cm long; *rachis often projecting as a bristle above the base of the terminal spikelet.* **Spikelets** 9–14 mm long. **Leaves** *flat when fresh, rolled under when dry, 0.4–1.5 cm wide, smooth, fleshy, very tough.* **Stems** leafy to the top, giving off a rank odor when bruised.
OCCURRENCE: Occasional; MDI, IAH, SCH.
OTHER NAMES: Saltwater Cordgrass

Saltmeadow Cordgrass • ***Spartina patens***

Rhizomatous, perennial herb of saltmarshes, coastal beaches, and shores, 15–80 cm tall. **Inflorescence** with spikelets arranged on one side of the rachis. **Spikelets** 9–13 mm long. **Leaves** *green when young, usually 4 per stem, very fine, the edges turned under, smooth on the back, 0.5–2 mm wide.* **Stems** *arising from persistent leaves of the previous year.*
OCCURRENCE: Occasional; MDI, IAH, SCH.
OTHER NAMES: High-water Grass

Freshwater Cordgrass • *Spartina pectinata*

Long-rhizomatous, perennial herb of marshes, shores, swamps, and wet gravel, 0.6–2 m tall. **Inflorescence** of 5–60 spikes, each spike 2–11 cm long including the awns and 5–8 mm wide. **Spikelets** arranged on one side of the rachis; *upper glume with an awn 3–10 mm long.* **Leaves** *hard, >30 cm long, with a very long taper to the tip, keeled, flat but quickly involute in drying, rough on the margins.* **Stems** *0.5–1 cm wide at base.*
OCCURRENCE: Occasional; MDI, IAH, SCH.
OTHER NAMES: Slough Grass, Prairie Cordgrass

Fernald's Mannagrass • *Torreyochloa pallida*

Trailing, matted, perennial herb of swamps and shallow water, 0.3–1 m tall. **Inflorescence** *a panicle, 7–30 cm long.* **Florets** *with lemmas strongly 5-nerved.* **Leaves** *soft, pale green, 5–20 cm long and 4–10 mm wide; ligules 5–8 mm long.* **Stems** *loosely decumbent from creeping bases.*
OCCURRENCE: Uncommon; MDI.
OTHER NAMES: Pale False Mannagrass, *Glyceria fernaldii*

Annual Wildrice • *Zizania aquatica*

Simple or basally branched, annual herb of quiet water and shores, up to 3 m tall. **Inflorescence** *with purplish to tan staminate flowers on the upper branches of the panicle; carpellate flowers below.* **Leaves** *flat, long, 0.3–5 cm wide.* **Stems** slender to stout, simple or basally branched, soft.

OCCURRENCE: Uncommon; MDI.

OTHER NAMES: Indian Wild Rice, Southern Wild Rice

HISTORICAL RECORDS OF PLANTS IN THE ACADIA PARK REGION

The following taxa were reported from the Acadia National Park region but have not been documented since 1980. If you know of the whereabouts of any of these species, please report them to the authors or Maine Natural History Observatory (www.mainenaturalhistory.org).

Acorus americanus
Agrimonia gryposepala
Agrostemma githago
Amaranthus albus
Anchusa officinalis
Antennaria parlinii
Antennaria plantaginifolia
Apios americana
Apocynum cannabinum
Arabis pycnocarpa
Atriplex littoralis
Berteroa incana
Bidens connata
Bidens vulgata
Botrychium angustisegmentum
Botrychium dissectum
Botrychium matricariifolium
Botrychium simplex
Bromus commutatus
Bromus hordeaceus
Bromus secalinus
Camelina microcarpa
Camelina sativa
Carex bushii
Carex haydenii
Carex hystericina
Carex michauxiana
Carex panicea
Carex tribuloides
Chenopodium simplex
Clematis virginiana
Clethra alnifolia
Coeloglossum viride
Conringia orientalis
Corallorhiza maculata
Cota tinctoria
Crataegus chrysocarpa
Cynosurus cristatus
Cypripedium parviflorum
Cypripedium reginae
Cystopteris tenuis
Dendrolycopodium hickeyi
Dichanthelium dichotomum
Dichanthelium linearifolium
Diphasiastrum complanatum
Dryopteris clintoniana
Eleocharis elliptica
Eragrostis cilianensis
Eriophorum viridicarinatum
Erythronium americanum
Eutrochium maculatum
Festuca trachyphylla
Fragaria vesca
Fumaria officinalis
Glechoma hederacea
Glyceria melicaria
Hedeoma pulegioides
Heliopsis helianthoides
Heracleum maximum
Hieracium piloselloides
Hippuris vulgaris
Holcus lanatus
Hudsonia tomentosa
Huperzia lucidula
Huperzia selago
Hydrocotyle americana
Hylodesmum glutinosum
Juncus dudleyi
Juncus filiformis
Juncus greenei
Kalmia latifolia
Lappula squarrosa
Lemna trisulca
Leonurus cardiaca
Lepidium densiflorum
Lilium canadense
Linaria dalmatica
Lindernia dubia
Linum usitatissimum
Liparis loeselii
Listera auriculata
Lobelia spicata
Ludwigia palustris
Lycopodiella appressa
Lysimachia arvensis
Lysimachia ciliata
Malva neglecta
Mentha canadensis
Mollugo verticillata
Muhlenbergia schreberi
Myriophyllum verticillatum
Nepeta cataria
Nicandra physalodes
Oenothera pilosella
Orobanche uniflora
Osmorhiza longistylis
Oxalis corniculata
Packera aurea
Panicum miliaceum
Parathelypteris simulata
Parietaria pensylvanica
Parthenocissus vitacea
Pastinaca sativa
Penstemon digitalis
Persicaria punctata
Platanthera aquilonis
Platanthera dilatata
Platanthera hookeri
Platanthera huronensis
Platanthera macrophylla
Platanthera obtusata
Platanthera orbiculata
Poa saltuensis
Polygala verticillata
Potamogeton zosteriformis
Potentilla canadensis
Prunus maritima
Pseudognaphalium macounii
Puccinellia maritima
Ranunculus aquatilis
Ranunculus bulbosus
Ranunculus recurvatus
Reseda alba
Ribes americanum
Ribes triste
Rorippa palustris
Rosa blanda
Rubus frondosus
Rubus pensilvanicus
Rubus semisetosus
Rubus setosus
Rubus vermontanus
Rumex altissimus
Rumex maritimus
Rumex occidentalis
Salicornia maritima
Salsola kali

Sanicula marilandica
Schedonorus arundinaceus
Schizachne purpurascens
Setaria italica
Silene antirrhina
Silena noctiflora
Silene nutans
Sinapis arvensis
Sisymbrium altissimum
Sisyrinchium angustifolium
Solanum nigrum
Solidago hispida
Solidago squarrosa
Spiranthes lacera
Spiranthes ochroleuca
Spiranthes romanzoffiana
Stachys arvensis
Stellaria borealis
Stellaria humifusa
Stellaria longifolia
Streptopus amplexifolius
Symphyotrichum ciliolatum
Symphyotrichum ericoides
Symphyotrichum lanceolatum
Symphyotrichum pilosum
Symphyotrichum tradescantii
Symphyotrichum undulatum
Taraxacum laevigatum
Thinopyrum pycnanthum
Tiarella cordifolia
Trifolium dubium
Triglochin palustre
Triodanis perfoliata
Trisetum spicatum
Urtica urens
Utricularia resupinata
Vaccaria hispanica
Veratrum viride
Verbascum phlomoides
Veronica persica
Vicia hirsuta
Vicia villosa
Viola labradorica
Viola renifolia

CULTIVATED SPECIES

Although others (Rand and Redfield 1894; Stebbins 1929a; Wise 1970a) reported the following taxa as escaping in the study area, we have excluded them from the catalogue because we consider them to be cultivated only, and not capable of freely reproducing or escaping outside garden conditions:

Actinidia arguta
Anchusa arvensis
Armoracia rusticana
Atocion armeria
Avena sativa
Betula lenta
Centaurea cyanus
Dianthus deltoides
Dianthus plumarius
Filipendula ulmaria
Helianthus annuus
Helianthus pauciflorus
Hemerocallis fulva
Hordeum vulgare
Humulus lupulus
Iberis umbellata
Isotrema macrophyllum
Linaria repens
Malva alcea
Mentha spicata
Myosotis arvensis
Myosotis sylvatica
Ribes rubrum
Rosa cinnamomea
Satureja hortensis
Secale cereale
Spiraea japonica
Swida sericea
Syringa vulgaris
Viburnum lentago
Viola tricolor

FALSE RECORDS

The following taxa were historically published as extant in the Acadia National Park region but were misidentified and are therefore excluded from the catalogue:

Arctium *lappa*
Argentina anserina
Asclepias incarnata
Bromus racemosus
Carex alata
Carex albolutescens
Carex baileyi
Carex bebbii
Carex brevior
Carex cristatella
Carex laevivaginata
Carex media
Carex pensylvanica
Cystopteris tenuis
Crataegus brainerdii
Crataegus coccinea
Dichanthelium commutatum
Elatine americana
Eriophorum gracile
Geranium carolinianum
Glyceria fluitans
Huperzia occidentale
Hypericum adpressum
Isoëtes riparia
Listera convallarioides
Lycopus virginicus
Nuphar advena
Plantago aristata
Polygonum oxyspermum
Rumex patientia
Rumex verticillatus
Salix fragilis
Symphyotrichum ericoides
Symphyotrichum praealtum
Symphyotrichum racemosum
Tripleurospermum inodorum

GLOSSARY

Achene: a dry, 1-seeded indehiscent fruit.

Acuminate: gradually tapering to a sharp-pointed tip, the sides more or less concave adjacent to the tip.

Acute: tapering to a short, pointed tip, the sides more or less straight to the tip.

Adnate: the fusion of dissimilar parts.

Alternate: structures borne at different levels, or one per node.

Annual: a plant that completes its life cycle in one year (germination, flowering, fruiting, and senescence). Look for single flowering stems and the absence of any nonflowering shoots or rhizomes.

Anther: the pollen-bearing portion of a stamen.

Anthesis: the period of flowering when pollen is shed.

Appressed: pressed tightly to another plant organ, usually refers to hairs when pressed close to the stem.

Aril: an appendage (usually fleshy) on a seed; a fleshy seed coat.

Ascending: directed upward or forward.

Bilaterally symmetric: a structure that can be divided through the center into two equal parts along only one plane.

Auricle: an ear-like lobe usually at the base of a plant organ, usually a leaf blade.

Awn: a terminal, bristle-like appendage.

Axil: the angle formed between the upper side of a plant organ (usually a leaf or bract) and the stem from which it grows.

Axillary: arising in an axil.

Barb: a small, rigid, reflexed, sharp projection, like the barb of a fishhook.

Basal: attached or grouped at the base.

Beak: a terminal projection on a 3-dimensional plant organ.

Berry: a fleshy fruit with 1 or more seeds and without a stony inner coat.

Biennial: completing a life cycle in two years, flowering and fruiting only in its second year.

Bipinnate: divided into pinnae and further divided into pinnules; twice pinnate.

Bipinnate-pinnatifid: divided into pinnae and further divided into lobed pinnules.

Bisexual: with both stamens and carpels present and functional in a flower; hermaphrodite.

Blade: the broad and flattened portion of a plant organ, such as a leaf.

Bloom: a white, waxy covering on a surface that can be rubbed away.

Bract: a reduced, variously-shaped, leaf-like structure subtending a flower or inflorescence.

Bracteole: a small or greatly reduced bract.

Bud: an undeveloped, unexpanded shoot, inflorescence, or solitary flower.

Bulb: an underground swelling at the base of a plant made up of fleshy, overlapping, modified leaves.

Bulbil: a small above-ground bulb-like structure, usually formed in a leaf axil, which can fall off and grow into a new plant.

Bulblet: a small bulb.

Callous: thickened or hardened.

Callus: the firm base of the lemma in the grass family (Poaceae).

Calyx: the whorl of sepals of a flower.

Capitulescence: the cluster of capitula on a plant.

Capitulum (pl. capitula): a dense cluster of sessile flowers, subtended by an involucre of bracts; found mostly in the aster family (Asteraceae).

Capsule: a dry fruit, usually several- or many-seeded, that splits into two or more parts to release the seeds.

Carpel: the organ bearing the ovules and seeds; usually composed of an ovary, style, and stigma.

Carpellate: bearing carpels.

Catkin: a dense spike of tiny, pendent, unisexual flowers, found mostly on trees and shrubs.

Cauline: borne on the above ground portion of the stem.

Cespitose: growing in dense tufts.

Channeled: with one or more deep grooves.

Ciliate: with a marginal fringe of hairs.

Clasping: surrounding the stem; usually refers to a sessile leaf with basal lobes that project around and appear to clasp the stem.

Compound: branched or composed of more than one like parts; regarding a leaf, divided into two or more distinct leaflets.

Concave: curved inward.

Connate: the fusion of similar parts.

Convex: curved outward.

Convolute: with rolled margins.

Cordate: heart-shaped, with two rounded, basal lobes and a basal notch.

Corolla: the petals of a flower.

Corymb: an inflorescence in which the outer flower-stalks are much longer than the inner ones, opening from the margins inward, creating a wide, flat- or round-topped inflorescence.

Costa: midvein of a pinna.

Costule: midvein of a pinnule.

Culm: a hollow or pithy aboveground stem.

Cyme: an inflorescence in which the terminal flower opens first, followed in succession by lateral and basal flowers.

Deciduous: falling off after the normal function; regarding a woody plant, dropping all of its leaves in autumn, and produces new leaves from buds the next spring.

Decumbent: horizontal at the base but tends to turn upwards at its tip.

Dichotomous: splitting into two; usually refers to a branching pattern.

Dimorphic: having two forms.

Dioecious: with only staminate flowers or only carpellate flowers on an individual plant.

Disc flower: one of the tubular flowers in a flower head in the aster family (Asteraceae); usually bisexual.

Dissected: divided into segments.

Distal: at or toward the tip.

Divergent: spreading.

Divided: lobed or separated to the base into distinct parts.

Drupe: a fleshy fruit, resembling a berry, containing a seed enclosed in a hard, stony, inner fruit wall.

Elliptic: widest at the middle and tapering at both ends.

Entire: without teeth or lobes along a margin.

Evergreen: remaining green throughout the winter and functional the following growing season.

Exfoliate: to shed or peel in thin layers; usually refers to bark.

False indusium: the edge of a pinnae or pinnule that folds under to enclose the sori.

Fascicle: a bundle or compact cluster of leaves, such as the leaves of pines.

Filament: the stalk of a stamen.

Filiform: thread-like.

Floret: an individual flower within a dense cluster; a small flower found in the capitulum of the aster family (Asteraceae).

Follicle: a dry fruit, derived from a single carpel, splitting open along one seam at maturity.

Free: not attached or fused to a different kind of plant organ.

Frond: a fern leaf, including both the blade and the stipe.

Glabrous: without scales or hairs.

Gland: an enlarged tip to a hair or a depression on a plant organ that produces a sticky or oily substance.

Glaucous: covered with a whitish or waxy coating.

Glume: one of the paired bracts at the base of a grass spikelet.

Herbaceous: not woody, dying back to the ground each winter.

Hip: a fruiting structure composed of an enlarged, fleshy floral tube (hypanthium) enclosing the achenes, as in roses.

Hirsute: covered with thick, stiff hairs.

Imbricate: overlapping in a pattern resembling tiles on a roof.

Indehiscent: not naturally opening at maturity along lines or pores.

Indusium (pl. indusia): a thin structure that covers and protects the sorus in ferns.

Inflorescence: an entire flower cluster on a stem or in an axil, including pedicels and bracts.

Involucre: a whorl of bracts at the base of a flowering head, often forming a cup-like structure.

Involute: with margins rolled inward toward the upper surface.

Keel: a central ridge on the underside of a structure; in the pea family (Fabaceae), the two lower petals that form the shape like the underside of a boat.

Lanceolate: narrow overall, but slightly wider below the middle and tapering to the tip.

Legume: a dry, pod-like fruit that splits open along one suture at maturity; characteristic of the pea family (Fabaceae).

Lemma: the lower of the two bracts enclosing a grass floret, often partially encloses the palea.

Lenticel: a slightly raised pore in the bark of a stem.

Liana: a woody trailing or climbing, vine-like plant.

Ligulate: having ligules.

Ligule: an appendage present on the upper side of a leaf, at the junction of the blade and sheath; the flattened portion of the ray flower in the aster family (Asteraceae).

Lobed: with large, projecting segments of an organ and sinuses between the segments that do not reach the axis or base.

Locule: the compartment within an ovary containing the developing seed.

Megaspore: a large spore; the larger type of spore in the quillwort family (Isoëtaceae).

Monoecious: having staminate (pollen-bearing) and carpellate (seed-bearing) flowers separate but on the same plant.

Mucro: a short, sharp, slender point.

Mucronate: having a small, bristle-like point.

Node: the point on a stem where a leaf or leaves are attached.

Nut: a hard, dry, one-seeded, indehiscent fruit.

Nutlet: a small nut.

Oblong: longer than wide and mostly parallel sided at least in the central portion.

Obovate: egg-shaped but widest above the middle, tapering gradually to its base and suddenly to its tip.

Obtuse: blunt or rounded at apex; with the margins coming together at the apex at more than a 90 degree angle.

Ocrea (pl. ocreae): the tubular sheath, formed from the stipules, at the nodes; characteristic of the buckwheat family (Polygonaceae).

Opposite: arising in pairs, on opposite sides of the stem.

Orbicular: nearly circular in outline.

Oval: widest at the middle and approximately 2 times as long as wide.

Ovary: the carpels of a flower collectively; after pollination and fertilization, the ovary develops into the fruit.

Ovate: more or less egg-shaped in outline.

Ovule: the tiny egg-containing bodies attached inside the ovary; after pollination and fertilization, the ovules develop into the seeds.

Palea: the upper of the two bracts enclosing a grass floret, often partially enclosed by the lemma.

Palate: a swelling on the lower lip of an asymmetric flower.

Palmate: with leaflets all radiating from a common point in a compound leaf.

Panicle: a branched raceme, with flowers maturing from the bottom to the top.

Papilla (pl. papillae): a short, blunt, nipple-shaped bump or projection on a surface.

Papillose: bearing minute papillae.

Pappus: a crown of hairs or bristles fused to the tip of the achene in the aster family (Asteraceae).

Pedicel: a stalk of a single flower.

Pedicellate: with a pedicel.

Peduncle: a stalk of an inflorescence.

Pendulous: hanging downward.

Perennial: living 3 or more years, generally flowering each year.

Perianth: the sepals and petals of a flower collectively.

Perigynium (pl. perigynia): a specialized bract of the carpellate flowers whose margins are united to form a sac-like structure enclosing the carpel or achene; in the sedge family (Cyperaceae).

Petal: one of the inner whorl of floral blades that surrounds the stamens or carpels of a flower, usually colored or white.

Petaloid: petal-like in appearance.

Petiole: a stalk of a leaf.

Pilose: bearing long, soft hairs.

Pinna (pl. pinnae): one of the primary subdivisions of a pinnately compound leaf fully divided to the rachis.

Pinnatifid: with the blade lobed but not fully cut to the rachis.

Pinnate: with a leaf blade fully divided into separate pinnae arranged along the leaf stalk.

Pinnate-pinnatifid: with a leaf blade divided into deeply lobed pinnae.

Pinnule: a distinct sub-division of a pinna, fully divided to the costa.

Pinnulet: a subdivision of a pinnule, fully divided to the costule.

Pith: the cylinder of soft tissue at the center of some stems and roots.

Plumose: feather-like.

Pome: a fleshy berry-like fruit derived from the swollen cup-shaped receptacle of the flower, found in the rose family (Rosaceae).

Prickle: a small, sharp epidermal outgrowth.

Pseudowhorl: a cluster of leaves falsely appearing whorled.

Pubescent: with hairs of any size or texture.

Quadrangular: 4-angled.

Raceme: an elongated inflorescence with individually stalked flowers, opening from the base towards the tip, which can continue to form new buds.

Rachis: the main axis of a compound leaf or inflorescence.

Radially symmetrical: with structures radiating from a common point, like the spokes of a wheel.

Rank: a vertical row.

Ray flower: a flower with one long, flat, strap-shaped petal, found in some species in the aster family (Asteraceae).

Recurved: bent backward or downward in a curve.

Reflexed: bent sharply downward, outward, or backward.

Remote: widely spaced or separated.

Retrorse: angling backward or downward.

Revolute: with the margins rolled under.

Rhizome: a creeping, underground, horizontal stem.

Rosette: a dense, radiating cluster of leaves, usually at ground level.

Rugose: wrinkled.

Sagittate: shaped like an arrowhead, with basal lobes pointing downward.

Samara: a dry, indehiscent winged fruit.

Saprophyte: a plant that nourishes itself on decomposing humus, usually through a partnership with a fungus.

Scabrous: rough to the touch.

Scale: a small, flat structure that is not leaf-like.

Secund: with flowers or branches on only one side of an axis.

Sepal: one of the outer whorl of floral blades that surrounds the petals of a flower, usually green.

Septate: divided by internal partitions.

Serrate: with sharp, forward-pointing teeth.

Serrulate: with minute, sharp, forward-pointing teeth.

Sessile: without a stalk.

Sheath: a structure that surrounds all or part of another, usually a leaf or bract base that surrounds a stem.

Silique: an elongate, dry, pod-like fruit that separates along two seams, found in the mustard family (Brassicaceae).

Simple: undivided.

Sinus: the indentation or cut between two lobes of a structure.

Sorus (pl. sori): a cluster of sporangia, commonly appearing as spots on the underside of a fern blade.

Spadix: a dense, erect, spike-like inflorescence, subtended or enclosed by a spathe, found in the arum family (Araceae).

Spathe: a large bract under or enclosing an inflorescence of the arum family (Araceae).

Spike: an unbranched raceme, the individual flowers without stalks or nearly so, maturing from the bottom towards the tip.

Spikelet: a small spike-like inflorescence or section of an inflorescence; one flower cluster of a grass or sedge.

Sporangium (pl. sporangia): a small, thin-walled, spore-holding case.

Sporophyll: a modified leaf that bears sporangia at its base.

Spur: a hollow projection from the back or base of a petal or sepal, usually containing nectar; a short, slow-growing woody twig projection.

Stamen: the pollen-producing organ of a flower, consisting of the anther and filament.

Staminate: bearing stamens.

Stellate: star-shaped; branching 3 or more times at the base.

Stigma: the portion of the carpel at the top of the style that receives pollen.

Stipe: a stalk-like structure.

Stipitate: borne on a stipe.

Stipule: a leaf-, scale-, or spine-like appendage at the base of a leaf stalk; found in pairs.

Stolon: a horizontal, aboveground stem, rooting at the nodes.

Striate: streaked or marked with fine parallel lines.

Strobilus (pl. strobili): a specialized region of a stem bearing sporophylls.

Style: the stalk-like structure that connects the stigma to the ovary.

Subdioecious: nearly dioecious.

Subopposite: nearly across from one another.

Suborbicular: nearly circular in outline.

Subsessile: nearly sessile.

Subtend: to occur at the base, often refers to bracts at the base of a flower or inflorescence.

Tepal: one of the units of the perianth when the sepals and petals are not differentiated by size or color.

Terminal: at the tip.

Trifoliate: having 3 leaflets.

Trigonous: 3-angled.

Tripinnate: with the leaf blade divided into pinnae and further divided into pinnulets.

Truncate: square-ended.

Tubercle: a small swelling or projection.

Umbel: a flat-topped or domed inflorescence with several branches joining from the same point at the top of the main stem.

Undulate: with a wavy margin.

Unisexual: bearing either carpellate or staminate structures but not both.

Valve: a segment of a fruit, the segments separating at maturity.

Vascular bundle: a cluster of connective tissue that conducts nutrients, sugars, and water through a plant.

Villous: bearing long, soft, shaggy, unmatted hairs.

Whorled: with three or more structures originating at the same node on a stalk.

Winter-annual: a species that germinates in the fall and completes its life cycle the following year.

INDEX

B

D

E

F

I

J

K

L

M

N

O

P

S

T

U

V

W

X

Y

Z